Dom Pedro

DOM PEDRO

The Struggle for Liberty in Brazil and Portugal,

1798–1834

Neill Macaulay

Duke University Press, Durham

1986

© 1986 Duke University Press
All rights reserved
Printed in the United States of America on
acid-free paper ∞
Library of Congress Cataloging-in-Publication Data
Macaulay, Neill.
Dom Pedro: the struggle for liberty in Brazil and
Portugal, 1798–1834.
Bibliography: p.
Includes index.
1. Brazil—History—1763–1821.   2. Brazil—History—
1822–1889.   3. Portugal—History—1789–1900.   4. Pedro
I, Emperor of Brazil, 1798–1834.   5. Brazil—Kings and
rulers—Biography.   1. Title.
F2534.M24   1986   981'.04'0924 [B]   86-16711
ISBN 0-8223-0681-6

To Cope and Rosemary

Contents

Preface

Two years before the end of the eighteenth century, Brazilians for the first time were publicly called to arms against royal absolutism. Posters appeared on walls and public buildings in Salvador da Bahia, largest city of Portugal's huge South American empire, urging the people to rise up against their colonialist oppressors, to establish a "democratic government, free and independent." The people did not rise up and the revolution did not occur in 1798. But within a decade Brazil was freed of the more onerous economic restrictions of the colonial system, and the early 1820s saw the first flowering of political liberty in both Portugal and Brazil. Portuguese freedom soon was crushed by a counterrevolution, but Brazilian independence was firmly established under a constitutional monarchy that would guarantee free speech and other basic rights of citizens until near the end of the century. In Portugal, the definitive nineteenth-century triumph of liberalism came in 1834, when the reactionary forces of Dom Miguel capitulated to the constitutionalists led by his brother Dom Pedro. Prior to his Portuguese victory, Dom Pedro had declared Brazilian independence, devised and promulgated constitutions for both Portugal and Brazil, and ruled the latter country for nine years as its first emperor. He died of natural causes four months after the constitutionalist triumph in Portugal, and three weeks short of his thirty-sixth birthday.

Dom Pedro was not personally responsible for the transformation of the Luso-Brazilian world during his lifetime, 1798–1834. But his adherence to the liberal cause, which lent it his legitimacy as heir to the Portuguese throne, facilitated the changeover from royal absolutism to constitutional monarchy in Brazil and in Portugal. The liberal tide was running strong in Europe and America in the 1820s and Dom Pedro was swept up in it; he can only be understood in the context of his times. This volume, then, is less concerned with the royal person than with his milieu and the economic and social forces that shaped it. The book examines an epoch in Luso-Brazilian history by following the trajectory of its preeminent figure, an approach that provides unique opportunities to view the cultural transition from the old order to the new.

Leopold von Ranke said that all decades are equal in the eyes of God. But for the mortal who searches the past for clues to the future, some decades are more significant than others. Chronological proximity is no indicator of vitality: the 1920s are as dead as Mussolini, but the 1820s are as alive as tomorrow. This is true for Brazil and Portugal, both reemerging today as liberal states after a long corporatist apostasy. Looking back over the last two or three centuries from the heights of the 1980s, one is struck by the realization that all those coercive states established in the fifty years after 1914 are no more than aberrations, withering vestiges of a counterrevolution that slowed, but could not stop, the world's march toward liberty.

Dom Pedro, like the liberalism he served and the world in which he lived, was imperfect—and imperfectible. The certainty of imperfection requires constant scrutiny of government by a vigorous political opposition and a free press. Criticism of Dom Pedro was freely expressed and often vehement; it prompted him to abdicate two thrones. His tolerance of public criticism and his willingness to relinquish power set Dom Pedro apart from his absolutist predecessors and from the rulers of today's coercive states, whose lifetime tenure is as secure as that of the kings of old. A regime of liberty, as Dom Pedro realized, offers the most efficient means for coping with the problems of an ever-changing world and exploiting its opportunities for the common good. Compared with all others, the liberal creed is modest; it does not promise the millennium, the day when history stops and the earth becomes paradise.

Successful liberal leaders like Dom Pedro may be honored with an occasional stone or bronze monument, but their portraits, four stories high, do not drape public buildings; their pictures are not borne in parades of hundreds of thousands of uniformed marchers; no "-isms" attach to their names. The liberal regime, which each day requires millions of uncoerced individual decisions, does not promote mass demonstrations or personality cults. The coercive regime demands conformity and condemns its subjects to economic under-development, technological backwardness, and war. There is no danger of war between liberal states, but from Berlin to Peking, from Albania to Vietnam, there is scarcely a coercive state that is not at, or near war with, or under the military occupation of, a coercive neighbor. The flawed ideology of liberalism, which Dom Pedro imperfectly served, is still the world's best hope for peace and happiness. This book is about one phase of the long struggle for liberty, and about one man's participation in that struggle.

The chronological organization that I have chosen permits the simultaneous examination of the concurrent developments that combine to shape reality at any given instant. It is not an easy form for the historian; it demands continual analysis and interpretation of occurrences in many areas and repeated reassessment of their shifting relationships. But this approach offers the best chance of avoiding the weaknesses that characterize much academic history: the fixation on one aspect of development or on one source or category of historical documentation; the application of a single, constrictive methodology; a tendency to one-cause explanations or, conversely, to ambiguity cloaked in the mock certainty of professional jargon. The analyst who sets out to assimilate elements from such diverse fields as economics, religion, political theory, psychology, military and naval science, music, and popular culture will not find the various specialty languages very helpful; eventually he must turn to a lingua franca—standard English in the case of this book. An absence of jargon does not, however, imply an absence of interpretation.

Some basic interpretations incorporated in the narrative have to do with the nature of the Luso-Brazilian society. Slavery permeated Brazilian society in the early nineteenth century, but more people in Brazil were free than were enslaved. Most important is the fact that Brazil had a land-abundant economy and, consequently, a population that placed a high value on leisure. This consideration underlies the book's discussions of slavery, the slave trade, immigration, representative government, the Bank of Brazil and development policy, and the cultural conflict between Brazilians and Portuguese. The situation in Portugal was different, and was reflected in the differences between Portuguese nobility and Brazilian plutocracy, between Old World peasants and New World subsistence farmers, between Portuguese merchants and Brazilian planters. What is surprising is the degree to which leaders on both sides of the Atlantic were open to new ideas.

In Portugal the Bragança monarchy appointed noted liberals to high government positions, their availability giving the crown the flexibility it needed to change course under the pressure of external events. Transferred to Brazil, the Portuguese government implemented sweeping economic reforms and tolerated some freedom of expression.

The Brazilian government that succeeded it expanded these reforms and guaranteed more freedom. In Brazil and Portugal there were simultaneous liberal revolutionary movements, with little philosophical difference between them. The separation of Brazil from Portugal was the work of Brazilian interest groups, including bureaucrats and intellectuals accustomed to government service, trained by the Bragança monarchy. Given its size, wealth, and the ability to govern itself—either as one national unit or as several sovereign states—Portuguese America could no longer be ruled from Lisbon, no matter what the ideology of the government there. The common identity of Brazilian and Portuguese liberalism was underscored when the founder of the Brazilian state returned to Portugal and led the liberal movement there.

In Brazil the main issue was neither liberalism nor independence from Portugal, but national unity. Despite continental trends and the dictates of economic reason, most of Portuguese America stayed together after the Brazilian declaration of independence in 1822. That the sugar- and cotton-exporting provinces of the Northeast, hard pressed to meet international competition from new producers in Cuba and the United States, would remain in a disadvantageous customs and currency union—dominated by southern Brazilian coffee interests who enjoyed a near monopoly as sellers on the world market—defies the prescripts of social science. The anomaly is of the kind that leads biographers to attribute too much influence to the actions of individuals on the course of history. I have tried to avoid that trap; it is up to the reader to say whether or not I have succeeded.

The reader familiar with dependency theory—fashionable in academic circles in the 1960s—will discern my rejection of that concept as applied to Brazil after 1808 and Portugal after 1820. Despite some constraints imposed by British power, both nations had considerable freedom of action, and they maneuvered adroitly on the international scene, played foreign governments off against one another, and generally determined their own domestic development. Economically, Portugal suffered with the loss of Brazil, but hard times did not affect the resolve of Portuguese governments—whether liberal, conservative, or reactionary—to resist the will of Great Britain. And Brazil never became part of a British "informal empire." The British barred Brazilian sugar from their market, bought most of their cotton from the United States (after 1815), and drank precious little coffee. Although some Britons extracted profits from Brazilian coffee, they had not created this lucrative export business and were not essential for its continuance. Nor were Brazilians dependent on British imports; they bought manufactured goods from Britain because that was where they got the best value for the money they earned from their exports to the United States and continental Europe. Whenever the costs of manufactured goods, capital, or technology were raised in Britain, the Brazilians switched to alternate sources of supply. The miniscule tariff advantage given British imports during 1810–44 hardly made Brazil a dependency of Great Britain. In short, the people who fought for liberty in Brazil and Portugal were not puppets manipulated by a foreign power.

Conceived in José Honório Rodrigues's graduate seminar in Brazilian history at the University of Texas in 1963, this book has had a long gestation: there were projects that I had to get out of the way before I could give it full attention. In the meantime, my former professor made the task immeasurably easier by publishing volume upon magnificent volume of his own research findings on the Brazilian independence and early empire periods. While José Honório furnished the inspiration for my work, the National Endowment for the Humanities and the University of Florida's Center for Latin American Studies provided funding, with a research fellowship and travel grants to Brazil, Portugal, and Britain. Archivists and librarians on three continents have made special efforts to facilitate my labors; I am particularly grateful to José Gabriel at the Arquivo Nacional in Rio, to Dona Maria and Dona Áurea at the Imperial Archives in Petrópolis, and to the University of Florida Library's John Brown, Geraldine Collins, Barbara Bundersen, Rosa Mesa, and Dona Renninger. For word processing the manuscript I am indebted to Mern Johnston-Loehner, whose patience and good humor are as appreciated as her dedication and efficiency. I am similarly grateful to Marjorie Summers, who drew the maps. Colleagues, students and friends who read portions of the manuscript, offered suggestions or advice—not always taken, but invariably appreciated—or who otherwise made notable contributions to this project include Dave Bushnell, Hugo De Clercq, David Fleischer, Al Hower, António de Oliveira Marques, Gene Ridings, and Bill Woodruff. I thank them for their help and simultaneously absolve them of responsibility for the interpretation I have placed on the developments examined herein. Equally blameless for any wrongheadedness on my part is my longtime collaborator and spouse, Nancy Macaulay; without her encouragement and support this book would have remained unwritten.

Neill Macaulay
Gainesville, Florida
1986

1 The Exodus

His soul on fire, and resolutely bent on emigration.
Little did I think
His placid, lamb-like spirit could assume
The lion's port, and be at once the king.
J. Woolcot, *The Fall of Portugal, or the Royal Exiles*

Brazilian gold and diamonds financed the construction of the Portuguese royal palace at Queluz. When it was built in the middle of the eighteenth century, crown revenues from the far-flung mines of Portugal's sprawling South American colony were at their height. The royal treasury, however, received a relatively small share of the production of the mines—theoretically one-fifth, actually much less. While the "royal fifth" was expended for such purposes as building palaces, most of the Brazilian mineral wealth flowed through Portugal in private channels, and much of it wound up in England as payment for British manufactured goods. Thus, the English industrial revolution was to a significant extent financed by gold from Portuguese Brazil.[1]

Britain was Portugal's principal trading partner at the time the Queluz palace was built, and would remain so for years to come. British influence on Portugal was not limited to economics: Britain was Portugal's oldest ally and its traditional protector against neighboring Spain, which could not give up the idea that Portugal should be part of a unified Iberian kingdom, ruled from Madrid. In the eighteenth century, with a Bourbon king on the throne in Madrid, Spain joined Bourbon France in a "family pact" directed against Britain and, incidentally, against Britain's ally, Portugal. Between 1703 and 1763 Portugal was drawn into three major wars on Britain's side against Spain and France.

Official Portuguese hostility toward France did not extend to the aesthetic realm: French influence on the design of Queluz palace, ten kilometers northwest of Lisbon, was unmistakable. The architect responsible for the west wing of the palace, completed shortly before Portugal entered the Seven Years War, was a Frenchman, Jean Baptiste

Robillion; Queluz's west wing strongly suggested the French palace at Versailles. The formal gardens, the trellises, the citrus groves, the cascades and spewing fountains surrounding Queluz bore further resemblance to Versailles. Yet despite these outward appearances, Queluz palace was essentially Portuguese. The three-part southeast wing (which housed the throne room), with its hipped roofs and ogee pediments, its garlanded windows and eccentric facades, was typically Lusitanian rococo. "Everywhere formality is suggested," one visitor noted, "and then avoided by the picturesque use of different levels and unexpected departures from symmetry."[2] The palace, though huge in scale, was so scattered and compartmentalized as to seem almost dainty. Although it had more mirrors than Versailles, they were smaller and seemed to reflect inward: Queluz was an intimate, private place. This definitely was not the residence of the Sun King.

The first sovereigns to reside regularly in Queluz palace were Queen Maria I and King Pedro III, who was both Maria's uncle and husband and ruled Portugal jointly with her. Maria, as crown princess, had shown signs of mental instability; her marriage to the even-tempered Pedro and the sharing of power were arranged to ensure that the kingdom would not suffer erratic rule. The queen apparently did not resent the arrangement, and on matters of state she was of one mind with her husband, to whom she was genuinely devoted. Maria and Pedro came to the throne in 1777 determined to weaken Portugal's alliance with Britain and to make peace with Spain. During their first year they concluded a treaty of friendship with Spain, which in effect kept Portugal out of the War of the American Revolution, which Spain soon entered on the side of France and the United States. The treaty of friendship was a wise move for Portugal, as the American Revolution was the only eighteenth-century war that Britain lost. The treaty of 1777 also provided for the marriage of Maria and Pedro's second son, Dom João, to a Spanish princess, Carlota Joaquina.

The death of King Pedro III in 1786, the result of a stroke, was a great blow to Queen Maria. Two years later her older son, the crown prince, died from smallpox. Then came the unsettling news of the French Revolution. When she learned of the executions of the queen and king of France, the queen of Portugal jumped to the conclusion that a similar fate awaited her. Not only was she going to die at the hands of the mob, but, she convinced herself, she was also going to hell. As the queen's shrieking laments echoed through the halls of

Queluz palace, her surviving son, Dom João, took up the reins of government. From 1792 Prince João ruled Portugal in his mother's name, although he was not formally proclaimed regent of Portugal until 1799, when Dona Maria was pronounced incurably insane.[3] It befell Dom João to guide Portugal through the tumultuous era that dawned on Europe with the French Revolution and reached its zenith of peril—for "legitimate" monarchies—with the rise of Napoleon Bonaparte.

Under Prince João, Portugal joined Spain—his wife's homeland—Britain, and various other European monarchies in declaring war on revolutionary France in 1793. After Spain made a separate peace with France in 1795, Dom João's Portugal attempted to do likewise, at the same time trying to assure Britain of its continued friendship. While Portugal pursued neutrality, Spain allied itself with the French republic and went to war with Britain in 1797. Shortly afterwards Portugal made peace with France. Pressure from France and Spain then mounted on Portugal to break its ties with Britain. Unwilling to choose between Britain and the Spanish-French combination, Dom João resorted to delaying tactics. Finally, in 1801 France and Spain declared war on Dom João's kingdom and the Spanish army invaded eastern Portugal. The war between Portugal and Spain put a new strain on the troubled marriage of Prince João and the Spanish infanta, Carlota Joaquina. The war in Iberia, however, was brief; it ended a few months after it began, with Dom João agreeing, by the Treaty of Badajoz, to cede some territory to Spain and to close Portugal's ports to all British ships.[4] A general European settlement, the Peace of Amiens, was concluded the next year, 1802, and the ports were reopened.

Following the Peace of Amiens, the dictator of France, Napoleon Bonaparte, attended to some colonial matters and ostensibly pursued various nonmilitary projects in France and in Europe. But the threat of a new war hung heavy over Europe; neither France nor Britain regarded the Peace of Amiens as more than an expedient truce. Military and diplomatic preparations for the next conflagration were pursued on both sides. Britain broke the peace of 1803 by declaring war on France, and new pressure was brought on neutrals like Portugal to take sides. Napoleon, shortly after crowning himself emperor of France in 1804, named one of his trusted lieutenants, his former aide-de-camp, General Andoche Junot, as his ambassador to the Portuguese court. Ambassador Junot presented his credentials to the

Prince Regent at Queluz palace on the afternoon of 24 April 1805.[5]

Andoche Junot, a Burgundian, son of a well-to-do farmer, had served Napoleon since the siege of Toulon in 1793. During the Italian campaign, in a cavalry engagement, he received a saber blow to the face, which left a prominent scar that extended from his temple almost to the bottom of his left cheek. The noble marks of four other wounds, according to his wife, also decorated his fair countenance. Tall and erect, this handsome, battle-scarred, thirty-three-year-old veteran strode into the throne room of Queluz palace dressed in the uniform he had worn to Napoleon's coronation. The new ambassador dazzled the Portuguese court.[6]

Junot's full-dress uniform—intensely admired by the prince regent and his six-year-old son and heir, Prince Pedro—was that of a colonel general of hussars. The jacket and trousers were blue, richly embroidered with gold. The jacket was trimmed with blue-fox fur. Draped over Junot's left shoulder was a white cloak with red facings. The ambassador's sleeves displayed the gold chevrons of his military rank, arranged in an oak-leaf pattern. A magnificent heron plume, a gift from the Empress Josephine, adorned his shako, which Junot did not take off in the presence of Portuguese royalty. The ambassador meant no offense: a French officer's shako, the Portuguese foreign minister explained to the prince regent, "is never removed, even in the presence of God."[7]

The resplendent ambassador was presented to Dom João's wife, the Princess Carlota Joaquina, to their son and heir, Dom Pedro, and to various other members of the royal family, but not to the mad Queen Maria, who was confined to quarters. On the following day the prince regent's valet appeared at the French ambassador's residence in Lisbon with an unusual request: Dom João wished to borrow General Junot's uniform, so that his tailor might use it as a model in making uniforms for himself and for Dom Pedro. The ambassador acceded to the request, though he doubted that the short and fat prince regent would look good in a hussar's uniform: Dom João was not handsome. "My God!" Junot exclaimed to his wife on his return home to Queluz palace, "How ugly he is!" He found Dom João's short and wiry consort no prettier: "My God! How ugly the princess is! My God! How ugly they all are! There is not a single comely face among them, except the prince royal."[8] The prince royal, Dom Pedro, a handsome child, would look good in a hussar's uniform.

Dom Pedro at age six
From Octávio Tarquínio de Sousa, *A vida de Dom Pedro I* (Rio de Janeiro, 1972). Reprinted by permission of Livraria José Olympio Editora S. A.

Dom Pedro, like his father, Dom João, was a second son. He had two older sisters. Carlota Joaquina gave birth to Dom Pedro on 12 October 1798 in the southeast wing of Queluz palace, in a rather small, square bedroom with a circular and concave ceiling mounted on mirrored columns that made the room appear large and round. This was the "Don Quixote chamber," so called because its walls were adorned with paintings of scenes from Cervantes's novel. At his baptism, conducted in the nearby music room, the infant prince received the name Pedro de Alcântara Francisco António João Carlos Xavier de Paula Miguel Rafael Joaquim José Gonzaga Pascoal Cipriano Serafim de Bragança e Bourbon. The death of his six-year-old brother in 1801 left Dom Pedro second in line for the Portuguese crown, after his father, the prince regent. In the meantime, Carlota Joaquina had borne two more daughters, in 1800 and 1801, and, in 1802, she gave birth to another son, Dom Miguel. More daughters came in 1805 and 1806. In thirteen years the Spanish-born princess had presented Dom João with nine children. The prince regent, however, could not be sure that he was the father of all these offspring. The paternity of Dom Miguel and the last two females was especially in doubt. But, apparently there was no question about Dom Pedro; he was definitely Dom João's son.[9]

The marriage of Dom João and Dona Carlota Joaquina was vexatious from the start. The Spanish infanta was ten years old at the time of the wedding; consummation of the marriage was delayed until the bride reached puberty, five years later. In the meantime, the couple lived apart. Dom João resided at the royal palace and monastery at Mafra, and Dona Carlota lived at Queluz palace in the custody of her mother-in-law, Queen Maria. Though unattractive—official portraiture blurred her frizzy hair and softened her sharp, harsh features —Princess Carlota was no wallflower. A lively, assertive girl, she was in virtually every respect unsuited for the equally unattractive but contemplative and phlegmatic Prince João, who was eight years her senior. The marriage was a matter of state, and Dom João was determined to do his duty and make the best of it. Dona Carlota began to provoke the prince early: in one encounter at the time of the wedding, the bride bit the groom savagely on the ear and threw a candlestick in his face. In April 1790, following the princess's first menstrual period and after a formal palace ceremony, the couple began their conjugal life.[10]

Dona Carlota left no doubt that she disliked her husband. The arrival of children did little, if anything, to change her attitude. After the 1802 birth of Dom Miguel, reputed to be the son of the marquis of Marialva,[11] Dona Carlota unofficially moved out of the Queluz palace and began spending most of her time at the royal country estate at Ramalhão. Dom João followed suit by abandoning Queluz for his favorite retreat, the palace-monastery at Mafra. His children and his mother, the mad queen, remained at Queluz. The young Dom Pedro saw his parents on the occasions that brought them back to Queluz, usually affairs of state like the presentation of French Ambassador Junot in 1805.[12]

The care and upbringing of Dom Pedro was left to nursemaids and tutors. The royal infant was assigned one full-time wet nurse, and two other lactating ladies were held in reserve: the princeling had six teats to sustain him. As he grew older, spiritual and intellectual nourishment was offered by several instructors, including the septuagenarian Doctor José Monteiro da Rocha, ex–Jesuit priest and retired professor of mathematics at the University of Coimbra, and Friar António da Nossa Senhora de Salete, a Franciscan whose teaching specialty was Latin grammar and literature.[13] Although the prince developed a taste for Virgil, his lessons at Queluz otherwise affected him little. He was a poor student, temperamentally inclined to reject academic instruction. His irregular family situation, far more than his formal studies, shaped his character. Dom Pedro was fond of his father, and when he became aware of such things, he resented his mother's humiliation of Dom João.

By nature passive, Dom João endured his wife's insults in the interests of the state. He was a conscientious ruler who met regularly and at length with his ministers and councillors of state, carefully weighed all matters before him, and whenever possible did nothing. His style of governing was appropriate for Portugal at a time when strong action—a bold move, the impulsive seizing of a perceived opportunity—could have brought the kingdom to ruin. Exasperated foreign statesmen, whose primary interest was not the preservation of the Portuguese monarchy, were apt to regard Dom João as a sluggard and a dolt. A disinterested observer, after considering Portugal's precarious position, wedged between a continent dominated by the French army and an ocean ruled by the British navy, would be more likely to appreciate the prince regent's statecraft. And those who were not completely distracted by his homely face and absurd figure—huge head,

7

round body, short legs, tiny hands and feet—might discern his keen intelligence and admirable personal qualities. William Beckford, who visited Dom João at Queluz palace in 1794, found the prince to be affable, shrewd, and highly articulate: "there was a promptitude, a facility in his diction, most remarkable." In lighter moments "a quaint national turn of humour added zest to his pleasantries."[14]

Dom João's cherished refuge was the massive palace and monastery complex—built on a gridiron pattern like Spain's Escorial—at Mafra, thirty kilometers northwest of Lisbon and twenty-two kilometers north of Queluz. There, in the company of Augustinian and Franciscan friars, the prince regent regularly attended mass and vespers, received communion, marched in religious processions, and sang in the choir.[15] Unlike his demented mother, Dom João was not a religious fanatic, but he did take great pleasure in religious ceremony and especially music. He had inherited the predilection of the Portuguese royal family of Bragança for sacred music: his ancestor, João IV, was credited with playing all musical instruments and with composing the Christmas carol "Adeste fidelis." Nourished by generations of royal patronage, the church music in Portugal at the time of Dom João's regency was "the best in Europe."[16] But Dom João and his attendants at Mafra did not occupy themselves exclusively with sacred sounds; the friars staged secular comedies for the enjoyment of the prince regent, put on sumptuous banquets, and organized hunts. An avid hunter, Dom João was one of the few European rulers at the turn of the nineteenth century who still practiced the medieval sport of falconry. His love of hunting, seemingly at odds with his generally sedentary nature, might be explained by the relish with which he devoured the yield of the hunt: it was not the sport, but the anticipation of eating that drove the prince regent into the field. Venison and game fowl were among his favorite foods, which also included roast chicken, of which he consumed prodigious amounts. Dom João was a big eater—a glutton, in fact.[17]

Gluttony was not among the vices of Dom João's wife, though she too was a hunter. Unlike her husband, who gave up horseback riding in 1805 because of leg troubles and hemorrhoids, Carlota preferred the mounted chase. An accomplished equestrian, she amazed young Madam Junot, the French ambassador's wife, by taking a skittish horse, mounting him astride like a man (her petticoats were split fore and aft), quickly dominating the beast, then charging off in a mad gallop.[18] Sport was important to Carlota Joaquina: she once commanded the visiting William Beckford to run a footrace with the marquis of Marialva and two of her female attendants. After winning the race, the Englishman was ordered to dance the bolero with another of Carlota's attendants, an Andalusian girl, to the accompaniment of castanets and female voices. In music, the princess preferred the profane to the sacred. In men, she preferred almost anyone to Dom João. The graceful young marquis of Marialva was one of her favorites, and was probably the father of one or more of her children.[19]

What the marquis saw in the princess could not have been physical beauty, for her homeliness was legendary. Madame Junot was struck by Dona Carlota's small stature, "four feet ten inches at most," and misshapen form: her breasts, arms, and legs were out of alignment, as one side was taller than the other. The ambassador's wife also took malicious note of the princess's "bloodshot" eyes, "vegetable" skin, "bluish" lips, huge teeth, large mouth, and "mane" of "dry, frizzy hair . . . which had no color."[20] Dona Carlota's adult portraits show a woman of trim figure and angular face, with large, dark eyes, black hair, and the suggestion of a moustache. William Beckford, less concerned with Carlota's appearance than with her character, deplored "her restless intrigues of all hues, political as well as private—her wanton freaks of favouritism and atrocious acts of cruelty."[21] Her favorite son, after the death of her firstborn, was the child born shortly after that loss, Dom Miguel. Dom Pedro was passed over in his mother's affections.

General Junot was by preference a soldier rather than a diplomat. Before he accepted the Lisbon post, he had gotten Napoleon's promise that he would be recalled to military service "at the sound of the first cannon shot." The cannons began to roar in the fall of 1805, after Britain had concluded military alliances with Russia and Austria aimed at expelling the French from Germany and Italy. In October, Junot received authorization to turn over the Lisbon embassy to a chargé d'affaires and join Napoleon in Bavaria. But before the general could catch up with the emperor's forces, they had defeated the Austrians in Bavaria and had driven deep into the Hapsburg Empire. Junot joined Napoleon's headquarters in Moravia on the eve of the battle of Austerlitz, in December 1805. At Austerlitz the combined Austrian and Russian armies were routed, which compelled the Russians to withdraw to their motherland and the Austrians to sue for peace. Following the battle of Austerlitz, Junot was sent to Parma to deal with an Italian rebellion against Napoleonic authority. Having restored order in Parma, Junot was summoned to France in July 1806, and was made military governor of Paris. In August 1807, after some unpleasantness with Napoleon and Marshal Murat over his supposed affair with the emperor's sister Caroline, who was married to Murat, Junot was transferred to command of a reserve corps in southern France, at Bayonne, and ordered to prepare for an invasion of Portugal.[22]

Napoleon could not invade Britain because of the supremacy of the British navy, incontestably established at the Battle of Trafalgar in October 1805, when Lord Nelson demolished the combined fleets of France and Spain. Unable to get his troops across the channel to England, Napoleon proceeded to wage economic warfare against the British on the continent of Europe: he declared the ports of Europe closed to British commerce. By July 1807 the boycott of British trade, Napoleon's "continental system," was joined by all the Christian states of mainland Europe except Sweden, Denmark, and Portugal. The holdouts were menaced by both France and Britain. Denmark decided to give in to Napoleon, which prompted the British to attack Copenhagen in September 1807 and capture the Danish vessels in the harbor, including eighteen ships-of-the-line; the British then sailed away with their prizes, leaving the Danes to join the continental system. Should Portugal follow Denmark in capitulating to France, the implication was clear, Britain would repeat its Copenhagen actions at Lisbon.[23]

Portugal had received an ultimatum from France and Spain on 12 August 1807. The note was presented to Dom João's foreign minister, António de Araújo de Azevedo, by the French chargé d'affaires and the Spanish ambassador in Lisbon. France and Spain demanded that Portugal break diplomatic relations with Britain, which would amount to a declaration of war, and close its ports to all British vessels. In addition, Portuguese authorities were to arrest all British subjects in Portugal and confiscate their property. If these demands were not met by 1 September 1807, France and Spain would go to war with Portugal.[24] Foreign Minister Araújo, an astute diplomat who was perceived as pro-French, engaged the French and Spanish envoys in lengthy discussions. He assured them of Portugal's intention to meet their demands, while pointing to innumerable difficulties in the way of full and immediate compliance. In this manner, he managed to get the deadline postponed, on a day-to-day basis, until the end of September.[25]

In the meantime, Dom João met with his council of state and considered various courses of action. The prince regent and his advisers decided to rush repair work on the Portuguese naval squadron in Lisbon harbor (only eight of twelve ships-of-the-line were seaworthy) and have the vessels take on provisions for a possible voyage to Brazil. Dom João agreed that his heir, Dom Pedro, should be sent to safety in Portugal's South American colony, and he ordered a proclamation drawn up to announce the move; he did not, however, set a date for the prince's departure. Some members of the council of state felt that the young prince should be joined by the rest of the royal family and the entire Portuguese government in moving to Brazil. An undertaking of that magnitude would require help from the British navy; Dom João wanted to know if and when Britain could provide such assistance. Some of the prince regent's advisers suggested that they might avoid a French-Spanish invasion and any need to transfer the government to Brazil, if the British would agree to a simulated state of war between Portugal and Britain, whereby Portugal would formally declare war on Britain, but take no meaningful action against British shipping or property. Foreign Minister Araújo was authorized to take up these matters with the British representative in Lisbon.[26]

The British minister plenipotentiary ad interim in Lisbon in 1807 was Percy Clinton Sidney Smythe, sixth Viscount Strangford, a twenty-seven-year-old Irish peer whom Lord Byron addressed in verse as "Hibernian Strangford, with thine eyes of blue, and boasted locks of red or auburn hue."[27] From 1802 until 1806, when the British minister plenipotentiary accredited to the Portuguese court (Britain seldom gave ambassadorial rank to its diplomatic envoys in the nineteenth century) returned to London, Lord Strangford had been secretary of the British legation. As legation secretary, the unmarried Strangford, according to Madame Junot, divided his time between sleeping and translating Portuguese poetry. His versions of the sixteenth-century poetry of Luís de Camões, the first volume of which was published in 1803, were widely read in the English-speaking world. Madame Junot further noted that Strangford was absentminded and nearsighted. Others characterized him as vain, childish, flighty, and conniving.[28] He was also very lucky: the course of events ran so strongly in Britain's favor that his worst gaucheries—in Portugal and later in Brazil—could not alter it.

Lord Strangford heard Foreign Minister Araújo's request that Britain provide assistance should Portugal find it necessary to transfer its government to Brazil. Araújo appealed to the young viscount with a vision of the results of such a move: the establishment in South America of a "great and powerful Empire, which, protected in its infancy by the naval supremacy of England, may rise, in time, to compete with any other Political Establishment in the Universe." The new empire, Araújo suggested, certainly would award its benefactor, Britain, exclusive trading privileges. The Portuguese foreign minister went on to warn Strangford that time was running out in the Portuguese negotiations with the French and Spanish envoys; soon Portugal would have to take some measures to comply with Napoleon's ultimatum. In order to prevent or at least delay a French-Spanish invasion, Portugal might have to formally close its ports to British ships and sequester—not confiscate—some British property. Strangford doubted that such measures would be acceptable to either his government or Napoleon.[29] The British government, in fact, did not categorically reject the idea of a simulated war between Portugal and Britain as a means of buying time while preparations were made to transfer the Portuguese court to Brazil, which London was happy to facilitate. Strangford was instructed to convey a British pledge of assistance directly to the prince regent, and to get his firm commitment to move to South America.

Dom João received Lord Strangford at Mafra on 25 September. The prince regent listened to the envoy's discourse on the futility of his trying to appease Napoleon and the necessity of his embarking for Brazil without further delay. This he could not do, Dom João responded, for "every feeling of religion and duty forbade him to abandon his People until the last moment"—until he had made every effort to prevent a foreign invasion. Should his efforts fail, he was resolved to withdraw to Brazil, but not before "the actual arrival of danger." He was glad to know that he could count on British help in transporting his court across the Atlantic. He appreciated British friendship, Dom João assured Strangford, though he realized that Britain stood to gain from "the foundation of a new Empire in the Brazils." As Portuguese colonies, the Brazilian provinces were closed to foreign shipping, but as the seat of the Portuguese monarchy, Brazil would have to be opened to direct foreign trade, because Brazilian commerce certainly could not be funneled through a mother country under enemy occupation. Dom João trusted that Britain did not "intend to oblige him to sacrifice his European Possessions merely that she might have the advantage of trading with his Colonies, and of repairing in the new World the losses which her Commerce had sustained in the old." He hoped the British would be magnanimous if he were forced to close Portugal's ports to their ships. The prince regent indicated that he would meet the French–Spanish demand, and if that failed to forestall the threatened invasion, then he would implement his plan to move to Brazil.[30]

The normally placid Dom João displayed "strong agitation and anxiety" during his conversation with Strangford, according to the British minister's report to London. The young viscount sought to take advantage of the prince's discomfiture, he reported, by appealing "to almost every feeling and prejudice by which I knew His Royal Highness to be governed; to Pride of Ancestry, to Paternal Affection, and to Superstition." Strangford reminded Dom João that "the two former occasions on which he had yielded to the Enemies of England were severally marked by a sad and disastrous Event" in the Portuguese royal family. Apparently, Strangford was alluding to Dom João's 1797 peace with France, which preceded Queen Maria's final lapse into insanity and the finding of a board of physicians that her condition was incurable, and to Portugal's 1801 treaty with Spain and France, which was followed by the death of Dom João's firstborn son. "Such awful coincidences," Strangford intoned to the supposedly gullible prince, must be considered "something more than accidental." Dom João was unmoved—Strangford's later boasts to the contrary notwithstanding. The prince regent intended to try to come to terms with France and Spain, and was as determined as ever not to abandon Portugal before the country was actually invaded. The British minister insisted that the prince regent at least send his heir, Dom Pedro, to Brazil, as a sign of good faith to Britain, and to put France and Spain on notice that his own retreat to Brazil "was not only possible but probable." Dom João said that this was under consideration; he would inform Strangford when he had made his decision. That was the only commitment that Strangford extracted from Dom João during their interview of nearly an hour and a half. Returning to Lisbon from Mafra, Strangford immediately went to see Dom João's personal physician, who conspired to use his influence to try to bend the prince regent to the will of Great Britain.[31]

The Marquis of Marialva
From Ángelo Pereira, *D. João VI: Príncipe e rei* (Lisbon, 1956).

Following Dom João's interview with Strangford, the Portuguese minister in London was instructed to negotiate a secret treaty to compensate Britain for the closing of the Portuguese ports, and to provide for British assistance in moving the Portuguese court to Brazil, should either of these steps become necessary.[32] Before these negotiations got underway in London, the patience of the French chargé and the Spanish ambassador in Lisbon ran out. On 30 September they broke off negotiations and departed Portugal, leaving the country technically in a state of war with France and Spain. Still the continental allies made no overt military move against Portugal, and Dom João clung to the hope that he might yet avoid a Napoleonic invasion. On 20 October the prince regent announced that Portugal would join the continental system and close its ports to British naval and merchant vessels.[33] That did not satisfy Napoleon. At the beginning of November it was learned in Lisbon that General Junot had left Bayonne with a large French force and was marching across Spain toward Portugal.

Should Junot cross the border into Portugal, Dom João and his advisers agreed, they all would sail to Brazil. But they decided to make one last effort to forestall the impending invasion: they would comply fully with the French–Spanish ultimatum. On 8 November, after Strangford had been forewarned, Dom João issued the order to detain British subjects and impound their property. The British minister, having received his passport, hired a small fishing vessel at Lisbon and set sail down the Tagus river toward its mouth on the Atlantic, a distance of about twelve kilometers. Thus, Portugal had broken diplomatic relations with Britain, as the ultimatum had required. But since diplomatic ties with Spain and France also were severed, the Portuguese had no regular channels through which to notify Napoleon that they had complied with his demands, and to urge him to call off his invasion. So the marquis of Marialva was dispatched to Paris as ambassador extraordinary to present the Portuguese case to the French emperor.[34]

The marquis of Marialva was well connected with the Portuguese royal family. Sometime lover of Princess Carlota, he was in 1807 her husband's *estribeiro mor* (master of the horse). Marialva was entrusted with a fortune in Brazilian diamonds, which he was to carry through Spain and France to Paris, where he was to distribute them to Napoleon and important members of his court as a goodwill offering from the royal house of Bragança. Dom João was now virtually certain that

Napoleon intended to depose the Braganças and place one of his own relatives on the Portuguese throne. To change the French emperor's mind, Marialva was to offer not only the diamonds, but a means by which a descendant of the Bonapartes could occupy the Portuguese throne legitimately: he was to propose the marriage of Dom Pedro to the daughter of Napoleon's sister, Caroline, and Marshal Murat.[35] The French emperor at least might stay his hand against Portugal while he considered the proposal. Marialva left Lisbon overland for Paris on 16 November, the same day that Rear Admiral Sir Sidney Smith arrived at the mouth of the Tagus river with a British squadron.

Admiral Smith's orders were to prevent the Portuguese naval and merchant vessels in the Tagus river from falling into Napoleon's hands. He was either to escort the Portuguese ships to Brazil, if Dom João decided to transfer his government there, or he was to capture or destroy them (apply the Copenhagen solution), if the prince regent refused to leave the country. Dom João had insisted all along that he could not abandon his kingdom before French troops actually crossed its borders. This was explained to the admiral by Lord Strangford, who boarded Smith's flagship, the *Hibernia*, at the mouth of the Tagus. Sir Sidney and Lord Strangford agreed to put Lisbon under a strict blockade while the viscount sought an interview with Dom João to notify him that he must embark immediately for Brazil or surrender his ships.[36]

With the deepening crisis the prince regent left Mafra and took up residence at Ajuda palace, near the waterfront in Lisbon. There, on 23 November, he received the news that Napoleon had declared the Bragança family dethroned and that General Junot's troops had crossed the border into Portugal. The time for action had arrived. The prince regent conferred with his council of state, and on the night of 24 November ordered Foreign Minister Araújo to execute plans for the embarkation of the royal family. The ships would sail, Dom João decreed, on the afternoon of 27 November; Lord Strangford was to be summoned to hear Dom João's declaration of friendship for Britain and his request for immediate assistance in transferring the royal court to Brazil.[37]

The ships had been standing by, provisioned for a voyage to Brazil, since August. Most members of the royal family had long been aware that the move was probable and had prepared themselves for it. But the innumerable courtiers, for as long as possible, had been kept in the dark, both as to whether their rulers would actually embark, and as to who would be allowed to accompany them if they did. As the belongings of the royal family began moving to the docks there was a mad scramble by courtiers to secure passage on the ships. Matters were complicated by unrelenting rains, which transformed into rivulets or quagmires of mud and loose cobblestone the narrow streets that wound around Lisbon's seven hills to the docks on the Tagus. Hundreds of coaches and wagons jammed the approaches to the river in the rush to deliver passengers and baggage in time to make the sailing. The belongings of those who were sailing and of those who hoped to be sailing piled up on the wharves in disorganized, rain-soaked heaps.[38]

On the morning of 27 November Dom João proceeded to the navy sector of the harbor, to Sodré quay, in a closed carriage driven by a coachman who forsook the royal livery for street clothes so as not to attract the attention of the Lisbon populace, now grown sullen and resentful in the knowledge of its impending abandonment. Dona Carlota, proceeding directly from Queluz with her two sons and youngest daughter, arrived shortly afterwards, in her ostentatious *oitavado* (figure eight) carriage. The princess was as unhappy about her departure as were the plebeans who appeared in the streets now that the rains had stopped and who stared in silent anger at her passing carriage. Since September, when Dom João informed her that they might be going to Brazil, Dona Carlota had been appealing to friends and relatives to intercede with the prince regent to convince him that she should be allowed to return to Spain with her daughters.[39] Dom João would have been delighted to be free of his wife, but the interests of the Bragança monarchy required that the entire royal family escape the grasp of those now sworn to destroy it, the rulers of France and Spain. Not only the princess, but the demented queen, the highest symbol of Bragança legitimacy, had to make the trip to Brazil.

Dona Maria had moments of lucidity as she was driven through Lisbon to the docks. "Don't go so fast!" she screamed at her coachman. "The people will think we are fleeing."[40] When the carriage stopped at Sodré Quay, where Dom João and Dom Pedro awaited her, however, she refused to get out. The sight of her son and grandson did not reassure her. "I don't want to!" she yelled repeatedly. Finally, uniformed officers dragged their kicking and screaming sovereign out of the carriage and past a somber Dom João and a wide-eyed Dom Pedro to the royal galley that would row them to the anchored flagship of the

Portuguese fleet, the eighty-four-gun *Principe Real*. Carlota Joaquina had already boarded another naval vessel, the *Afonso de Albuquerque*, along with four of her daughters. The two remaining daughters and various relatives were berthed on a third ship-of-the-line, the *Rainha de Portugal*. Accompanying Dom João on the *Principe Real*, besides the queen and Dom Pedro, were Dom Miguel and all the councillors of state. Other royal officials were distributed among five other ships-of-the-line, eight lesser warships, and the thirty merchantmen that were to sail with the fleet.[41]

The royal family and the principal officials were aboard the ships by noon on 27 November, the date Dom João had set for the departure. But they could not sail because of a prevailing southwesterly, which began blowing on the afternoon of 27 November, bringing more rain. Also, arrangements with the British, who were blockading the mouth of the Tagus, were not made until 28 November, when Dom João conferred with Lord Strangford aboard the *Principe Real*. Admiral Smith's squadron would inspect the Portuguese vessels as they crossed the bar, provide supplies and other assistance as needed, and detach four British ships-of-the-line to escort them to Brazil.[42]

As the Portuguese vessels in the Tagus awaited favorable winds for sailing, more courtiers scrambled aboard. Among them was the Brazilian-born Felisberto Caldeira Brant Pontes, lieutenant colonel in the Portuguese regular army and owner of vast estates in Brazil.[43] Lower on the social and economic scale were passengers like António Gomes da Silva, a goldsmith employed by the royal family, who traveled with his wife and adopted son, Francisco.[44] Favored artisans and servants joined court luminaries in seizing the opportunity to escape the French occupation and accompany the royal family to Brazil. By 29 November some 10,000 Portuguese were on the ships in the Tagus. Many were unable to get their baggage aboard, for priority was given to loading essential government property, like the royal archives, library, and printing press.[45]

In the meantime, General Junot was closing in on Lisbon. The rain that hindered the loading of the Portuguese ships also slowed the pace of his 23,000 French soldiers—mostly ill-trained conscripts, poorly equipped and lightly armed. Wagons and artillery were left by the wayside as Junot's vanguard plunged through the mud of the upper Tagus valley toward Lisbon. Days of forced marches left many of his men shoeless; rain and immersion in the swirling floodwaters of the

Tagus and its tributaries left most without a speck of dry gunpowder. However vulnerable, Junot's troops were identified with the war machine that had smashed the armies of Prussia, Austria, and Russia: Portuguese arms would not attempt to obstruct their march on Lisbon. Junot's precise destination was the Portuguese capital's downriver suburb of Belém, where a massive square tower, crammed with artillery on six levels, monitored traffic in and out of Lisbon harbor. By seizing the sixteenth-century Tower of Belém, Junot could seal off the port, and thus prevent the sailing of the Portuguese warships and merchantmen and thwart the escape of the Bragança family—as Napoleon had ordered.[46]

As long as the winds blew from the southwest the ships could not sail. But the morning of 29 November dawned bright and clear and the winds shifted; a wind from the northeast—a "Spanish wind" —now prevailed, blowing directly down the Tagus and out into the Atlantic. Fully realizing the implication of the change in the weather, Junot pushed his exhausted troops to the limits of their endurance. On the morning of 30 November the battle-scarred Burgundian and his 1,200-man vanguard entered Lisbon through its northeastern gate, and meeting no resistance, dashed across the city and occupied the Tower of Belém. There was only one Portuguese vessel to be seen on the river, the merchantman *Chocalho*, dancing over the waves under full sail, making for the Atlantic. The enraged general personally directed artillery fire on the fleeing vessel, and disabled her with a cannonball through the rigging, which forced her to surrender. She carried no one of importance. The ships she had belatedly attempted to join were safely on their way to Brazil, under British escort, carrying Dom João, Dom Pedro, and the rest of the Portuguese royal family. They had gotten away with time to spare.[47] With consummate skill, Dom João had played the weak hand that fate had dealt him. He won, among other things, exemption from the humiliation that awaited his dim-witted in-laws in Spain: dethronement and imprisonment in Napoleon's France. General Junot lost, and his failure to halt the exodus cost him his chance for a marshal's baton. The diamond-laden marquis of Marialva also failed to complete his mission, though his career, unlike the general's, did not suffer for it. Detained in Madrid, Marialva was unable to continue on to Paris and propose to the French emperor that Dom Pedro marry Napoleon's niece.[48] When Dom Pedro did marry—in Brazil, nine years after the escape from Portugal—his bride was Napoleon's sister-in-law.

2 The New Kingdom

For thy city lost an empire will we gain.
—Virgil, *Aeneid*

Dom Pedro was aboard the *Principe Real* as she ran with the Spanish wind down the Tagus and across the bar into the Atlantic Ocean, Portugal's royal standard fluttering from her mainmast pole, on the bright, nearly cloudless morning of 29 November 1807. Standing offshore was Rear Admiral Sir Sidney Smith's British squadron, which greeted the Portuguese flagship with a twenty-one-gun salute. The deck on which the young prince stood trembled as Portuguese guns thundered a return salute. Then the ships of two nations mingled, the *Principe Real* seeking out the *Hibernia*, Admiral Smith's flagship. A boat was lowered from the *Principe Real* as she maneuvered about the *Hibernia*, to take Lord Strangford to the British vessel. The viscount, after a brief visit to the *Hibernia*, returned to the *Principe Real* with Admiral Smith, whom he presented to Dom João. The prince regent received Sir Sidney, Strangford later noted, "with the utmost condescension and kindness."[1] Dom João then presented his heir to the British admiral.

Dom Pedro looked on as his father and Sir Sidney discussed arrangements for the voyage to Brazil. At one point during the conference, which lasted close to three hours, the admiral suggested that the prince regent transfer to one of the British warships, where he and his party might be more secure. Dom Pedro, according to an apocryphal account, was so incensed by the suggestion that he intervened in his elders' conversation to insist that the Braganças remain aboard the *Principe Real*; having abandoned their kingdom, they could not now desert their flagship—that would be the ultimate humiliation.[2] Dom João, however, did not need a sermon from his nine-year-old son to make him aware of the importance of the *Principe Real* as the transitional locus of Portuguese sovereignty; on that vessel he had deliberately placed Portugal's incapacitated monarch, Queen Maria, and all her male heirs: himself, Dom Pedro, and Dom Miguel. They would remain together on that floating piece of Portugal, under the prince regent's control, until they disembarked on Portuguese soil in Brazil. Had the *Principe Real* gone down in the Atlantic, the Bragança dynasty would have gone down with her.

A test of the seaworthiness of the *Principe Real* and her over-loaded sister ships came soon after they had merged with the British squadron. As Admiral Smith and Dom João conferred on the after-noon of 29 November, clouds began to gather and a heavy swell arose. The wind veered westerly and by nightfall was at gale force. The combined fleet had to stand out into the Atlantic, or risk being dashed against the rocky Portuguese coast. Painfully, the ships beat away from the mainland—pounded by heavy seas, pelted by driving rain, and heeling over fearsomely in the furious west wind. The storm lasted through the night and for most of the next day.[3]

By 1 December the storm had passed, although the sea remained rough and the wind strong from the west. An inspection of the Portu-guese fleet by Admiral Smith and his officers found one small warship, a brig or schooner, so damaged that she was no longer seaworthy; she limped back to Lisbon, a consolation prize for the French. One ship-of-the-line was advised to sail to England for repairs, but the advice was ignored and she remained with the other Portuguese vessels, which were judged fit to cross the Atlantic to Brazil. Sir Sidney assigned four of his ships-of-the-line to escort them and to relieve them of some of their passengers. Another British vessel was dispatched as a courier to England, with Lord Strangford aboard. The rest of the British men-of-war would remain with their admiral off the coast of Portugal to confront the French; two of Smith's ships transferred a small amount of provisions to their Brazil-bound allies before they parted company on 5 December.[4]

The voyage to Rio de Janeiro was to be by way of São Tiago island—a rendezvous and reassembly point for the fleet, off Africa's Cape Verde—and Bahia, in northeastern Brazil. One Portuguese warship, the seventy-four-gun *Medusa*, was dispatched ahead of the fleet, with instructions to bypass São Tiago and sail directly to Brazil to inform the colonial authorities of the impending royal arrival. The remaining seventeen Portuguese and four British warships and thirty-odd merchant vessels reached south toward São Tiago in rough seas, the westerlies abeam and blowing steadily at a moderate gale. On 11 December, near latitude 33° North, a terrific storm blew up. Buffeted by tremendous winds, the ships of the fleet were scattered over a vast area of heaving, rain-shrouded sea. When the weather cleared on 12 December, most of the vessels, including three British escorts, proceeded as planned to São Tiago. But the storm had left the *Principe Real* and several others—including the *Rainha de Portugal* with Dona Carlota aboard, and the British escort *Bedford*—together far out in the Atlantic, squarely in the path of the northeasterly trade winds. Rather than beat back toward Africa, they would take advantage of their position and set sail for South America. They enjoyed fine weather and smooth sailing the rest of the way to Brazil.[5]

Dom Pedro responded to the shipboard environment in a manner befitting the heir to the throne of a great maritime nation. The *Principe Real*, with her length of sixty-seven meters and beam of sixteen and a half meters, her poop, quarterdeck, forecastle, three gun decks, and cavernous hold, gave him plenty of space for roaming and exploring. He scampered about this wooden leviathan, mixing with the crew—more than a thousand, including sailors and marine guards—observing them at work and questioning their officers about the mechanics of sailing and the mathematics of navigation. The officers indulged their lively young prince, teaching him to calculate longitude and giving him opportunities to display his considerable manual dexterity in performing nautical tasks. Dom Pedro clearly preferred line and capstan to pen and copybook, and apparently little regretted his separation from his tutor, the aged Doctor Monteiro da Rocha, who remained in Portugal. But among the *Principe Real*'s 412 passengers was a comparably learned cleric, Friar António de Arrábida, erstwhile royal librarian at Mafra, who offered the prince religious and academic guidance during the Atlantic crossing. A man of recognized piety, the tall and slender Franciscan was also noted for his urbane manners and tastes and intellectual interests ranging from botany to political theory. He was thirty-six years old when, aboard the *Principe Real*, he established an easy rapport with the boy-prince, the beginning of a long-lasting relationship with Dom Pedro, as his confessor and mentor. On the Atlantic crossing Friar Arrábida encouraged the prince to pursue his interest in Virgil's *Aeneid*, perhaps pointing out the similarities between their voyage and that of the displaced Trojans. When Dom Pedro was not minding the business of the ship's crew, he might be found seated before the mainmast reading the Latin epic.[6]

The *Principe Real*'s course was only slightly more westerly than that taken three centuries earlier by Pedro Alvares Cabral, the discoverer of Brazil. Cabral, following up Vasco da Gama's 1498 voyage around Africa to India, stood far out into the South Atlantic, to skirt the horse latitudes that had slowed his predecessor. In April 1500 Cabral sighted and touched the South American mainland some 500 kilometers south of Bahia. After formally claiming the land for Portugal, he resumed his voyage to India. Colonized by Portuguese in the sixteenth century, the country got its name from the dyewood—*pau brasil*—that was its first major export. During the seventeenth century Brazil became the world's leading producer of sugar, and in the eighteenth century of gold and diamonds. The Brazilian sugar industry declined with the growth of West Indian competition in the late seventeenth century, but revived a hundred years later as revolutionary turmoil disrupted Caribbean production. An earlier revolution, in British North America, had created a lucrative market in England for another Brazilian product, cotton. The rise in Brazilian sugar and cotton exports continued into the nineteenth century, while shipments of gold and diamonds dwindled, due to mine exhaustion. Under the colonial system, all Brazil's trade had to go through Portugal. But now that Portugal was under French occupation, the system would have to be changed. Dom João would attend to that matter shortly after landing in Bahia.

In January 1808 as the *Principe Real* neared the Brazilian coast, she was hailed by a brigantine sent out from Recife by the governor of the province of Pernambuco. The governor had been advised of the fleet's approach by the captain of the advance ship *Medusa*, which, having been damaged in the storm of 11 December, put in to Recife for repairs before proceeding to Bahia. The brigantine brought fresh provisions, including tropical fruits, which were greatly appreciated by the ocean travelers. The young Dom Pedro, one might say, received his first taste of Brazil from Pernambuco; unfortunately, his later experiences with that province would not be as sweet as its mangoes and cashew fruit. The future emperor's first view of Brazil was probably of the coast of Bahia. On 22 January the *Principe Real* and four accompanying vessels sailed into All Saints Bay and dropped anchor in the harbor of Salvador da Bahia.[7]

Bahia, like Lisbon, was a multi-level city. The main government buildings, the cathedral, and most residences were on a promontory that rose eighty meters above the dockside area. Beyond the city, with its whitewashed structures seemingly stacked one on the other and intertwined with bright-green tropical foliage, lay the shimmering expanse of the bay, and the land embracing it—rolling gently to the horizon, displaying a patchwork of sugarcane fields, citrus groves, tobacco *veigas*, pasture, and native forest. The entrance to the bay was from the south, with the city rising on the east and the large island of Itaparica lying low in the west. A fort at the foot of the promontory offered the city little protection, as its guns could not command the ten-kilometer breadth of the channel. Bahia was vulnerable to attack from the bay and from the ocean beaches northeast of the city. In the seventeenth century, when it was the colonial capital of Brazil, Bahia had been twice captured by the Dutch, who, on another occasion, imperiled the city by occupying Itaparica. The Bahians who enthusiastically welcomed the Portuguese ships in 1808 hoped that the prince regent would remain in their city and make it his capital. But security considerations made this impossible.[8]

Transported in a few weeks from the blustery onset of winter in Europe to the eternal summer of tropical South America, Dom Pedro found himself in surroundings that fairly epitomized the Portuguese empire. The architecture of Bahia was basically Portuguese, with some adaptations, like verandas, from India. The landscape was graced with citrus and banana plants from southern Europe and North Africa; with native papaya plants and imperial palms, towering on smooth, pearly trunks to heights rarely attained by Mediterranean species; and with India's supple coconut palms—their elongated, feathery fronds supported on sensuously curved but spiny trunks—and densely foliated mango trees, which mercifully interposed their splendid canopies between sun and earth, casting shadows so dark as to amaze even the most erudite visitor to the tropics.[9] Native American hardwoods from the rain forest south of the city provided worm-resistant raw material for the colony's important shipbuilding industry; the *Principe Real* had been built in Bahia and launched into All Saints Bay in 1791. Africa was well represented in Bahia by its people, for the city was the center of Brazil's thriving slave trade, the main entrepôt for human property acquired on the Guinea coast, often in exchange for Bahian tobacco. Although most of the slaves landed at Bahia were destined for the sugarcane fields of northeastern Brazil or for the mines of the south, enough were retained in the city to make its population, by the time the Portuguese royal family arrived, one of the New World's darkest: of some 100,000 urban Bahians, about 40,000 were black and 30,000 mulatto.[10]

Dom Pedro first set foot on Brazilian soil at about four o'clock in the afternoon of 23 January 1808, when he left the *Principe Real* to accompany his parents and siblings to the Bahia cathedral for a Te Deum mass. As their carriages wound their way from the docks to the upper city, the royal visitors were wildly cheered by the Bahian multitudes. After the religious ceremony, "in which all the musicians of the city of Bahia played," the royal party returned to the ships. The next day Dom Pedro disembarked with his father and his demented grandmother for a month's stay at the local governor's palace. Dona Carlota, who found this quintessential colonial city little to her liking, did not go ashore again until 28 January, when she left the *Afonso de Albuquerque* to take up lodging at the law court building.[11]

The presence of the Portuguese royal family in Brazil drastically altered the relationship between colony and mother country. For the first time in his life, the prince regent was free to act in accordance with his own judgment of what was best for his realm. His feet were firmly set on some of Brazil's richest soil, the cheers of his Brazilian subjects rang in his ears, and he was thousands of kilometers from any French or Spanish army, with only one British warship in sight and no British minister to badger him. In Portugal, Lord Strangford had sought to persuade Dom João to open Brazil to British trade. In the viscount's view, the flight of the Portuguese royal family to Brazil was to escape French, not British, domination; indeed, the Portuguese court in its New World setting was supposed to be so beholden to Britain as to accede to the rerouting of Brazilian trade into British channels: Britain was to replace Portugal as Brazil's mother country.[12] But when the Portuguese court sailed for South America, Lord Strangford sailed for England, to report to his superiors and stake out his claim to diplomatic glory. Until Strangford rejoined the Portuguese court in Brazil eight months later, Dom João was on his own. The prince regent took advantage of the proconsul's absence to proclaim Brazil's economic independence: by royal decree issued in Bahia on 28 January 1808 he opened the ports of Brazil to direct trade, on an equal basis, with all nations at peace with the Portuguese crown.[13] The prince regent's decisive action removed Brazil from legal subjugation to the trading system of another country. It was the first step toward Brazil's full independence, which would be declared in less than fifteen years by Dom João's son and heir, Dom Pedro.

From the governor's mansion in Bahia and on excursions about the city with his father, young Dom Pedro looked upon scenes quite different from those he might have observed in Portugal. Wheeled vehicles, like the carriages that transported the royal family, were fairly rare in Bahia, as were horses and mules. The clatter of hooves and the creak of wheels inevitably attracted throngs of curiosity seekers who lined the narrow streets, and recognizing the royal personages, cheered them lustily. Those who could, ran along beside and behind the carriage. By handing out coins to the Bahians who followed for long distances, Dom João encouraged these impromptu escorts. Excursions beyond the city were especially pleasant at this time of year, February. The orange trees were in bloom and the scent of their blossoms was in the air. Usually, the royal party would return to the governor's residence by nightfall, but on a boat trip to Itaparica, Dom João and Dom Pedro had to spend the night on the island, in a government-owned house; unfavorable winds prevented their return to the city until the next day.[14]

Dom Pedro and his father traveled between the waterfront and the upper city by carriage, but most Bahians of means commuted in sedan chairs or litters carried by black slaves. Ships' cargoes were conveyed from dockside to the upper city in a sledge pulled up a slide by a windlass operating on a counterpoise system. Smaller burdens were transported suspended from a pole carried on the shoulders of a pair of black men. Individual blacks and mulattoes, males and females, went about the city with large baskets, jugs, and trays loaded with goods, balanced on their heads. White women were seldom seen in public, but black and mulatto women were everywhere, and they were striking in their appearance. The *bahiana* dress consisted of a kind of turban, to cushion the burdens carried on the head; a thin muslin blouse, bordered with lace at the cuffs and collar; necklaces of gold chain or strings of beads; two or three colorful, lace-trimmed, cotton skirts or petticoats, drawn in at the waist and cut just above the ankles; and backless, slightly elevated slippers. The bahianas moved with extraordinary grace, and never ceased to amaze foreigners with their displays of dorsal flexibility. Black males amused themselves by watching the bahianas and by practicing *capoeira*, a knife- and foot-fighting dance, to the beat of a drum and the twang of a single-string *berimbau*.[15] Dom Pedro was destined to grow up in a country whose sights, sounds, and smells were quite distinct from those of his native Portugal.

Reembarking at Bahia on 26 February 1808 the royal exiles

began the last leg of their journey to Rio de Janeiro. Their ships ran easily with the Brazil current to Cape Frio, rounded it, and a week out of Bahia, stood at the entrance to Guanabara Bay. Though scarcely two kilometers wide, the passage was unmistakable, marked by the incredible Sugar Loaf, a massive, egg-shaped boulder, rising 400 meters out of the sea and leaning back against a jungle-topped granite shoulder about half its height. Opposite the Sugar Loaf lesser rocks formed the eastern edge of the channel, which was so deep and well defined that pilots were not needed. Forts on the eastern rocks and at the foot of the Sugar Loaf effectively commanded the entrance to the bay; their guns roared in salute at midday on 7 March 1808, as a sea breeze wafted the Portuguese vessels past them and into the harbor at Rio. There the vessels proceeding from Bahia were reunited with their sister ships that had sailed directly from São Tiago. The royal passengers transported by these vessels, which had anchored at Rio seven weeks earlier, had only recently gone ashore, on 22 February, after learning of the safe arrival of their sovereign in Bahia. Dom João received the viceroy of Brazil, the count of Arcos, aboard the *Príncipe Real* on the afternoon of 7 March, and plans were discussed for the gala disembarkation of the royal family the next day. That night the great event was heralded by a magnificent display of fireworks.[16]

In Rio de Janeiro, unlike Bahia, the cathedral and principal government buildings were on the waterfront, at the northeast end of a low-lying corridor, about a kilometer wide, that ran for three kilometers between two ranges of hills to the swampy estuary of the Rio Comprido. The business district and most of the city's residences were located on this plain, where the narrow streets were straight and intersected each other fairly regularly, usually at right angles. On the hills were scattered a few churches, monasteries, and villas, and on the Morro do Castelo, the hill above the viceregal palace, stood a fort, observation post, and signal tower. Behind the hills and the bay stretched a panorama of jungle-clad mountains, whose wildly disparate configurations were reflected in their names, from Hunchback to Finger of God.

Under a blazing sun on the afternoon of 8 March 1808 the royal family—Dom João, Dona Carlota, and their children, but not the mad queen—transferred from their ships at anchor in Rio harbor to a brigantine that took them to the quay at the Largo do Paço (Palace

Square). Soldiers lined their way, bands played, crowds cheered, rockets flared, and cannons boomed in salute as the royal family disembarked and paraded, under a silk canopy carried by the city councilmen of Rio, across the square to the cathedral to offer thanks to God for their safe arrival. After the religious ceremonies, Dom João and Dom Pedro got into a carriage and were driven a short distance through the exuberant multitude to the viceroy's palace, with other members of the royal family following in other vehicles. The royal family was lodged in the palace, which the count of Arcos, the young and energetic viceroy, had expeditiously prepared for them. Under his direction it had been refurbished and expanded by annexing the adjacent city jail and Carmelite monastery, removing the prisoners and friars, and linking the three buildings with covered walkways. An apartment in the palace was reserved for the queen, who was judged well enough to disembark on 10 March. The earlier welcoming ceremonies were repeated for the demented monarch, who held up well, except for shrieking in terror as the cannons fired.[17]

At the Rio palace, young Dom Pedro, for the first time in years, found himself under the same roof with his father and mother, his grandmother, and all his siblings. This situation, however, would not last long. Neither of the boy's parents was disposed to continue living in the same house with the other, and both quickly decided that the viceregal palace and the area in which it was located, did not meet their residential requirements. Despite the count of Arcos's alterations, the palace remained an undistinguished stone structure of three stories, counting an attic, whose living quarters—mainly converted offices and meeting rooms—were scarcely more appealing to the Braganças and their attendants than were the cells of the appended jail and monastery. Including royalty, courtiers, and servants, nearly 300 people were crammed into this "miserable abode for royalty" that was "dignified with the name of a palace."[18]

Outside the palace was a treeless plaza paved with gray granite stones, like the adjacent streets. Jammed together along the narrow streets were modest one-story houses of plastered and whitewashed granite, with red-tile roofs; two-story buildings, with shops, warehouses, and taverns below and residences above; and an occasional three-story structure or church. One had to look up to the hills to see greenery. There were no sidewalks and the paved streets sloped inward to form the channels through which the waste water of this city of

60,000 to 100,000 people flowed, when it did not collect in stagnant pools, which, because of the lowness of the terrain, were virtually impossible to drain. The heat of Rio's tropical location quickened the rotting of the filth in the streets, while the frequent rains only washed the noxious refuse into puddles that emitted "the most putrid exhalations."[19] Rio was a dirty, stinking, unhealthy city, and the royal family soon dispersed to residences in the suburbs—except for the mad queen, who was kept in the downtown palace.

A wealthy local merchant presented to the royal family a country estate, Boa Vista, located five or six kilometers west of the city on a wooded ridge between Corcovado Mountain and Guanabara Bay. Another public-spirited gentleman offered a beach house at Botafogo, a sheltered inlet just inside the bay, facing the Sugar Loaf, about four kilometers south of town. Dom João accepted the country estate and moved there with his sons, Dom Pedro and Dom Miguel, and his nephew, the Spanish infante, Don Pedro Carlos. Dona Carlota withdrew to the beach house with her daughters.[20]

The oldest of the princes at Boa Vista was the Spanish Don Pedro Carlos. Twenty years old and living with the Portuguese royal family when Spain and France invaded Portugal in 1807, he willingly accompanied the Braganças to Brazil. About the time the infante arrived with the Portuguese in Rio, Spanish King Carlos IV abdicated the Spanish throne and his son, Don Pedro Carlos's uncle, was proclaimed King Fernando VII of Spain by patriots determined to block Napoleon's now obvious design to take over their country. Fernando VII, however, proved inept as a leader and wound up, with his father, a prisoner of Napoleon in France. Napoleon proceeded to proclaim his own brother, Joseph Bonaparte, to be king of Spain, but Don Fernando's partisans rejected him and launched a war of national liberation against the occupying French army. In May 1808, the patriots began forming a government in unoccupied territory to rule Spain and its empire in the name of the absent king, an undertaking that was encouraged and supported by the British. As news of these events reached Rio, Dom João and his advisers considered the idea of setting up a court for Don Pedro Carlos, the only male member of Spain's royal family to escape French captivity, in one of the Spanish American viceregal capitals, like Buenos Aires.[21]

The objectives of the British in Spanish America were to open its ports to British trade, while at the same time securing the allegiance of the colonials to their ally, the emerging patriot government in Spain. This policy was well enough understood by Lord Strangford, who arrived in Rio from London in July 1808 to resume his post as minister plenipotentiary to the Portuguese court. The policy was not so clear to Admiral Sir Sidney Smith, whose British squadron had dropped anchor in Rio harbor two months earlier; Sir Sidney's orders were to attack the French and their allies in South America. While French Guiana was Napoleon's only outpost on that continent, Sir Sidney was more concerned with Buenos Aires, site of a British military disaster two years before, which he believed was in danger of falling under French domination. To forestall this, the admiral favored using his forces to seize Buenos Aires and install there Don Pedro Carlos and his aunt, Dona Carlota—the imprisoned King Fernando's sister—as joint regents of Spanish America. Lord Strangford was adamantly opposed to the proposal.[22]

There was no love lost between Sir Sidney Smith and Lord Strangford. The admiral already despised the devious Hibernian for falsely taking credit for the emigration of the Portuguese royal family to Brazil. Now he saw the viscount's opposition to the Buenos Aires plan as motivated by nothing more than a childish determination to prevent himself from being upstaged as Britain's main man at the Portuguese court. Strangford worked assiduously to turn Dom João against the plan. The prince regent was ambivalent: although he wanted to stop the spread of French domination and influence, and possible republican subversion, and he would have liked to send his wife even farther away than Buenos Aires, he was also well acquainted with Dona Carlota's ambition and aggressive instincts, and could envision a threat to the security of Portuguese Brazil should she become ruler of neighboring Spanish America. At the least, he had reason to fear that she would be in a position to thwart his own designs on nearby Spanish territory. Also, Dom João did not want Don Pedro Carlos involved in his wife's possible schemes; he was greatly fond of the youth and would be reluctant to relinquish custody of him to the dissolute Dona Carlota. Don Pedro Carlos, frail and unassertive, returned his uncle's affection, and shared Dom João's distaste for Dona Carlota and her intrigues.[23] But the princess had a bold and determined ally in the English admiral.

Lord Strangford accused Sir Sidney Smith of "romantic" involvement with Dona Carlota.[24] Perhaps he did not mean this in the amorous sense. The princess was even less physically attractive in Brazil than she had been in Portugal. With age her features were becoming more gaunt and her facial hair more pronounced. The hair on her head had been sheared on the Atlantic voyage to combat an infestation of lice, and it was just beginning to grow out when she entered the relationship with Sir Sidney. They prepared their case at her beach house in Botafogo and the admiral argued it before Dom João on visits to Boa Vista and Santa Cruz, another country place the prince regent had acquired. Sir Sidney got nowhere with Dom João or Don Pedro Carlos; apparently the only positive response he received was from six-year-old Dom Miguel, Dona Carlota's favorite son, who indicated that he would not mind leaving his father's household to accompany his mother to Buenos Aires. Maybe the child was resentful of Dom João's favoritism for Dom Pedro and Don Pedro Carlos. In any event, the admiral took an interest in the lad, brought him presents, and selected for him an English teacher, whom Dom João accepted.[25]

On the Buenos Aires proposal, the prince regent remained noncommittal. Finally, in October 1808 Sir Sidney presented Dom João with a document written and signed by his wife, announcing that she was going to Buenos Aires to establish herself as regent of Spanish America, and that she was taking Dom Miguel and all her daughters with her. Whether or not her husband gave his permission, she intended to carry out her plan, with the help of Admiral Smith and the British squadron. Sir Sidney claimed that he had secret orders from the British admiralty authorizing the operation, and he and the princess began making preparations for the expedition. Strangford appealed to London to revoke Smith's orders, while the admiral insisted to his navy superiors that the operation was essential for advancing British interests in South America, that Dona Carlota had private assurances of support from the leading citizens of Buenos Aires, and that the project had Dom João's approval (perhaps he innocently misinterpreted the prince regent's silence). Strangford and the Foreign Office prevailed: early in May 1809 Smith received orders from the admiralty relieving him of his command and ordering him back to England. He delayed his departure long enough to learn of the success of a joint British-Portuguese expedition he had sent to seize French Guiana. Finally, on 21 June, having bid Dona Carlota a sad farewell, he sailed from Brazilian waters, never to return. Strangford, not content with his victory, used his influence in London to deprive Smith of his commander's share of the prize money from the sale of enemy vessels captured in Guiana.[26]

Sir Sidney Smith had recommended the English teacher who was named for Dom Miguel, but it was one of Lord Strangford's collaborators who was appointed language instructor and principal tutor to Dom Pedro. João Rademaker, a "supremely cultured polyglot,"[27] who reputedly spoke all the languages of Europe, appeared in Rio after relinquishing the post of Portuguese minister to Denmark. He accepted the position of royal tutor in October 1808. As a diplomat, João Rademaker was, according to John Hann, "either the complete incompetent or an archscoundrel." He was, in fact, Strangford's agent in the Portuguese foreign ministry and at Dom João's court at Boa Vista, where he was well placed as tutor to the prince regent's heir and favorite son. Striving diligently to preserve his advantageous position in the royal household, Rademaker was, by all accounts, an excellent teacher for Dom Pedro. Hardly an ardent student, the prince nevertheless responded positively to the patient pedagogy of the cosmopolitan Rademaker, whose Dutch forebears had settled in Portugal in the seventeenth century and engendered for their adopted country a progeny of peripatetic diplomats, clerics, and army officers.[28]

While under the tutelage of Rademaker, Dom Pedro maintained his relationship with Friar António de Arrábida, who continued as the prince's confessor, religious preceptor, and general confidant. The Franciscan was otherwise engaged in scientific work: collecting and classifying specimens of the native flora and advising Dom João in the establishment of the Royal Botanical Garden near Rio. To Dom Pedro, Friar Arrábida imparted a sincere religious faith coupled with a respect for secular knowledge. The boy's rambunctious nature—his father would not allow him to be disciplined—could be overcome, temporarily, by a skillful appeal to these sentiments. Rademaker managed to expose Dom Pedro to some of the elements of mathematics, logic, history, geography, and political economy. The prince continued to study Latin, which he read with some facility, and took up French and English under Rademaker. The royal pupil was supposed to spend two hours a day in formal study, but when he became bored with a lesson, or thought of something better to do, he would simply dismiss his tutor and pursue his whims. Helping the prince with his lessons and encouraging him in his studies was his governess, Dona Maria Genoveva do

Rêgo e Matos, who had accompanied the royal family on the Atlantic crossing. At Boa Vista Dona Maria Genoveva, in effect, assumed the role of mother to Dom Pedro; she was subject to his tantrums, but she received and returned his love.[29]

Dom Pedro tended to become bored at public functions, but ever conscious of the fact that he was a future king, he endured them with good grace, for the most part. Seated in a chair beside his father's improvised throne, he would play his role in the traditional Portuguese *beija mão*—the ceremony held from time to time in which subjects of the prince regent were invited to the palace to file past him and kiss his hand, and that of any other available member of the royal family. Dom Pedro's extended hand received the kisses of adults, but if he were approached by a child, his hand was apt to fly up and administer a sharp blow to the youngster's chin. The prince usually managed to suppress his laughter as his surprised victim would be led away by parents trying to avoid a scene. Such behavior did not set a good example for Dom Pedro's younger brother, Dom Miguel. Acutely aware of his inferior position in the line of succession, Dom Miguel did not have the likelihood of ascending to the throne to act as a check on his malicious impulses. Four years younger than Dom Pedro, he managed to keep up with his brother in mischief making. At the age of seven he was firing a pair of miniature cannon—unwisely presented to him by Sir Sidney Smith—at the legs of attendants at the royal court.[30]

Dom Pedro and Dom Miguel had the same teachers, for whom the younger prince demonstrated even less aptitude for academic learning than did his brother. Dom Pedro was a poor speller, but his brother was worse; after years of instruction he persisted in misspelling his own name as "Migel." Either boy probably would have done much better in military training, but none was offered them. They delighted in playing soldier. At the huge plantation and cattle ranch at Santa Cruz—some eighty kilometers west of Rio, on the trail to São Paulo —where Dom João began spending his summers in 1808–9, the princes mobilized rival armies of slave children and went at each other with sticks and rocks on battlefields beyond the sight of adults. The play was rough and both leaders took their share of blows. An injury that incapacitated Dom Pedro for several days came to the attention of the royal physician; the doctor was sure that it resulted from the blows of clubs, but the prince insisted that he got it falling off a horse. In truth, both princes were reckless horsemen and took numerous falls in their pursuit of equestrian thrills.[31]

There were far more horses and mules in the province of Rio de Janeiro and adjacent São Paulo than there were in Bahia. Mules were necessary to pack supplies over the coastal mountains to the mining districts and bring out the gold and diamonds. Horses were needed to breed mules and to mount hundreds of cavalrymen and dragoons assigned to police the trails and escort mule trains bearing crown revenue. People from São Paulo—*paulistas*—had discovered the mines of Minas Gerais after more than a century of roaming the savannas of central Brazil on foot. Later pushed out of Minas Gerais by hordes of newcomers from Bahia and other parts of the Portuguese empire, some paulistas went into the horse and mule business, importing the animals from the pampas to the south and selling them to merchants and government buyers at Sorocaba, São Paulo, which became the site of Brazil's largest livestock fair. Horses and mules purchased at Sorocaba were driven past the royal family's summer home at Santa Cruz on their way to markets in Rio de Janeiro.

The society of Rio de Janeiro was not horse oriented like that of the southern pampas, but neither was it as slave dependent as that of Bahia. People were carried about in Rio on the shoulders of slaves, but there was also some coach traffic. Men rode horses and drove pack mules, and mounted soldiers were frequently seen on the streets. This was a contrast to Bahia, where despite the immensity of the province there was no cavalry when the royal family arrived in 1808.[32] Although the sugar planters around Rio, like those of Bahia, utilized mainly the energy of slaves and oxen in their mills and fields, they were more apt than Bahians to purchase horses and mules for their personal use. Because straddling an equine was not as comfortable as lounging on a covered litter carried on the shoulders of slaves, some planters would have a litter rigged up between two mules, to be led by a slave, for a journey to Rio.[33] Such effeminacy disgusted Dom Pedro and Dom Miguel, who shared the hard-riding proclivities of their Spanish mother.

Dom Pedro and Dom Miguel were attracted to the stables and corrals of Santa Cruz, a latifundium of some 23,000 hectares that had belonged to the Society of Jesus until the Portuguese crown expelled the Jesuit fathers from Brazil and confiscated the order's property in 1759. Considerably run down from its prime condition under the Jesuits, Santa Cruz in 1808 supported seven to eight thousand head of

Dom Pedro at age 16 or 17: Watercolor by Jean Baptiste Debret
Fundação Dr. Ricardo do Espírito Santo Silva, Lisbon

semiwild cattle on extensive pastures cleared from the forest. There were more than a thousand slaves at Santa Cruz but few horses, when Dom João took over the property and authorized the purchase of work animals. Many of the newly acquired horses were unbroken, and breaking them to saddle, cart, or plow became a favorite recreation of the royal brothers. Stableboys and grooms became their preferred companions. Dom Pedro, in his late teens, broke four pairs of horses to harness in one morning. On horseback both princes were fearless and indefatigable, risking themselves and their mounts in chases through woods and over unknown terrain, baiting bulls, pursuing wild animals, riding for hours without pause in all kinds of weather and after dark. Dom Pedro was concerned with virtually everything related to the care and feeding of horses; he became an expert farrier, perhaps one of the best in Brazil.[34]

Dom Pedro was a fine horseman, but he was not a great horse trainer. He enjoyed the contest of wills with a large beast and his inevitable victory over the brute. After dominating an animal, he would teach it only a few commands; his objective was to train the horse to ignore all distractions and surmount all obstacles in order to carry him, or pull his carriage, at the fastest possible speed. Obsessed with speed and stamina, he was little interested in exhibitions of eye-pleasing gaits or fancy maneuvers in a sandy arena. Once he was presented a team of finely trained carriage horses from Europe, and he was unable to drive them; he claimed they had not been broken. In truth, they had not been broken to his style. Dom Pedro's primitive style brought him some hard knocks and broken ribs. As a youth he acknowledged that he had been thrown from horses thirty-six times. His rough early life may have aggravated a congenital epileptic condition; by the time he was eighteen he had suffered six grand mal seizures.[35]

Among Dom Pedro's less strenuous recreational activities were furniture making and wood carving. He used the power of his position to procure the best materials, and he received from the count of Arcos, then governor of Bahia, some of that province's famous hardwoods. In a letter to the former viceroy, whom Dom Pedro had admired since the royal family's first days in Rio, he declared that he was Arcos's friend "as a man, not as a prince."[36] (The writer was not quite fourteen years old.) The frigate *Principe Dom Pedro*, launched at Bahia in 1811, would sport a figurehead of her namesake, carved by the prince himself. Dom

Pedro had a certain aptitude for the visual arts: his carved figures were competent and his pen–and–ink drawings not bad.[37]

The prince's creative drive took him into the fields of poetry and music. In the former he tended to sacrifice logic and measure to rhyme, and produced mostly doggerel. In the latter he produced sweet sounds and demonstrated real talent. He had a good singing voice and learned to play a number of musical instruments, mostly on his own. He received some instruction from Padre José Maurício Nunes Garcia, director of music at the Rio cathedral, whom Dom João named royal chapel master in 1808. Padre José Maurício was a Brazilian of humble origins, a mulatto, whose religious superiors, perceiving divine inspiration in the exquisite sacred music he composed and directed, had decided to ignore his production of illegitimate offspring. Dom João, a discerning music critic, praised the work of José Maurício, but when the prince regent's court composer from Portugal, Marcos Portugal, finally made the trip to Rio in 1811, he displaced the mulatto priest as royal music director and teacher of Dom Pedro. A prolific composer of operas as well as sacred music, Marcos Portugal introduced Dom Pedro to a wide variety of secular works and encouraged the prince in his own compositions. The instruments that Dom Pedro mastered included the clarinet, flute, violin, bassoon, trombone, and harpsicord. He also played the guitar, which had no place in masses or operas, but was used to accompany popular songs and dances, like the Portuguese-gypsy *fado*, the Luso–Brazilian *modinha*, and the Angolan *lundu*, lascivious forerunner of the samba, which began with an "invitation to dance," the partners rubbing belly buttons, and was banned by the church.[38] The sexual initiation of the prince, who, not yet fourteen, declared that he was to be regarded as a man, might well have followed some clandestine dance on a packed–clay patio among the slave huts of Boa Vista or Santa Cruz.

In other areas, Dom Pedro's education proceeded slowly. Under Rademaker's tutelage he learned to speak passable French and to read English, and was introduced to some of the important literary and philosophical works in those languages. Dom Pedro, it was said, was just beginning to respond to Rademaker's intellectual stimulation when, in 1814, the tutor suddenly died, poisoned by a female slave.[39] Coincidentally, Rademaker's secret master, Lord Strangford, was recalled at this time to London on Dom João's demand. After years of patiently

Dona Carlota Joaquina, Queen of Portugal and Brazil
From Tobias Monteiro, *Historia do imperio: A elaboração da independencia*
(Rio de Janeiro, 1927).

suffering the Hibernian's sleepy arrogance and shrinking from the British veto he wielded, the prince regent at last was able to get rid of him and put in motion his own bold plans for the aggrandizement of Brazil.

Sir Sidney Smith's departure in 1809 had been a blow to Dona Carlota, but it did not destroy her ambition to make herself ruler of Spanish America. She continued to correspond secretly with prominent figures and potential supporters in Buenos Aires and other Spanish colonial cities. In the meantime, Lord Strangford pressed her husband to grant Great Britain sweeping concessions in Brazil. The result was the so-called Strangford treaties of 1810, whereby British goods were guaranteed unrestricted access to Brazilian markets on payment of duties of no more than 15 percent ad valorem, with Dom João granting Britain most-favored-nation trading status in Portugal and its empire. To promote British-Brazilian commerce, British subjects were allowed to settle in Brazil and were granted the privileges of extraterritoriality: not subject to Portuguese jurisdiction, they could be brought to trial only before judges of their own nationality elected by British residents in Brazil. In other provisions galling to the Brazilians and Portuguese, subjects of Portugal were prohibited from engaging in the transatlantic slave trade from parts of Africa that did not belong to Portugal, and Dom João promised to cooperate with the British in efforts gradually to put an end to the traffic everywhere in the world.[40]

Great Britain, following the examples of Denmark and the United States, had prohibited the importation of slaves from Africa into its own territories after 1 March 1808, and backed by the authority of its preponderant navy, had set out to persuade other nations that they should do likewise. Brazil, by far the largest importer of Africans in the Western Hemisphere, was the prime target of those Britons who for various humanitarian, religious, and economic reasons were determined to halt the infamous commerce. In the three centuries prior to 1810, perhaps five million slaves had been landed in Brazil, shipped from Portuguese trading posts along the west African coast, from Cape Verde to the Bight of Bonny, or from the Portuguese colonies of Angola and Mozambique in southern Africa. In addition, Portuguese slavers at times supplied labor to Spanish and other European colonists in the Caribbean. Brazil's appetite for imported forced labor was voracious; in Brazil, unlike the southern United States, the slave population did not reproduce itself. For all the imports, Brazil's black slave population—concentrated in the Northeast, Minas Gerais, and Rio de Janeiro—numbered little more than a million in 1810. Since the rest of Brazil's people—some three million whites, "civilized" Indians, mestizos, and free blacks and mulattoes—had an understandable aversion to plantation labor, Brazilian planters saw no way of maintaining sugar and cotton output, or embarking on large-scale coffee production, as Dom João was recommending, without a steady infusion of slaves from Africa.[41] The prince regent seemed to agree; the British had forced him to make the slave-trade commitment and they would have to force him to carry it out.

The British also had pulled Dom João unwillingly into an alliance with the patriot government in Spain, the central junta of Seville. Dom João, no less than his wife, sought to undermine the authority of the junta, which, by 1809, all the Spanish colonies had recognized. The prince regent hoped to install his favorite nephew, Don Pedro Carlos, as regent of Spain and its empire, and he looked for ways to strengthen the youth's claim to the Spanish throne itself, should Fernando VII not survive French captivity. Dona Carlota—who, if one discounts an arguable Spanish law denying the crown to females, was much better positioned in Spain's line of succession—detested Don Pedro Carlos and was outraged when Dom João proposed that he marry their eldest daughter, Dona Maria Teresa. The wan Don Pedro Carlos displayed uncharacteristic enthusiasm for the match, and he and his uncle prevailed; Dona Maria Teresa accepted the proposal, although she was not unaware of the anguish of her mother, to whom she was fairly close. The wedding was held in the Royal Chapel (formerly that of the Carmelites) and celebrated on the Palace Square with all manner of pageantry and fireworks for an entire week in May 1810. Afterwards, the couple retired to an apartment Dom João had reserved for them at Boa Vista, and the next year they produced a son, Dom Sebastião. Palace gossips worried that Don Pedro Carlos was undermining his already precarious health in excessive conjugal activity with Dona Maria Teresa. In any case, the young husband succumbed to a "violent nervous fever" and died on 26 May 1812. A heartbroken Dom João declared six months of official mourning for Don Pedro Carlos.[42]

By this time the situation in the Spanish colonies in South America had changed dramatically. Reacting to news of the dissolution of the central junta of Seville in the face of a massive French offensive in Spain, the leading citizens of Buenos Aires and most other colonial capitals in Spanish South America organized their own autonomous governments in the name of the imprisoned King Fernando and expelled the royal officials who objected. Among these was the viceroy of La Plata, who was put aboard a Spanish ship at Buenos Aires and sent back to Europe. As it turned out, Napoleon's army did not succeed in overrunning all of Spain in 1810, and a new patriot government, the Regency, was firmly established in the port of Cádiz, under the protection of the British army and navy. To legitimize itself, the Cádiz government summoned a *cortes* (parliament) of delegates elected from the colonies as well as from the provinces of Spain. The Buenos Aires junta denied the authority of the Cádiz government and refused to send delegates to the cortes. Dona Carlota hoped that the Buenos Aires junta would invite her to be Queen of La Plata, but most of its members preferred constitutional government to the absolute monarchy that she offered, so the invitation was not forthcoming.[43]

The Cádiz government tried to reestablish Spanish authority over the viceroyalty of La Plata by sending out a new viceroy, who set up his court at Montevideo, in the province of Uruguay. There the viceroy came under attack by an army raised by the government in Buenos Aires, and by an irregular force led by the Uruguayan gaucho, José Gervasio Artigas. Dom João, over Strangford's objections, sent a Portuguese army expedition to Uruguay to help the Spanish viceroy combat the forces of Buenos Aires and Artigas. Strangford realized that the prince regent had ulterior motives in dispatching the expedition: Dom João aimed to bring Uruguay under his own control, and then annex it to Brazil—something the viscount and his superiors in London were determined to prevent.[44] The expansion of Brazil was not in Britain's interests; a larger and stronger Portuguese state in South America might break the chains so assiduously forged by Lord Strangford and go on to threaten British hegemony elsewhere on the continent.

Uruguay was a tempting prize for Dom João. The area originally had been settled by the Portuguese in 1680, and in the subsequent century of intermittent warfare between Spain and Portugal, it changed hands several times. In 1777 Portugal ceded Uruguay to Spain by treaty, but in the 1801 war Portuguese forces pushed the border of Brazil some distance south along the coast at the expense of the Spanish province. In Dom João's view, the natural and historical southern boundary of Brazil was the Río de la Plata, which meant that all of Uruguay was destined to be Portuguese. To help fulfill that destiny, the prince regent dispatched troops to Uruguay, ostensibly to defend the Spanish viceroy in Montevideo. After several months of desultory fighting between his forces and those of the uneasy alliance of Artigas and Buenos Aires, in 1812 Dom João was prevailed upon by Lord Strangford to send an emissary to Buenos Aires to seek a negotiated end to the conflict. On Strangford's recommendation, the prince regent assigned the mission to João Rademaker, Dom Pedro's tutor. Disregarding the orders of the government he was supposed to be serving, Rademaker acted on Strangford's secret instructions and immediately signed a truce between the forces of Rio de Janeiro and Buenos Aires; he then arranged for the evacuation of all Portuguese troops from Uruguay without securing the withdrawal of those of Buenos Aires. Although Rademaker's settlement ignored Dom João's interests, as well as those of the Spanish viceroy, Strangford pressured the prince regent to accept it. Also left out was Artigas, who soon declared the independence of Uruguay and continued his struggle against Spain, Buenos Aires, and the Luso-Brazilians. In the meantime, Rademaker rushed back to Rio to inform Strangford that he had learned of a plot by partisans of Dona Carlota to assassinate the leaders of the government of Buenos Aires and take over the city in her name. Word was passed to the authorities there who arrested the conspirators and had them shot.[45]

Thwarted in her Río de la Plata intrigues, Dona Carlota seemed to take out her frustrations on the diplomatic corps in Rio. She traveled often between her house in Botafogo and the city palace, and took regular drives in Rio's southern suburbs, where most foreign diplomats resided. Like everyone else, foreigners were required to dismount, uncover, and kneel as the princess's carriage passed, preceded by a pair of burly outriders whose job was to insure that Dona Carlota received the royal honors due her. Consuls, legation secretaries, and ministers were ordered out of their coaches, or down from their horses; if they did not comply, they received a thrashing. Most complied, under protest. The Russian minister was so annoyed by the repeated humiliation that he moved out of the neighborhood. The near-sighted Lord Strangford, perhaps slow to recognize the royal carriage and react accordingly, was assaulted by the princess's sword-wielding guards, who forced him down from the saddle and left him fuming in the dust raised by the passing vehicle. "The only redress which his Lordship obtained, was the imprisonment of the guards for a short time."[46]

Dom João VI, King of Portugal and Brazil
From Ángelo Pereira, *D. João VI: Príncipe e rei* (Lisbon, 1956).

While Strangford nursed his bruises in Rio, the settlement he had ordered for Uruguay collapsed. The dauntless Artigas swept all before him in 1814 and entered Montevideo in triumph. In the meantime, another war had become a cause for concern in Rio as Yankee privateers and United States Navy warships cruised along the Brazilian coast preying on British shipping. The Portuguese, while allied with the British against the French, remained neutral in the War of 1812 between Britain and the United States—although Dom João complained about the intrusions of Americans into Brazilian territorial waters in pursuit of prey, and their occasional seizure of Portuguese vessels, taken for British ones. A bumptious United States minister to the Portuguese court did little to ease the strained relations between the two nations, although he did receive some credit from fellow diplomats in Rio for facing down Dona Carlota. He was Thomas Sumter, Jr., son of the Revolutionary War hero, the Gamecock of South Carolina, and he shared his father's aversion for royalty. One day in September 1815, as Dona Carlota's carriage approached him, Sumter defiantly remained astride his horse, and when her guards came to haul him down, he drew his two pistols and made them back off. Unprepared for an American-style shoot-out, Dona Carlota and her entourage withdrew and, a few days later, Dom João issued orders limiting the obeisance required of foreigners to that which they would render their own sovereigns.[47]

Lord Strangford was not in Rio to experience mixed feelings about the humiliation of Dona Carlota by the disagreeable Sumter. The Hibernian had overstepped the bounds of propriety, even for a proconsul, in vetoing Dom João's choice for Portuguese foreign minister and in badgering the prince regent to leave Brazil and return to Portugal in 1814. Napoleon had been defeated; the French were gone from the Iberian peninsula; Fernando VII had taken his seat on the Spanish throne, dismissed the Cortes, and torn up the constitution it had adopted in his absence. Things were returning to normal. It was time for Dom João to move his government back to Lisbon—or so thought the Tory Liverpool-Castlereagh government, and Strangford heartily agreed. But Dom João disagreed, and he outmaneuvered them by appealing directly to the prince regent of Great Britain for the removal of the disrespectful Strangford. The future King George IV, during the great revival of respect for legitimate monarchs that followed Napoleon's first abdication, deplored the abuse of his Portuguese cousin by the British minister and urged the viscount's removal. His government complied, and Lord Strangford embarked in Rio for England on 8 April 1815.[48]

Dom João had an excellent perception of the temper of his times, and he seized the opportunities offered him. Rather than return to Portugal, he would stay in Brazil, where he would be better able to resist British pressure in the postwar world. To break away from Britain, he would seek support from Austria and restoration France. In South America he would smash Artigas and conquer Uruguay. He would declare Brazil a kingdom and make Rio de Janeiro a city fit for a king. He would remodel the city, enlarge the palace at Boa Vista, and bring over French artists and Austrian musicians. He would do all this and much more.

The kingdom of Brazil, coequal with the kingdom of Portugal in the Portuguese empire, was proclaimed in Rio de Janeiro on 17 December 1815, the eighty-first birthday of the mad Queen Maria. Courtiers and officials assembled outside the city palace and troops were drawn up in the plaza to hear the reading of the prince regent's decree, which was dated the previous day. The proclamation set off three days of celebration in Rio de Janeiro. Three months later the queen died and the kingdom acclaimed its first king, Dom João VI. Among those congratulating the new monarch was his seventeen-year-old son and heir, Dom Pedro. "Posterity, that incorruptible posterity, that spares not even kings," intoned the new crown prince, "will note in Your Majesty an infinite number of moral and political points of contact with the heroes of the *Aeneid*; like Aeneas, Your Majesty, after a long voyage, came to lay the foundations of a state that is bound one day to be the foremost of the world."[49]

3 The Crown Prince

Dost thou hear, Hal? Never call a true piece of gold a counterfeit:
Thou are essentially made, without seeming so.
Shakespeare, *Henry the Fourth, Part One*

Dom Pedro at age seventeen had what was called *boa presença* (good appearance). He had reached his adult height, somewhat above the male average for his time and place, after an adolescent spurt of growth about a year earlier, and now his frame was filling out; his build was still slender, but with broad shoulders, an ample chest, and powerful upper arms. His hair was a lustrous brown, thick on his head, and very curly; sideburns were forming and there was a trace of a moustache above his slightly protruding upper lip. His nose was straight and prominent, and his chin was a bit receding. After years under a tropical sun, his complexion was still light, his cheeks rosy. His large, dark, sparkling eyes gave an impression of *candura* (innocence), which was certainly misleading. His good appearance owed much to his bearing, proud and erect even at an awkward age, and his grooming, which was impeccable. Habitually neat and clean, he had taken to the Brazilian custom of bathing often. His clothes were well tailored and stylish.[1] For all his hard living and rough riding, the crown prince of Portugal and Brazil was something of a dandy.

The personal habits of Dom Pedro seemed the very antithesis of those of his father. Dom João was notorious for wearing clothes until they literally rotted off his body; he would stuff whole roast chickens into his pockets. Never in his life, it was said, had the king ever taken a complete bath with soap and water. He suffered from various rashes and skin diseases, and uninhibited by the presence of others, would thrust his hand inside his clothing and scratch wherever he itched. A tick bite that Dom João received at Santa Cruz became infected and produced a painful swelling in his leg, for which the palace physician prescribed saltwater hydrotherapy. The king consented to the treatment only after elaborate preparations had been made: he was provided with a wooden tub that was placed inside a portable bathhouse that was lowered into the waters at São Cristóvão Beach, near Boa Vista. His son, Dom Pedro, however, liked to swim nude in the surf at Flamengo Beach, and did not seem to care who saw him.[2]

Dom João gave scant thought to the education of his heir. He did not consider it a matter of great importance and instructed Friar Arrábida, who succeeded the poisoned Rademaker as director of Dom Pedro's education, not to push too much learning on the lad. The prince pursued the study of French under Father Renato Pedro Boiret, a worldly cleric who was renowned for his afternoon tea parties. Dom Pedro read Benjamin Constant de Rebecque on the philosophy of government and General Maximilièn Sébastian Foy on the campaigns of Napoleon. He practiced writing French by composing at least one letter to his mother in that language.[3]

Dom Pedro, living with his father at Boa Vista, corresponded fairly regularly with his mother, now the Queen of Portugal and Brazil, residing at Botafogo Beach or at one of her country villas. His letters were brief, no more than a page, sometimes consisting of a single sentence: "My Mother and my *Senhora*, I hope that Your Majesty has been well and will continue to be. From this, your humble son who kisses your hand, Pedro." Less perfunctory were notes transmitting gifts of flowers or game birds the prince had shot, intervening in behalf of a servant who wanted to be transferred from one royal household to the other, or inquiring specifically about the health problems of the queen or of one of the princesses living with her.[4]

Except for their common heritage of epilepsy, Dom Pedro seemed to escape the variety of ailments that afflicted his siblings, including Dom Miguel, who suffered persistent coughs and fevers and was thought to be tubercular. Dom João's archivist, Luís dos Santos Marrocos, who detailed the illnesses of the royal family in letters to relatives in Lisbon, had little to say about Dom Pedro in this regard, noting only his seizures and a skin infection he contracted in 1815, which left his face slightly marked. Among the Braganças, whatever their ailments, only the octogenarian Queen Maria and her seventy-six-year-old sister, Dona Mariana, died in Brazil—although Dom Pedro's oldest sister, Dona Maria Teresa, lost her husband, the Spanish infante Don Pedro Carlos. After Don Pedro Carlos's death, his widow joined Dom João's household with her infant son, Dom Sebastião. Dona Maria Teresa, the most intelligent and capable of the princesses, became Dom João's private secretary and confidante on matters of state.[5]

Dom João, his sloppy appearance and other unattractive traits notwithstanding, set for Dom Pedro a worthy example of regular habits, piety, work, and devotion to duty. Arising each morning at six, he would proceed with his Portuguese valet to the royal chapel to hear mass, after which he would be shaved by the valet, eat a hearty breakfast, and receive family members and palace functionaries like Archivist Marrocos, who boasted that he regularly kissed the royal hand at seven o'clock. Later in the morning the king met with his closest advisers, including Dona Maria Teresa, to discuss the more pressing problems of the hour and arrange the rest of the day's schedule. At midday Dom João sat down for dinner with his sons and grandson, while all the palace staff stood in attendance. The main dish was almost surely to be Dom João's favorite, roast chicken, which the king ate without the help of knife or fork, and washed down with water (he seldom drank wine). Before dessert was served there was a ceremonial washing of His Majesty's greasy hands, with Dom Pedro holding the silver basin, Dom Miguel pouring water from a pitcher, and little Dom Sebastião standing by with a towel. After dessert, usually fruit from the royal orchards at Boa Vista or Santa Cruz, the king retired for an hour's nap. Afterwards he received petitioners and other visitors until about five o'clock, when, if it was not raining, the royal carriage would be summoned and Dom João would go for a drive. While his mother was living, Dom João tried to see her every day; either he would drive to the city palace where she resided, or she would be brought out to Boa Vista.[6]

Dom João would return from his afternoon drive at nightfall and go directly to the chapel for vespers. After prayers and another big meal—he also snacked throughout the day—Dom João might preside over a meeting of his council of state. This was the body that made policy and formulated laws in the name of the king. All members were appointed by Dom João and served at his pleasure; they included some cabinet ministers, ecclesiastics, and an occasional member of the royal family, like Dona Maria Teresa (Dom Pedro was not invited to attend a meeting of the council of state until 1821). Although the final decision on any matter was the king's, it was likely to be the result of a consensus arrived at after the discussion of a wide range of views. Decisions of the council of state were conveyed in the king's name to the king's ministers—the heads of the various executive departments of government—who carried them out. When there was no meeting of the council of state, Dom João would occupy himself with official visitors or paperwork until eleven o'clock, his bedtime.[7]

The royal residence at Boa Vista was no more than an oversized Brazilian country house when the Braganças occupied it in 1808. It was a two-story rectangular structure with a veranda supported by twenty columns and a three-story pavilion at the main entrance. The only major improvement made before 1815 was the addition of a gate and wall enclosing the adjacent garden of citrus, coffee, banana, mimosa, and other flowering plants. At the time of the proclamation of the kingdom of Brazil, work was underway to give the structure a gothic facade to make it look more like a European palace, and plans had been drawn up for a three-story annex and more pavilions. On the inside, there had been some redecorating early in the royal occupancy to enhance the throne room and the council of state chamber.[8]

In the city of Rio de Janeiro, Dom João's government had made some improvements by the time of the proclamation of the kingdom. But the city's most impressive structure at that time, the Carioca Aqueduct, antedated the arrival of the royal family. Built in the 1750s, the aqueduct carried water from a covered reservoir on the lower north slope of Corcovado Mountain to a large public fountain at Carioca Plaza, a vertical drop of nearly 200 meters in a distance of five kilometers. The covered, stone-masonry channel cut through some hills, skirted others, and spanned a major gap on two ranges of arches, one above the other, and each as tall as a two-story house. Although the aqueduct also supplied water to three smaller fountains in the city, including one at the Palace Square, it was at the Carioca Fountain that carriers for most of the city's households gathered with barrels and large jars to fetch a day's supply of potable water. As the liquid gushed from eleven overhead brass pipes, there was pushing and shoving below and sometimes fights between muscular slave water carriers, irritated or bored after waiting in line for as long as an hour or more. The fountain runoff flowed into a shallow tank where half-naked blacks and mulattoes, of both sexes, washed clothes. From the fountain to which the city's multitudes were drawn, the people of Rio got their name: *Cariocas*. Dom João, who appreciated good drinking water, resolved to give the Cariocas better access to the stuff. He ordered construction of a new aqueduct from the Rio Comprido to the Campo de Santana, on the northwest edge of the city, and presided over the inauguration of a fountain there on 13 May 1809. The fountain was a boon to the residents of that neighborhood, but the new aqueduct was inferior to the older one in the quality and quantity of the water it delivered, and in its construction, which was of wood. Plans were developed for a more permanent structure to bring water to the Campo de Santana from the Rio Maracanã.[9]

A more urgent project—after the arrival of Maestro Marcos Portugal in 1811—was the replacement of the city's modest opera house with an adequate royal theater. This was accomplished on 12 October 1813, Dom Pedro's birthday, when a new theater, nine blocks from the city palace, was inaugurated with most of the royal family in attendance. The opera featured was *The Oath of the Gods*, by Marcos Portugal. Two years later, at the time of the proclamation of the kingdom of Brazil, high priority was given to musical improvements. An organ was ordered for the Royal Chapel and Italian castrati were recruited to sing in the choir. A marching band, the first to appear in Brazil, was organized in Portugal and shipped to Rio. In Paris, the renowned Austrian pianist and composer, Sigismund von Neukomm, was contracted for Brazilian royal service, along with some of France's most talented painters and sculptors. Perceiving a boom in the visual and performing arts in Brazil, dozens of French and other European artists, musicians, singers, actors, and dancers booked passage to the new kingdom.[10] They enlivened the nightlife of Rio de Janeiro.

Rio's coffee houses, restaurants, and taverns were meeting places for men of all colors and black and mulatto women. Respectable white women, at least until the French arrived, did not appear in public places other than church or the theater. Prostitutes of various colors were found "in every quarter and in every street" and were, according to a visiting Frenchman, "perhaps, as numerous as at Paris." Carioca streetwalkers did not openly solicit customers, but advertised their profession by a distinctive mantilla they wore, which was trimmed in black velvet.[11] Taverns were open to the street, except when some activity frowned upon by the police, like gambling or lascivious dancing, was going on; then a curtain might be pulled across the establishment's wide entrance. Whenever possible, however, the circulation of air was promoted to mitigate the tropical heat, and to dispel the smoke and foul odor of whale-oil lamps. Foreign sailors might light up pipes, and visiting Spanish Americans, cigars, but most of the tobacco consumed by tavern clientele would be smokeless, snorted in the form of snuff. For drink, the best establishments offered beer imported from Sweden, a variety of Portuguese wines, rum, and imported liquors. Places catering to the poorest segment of society, blacks, sold mostly *cachaça*, a cheap distillate of fermented sugarcane juice. Lemonade or orangeade was usually available to mix with cachaça or other spirits. In the better establishments customers consumed great quantities of Portuguese *vinho verde*, green wine, mixed with the excellent Carioca water. Musical entertainment, improvised by the clientele, was limited to Afro-Brazilian songs and rhythms in the poorest places, but elsewhere included fados and modinhas as well as the ubiquitous Angolan lundus.[12]

Dom Pedro, crown prince of Portugal and Brazil, appeared on the Rio tavern scene in the guise of an ordinary citizen, usually in the company of one or more grooms or other low-level employees of the palace at Boa Vista. One night, according to a story repeated by at least one reputable historian,[13] Dom Pedro and a companion, both dressed in the wide capes and broad-brimmed hats worn by horsemen from São Paulo, entered the Bugle Tavern on Violas Street. Taking seats at a rough wooden table, the counterfeit paulistas gave their attention to a guitar duel then in progress. Two Cariocas were competing for the applause of the audience, making up verses as they strummed their instruments. One, a large black man, had a flash of inspiration as he caught sight of Dom Pedro sitting with the collar of his paulista cape pulled up about his face. Looking directly at the disguised prince, the black guitarist broke into a grin and began singing

A paulista is a sneaky bird,
Without faith or the guts to peck:
The kind you go after with a stick,
Giving blows or chops to the neck.[14]

The audience, all eyes on Dom Pedro, burst into riotous laughter. The enraged prince jumped up, threw back his cape, revealed his identity, and ordered his companion to "lay the club on this scoundrel!" But the immobilizing shock of recognizing the crown prince had lasted only a split second, and the offending guitarist was already running out the front door, followed by most of the tavern's male clientele; women dived under tables to avoid being trampled in the mad scramble for the exit. Of those who had insulted the teenaged prince with their laughter, only one man remained: a tall, lean Portuguese about twenty-five years old wearing a big Catalonian hat. The prince's companion went after him with club raised, but the Portuguese neatly sidestepped his assailant, tripped him, and sent him sprawling across the floor. In a flash, the Portuguese picked up the stunned bodyguard by his clothing and heaved him out the back door, onto the tavern's patio. Turning to the furious prince, the unruffled stranger doffed his sombrero and took a deep bow, describing a great arc in the air with the hat, almost touching the floor, and with only a trace of a smile on his lips, said softly, "Francisco Gomes da Silva offers Your Highness his compliments and his services."

Dom Pedro could not contain himself: he broke into loud guffaws and then declared happily, "Joker, you are a man!" Thus, Brazil's Prince Hal found his Falstaff, and gave him the name by which he would forever be known: *O Chalaça*, (the Joker)—or so goes the story.

Actually someone other than Dom Pedro might have conferred that appropriate sobriquet on Francisco Gomes da Silva, and the prince could have made his acquaintance at one of the royal residences, since Chalaça was employed as a palace servant, though one of many, from 1810 to 1816. The adopted son of a goldsmith who had sailed for Brazil with the royal family in 1807, Francisco Gomes da Silva was a protegé of Dom João's Chamberlain, the Viscount Vila Nova da Rainha, who might have been Chalaça's father. The viscount's patronage, however, could not save Chalaça from being fired as a royal houseboy in 1816 for seducing a palace matron at Santa Cruz. Before the end of the year, as his friendship with Dom Pedro blossomed, Chalaça was reinstated in government service as a clerk in the treasury department. At one time Chalaça had a financial interest in the tavern on Violas Street, whose principal owner was Maria Pulqueria, the widow of a Portuguese army bugler and the Joker's occasional mistress. Chalaça was part owner of another tavern on the square across from the city palace. But he was best known as a wit, storyteller, prankster, guitarist, singer of ballads, dancer of lundus, womanizer, and brawler. He would contribute to the education of Dom Pedro, eight years his junior, and the two would share many adventures. Chalaça's wisecracks could get them into trouble; on at least one occasion the prince had to wade into a tavern fight to rescue the Joker. In a tight situation, the hard-drinking Chalaça could count on the relative sobriety of his royal friend, who throughout his life, drank only moderately.[15]

Dom Pedro and Chalaça regularly attended the new Royal Theater, which was as large as the Paris Opera, with orchestra seating for 1,020, and 112 boxes, but no public galleries. The Royal Theater presented several attractions daily from a repertory of operas, light operas, symphonies, ballets, tragic dramas, and comedies. The crown prince conceived a passion for the actress Ludovina Soares da Costa. At length he arranged a rendezvous with Ludovina at her house. When the eager prince arrived at the appointed hour, the actress met him at the door and led him into a room, which, to Dom Pedro's great surprise, was filled with members of her theater company, including her husband, all holding lighted torches and awaiting the honor of meeting His Royal Highness. Realizing that he was the victim of a jest—one worthy of the Chalaça—Dom Pedro made the best of it and greeted them all with good humor.[16]

Upper-class Brazilian and Portuguese fathers kept close watch over their daughters when the crown prince was around; at least one went so far as to bar Dom Pedro from his home. The young prince pursued their wives as well as their daughters, when the opportunity presented itself. If he spotted slaves carrying a sedan chair with the curtain drawn—a good indication that a lady was inside—Dom Pedro might ride up, pull back the curtain, and, if he liked what he saw, flirt with the occupant. Some prominent women apparently gave in to the prince's advances, including the wife of General Jorge de Avilez, commander of the Rio de Janeiro army garrison.[17]

Dom Pedro's first extended affair was with Noémi Thierry, a young, unmarried French ballerina. His passion for the fair Noémi lasted for months, at least, and resulted in the ballerina's pregnancy. The facts of the relationship, which the prince did not attempt to conceal, were well known in Rio and were potentially embarrassing to Dom João's government, which was trying to arrange the marriage of Dom Pedro to a European princess. Finally, for reasons of state, the prince and the ballerina agreed to end their affair. A sizable sum of money was appropriated from the royal coffers for Noémi and her unborn child, and she was put on a ship for Pernambuco, where she was entrusted to the care of the provincial governor. The child she was carrying was stillborn in Pernambuco, and Noémi disappeared from public view, perhaps returning to France. On 13 May 1817, Dom Pedro was married by proxy to the Austrian Archduchess Leopoldina von Hapsburg, the bride won for him by the marquis de Marialva.[18]

The marquis of Marialva, Dom João's master of the horse and Dom Miguel's reputed father, was in Spain on his way to France to propose to Napoleon the marriage of Dom Pedro to the French emperor's niece, when he learned, in late 1807, of the flight of the Braganças to Brazil and General Junot's occupation of Lisbon. With France and the fugitive Portuguese court at war (though not declared by the latter until May 1808), Marialva's mission lost its rationale and the marquis returned to Portugal, where he cast his lot with the occupation regime. He was not alone: Marcos Portugal dedicated an opera to Napoleon, and the gallant General Gomes Freire de Andrade, outraged by what he considered the desertion of the Portuguese royal family, offered his services to the French emperor. In May 1808 the marquis of Marialva was a member of a high-level Portuguese delegation sent to France to congratulate Napoleon on his victory in Portugal, thank him for freeing the country from English domination, and discuss the formation of a post-liberation regime. The Portuguese delegation arrived at Napoleon's residence in Bayonne just as the emperor was disposing of Spanish King Fernando VII and ex-King Carlos IV by imprisoning them in France. The emperor decided to do the same with the representatives of the Portuguese elite: he ordered Marialva and his companions interned in France. Thus, the marquis remained a prisoner of the French until the fall of Napoleon in 1814.[19]

The Spanish and Portuguese prisoners were dispersed to various chateaux in France, with the most important, King Fernando and his brother, Don Carlos, interned at the private estate of Napoleon's former foreign minister, the wily Charles-Maurice de Talleyrand, who treated them as royal guests. Eventually, the marquis of Marialva also came under the protection of Talleyrand, who was playing his usual double game, counseling Napoleon while plotting his overthrow. Marialva and Talleyrand, both bons vivants and kindred spirits politically, shared many tastes, including one for the music of Sigismund von Neukomm, Talleyrand's house pianist. After Talleyrand emerged as foreign minister of the restored Bourbon regime under King Louis XVIII, Dom João appointed Marialva as his ambassador to the French court. But to head his delegation to the European peace conference of 1814–15, the Congress of Vienna, Dom João appointed a statesman more acceptable to the British, Pedro de Sousa e Holstein, count and future duke of Palmela, who had served as an army officer with Wellington against the French in the Peninsular Campaign. Later, however,

Marialva also was sent to Vienna, as special envoy to Russian Czar Alexander I, another former house guest of Talleyrand, who was personally attending the congress.[20]

At Vienna Dom João's representatives found support from Russia and Austria as well as from France, for the proclamation of the kingdom of Brazil and the continuance of the Portuguese court in Rio—where it would be better able to resist British influence, while serving as a pillar of legitimacy on a continent wracked by revolution. But on the matter of the African slave trade, the sovereigns of Russia and Austria, greatly concerned with Christian morality, sided with Great Britain against the Luso-Brazilians. Under pressure from all sides, the Portuguese representatives at Vienna signed a treaty with the British foreign secretary, Lord Castlereagh, which banned Dom João's subjects from the transatlantic slave trade north of the equator, and committed Portugal to later negotiations to set a deadline for the complete abolition of the traffic between Africa and Brazil. Dom João ratified the treaty in Rio on 8 June 1815.[21]

On territorial matters, Dom João's government was willing to return French Guiana in order to consolidate its tacit alliance with Restoration France. In Europe, Portugal wanted Spain to return the border district of Olivenza, which it had seized in the 1801 war. If Spain would not give back Olivenza—and it would not—then it could not reasonably object to Portuguese annexation of Uruguay. Though he could not admit it, Dom João was willing to accept the trade-off. He wanted no trouble with Spain and agreed with Dona Carlota to the marriage of one of their daughters, Dona Maria Isabel, to Spanish King Fernando, and the wedding of another, Dona Maria Francisca, to the king's brother, Don Carlos—marriages between uncles and nieces, none of them very bright. The search for a bride for Dom Pedro, which began at the Congress of Vienna, was concerned with more distant relatives. Prospects included daughters of the Austrian emperor, the Russian czar, and the king of the Two Sicilies. The marquis of Marialva, whose talent for dealing with Europe's royal families was well appreciated by Dom João, was put in charge of the final phase of the search.[22]

In the meantime, Dom João set in motion his plans for the conquest of Uruguay. The British could not stop him; they had no minister plenipotentiary in Rio, only a chargé d'affaires. The government in London had been so sure of its power to compel Dom João to return to Portugal that instead of sending a replacement for Strangford to Rio, it dispatched George Canning, once and future foreign secretary, to Lisbon as British minister plenipotentiary. After waiting there nearly a year for the return of the runaway court, the great Canning finally gave up and went to France, leaving the kingdom of Portugal in the care of the British commander of the Portuguese army, Marshal William Carr Beresford. But nearly 5,000 of the best Portuguese troops, veterans of the Peninsular Campaign, were withdrawn from Beresford's command, on Dom João's orders, and shipped to Brazil to spearhead the Luso-Brazilian invasion of the Uruguayan republic of José Gervasio Artigas. Prospects for the operation were excellent: it even had the covert support of the government in Buenos Aires, which, disturbed by Artigas's growing influence in the northern Argentine provinces, tacitly dropped its own claims to Uruguay to encourage the Luso-Brazilians to eliminate the troublesome caudillo.[23]

Three squadrons of Portuguese cavalry and one battery of artillery sailed directly from Portugal to staging areas in southern Brazil, and four battalions of light infantry disembarked at Rio in March 1816 to train with two Brazilian regiments, one white and one free black. The veteran troops were accompanied by Marshal Beresford, who had vain hopes of persuading Dom João not to employ them in Uruguay. They arrived at Rio during the period of deep mourning following the death of Queen Maria, when a public celebration in the capital city would have been unseemly. But as the time for the troops' departure for the south approached, Dom João arranged to give them a royal send-off. All the members of the royal family, plus members of the diplomatic corps and other invited guests, went out to the training ground in Nitcrói, across the bay from Rio, to review the troops on 13 May, the king's birthday. Dona Carlota and her daughters—including Dona Maria Isabel and Dona Maria Francisca, whose proxy weddings to the Spanish king and his brother were announced at the parade —watched from carriages, while Dom João made a rare appearance on horseback, reviewing the troops with his sons, Dom Pedro and Dom Miguel. The two princes, tall in the saddle and resplendent in their army uniforms, evoked many admiring comments from onlookers. The parade began at noon and lasted for two hours, under a hot sun. Afterwards, guests and army officers passed through a tent on the parade ground to kneel and kiss the hand of the king, queen, princes, and princesses. Several hundred had done so when at four o'clock

Dom Pedro suddenly keeled over, his face frozen, eyes staring straight ahead, and began thrashing about on the ground in delirious convulsions, foaming at the mouth. Stunned spectators looked on as attendants carried the spasmodic prince to a nearby house; two hours later he had recovered from the seizure, though he was very tired. A few weeks later, after the troops had embarked for southern Brazil, Beresford left for Europe with the royal brides. The war began in September 1816, with preemptive strikes by Artigas into the Brazilian province of Rio Grande do Sul, followed by the long-awaited Luso-Brazilian invasion of Uruguay.[24]

As the campaign in Uruguay was beginning, the search for a bride for Dom Pedro was coming to a conclusion. By March 1816 the possibilities had been narrowed to a princess of the Bourbon house of the Two Sicilies and the three unmarried daughters of the Hapsburg emperor of Austria. Dom João preferred for his son one of the Austrian archduchesses, the marquis of Marialva was told, "because of the superior character of the sovereign," their father, "for reasons of kinship," and because of what the Portuguese ruler knew about "the regular education of those princesses." The Hapsburg emperor, Franz I, was indeed a man of exemplary character, in addition to being the sovereign of one of Europe's five great powers. A comparative survey of the latest performances of royal issue would indicate that Hapsburg blood was superior to Bourbon blood, of which, Dom João might lament, there was already too much in the veins of his progeny. And a Hapsburg princess would bring to a marriage with Dom Pedro the broad and systematic training in languages, arts, and sciences that the crown prince of Portugal and Brazil so sadly lacked. The marquis of Marialva was ordered to proceed from Paris to Vienna for a closer look at the young archduchesses, and if conditions were favorable, to negotiate a marriage contract.[25] He arrived in the Austrian capital in November 1816.

One of the three Hapsburg prospects was eliminated when she married an Italian prince before Marialva arrived in Vienna. The youngest, Carolina, had not reached puberty, and the remaining archduchess, Leopoldina, was promised to a minor German prince, a nephew of the king of Saxony. Marialva decided to go for Leopoldina. He had to convince the Hapsburg monarch that the united kingdom of Portugal and Brazil far exceeded the kingdom of Saxony in wealth, potential power, and strategic importance — which was not hard to do, since Clemens von Metternich, the powerful Austrian foreign minister, had already assured the emperor that such was the case. But Marialva also had to convince the Archduchess Leopoldina of the desirability of a marriage to Dom Pedro, for the emperor insisted that his daughter have the final decision in the choice of a husband. So the marquis came to Vienna loaded with evidence of the wealth of Brazil and with portraits of Dom Pedro and tales of the prince's sterling qualities. He was entirely successful. His first interview with Metternich was on 7 November, with Emperor Franz on the tenth, and with Archduchess Leopoldina on the thirteenth; on 29 November 1816, the marriage contract was signed.[26]

The agreement was kept secret; new marital arrangements had to be made for the jilted Saxon prince, and the contract had to be ratified by Dom João and Dom Pedro. In his reports to Rio, Marialva referred to the admirable intellectual, scientific, and artistic attainments of the archduchess, to her "goodness," affability, and regal presence, but said nothing about her physical attributes. Marialva forwarded a portrait of the prospective bride to Dom Pedro, noting simply that it was a good likeness. The marquis was not going to deceive the crown prince, whose tastes in women ran from lithe Brazilian *mulatas* to French ballerinas. The portrait was of a blond, blue-eyed, nineteen-year-old German girl—fair skinned, heavy set (but not fat), with full lips and cheeks, and a rather thick neck. She was not beautiful, but neither was she ugly.[27]

Marialva's ceremonial entrance into Vienna to formally ask for the hand of the Hapsburg princess was scheduled for 17 February 1817. The marquis had orders from Rio to spend whatever was necessary to make a good impression. He took his instructions literally and orchestrated one of the grandest spectacles Vienna had ever seen. Finely wrought jeweled medallions were liberally distributed at the imperial palace and among the diplomatic corps. To special personages who preferred less ornamental gifts, Marialva handed out gold bars. Even the lowest-level functionaries received valuable presents: golden necklaces, diamond earrings, jewel-encrusted snuff boxes. For his grand entrance into the city, Marialva was able to assemble outside the Carinthian Gate a procession of forty-one carriages, twenty-four of which the marquis had had specially made for the occasion, each pulled by six horses and occupied by nobles of the realm or foreign diplomats, and each attended by two or four coachmen, outfitted in uniforms of red and silver, or blue and gold. Marialva rode in a lavishly decorated coach with glass windows imported from Paris. The next day, in a ceremony at the Hofburg palace, the Archduchess Leopoldina was officially betrothed to the crown prince of Portugal and Brazil. Her engagement gift from Marialva was a miniature portrait of Dom Pedro set in a frame of diamonds, suspended on a diamond necklace, which she put on immediately, showing great satisfaction. Excluding the value of 167 diamonds and some other gems that came from government stocks, the cost of the Marialva mission to the kingdom of Portugal and Brazil was at least 332 *contos* (the equivalent of about 348,600 Spanish or United States silver dollars). In addition, the marquis spent more than 106 contos of his own money—he was from one of Portugal's wealthiest families—for which he was not reimbursed.[28]

The archduchess officially became Dona Leopoldina, crown princess of the United Kingdom of Portugal and Brazil, on 13 May 1817, Dom João's birthday, when she was married to Dom Pedro in a proxy wedding in Vienna. Three weeks later she left Vienna for Livorno, where she and her party were to be met by the Portuguese warships assigned to carry them to Brazil. She seemed eager to embark on her New World adventure, having devoted long hours to the study of the Portuguese language, Brazilian history and geography, and the geology, flora, and fauna of tropical South America. Recognizing her passion for the subject, Marialva had assured the princess that her bridegroom also was fond of the natural sciences. That was misleading; "the only 'natural' thing Dom Pedro was interested in," one of Dona Leopoldina's biographers has written, a bit unfairly, "was the natural act of sex."[29] The princess, on her part, was inclined to romantic fantasy; she was "almost driven crazy" by the miniature she had received, she confided to her older sister, Marie Louise, the estranged wife of Napoleon; "I stare at it all day long." Dom Pedro was "more beautiful than Adonis," she gushed; "I guarantee you, now I am indeed in love."[30]

Dona Leopoldina's voyage to Brazil was delayed by political and military troubles in South America and in Portugal. In Uruguay the Luso-Brazilians had driven Artigas's forces from the coastal centers of population, but the caudillo refused to concede and was carrying on guerrilla operations in the interior, while representatives of his government were still issuing letters of marque authorizing foreign privateers to take Portuguese vessels. The privateers, mostly Americans from Baltimore, were creating havoc with Portuguese merchant shipping in the South Atlantic, but were unlikely to attack men-of-war like those assigned to fetch Dona Leopoldina: the 54-gun ship-of-the-line *São Sebastião* and the *Dom João VI*, recently launched and specially outfitted in Lisbon for the royal passengers, with thirty-six cannon and one hundred marine riflemen. The British, however, exaggerated all dangers in hopes of keeping Dona Leopoldina in Europe, to attract the Braganças back to Portugal. The news of a major uprising in the Brazilian province of Pernambuco gave the British-dominated government in Lisbon an excuse to hold up the departure of the *São Sebastião* and *Dom João VI* for Livorno: the vessels or their crews might be needed to suppress the rebellion in Brazil. Dona Leopoldina got word of the delay while she was in Florence, en route to Livorno, on 17 June.[31]

In the northeastern Brazilian province of Pernambuco there was resentment among merchants and sugar planters over new tax levies to pay for the war in Uruguay. And, with the Rio government's commitment of resources to the southern campaign, the needs of the troops stationed in Pernambuco were neglected: rations were short and pay was in arrears. The senior officers, mostly Portuguese, were unable to improve conditions, which exacerbated the resentment of their juniors, mostly Brazilians. Disgruntled army officers were cultivated by a civilian group that included Domingos José Martins, a merchant who had been initiated into Freemasonry in England, and José Inácio Ribeiro de Abreu e Lima, an ex–Carmelite friar better known as Padre Roma, who was devoted to the ideals of the French Revolution. A military revolt in the Pernambucan capital of Recife on 6 March 1817 resulted in the death of several senior officers, the expulsion of the royal governor, and the formation of a republican junta that included Domingos José Martins. Padre Roma was sent south, toward Bahia, to spread the revolution in that direction. The ex-Carmelite's son, José Inácio de Abreu e Lima, happened to be in a military prison in Bahia for insubordination.[32]

The governor of Bahia, Dom Pedro's good friend, the count of Arcos, acted decisively to stop the revolutionary contagion. His troops captured Padre Roma on a beach near the Bahian capital and shot him three days later on the governor's orders. Padre Roma's imprisoned son, who had asked to see his father, was forced to attend the execution. In the meantime, Arcos mobilized Bahian regular and militia units for an assault on Recife; his strike force was beefed up by four regular battalions sent from Rio at his urgent request. Recife fell to loyalist forces on 20 May 1817; Domingos José Martins and two other members of the republican junta were captured and taken to Bahia where they suffered the fate of Padre Roma. The kind-hearted Dom João soon ordered a halt to the summary executions; Padre Roma's son, Abreu e Lima, escaped from prison a few months later and went on to fight for the liberation of Spanish America under Simón Bolívar. Dom Pedro was impressed by the efficiency of Arcos's swift and brutal response to the rebellion.[33] The resolute action of the count of Arcos preserved the territorial integrity of the kingdom and saved Brazil from the fate of Spanish America, soon to be fragmented into more than a dozen republics.

The rapid suppression of the Pernambucan revolt was not foreseen in Portugal, where Masonic coreligionists of Domingos José Martins, friends of liberty and constitutional government, and Portuguese nationalists stepped up their conspiratorial activities against the British puppet regime of Marshal Beresford. Fearing a revolution, the English marshal ordered mass arrests of suspected subversives, which were carried out in the predawn hours of 26 May 1817. Among those seized was General Gomes Freire de Andrade, Freemason and ex-Bonapartist. The general was tried in secret, convicted of lese majesty, and hanged—along with eleven others, mostly army officers —without being allowed an appeal to the king. The extraordinary events in Lisbon made it difficult to argue that the Portuguese capital was a safer place than Rio for the royal family; the British suggested that Dona Leopoldina stay in Vienna. The princess, impatiently waiting in Florence, maintained that if there was trouble in Brazil, that was where she belonged, at her husband's side. The Portuguese warships finally left Lisbon on 6 July for Livorno, to pick up Dona Leopoldina and her party and carry them directly to Rio.[34]

The princess sailed from Livorno on 15 August 1817 on the *Dom João VI* with her ladies-in-waiting and other attendants. A new Austrian ambassador to the Rio court sailed on the *São Sebastião*, while various scientists and artists had departed for Brazil some weeks earlier aboard two Austrian navy frigates. One of these ships, the *Augusta*, waited at Gibraltar and joined the Portuguese vessels for the Atlantic crossing. The voyage took longer than expected, due mainly to the poor sailing qualities of the *Dom João VI*, and it was not until 5 November that the Portuguese-Austrian squadron entered the harbor at Rio.[35]

The authorities at Rio had had ample time to prepare a gala reception for the bride of Dom Pedro. As soon as the ships were sighted, the signal telegraph on the Morro do Castelo ran up huge streamers in the colors of Austria and Portugal. The vessels in the harbor were decked out in festive array, and the warships were primed for the traditional twenty-one-gun salute. The artillery of the forts at the entrance to the bay began the salute as the *Dom João VI* crossed the bar under full sail at five o'clock in the afternoon, and as she approached her anchorage at the naval arsenal, the warships in the harbor joined in the thundering chorus. The *São Sebastião* and the *Augusta* responded with twenty-one salvos for each fort. When the guns fell silent, the church bells of Rio could be heard ringing; these were soon drowned out by the roar of huge rockets launched from the Morro do Castelo into the darkening sky; the last missile burst above the city into pinwheels of exploding stars. As the sun was setting behind the Serra do Couto, the royal galley of the Braganças approached Dona Leopoldina's ship from the west. When the splendid barge was secured alongside the *Dom João VI*, the ebullient princess descended to greet her new family. She curtsied and embraced them all, starting with Dom João and Dona Carlota. Her young husband received her cordially, if not effusively; if he was disappointed at the first sight of her, as some have claimed, she was well pleased with him. Dona Leopoldina found Dom Pedro to be even more handsome than his pictures.[36] They would consummate their marriage after official landing ceremonies the next day.

At midday on 6 November 1817 the royal family went out to the *Dom João VI* where they had lunch with Dona Leopoldina. Afterwards they all boarded the gold-colored royal galley, taking seats in her plush stern cabin, to be rowed by oarsmen in silver helmets and scarlet jackets to the ramp at the Naval Arsenal, for their grand entrance into the city of Rio de Janeiro. At the ramp was the first of three highly ornamented arches, designed by French artists and architects and constructed of wood and plaster painted to look like marble. The royal party crossed from the galley to the ramp on a red-carpeted gangplank and strolled through the arch past saluting soldiers and dignitaries to the carriages that awaited them at the north end of the Rua Direita, at the base of São Bento Hill, which was lined by newly planted palm trees. A gilded carriage with crimson trim, drawn by eight white horses harnessed in crimson and gold, was reserved for the king and queen and the newlyweds; two six-horse coaches stood by for Dom Miguel and his sisters. Ninety other vehicles joined the procession, which was escorted down the Rua Direita to the city palace by a squad of cavalrymen. Sand had been spread over the cobblestones to cushion the ride, and flowers and sweet-smelling herbs were strewn in the path of the royal party. Flags, bunting, and tapestries hung from the windows of the houses along the street, the city's widest, which was lined with jubilant spectators, who fell to their knees as the royal vehicles approached. Little boys, dressed as the Greek gods of love and marriage, were stationed atop the arches to drop flowers and pour perfume on the king's carriage as it passed beneath.[37]

The procession covered a distance of less than a kilometer, ending at the Royal Chapel attached to the city palace, where the bishop pronounced a nuptial benediction. This was followed by a Te Deum mass with music composed for the occasion by Marcos Portugal. After that there was hand kissing in the city palace, appearances before the crowds in the square, and a state dinner. The day's activities took their toll on the king, whose bad leg was acting up; he cancelled a scheduled drive home to Boa Vista, fearing that the long, jolting carriage ride would aggravate his condition, and summoned the royal galley to the Palace Square Quay, to take the royal party to São Cristóvão dock, near the palace where they would spend the night. Festivities continued for two more days, at Boa Vista and in the city, and concluded with an opera and ballet at the Royal Theater. After that, Dom Pedro and Dona Leopoldina settled down to life at Boa Vista with Dom João, while Dona Carlota went back to her villa at Mata Porcos, to enjoy the attentions of a new lover, the young cavalry colonel, Fernando Brás Carneiro Leão.[38]

The family Dona Leopoldina joined in Brazil was unlike the one in Austria that she had grown up in. In the Bragança family, the father and the mother hated each other; the mother's infidelities and the father's unmanly tolerance of them were the subjects of malicious court gossip; the sons, neglected by their parents, were wild, poorly educated, seemingly driven by their basest instincts; the daughters were alternately pampered and disciplined by the mother, but received little academic instruction—some were virtually illiterate. The Hapsburgs, by contrast, were noted for their broad and rigorous academic training, their personal discipline, and high moral standards.

Although Dona Leopoldina's mother had died when the princess was ten years old, she had close relationships with the stepmother she acquired the next year, in 1808, and with her father, who carefully monitored her education. She had witnessed her father's anguish when her mother died, and again on the death of her stepmother, early in 1816. Sexual adventures definitely were frowned upon in the Hapsburg household, an attitude that perhaps affected the development of Dona Leopoldina's brother, the epileptic Crown Prince Ferdinand, who at age twenty-three still had shown no interest in girls.[39]

The Hapsburg family had suffered its share of calamities, with the premature deaths of several members, four invasions of its realm by France, and the sacrifice of the oldest daughter, Marie Louise, as the bride of the detested Napoleon. Dona Leopoldina's childhood was hardly idyllic. She was sustained by a love of family, a sense of duty, and a strong religious faith, which allowed wide swings between optimism and fatalism, but did not permit despair. Prior to leaving for Brazil she prepared a *vade mecum*, a manual of conduct to guide her in her new life. "I will conduct myself with all possible modesty," she resolved. "My heart will be eternally firm against the perverse spirit of the world." She would strive to avoid "wasteful expenditures, injurious luxuries, indecent ornamentation, and scandalous clothing and gossip." Dona Leopoldina asked God to keep her from ever being "alone with a man, however virtuous he might appear, in a secluded place," and from a "long and scandalous toilette."[40]

Dona Leopoldina's resolve to avoid overdressing and excessive makeup won no applause from her well-groomed husband, who, nearly two years her junior, rather liked painted ladies. And Dom Pedro, despite Marialva's assurances to the contrary, did not share her passion for collecting and classifying rocks, insects, and plant specimens. But they did have some common interests. She was an excellent equestrian and he seemed to enjoy their long, daily rides into the Tijuca Forest, even though the purpose of a trip might be to catch butterflies. Dona Leopoldina rode astride, like Dona Carlota, though with calm, cheerful mastery instead of the dramatic dominance of her mother-in-law. But for all her competence, learning, and discipline, Dona Leopoldina was afraid of the tropical thunder — the awesome explosions of lightning-heated air reverberating between granite mountains that were heard almost daily, and terrified many Europeans in Rio. Perhaps this weakness endeared her to her husband. He could not help but respond to her great love for him, her good nature, sweetness, and considerateness. And he found that she could help him develop his own skills in art and music. Dona Leopoldina was an accomplished portrait and landscape painter and a fine pianist. She recognized her husband's superior musical talent and encouraged him to study composition under Sigismund von Neukomm, the Austrian pianist and composer who had come to Brazil from France in 1816.[41]

From the voluminous and frank correspondence that Dona Leopoldina carried on with her relatives in Europe, it appears that Dom Pedro gave up tavern hopping and womanizing for some time after the consummation of their marriage. She begged her father not to believe the scandalous tales that he might hear about her husband. She admitted that there was some coarseness in his speech and manners, and that he was impetuous and given to fits of temper; this she attributed not to flaws in his character, but to his irregular upbringing in an environment of hostility between his parents. She might have blamed it on his epilepsy, except that her brother had the same affliction and did not exhibit similar behavior. Although Dom Pedro was on familiar terms with some of the worse riffraff in Rio, he was liable to take a horsewhip to any government functionary who did not show him the proper respect. Hyperactive and impatient, he disliked waiting and was intolerant of incompetence. Once, when his horse had thrown a shoe and a blacksmith was having trouble replacing it, Dom Pedro called the man a "swine," pushed him aside, seized his tools and did the job himself. At times he would humiliate or otherwise abuse a friend, but then he would apologize and embrace him. He could be sharp-tongued and mean, but normally he was good-humored and generous—generous with his time and efforts on behalf of others, but not with his money: he was parsimonious and kept a tight rein on household expenses.[42] Dona Leopoldina realized early on that life with Dom Pedro would not be easy.

Dona Leopoldina saw little of her mother-in-law, but became quite close to her father-in-law. Stable in personality, careless in appearance, modest, consistently kind, the king was perhaps nearer in spirit to the princess than was her husband. In any case, Dom João became her surrogate father and she became one of his great joys. He did everything possible to facilitate her scientific studies and the research of the naturalists she had brought with her from Europe. Dom João ordered four days of festivities to honor his daughter-in-law's twenty-first birthday, 22 January 1818. A bullring was set up in front of the Boa Vista palace and Dom Pedro and Dom Miguel supervised the procurement of bulls for the afternoon spectacles that began on the princess's birthday. The animals were fought from horseback by Portuguese emigrés—Brazilians never took to the sport—and there were some serious injuries among the *toureiros* during the four-day series; two reportedly died. Nevertheless, the Portuguese at the court considered the *corridas* a great success and persuaded the king to authorize the construction of a permanent bullring at the Campo de Santana.[43]

Two weeks after the bullfights there was another grand occasion, the *aclamação*, or formal enthronement of the king, at the city palace. It was not a coronation, for that practice had been discontinued in 1578, out of respect for the memory of King Sebastião, who lost his head and the crown that year on a battlefield in Morocco. In the 1818 ceremony Dom João accepted the petitions of the city and town councils of Portugal and Brazil that he reign over them, and took an oath to God. Then Dom Pedro and Dom Miguel knelt before the king, who was seated on the throne with scepter in hand, and a replacement crown on a table at his side. He wore a plumed hat and, for the first time, his royal robes. Dom Pedro and Dom Miguel swore fealty to him. Later they went to the palace balcony to receive the cheers of the multitude. Many honors, promotions, and new titles of nobility were handed out by the king in commemoration of this event. Such rewards were necessary to placate the Portuguese who were ill-reconciled to an indefinite stay in Brazil, and the Brazilians who were fed up with the parasitic presence of the Lusitanians. Wealthy Brazilians had welcomed the court to Rio in 1808, and had offered the royal family and government officials the use of some of their best urban and rural properties. Some Brazilians made outright gifts of houses or villas, some received nominal rents, but nearly all felt cheated by the Portuguese, whom they regarded as ill-mannered and ungrateful. Some of the Brazilians were mollified with patents of nobility, but many—like the merchant who gave up Boa Vista—received only membership in the Order of Christ, a knighthood that was extended to Portuguese-born functionaries of the lowest level. Wealthier Portuguese received titles of viscount or count; the nobility was greatly expanded by Dom João. In Portugal, it was said, it took 500 years for a family to produce a count; in Brazil it took 500 contos.[44]

The Brazilian upper class resented this purchased nobility and deprecated its culture, or lack of same. It was nobility typically Portuguese: "ignorant, unlettered, bullfighting, fado loving, dissipated, brawling."[45] Dom João had inflicted on Brazil this uncouth gang —which included his sons Dom Pedro and Dom Miguel—but he had also brought to Rio the Italian-style operas of Marcos Portugal, French ballets, and the magnificent voices of the Royal Chapel's Italian castrati, albeit at great cost. The Portuguese court had also attracted to Rio the celebrated Sigismund von Neukomm, native of Salzburg and student of Haydn in Vienna, chapel master to the czar in St. Petersburg, personal pianist to Talleyrand and music director with the French delegation to the Congress of Vienna, who arranged all the music for Talleyrand's receptions at the Kaunitz mansion, and whose joint concert with the Hapsburg chapel master, Antonio Salieri, received rave reviews in that music capital. The maestro's latest position was chapel master to the king of Portugal and Brazil and music tutor to the crown prince, but he and his colleagues were available for public performances and for soirées at the homes of wealthy Cariocas, foreign diplomats, or Portuguese emigrés whose interests transcended green wine and gory bullfights. Still absent from Rio's social calendar were grand balls, like those Dona Leopoldina had enjoyed in Vienna. The princess lamented to her sister Marie Louise: "I sincerely would like to dance a waltz once in a while."[46]

Dom Pedro, with his marriage to Dona Leopoldina and his almost simultaneous apprenticeship to Neukomm, entered a new world, though without severing his ties with the old one. His younger brother remained in the old world. While Dom Pedro practiced on his instruments, worked on his musical compositions, and read books procured for him by his wife—she was pregnant with their first child by the end of 1818—Dom Miguel carried on in his brother's tradition in the taverns of Rio. Friar Arrábida, hoping to attract the younger prince to study, set aside a luxurious reading room for him at the National Library and stocked it with fine new editions of the books he was trying to get his student to read. Some time later a visitor to Dom Miguel's reading room found little indication that it had ever been used: the pages of most of the books were still uncut. Though little fond of books, Dom Miguel had one dedicated to him: *Young People's Treasury*, a volume from the royal printing press that dealt with "Morals, Virtue, and good Manners." The English merchant, John Luccock, thought the dedication appropriate, for no one needed instruction in those subjects more than Dom Miguel. Years before, Sir Sidney Smith had predicted that Dom Miguel would be a hero if given the education he needed; otherwise he would turn out to be a tiger. By his late teens the prince had overcome or outgrown the infirmities that had plagued his childhood, and was exhibiting real ferocity—in his bullfighting, in his deer hunting, in driving six-horse carriages through the streets of Rio at breakneck speed. In later years his enemies would accuse him of many atrocities, like wiping out Brazil's first Chinese colony. This consisted of 200 or more agriculturalists whom Dom João brought from Macao to cultivate the tea that he was trying to grow in the Royal Botanical Garden. The tea plantation failed and the Chinese disappeared; Dom Miguel is supposed to have hunted them down with horses and hounds.[47]

Far removed from Dom Miguel's world were the soirées at the homes of Rio culturati, where arias sung by Royal Chapel castrati were the featured entertainment. Ladies in the latest Paris fashions, purchased in the French boutiques that appeared on Ourives and Ouvidor streets after 1815, made a great fuss over these strange creatures. They were magnificent sopranos or contraltos in choirs or operas, though not at Rio's Royal Theater, where impresarios did not employ them, perhaps because of the enormous salaries they commanded. "In conversation their tones are squeaking," noted an anonymous foreign visitor. This observer appreciated the singing of the castrati, but found them "disgusting" in other respects. "Their whole gait announces effeminacy," he wrote, "and their figures are remarkable for narrowness of shoulders, width of hip, and an extraordinary development of length of the femur and tibia; so much so that when sitting down their knees are nearly in a level with their chair."[48]

Another high-pitched voice on the Rio social scene belonged to the perfumed count of Galvêas. This nobleman's house was a veritable "den of iniquity," according to Archivist Luís Marrocos, whom the count tried to seduce. The queen referred to him as Dr. Pastorino, alluding to his fame as a shepherd of young boys. Others called him *O Doudo* (the Madman). An embarrassment to the court, the widowed count was urged to remarry and reorder his life. The prospective bride was the widow countess de Ponte, who said that before the wedding she would want to go into a coma. This was taken as a rejection, and the count was still single when he died suddenly in 1819, at the age of fifty-eight.[49]

Galvêas's principal critic at the court was the king's chamberlain and closest companion, Viscount Vila Nova da Rainha. Years later, some former servants at Boa Vista claimed that they had detected a homosexual relationship between Dom João and his chamberlain. The patents of nobility and other honors that Dom João bestowed on this otherwise undistinguished courtier and his two brothers, the Lobatos, might have been in return for sexual favors. But if the king did in fact engage in homosexual activity, he took great pains to hide it, in contrast to the queen's blatant adultery. Dona Carlota's transgressions apparently went beyond adultery: she was accused of ordering the murder of the wife of her lover, Colonel Fernando Brás Carneiro Leão, in 1820. A secret investigation into the ambush slaying of Gertrudes Carneiro Leão convinced the king that the queen had hired the assassin. Dom João destroyed the records of the investigation and ordered Dona Carlota confined indefinitely to her residence.[50]

The behavior of Dom Pedro, whose first child, a daughter, Dona Maria da Gloria, was born on 5 April 1819, was little criticized during this period. From all appearances, he was a model father, husband, and son. He lived with his growing family in a modest two-story house, newly constructed in the style of a medieval castle with a flagpole on top, on the grounds at Boa Vista, about 1,200 meters from the main palace. Dom Pedro took an interest in the management of the royal estates and continued to concern himself with the welfare of their slaves and employees. He was not much involved in matters of state. From Rio he followed the progress of Portuguese General Carlos Federico Lecor in pacifying Uruguay. An enlightened military governor and diplomat as well as an able general, Lecor managed to isolate Artigas and gradually wear him down. He did this with the collusion of the government in Buenos Aires, now the capital of the United Provinces of La Plata, the nation in de facto existence since 1810 that was formally launched with the Argentine declaration of independence from Spain in 1816. When a civil war broke out in La Plata in 1819, the hard-pressed Artigas abandoned Uruguay to take a hand in that more promising conflict. The caudillo's most competent lieutenant, Fructuoso Rivera, refused to follow suit, and fought on in Uruguay for a few more months. Finally, Rivera accepted an offer from Lecor and surrendered his forces to the Luso-Brazilians early in 1820. Rivera became a colonel of dragoons in Dom João's army, all armed resistance to the king in Uruguay promptly ceased, and Artigas soon wound up under permanent arrest in Paraguay.[51]

The royal family received bad news from Spain in March 1819. Dom Pedro's sister, Dona Maria Isabel, wife of Spanish King Fernando VII, had died in childbirth three months earlier. The horrible details of the queen's death were revealed later. In the last stages of pregnancy she suffered an epileptic seizure and lapsed into a coma, which the royal surgeon mistook for death, or at least moribundity. Eager to save the long-awaited male heir she was thought to be carrying, he performed a hasty cesarean section on his inert patient, hacking through tissue, arteries, and organs in his fervor to extract the treasured infant—which turned out to be a stillborn girl. The poor queen recovered consciousness before dying in great agony.[52] Thus, the regime of Fernando VII once again exhibited its mean-spirited stupidity and criminal incompetence. Spain endured this kakistocracy until January 1820, when the Spanish army revolted and forced the king to restore the Constitution of 1812—the charter that had been adopted during Don Fernando's internment in France and suppressed upon his return in 1814—and to appoint a liberal government and reinstate the Cortes.

The establishment of the new regime in Spain, with Freemasons prominent among its leadership, had its effect across the border in Portugal, where brother Masons, liberals, nationalists, and devotees of the martyred General Gomes Freire de Andrade were inspired to step up their plotting against the British-puppet government of Marshal William Carr Beresford. The marshal realized the seriousness of the situation and decided that the return of the king, or at least a member of the royal family, was urgently needed to prevent a revolution in Portugal. In May 1820 Beresford arrived in Rio and begged the king to go back to the mother country and save the monarchy. Dom João did not share the marshal's sense of urgency: he said he would give the matter of returning to Portugal some more thought; in the meantime, Beresford should take advantage of his sojourn in Brazil to inspect the principal military installations in the South American kingdom. By this time, Britain had finally appointed a minister plenipotentiary to the Rio court, Edward Thornton, who conveyed his government's dismay at the prospect of Portugal exploding in an anti-British revolution while the British commander of the Portuguese army was frittering away his time on an inspection tour in Brazil. If Dom João would not return to Portugal, or send his son, Dom Pedro, Thornton pleaded with him at least to send Beresford back without delay. The king consented and the marshal cut short his inspection tour and embarked for Lisbon on 13 August. He was too late. The revolution began in Oporto on 24 August and spread over the country in the next few weeks. By the time Beresford arrived at Lisbon on 10 October, a revolutionary junta was in power there and refused to let him land. He and the other British officers were expelled from the Portuguese army, and the junta scheduled elections for December, to choose delegates to a Cortes—the first Portuguese parliament since 1697, when the crown, bolstered by new gold revenues from Brazil, had dispensed with such assemblies. The new Cortes, besides exercising legislative power, was to sit as a constituent assembly and produce a constitution for the Portuguese nation.[53]

There was little that Dom João could do about the revolutionary outbreak in Portugal, which he first learned of on 17 October. The municipal juntas in northern Portugal informed Dom João that they had convoked a Cortes and petitioned the monarch to return to Lisbon and restore the unity of the state. British Minister Thornton urged the king to comply: to go back to Portugal, make his royal presence felt, and try to moderate the course of the revolution. Dom João's minister of internal affairs, Tomás António da Vila Nova Portugal, a Portuguese-born lawyer who had learned to enjoy life in Brazil, urged the king not to leave; if someone had to go, he could send Dom Pedro. The count of Arcos, who had left the governorship of Bahia to become Dom João's navy minister in Rio, indicated that he would be available to accompany the prince to Portugal, should the king decide to send him. If Dom João chose to go himself and leave Dom Pedro in charge of Brazil, Arcos would be willing to stay and assist his young friend. The king's advisers agreed that the monarch should not recognize the authority of the revolutionary juntas, but also that it would be unwise for him to challenge it, at this time. Consequently, Dom João issued a *carta régia* (royal letter) declaring that the juntas had no right to convoke the Cortes—that was the king's prerogative—but that Dom João recognized the utility of convening a Cortes in Portugal to formulate proposals for the governance of the realm, to be submitted to the king for his consideration. Therefore, the king sanctioned the Cortes and pardoned those subjects who had usurped his authority. When the Cortes had completed its work to the satisfaction of the king, Dom João or one of his "sons or descendants" would return to Portugal to rule over that component of the United Kingdom.[54]

On 23 December, the count of Palmela, formerly Dom João's representative at the Congress of Vienna and minister to Great Britain, arrived in Rio to become foreign minister, a post to which he had been appointed in 1817, but had avoided assuming due to an aversion to Brazil and to life at Dom João's court. An old-world aristocrat, one of the late Madame de Staël's lovers, friend of Benjamin Constant, connoisseur of fine cigars, Palmela liked to dabble in progressive ideas. The events of 1820 finally induced him to proceed from London to Rio via Portugal, where he consulted with members of the new government. In Rio, Palmela urged the king to send Dom Pedro to Portugal—not to try to rally the forces of absolutism against the Cortes, but to sanction its deliberations and provide guidelines for the constitution it was going to write. Palmela, virtually alone among the king's advisers, called on Dom João to recognize the legislative and constituent authority of the Lisbon Cortes and to accept the principle of constitutional rule, both for Portugal and for Brazil. A limited constitutional monarchy on the British model, Palmela believed, would best promote the prosperity, happiness, and loyalty of the king's subjects. The British minister in Rio agreed with Palmela on this point, and also favored sending Dom Pedro to Lisbon, as a first step in the repatriation of the entire court.[55]

By the end of 1820 Dom Pedro was ready to try his hand at politics. The count of Arcos, whom he visited regularly, encouraged him, but Dom João tried to keep him isolated from affairs of state; the king did not want to send the crown prince to Portugal, perhaps because Dom Pedro and the count of Arcos seemed so eager to go. Dom João knew his son to be impetuous, and he was wary of the assertive style of the prince's mentor. As usual, the king chose caution and delay, hoping the situation in Portugal would resolve itself, or that the European powers would crush the revolution for him. Palmela was impatient; he had drafted a set of guidelines for a Portuguese constitution and he wanted Dom Pedro to present them to the Cortes while there was still a chance of the deputies' accepting them. The question was not simply whether Dom Pedro would go to Portugal, but whether he would go and deal with the Cortes as an advisory body or as a constituent assembly with plenary powers to frame and adopt a constitution. Tomás António opposed conceding constituent authority to the Cortes and Arcos was ambivalent. After much debate, the king finally asked Dom Pedro what he thought. In an undated memorandum the crown prince stated his position forthrightly, but with the garbled syntax, careless punctuation, and misspellings that characterized his writings on less weighty matters. He favored a constitution under which all laws would be proposed by the crown and enacted by parliament, after discussion and approval by a majority of the deputies voting. However, he did not favor submitting guidelines for such a constitution to the Cortes in Lisbon. It would be "indecorous" and a "sure disgrace" for the king to recognize that self-proclaimed constituent assembly.[56]

In January 1821, while Dom João and his advisers debated the nature of Dom Pedro's proposed mission, Dona Leopoldina entered the picture to insist that if they send her husband to Portugal, she was going to accompany him—despite the fact that she was eight months pregnant. Dom Pedro supported his wife's position and thereby provided a reason for postponing the trip until after Dona Leopoldina's expected delivery date at the end of February—although she was willing to give birth on the high seas. The question of whether any member of the royal family should return to Portugal was answered negatively in a pamphlet published anonymously in French, at the instigation of Tomás António. The pamphlet denounced the Lisbon government and argued that Brazil was more important to the crown than was Portugal; it caused a sensation among the Rio intelligentsia. Then, on 17 February, news reached Rio of the revolutionary takeover of Bahia a week earlier. The officers and men of the artillery regiment in Bahia, obeying the call of their comrades in Portugal to proclaim the constitutional revolution, joined with Portuguese civilians and some native liberals in occupying the governor's palace and demonstrating in favor of the new government in Portugal and against royal absolutism. The royal governor lacked the decisiveness of his predecessor, the count of Arcos, and was slow to react to the insurrectionary challenge. When loyal infantrymen, under Brazilian General Felisberto Caldeira Brant Pontes, were finally committed to action, the rebels were well organized and repelled them with musket and artillery fire. They inflicted numerous casualties and killed General Brant's horse. Realizing the hopelessness of the situation, the governor and the general capitulated to a military-civilian junta and left for Rio a few days afterwards. There had been a similar revolutionary seizure of power in Belém, at the

Dona Leopoldina at the time of her wedding to Dom Pedro, 1817
Painting by Natale Schiavoni, Palácio da Ajuda, Lisbon

The Count of Arcos
From Tobias Monteiro, *Historia do imperio: A elaboração da independencia*
(Rio de Janeiro, 1927).

mouth of the Amazon River, early in January, but news of this event did not reach Rio or Bahia until six or seven weeks later.[57]

At a joint meeting of the ministry and the council of state on the day after the Bahia news was received, Palmela urged prompt action. The king should immediately proclaim constitutional rule in Brazil, Palmela argued, to bring the situation in Bahia under control and prevent revolts in other Brazilian provinces. The foreign minister had drawn up an outline, or set of "bases," for a Brazilian constitution, which the king should endorse and publish without delay. The document called for a representative system, with a division of powers between parliament and the crown, for the equality of citizens before the law, guarantees of individual freedom and property rights, and freedom of the press. The crown prince, Palmela urged, should sail within eight days for Bahia—accompanied by the count of Arcos, four or five warships, and some troops from the Rio garrison—to proclaim the bases of the constitutional regime, before continuing on to Lisbon to present a similar document to the Cortes. But the king hesitated to take so radical a step, and the crown prince would not leave until his wife was able to accompany him. Exasperated, Palmela handed in his resignation; as usual, the king took no immediate action on it.[58]

Dom Pedro, once eager to go to Lisbon, now seemed to be dragging his feet. Concern for his wife and unborn child perhaps contributed to his reluctance to leave, but his growing awareness of the political ferment in Rio probably played a greater part. Barred by his father from direct participation in the government, he was briefed on the continuing debate and deadlock by the count of Arcos, whose house he visited frequently. Chalaça and other friends of that ilk informed the prince of discussions in the taverns and coffee houses. They collected subversive handbills for their royal friend, who relayed them to the count of Arcos, accompanied by good-humored notes. Amusement, rather than indignation, was the reaction of Dom Pedro to the various schemes to establish constitutional rule in Rio, to compel his father to obey the will of the Cortes and return to Lisbon, or to prevent him from doing so. In fact, the crown prince might have sympathized with those who wanted the king to leave. A constitution, he believed, was essential, and should be a gift from the throne; perhaps he went a step further to conclude that if the occupant of the throne was unwilling to make the gift, he should vacate it in favor of someone who was. The Portuguese revolution had gone too far for the

The Count (later Duke) of Palmela
From Tobias Monteiro, *Historia do imperio: O primeiro reinado, I* (Rio de Janeiro, 1939).

crown prince to have any hope of controlling it; but in the absence of his father Dom Pedro might be able to direct the incipient Brazilian revolution. In any case, the prince's wide circle of associates in February 1821 included Francisco Romão de Góis, a Portuguese priest who was conspiring with Portuguese army officers to deliver a constitutionalist coup d'etat in Rio. The conspiracy was well advanced when on 25 February the king published a decree, dated 18 February, for the convocation in Rio of a Cortes composed of the municipal attorneys of the cities and towns of Brazil and the Portuguese Atlantic islands, to consider the constitutional proposals being debated by the Cortes in Lisbon, with a view to adapting them to the needs of the kingdom of Brazil.[59] The publication of this order spurred the coup planners to action, for it not only defied the authority of the Lisbon Cortes, but threatened the separation of Brazil from Portugal, something the Portuguese-dominated military was determined to prevent.

Before dawn on 26 February a loyal officer of the palace guard informed the king at Boa Vista that soldiers and artillery were being concentrated on the square in front of the Royal Theater in Rio. About the same time, Padre Góis awakened Dom Pedro with news of the troop movement. Father and son conferred immediately and the king dispatched Dom Pedro to the square to read to the troops a decree that had been prepared for such an emergency. Armed with the decree, Dom Pedro mounted a fast horse and galloped off on the five-kilometer ride into the city, accompanied by a single servant. The crown prince reined up at the Royal Theater just before five o'clock. The troops cheered as Dom Pedro swung down from the saddle and strode confidently onto the portico of the theater. "It's all done," he announced, waving the predated decree from the king. "The troops now can go to the barracks and the officers to kiss the hand of my august father."[60] Then he began to read the decree, by which the king promised to "adhere to and adopt for the kingdom of Brazil the constitution that the Cortes shall make, except for modifications that local circumstances might make necessary."[61] A civilian interrupted to declare that this did not satisfy the troops and the people. The spokesman, Marcelino José Alves Macamboa, a Portuguese lawyer and priest, demanded that the king publicly swear to uphold the Portuguese constitution without reservations, dismiss his council of ministers, and accept a junta of government composed of twelve men already chosen by the military and the people. Dom Pedro responded affably that he would relay these thoughts to his father. The crown prince did not object to the individuals indicated for the junta, most of whom were Portuguese-born moderates; perhaps an accommodation could be made. Dom Pedro mounted his horse and headed for Boa Vista palace with the list of names.[62]

At Boa Vista, Dom Pedro found Dom João in conference with Tomás António. The prince's energetic presence, his acute assessment of the situation, and his insistence that the king make further concessions to avoid total disaster, won both men to his point of view. The conservative, legal-minded Tomás António advised that the twelve names be distributed among the portfolios of the council of ministers; thus Rio would not get a constitutionalist junta, like Bahia's or Belém's, but the kingdom of Brazil would get a new ministry, appointed by the crown in accordance with ancient practice. The king agreed. To satisfy another demand, Dom João produced another predrafted decree, sanctioning in advance, without reservation, whatever constitution the Lisbon Cortes was going to produce. The decree was copied in Dom Pedro's handwriting, dated 24 August, and signed, along with the new ministerial appointments, by the king. With these documents Dom Pedro took to his horse and was off again for the theater plaza, which he reached, the second time that morning, around seven o'clock.[63]

This time Dom Pedro entered the theater to confer in the vestibule with the military and civilian leaders of the revolt, the ministerial appointees, members of the Rio city council, and other dignitaries who had been attracted to that place of high drama. Padre Macamboa and his more radical colleagues did not like the idea of their revolutionary junta being converted into a royal council of ministers, but the military leaders accepted the change and the appointees seemed to prefer it. The chief of the new cabinet was Silvestre Pinheiro Ferreira, a Portuguese-born philosopher, author, linguist, and diplomat. Silvestre replaced Palmela as minister of foreign affairs. The brightest star in Rio's somewhat limited intellectual firmament, Silvestre was already a councillor of state to Dom João and recently had been chosen to be the king's minister to the United States. A proponent of the "new ideas" of the nineteenth century, Silvestre, like his predecessor, was committed to peaceful and orderly change. Unlike the recently arrived Palmela, he was personally well known by Rio's constitutionalists, who looked to him for leadership. Silvestre and Dom Pedro agreed that the prince would go to the portico, read the new decree to the assembled troops and people, and take an oath to the unborn constitution in the king's name. After that he would take the oath in his own name, as would Dom Miguel, the new ministers, and all other government officials present.[64]

Dom Pedro's oath taking in the name of his father did not satisfy the crowd; they demanded that the king appear before them in person and swear to the constitution. Once again the prince mounted his horse and was off at a gallop for Boa Vista. Around eleven o'clock the crowds in the theater square spotted the king's carriage coming towards them, escorted by Dom Pedro on horseback. A great cheer went up—*vivas* to the king and the constitution—as the people ran to greet Dom João. To the consternation of the king, men from the crowd unhitched the horses from his carriage and began to draw it themselves, in a show of gratitude to their new constitutional monarch. The carriage was pulled by Dom João's citizen-subjects from the theater to the city palace, which was deemed a more suitable location for the king to take the oath to the constitution. Alighting from the carriage the king soon appeared at a palace window in the company of his family, including the queen. In a loud voice Dom João repeated the oath administered by the bishop, swearing to "observe, protect, and perpetually maintain the constitution, exactly as it shall be made in Portugal by the Cortes." The king was stoic, but the queen seemed delighted to take the oath—although no one despised constitutional rule more than she—probably because she realized that these proceedings would culminate in her long-desired return to Europe. The people in the plaza cheered, and that night and the next the royal family received thunderous ovations at the theater, between acts of Rossini's *Cenerentola* and Puccitto's *The Search of Henry IV*.[65]

To some, the events of 26 February 1821 seemed to have been orchestrated by the twenty-two-year-old Dom Pedro, perhaps with some behind-the-scenes direction from the count of Arcos. Maybe the crown prince, frustrated at being kept out of the government, had reached some understanding with the constitutionalists in the days preceding the coup. At any rate, one of the first official acts of Silvestre Pinheiro Ferreira, the new cabinet chief, was to ask the king to authorize Dom Pedro's attendance at all future meetings of the council of ministers and the council of state. Dom João readily consented. The king also resigned himself to returning to Portugal, bowing to the will of the cabinet majority. (Silvestre, fearing that anarchy or independence would follow the king's departure, cast a dissenting vote.) It was agreed that Dom Pedro would remain in Rio as regent of the provisional government of Brazil, with a council of ministers appointed by the king in consultation with the departing cabinet. A royal decree to this effect was published on 7 March, the day after Dona Leopoldina gave birth to a son, Dom João Carlos. The apprehensions that some Brazilians were beginning to feel about the possible consequences of the king's departure were put aside as they celebrated the arrival of the infant prince.[66]

Brazil, supreme in the Portuguese empire since 1808, resubmitted to rule from Portugal in 1821. The new regime in the mother country, however, was a representative one that provided for Brazilian participation in the government in Lisbon. The constitution that was being drawn up in Lisbon was frankly based on the Spanish Constitution of 1812, and Cortes deputies were apportioned and elected according to the provisions of that document: colonies were underrepresented and elections were indirect. On 7 March 1821, the day of the official announcement of the impending return of the king and his court to Lisbon, the Rio government also issued instructions for the election of Brazilian deputies to the Portuguese Cortes. Parish voters were to choose electors who would choose the electors of the *comarca* (district), who would name the actual deputies. In the days following the March decrees, enthusiasm for Portuguese constitutionalism waned among native Brazilians. After years of grumbling about the presence of the parasitic court in Rio, many Cariocas now realized that it had brought them important economic advantages that were likely to be withdrawn with the transfer of power back to Lisbon. The Rio city council and the chamber of commerce petitioned the king to reconsider his decision to leave; they urged him to stay in Brazil, or at least to delay his departure indefinitely. Such activity raised threats of another coup by Portuguese military commanders, to insure fulfillment of the king's promise to return to Portugal. Portuguese ideologues, like Padre Macamboa, were disgruntled because there was no citizens' participation in government after 26 February; the constitution that had been proclaimed that day still did not exist, and the government of Silvestre Pinheiro conducted the people's business in the manner of its absolutist predecessors. The new government, however, did proclaim freedom of the press, or, at least, the end of prior censorship of manuscripts bound for the printer.[67]

To allay the fears of the various groups, Silvestre decided to convoke a meeting of the parish electors of the Rio district, prior to the king's departure. Although the only prescribed duty of the parish electors was to cast votes for district electors in the selection process for Cortes deputies, Silvestre wanted to use the occasion to explain to the assembled electors, as the representatives of the people, the measures that were being taken for the transfer of power in Rio from the king's government to Dom Pedro's regency, and to ask their advice and consent. The public was invited to attend this debut of representative government in Rio, so a large meeting hall was needed. The new commercial exchange building, a symbol of Rio's expanding international trade, located on the waterfront between the city palace and the Naval Arsenal, was chosen for the convention, which was scheduled for Saturday, 21 April, the day before Easter. To accommodate the public, bleachers were erected on the exchange's huge trading floor, converting it into an amphitheater. In the meantime, the loading of the ships for the voyage to Portugal proceeded at a leisurely pace. The king remained unhappy about the coming trip, and Silvestre became increasingly apprehensive of the danger of Brazil's descending into anarchy after their departure.[68] He also probably feared losing his job when they arrived in Portugal.

Dom Pedro seemed confident that he could maintain order in Brazil after the departure of the Portuguese court. His belief that he enjoyed the support of the military was reinforced when, on Silvestre's suggestion, he met with the regular and militia officers in Rio and extracted from them a pledge to obey the orders of the ministry. To induce Bahia's military-civilian junta to submit to the authority of the Rio government, the king issued a decree legalizing the junta and all its actions. With the help of the count of Arcos, the prince believed that he could bring Bahia back into the fold. He appeared most concerned about the deplorable state of public finances, making pointed arguments for fiscal conservatism in meetings of the council of ministers. He proposed turning over all the royal family's jewelry, including his wife's, to the Bank of Brazil as collateral for loans to the royal treasury. The prince's proposal was enacted, but the ministry's order was evaded and most of the jewels wound up on the ships bound for Portugal.[69] The Bank of Brazil was stuck with the debt.

The final crisis of the reign of Dom João in Brazil came on 21 April 1821. When the assembly of parish electors convened at four o'clock that afternoon at the commercial exchange, the bleachers were filled with Portuguese shopkeepers, clerks, and other followers of Padre Macamboa. Throngs of like-minded individuals—their spirits elevated by jugs of wine supplied by sympathetic tavernkeepers—milled about outside the building, blocking the entrances, and cheering the news from inside as it was relayed to them. The presiding district judge was shouted down from the bleachers as he tried to present the afternoon's business. Among the 160 or so electors—mostly conservative types: merchants, landowners, army officers, doctors, lawyers—were a few well-prepared radicals, who took up the cry of the crowd, declaring that they had not come to do the bidding of an absolutist regime, but to establish a true constitutional government. Thoroughly intimidated, the judge stepped aside and allowed the radicals to organize the convention. Padre Macamboa, who was not an elector, appeared on the floor and assumed the role of "attorney of the people," to delirious cheers from the bleachers. Forty years old and broad of beam, Padre Macamboa was a powerful demagogue, but his talent for rabble-rousing was eclipsed by that of his acolyte, Luís Duprat, the twenty-year-old, Portuguese-born son of a French tailor. This slender youth, wearing spectacles à la Robespierre, mesmerized the crowd with his wild energy and revolutionary oratory. The electors, swept up in the emotion of the hour, or fearing for their lives, did the bidding of Macamboa and Duprat. Since Brazil had to have a constitution and the Portuguese constitution was not yet ready, the convention adopted the Spanish constitution, effective immediately and to remain in vigor until the Portuguese document arrived. The assembly, acting as a provisional parliament under the Spanish constitution, ordered the king to proclaim that document and swear to uphold it.[70]

Word of the proceedings at the exchange building soon reached the king's ministers, who assembled in emergency session at the Boa Vista palace. Dom Pedro joined the cabinet meeting, after taking the precaution of calling up a battalion of infantry and a battery of artillery and ordering them into positions between the palace and the city. At the meeting Silvestre suggested that adopting the Spanish constitution might not be a bad idea: it would not do any harm and it might satisfy the people. The other ministers seemed willing to go along, except for the navy minister, who said he did not know why, but he did not think they should proclaim the Spanish constitution. Dom Pedro was outraged; he did not think they should proclaim the Spanish constitution either. If Silvestre continued to argue for it, the prince declared, he was going to throw him out the window. Dom Pedro's robust reasoning did not sway the cabinet or reinvigorate the dispirited king; the crown prince left the meeting in disgust. As the ministers debated and received delegations from the rebel assembly, Dom Pedro began implementing the measures he felt were necessary to end the crisis. A delegation from the exchange building came to him to ask why troops were out on the road. "You will see," the prince replied.[71]

While the commanding general of the Rio military district was conferring with the cabinet at Boa Vista, his subordinate, Division General Jorge de Avilez, was dealing with Dom Pedro. At the exchange building the militants, awaiting word from the delegation they had sent to the palace to demand the promulgation of the Spanish constitution, filled positions in their provisional government and debated various matters, including a rumor that the absolutists had loaded great quantities of gold aboard the ships in the harbor. This wealth, Duprat declared, must not be allowed to slip through the fingers of the people. A resolution was adopted to close the harbor to all outgoing vessels; to implement the order, Duprat designated the highest-ranking military man present, seventy-eight-year-old General Joaquim Xavier Curado. The shock of receiving orders from a twenty-year-old civilian almost brought the general to his senses: he said that he only took orders from the king. But the king no longer ruled, Duprat reminded him: "Here only the people govern." The old general shoved off in a boat with a people's escort to do his revolutionary duty; he ordered one fort to fire on any departing vessels and was on his way to a second installation when he was captured in mid-harbor by a boatload of soldiers sent out by Dom Pedro.[72] Unaware of this development, people were singing in the streets

> With watchful eye and footsteps bold
> Let's go on board and get the gold.[73]

At Boa Vista, around ten o'clock, the king and the cabinet gave in to the rebels and adopted the Spanish constitution. The delegation returned to the exchange building with a freshly printed royal decree, signed by the king, ordering that the Spanish constitution be "strictly and literally observed" in Brazil until the arrival of the Portuguese one.[74] A wave of jubilation swept the assembly, which, under the direction of Duprat and Macamboa, went on to formulate ever-more-radical demands. Silvestre, who had hoped that the electors would adjourn their meeting in gratitude after the concession on the constitution, was sorely disappointed. Still, he was reluctant to use force to dissolve a legal assembly, which he himself had convoked. He and the district military commander discussed surrounding the exchange building with troops to encourage more reasonable behavior inside. Meanwhile, Dom Pedro and General Avilez were taking matters into their own hands.[75]

At four o'clock on Easter morning, 22 April, a company of soldiers marched up to the door of the commercial exchange building. Before the commander could read an order dissolving the assembly, a shot rang out and a soldier fell dead. General Avilez urged restraint on his men as they charged into the building with bayonets fixed, amidst great tumult and confusion. Several people reportedly were killed inside the building, although only one was identified—a Portuguese wine merchant. Many more were wounded and some militants may have drowned after jumping out of windows and attempting to swim away or escape on boats in the harbor. Duprat and Macamboa were captured, but several other ringleaders managed to get away. It was all over by five o'clock.[76]

By eight o'clock on Easter morning, a draft decree in Dom Pedro's handwriting, revoking the royal order of the previous night that promulgated the Spanish constitution, was circulating at Boa Vista palace. At the crown prince's insistence, and over Silvestre's objections, the king issued the decree nullifying the one of the previous day. By way of explanation, it noted that the delegates who came to the palace on 21 April had presented themselves as representatives of the people, but "it can be seen today that that representation was made on the orders of evil-intentioned men who desired anarchy." Therefore it was best to reinstate the former system, which authorized the departing king to appoint and instruct the government of the crown prince, pending the arrival of the Portuguese constitution. At three o'clock on the afternoon of 22 April Dom Pedro read this decree to the troops drawn up on the Campo de Santana.[77] By his decisive actions of the preceding twenty-four hours, the prince had made himself master of Rio de Janeiro. For him to maintain that position and bring the rest of Brazil under his control, it was necessary that his father and the Silvestre ministry get out of the country without further delay.

Preparations were accelerated for the sailing of the ships that

would take the Portuguese court back to Europe. The royal family
—the king, queen, Dom Miguel, the princesses, Dom Sebastião
—embarked on the *Dom João VI* in the darkness before dawn on 25
April. Dom Pedro and Dona Leopoldina came on board to bid them a
tearful farewell. When the squadron of twelve vessels set sail the next
day, 26 April, some 4,000 courtiers, government officials, foreign
diplomats, and their relatives and servants were aboard, along with the
royal treasury and specie surreptitiously withdrawn from the Bank of
Brazil. Prior to embarking, the king issued a decree naming a council
of ministers for his son's government; it was headed by the count of
Arcos. Dom João and Dom Pedro met privately for the last time on
the day before the king's embarkation. As Dom Pedro recalled the
scene in a letter to his father the following year, they discussed the
possibility of Brazilian independence. Dom João feared that Brazil
might fall into the hands of adventurers like Macamboa and Duprat.
Should separation from Portugal occur, the king indicated that he
would prefer that the Brazilian independence movement be led by
Dom Pedro, who would respect his father. A statesman who served
both father and son, but who was not present at that meeting, put into
the king's mouth the words that the situation demanded: "Pedro,
Brazil soon will break with Portugal: If that happens, put the crown on
your own head, before some adventurer grabs it."[78]

4 Independence or Death

*I know my mother's a bitch,
but she brought me into this world without fear.*
Dom Pedro I, Emperor of Brazil

When the ships transporting the Portuguese court sailed from Rio on 26 April 1821, they were accompanied past the harbor forts—which rendered the usual salutes—by the paddle-wheeled steamer *Bragança*, which carried sightseers at four silver dollars a head. Dom João and his family departed Brazil as they had arrived, by the old technology, but they were escorted out by the power of the nineteenth century, applied to a vessel bearing their name and captained by an Englishman—not a Royal Navy officer, but a private entrepreneur. Samuel C. Nicoll's *Bragança*, which was built in New York, was not the first steamer in Brazilian waters. That honor belonged to a smaller vessel launched in Bahia and fitted with an engine ordered from England by General Felisberto Caldeira Brant Pontes, the ill-fated military commander of the province. General Brant's steamboat made her first run on All Saints Bay in 1819, the year before Captain Nicoll's *Bragança* arrived in Rio.[1] Thus the age of steam dawned on the shipyards of Bahia, Brazil's largest and oldest industrial complex.

Prior to the coming of the Portuguese court, shipbuilding was one of the few manufacturing activities that the government encouraged, or even permitted, in Brazil. Sugar processing also was consistently promoted, and at times the crown licensed textile workshops to make military uniforms in Brazil, or ironworks to produce essential horseshoes or mining implements, but for most of the period before 1808 such activity was forbidden in the colony. Manufacturing in the Portuguese empire was reserved for the mother country. Manufactured goods not produced in the mother country were purchased abroad and shipped through Portugal to Brazil, providing unwarranted profits to Portuguese middlemen at the expense of Brazilian consumers. Under the colonial system, Brazil was not permitted direct commerce with the outside world—except for the African slave trade. This system ended with Dom João's opening of Brazilian ports to the commerce of all friendly nations, and his lifting of the ban on Brazilian manufacturing, both proclaimed early in 1808. Skilled foreigners were encouraged to settle in Brazil at this time, and they contributed greatly to the expansion of commerce, industry, and agriculture—as well as to the enhancement of the fine arts—in various parts of the country. The impact was greatest on Rio de Janeiro, where 354 foreign ships called in 1820, compared with 90 in 1808, and practically none in earlier years, when the only non-Portuguese vessels permitted in Brazilian harbors were allied men-of-war or ships in distress. During the 1808–20 period, despite a decline in gold and diamond shipments, the annual value of Brazilian exports edged up to 19 million silver dollars, and was consistently exceeded by that of imports, mostly of non-Portuguese origin that entered through the port of Rio. By 1821 Rio had more than 3,000 foreign residents, with the largest contingents coming from France, Britain, Switzerland, and the German states. Immigrants engaged in the export–import trade and set up factories to make bricks, mill flour, and cast iron. The population of Rio kept pace with the economic growth, and by 1819 the city, with 113,000 residents, had supplanted Salvador da Bahia as Brazil's largest.[2]

There was a building boom in Rio during the Portuguese court's residence. Tax relief was granted to encourage private housing construction, and the government paved city streets, improved suburban roads, built bridges, drained swamps, and built the Maracanã aqueduct. Public funds were expended in improvements on the king's palaces and expansion of the naval arsenal, and in the construction of new army barracks, the Royal Theater, the bullring, the commercial exchange, and a treasury building. An existing structure, belonging to the Third Order of the Carmelites, was used to house Dom João's collection of 60,000 books, which was opened to the public as the National Library.[3]

Dom João was concerned with the dissemination of useful knowledge in Rio and in the rest of Brazil. The printing press he brought with him from Portugal was the first to go into operation in Brazil. Besides publishing government decrees, the royal press put out a semiweekly newspaper, *A Gazeta*, and a fortnightly literary review, *O Patriota*. It also printed books; one of its first was a Portuguese translation of Adam Smith's *The Wealth of Nations*, in 1811. Brazil's second printing press was a privately owned one, set up in Bahia in 1808, that brought out the second Brazilian edition of *The Wealth of*

Nations in 1812, during the governorship of the count of Arcos. Under the count's enlightened administration a public library was opened in Bahia and the provincial newspaper, Brazil's second oldest, was patronized by the government. Printing presses, but no periodicals, were established in Recife and several other provincial capitals before 1821. Rio got its second press, a private one, in 1816. Until 1821 nothing could be published in Brazil without a government stamp of approval; however, the hand of censorship lay fairly lightly on the Brazilian press, and the uncensored *Correio Braziliense*, published monthly in London by the Brazilian journalist Hipólito da Costa circulated openly in Brazil. Hipólito and his colleagues in Brazil used a great deal of restraint in dealing with matters sensitive to the crown, and Dom João and administrators like the count of Arcos tended to agree with the Bahian who argued that the spread of knowledge essential to economic growth required "the freedom to think and publish thoughts by all known means, principally that of the press."[4] There was a veritable explosion of information during Dom João's stay in Brazil.

In other ways, direct and indirect, the regime of Dom João promoted education and scientific research in Brazil. The country's first medical college was established in Bahia by royal decree issued by Dom João while he was there in 1808. A second royal medical college and army and navy academies were established in Rio. Members of the French artistic mission made up most of the faculty of the Royal Academy of Fine Arts, in Rio. Primary and secondary education remained largely a private matter, with classes conducted in homes by itinerant teachers, but these increased in number after 1808 and were able to advertise their availability in the Rio *Gazeta*; some specialized in teaching reading and writing to females and slaves. The crown sponsored the research of natural scientists in various parts of Brazil and established the Royal Botanical Garden near Rio. Mineralogists looked for new mineral deposits to exploit, and botanists and zoologists studied the adaptation of useful foreign plants and animals to the Brazilian environment. Chinese tea and Arabian camels were introduced during the reign of Dom João in Brazil, but neither caught on. Nearly a century earlier another exotic import—Afro-Asian coffee—entered Brazil from French Guiana. This was the plant that began to transform the Brazilian economy in the time of Dom João.[5]

Dom João handed out numerous royal grants of land near Rio and over the coastal mountains in the Paraíba river valley for the cultivation of coffee. The unnavigable Paraíba, which originated in São Paulo and formed the border of the provinces of Minas Gerais and Rio de Janeiro before emptying into the Atlantic, north of Rio, was to become Brazil's "River of Coffee." The coffee flowed to the port of Rio, whence it was shipped to markets in Europe and the United States. Rio's annual coffee exports, which amounted to less than half a tonne in 1800, grew to 6,763 tonnes in 1820; the value of this coffee was more than half that of the sugar shipped from Rio that year. Sugar, Rio's traditional agricultural export, steadily lost ground to coffee in the years that followed. Exports from Rio included produce from neighboring São Paulo and Minas Gerais. The gold mines of Minas Gerais had all but ceased producing, and diamond production was dwindling, when coffee planting was introduced and helped save the provincial economy. The opening of iron mines and the establishment of iron smelters and foundries during the time of Dom João took up some of the economic slack in Minas Gerais, as did an expansion of cotton planting for export, and food agriculture and dairying to feed the burgeoning population of the nearby royal capital. By 1820 mule trains that once brought gold from Minas to Rio were carrying cotton or cheese. Unlike the more distant mining provinces of Goiás and Mato Grosso, Minas Gerais did not lose population when the gold and diamonds played out. In fact, Minas remained Brazil's most populous province, although it had no cities comparable in size to Rio or Bahia.[6]

São Paulo, like Minas Gerais, took part in the Paraíba valley coffee boom. The paulista horse and mule business grew with expanding demand for the animals in civilian and military markets in Rio. Near the paulista livestock center of Sorocaba, Brazil's first pig-iron mill went into operation in 1818, and the king chose the city of São Paulo as the site of an arms factory. The war in Uruguay bolstered the economy of Rio Grande do Sul, where ranchers supplied animals to feed and mount the Luso-Brazilian army. As military operations were suspended in January 1821, Brazilian and international demand for the cattle products of Uruguay and Rio Grande do Sul were growing. European leather-goods industries and machinery and pump manufacturers consumed great quantities of South American cowhides, and candle and soap makers provided lucrative markets for tallow. Plantation owners in Brazil and Cuba were beginning to buy the dried salted beef jerky of the southern pampas to feed their slaves.[7]

In contrast to the South, the Brazilian North and Northeast

faced bleak economic prospects at the time of the king's departure for Portugal. In Bahia the troubles began with Dom João's ratification of the treaty prohibiting the slave trade north of the equator in 1815. This threatened to deprive Bahian slavers of their traditional source of supply, the West African states north of the line. Although the trade would continue illegally for many years, the treaty frightened capital out of the business and dealt a severe blow to the Bahian tobacco industry, which had concentrated on a product especially made for the West African trade. The bottom fell out of the market for the twisted, molasses-soaked "rolls" preferred by African chiefs, forcing Bahian planters to switch to the production of leaf tobacco for the European market. Bahian leaf tobacco sold at a considerable discount to the Cuban and Virginian varieties, and in 1820 exporters were rejecting more than a third of the leaf offered them in Bahia.[8]

Tobacco and slave trading, however, were less important to Bahia than was sugar, which dominated the economy of that province and all of northeastern Brazil. To bolster this industry, Dom João's agronomists experimented with new varieties of sugarcane from Asia, and in 1815 Bahia's first steam-powered sugar mill went into operation. Two years later Pernambuco got its first steam-powered sugar mill. But Brazil's chief competitor in world sugar markets, Cuba, soon adopted steam power and wiped out the Brazilian technological edge. Sugar production in Cuba was already soaring, and the island's location — much nearer North American and European markets than Brazil — gave it an important transportation advantage. Prices dropped, and in 1820, despite increased Brazilian production, Brazil's export earnings from sugar, the mainstay of the country's economy since the sixteenth century, began to decline.[9]

The decreasing profitability of sugar affected producers from the coast of São Paulo north to Maranhão. In the southernmost range of the sugar belt, coffee and cotton were the alternative export crops, but in the North, from Pernambuco to Maranhão, cotton alone was the established option. This option lost its attractiveness as the price of cotton dropped in tandem with that of sugar after 1817. The United States had the same advantages over Brazil in cotton that Cuba had in sugar. The end of the War of 1812, in 1815, reopened the British cotton market to American exporters, just as Carolina and Georgia planters were expanding into Alabama, Mississippi, and the Louisiana Purchase territories. They opened to cotton production that huge, fertile region that was tied together and linked to the outside world by navigable rivers. In the vastness of central Brazil, where the soil was thin and the rivers provided no access to the sea, the sparse population was little concerned with the dim export prospects of sugar, tobacco, and cotton. The people who remained in Mato Grosso and Goiás after the closing of the mines turned to subsistence farming or the raising of cattle for local consumption. In the far North, the forest products of the Amazon basin—herbs, spices, Brazil nuts, cacao, wild animal pelts, rubber—weighed little in Brazil's international trade balance in 1821.[10]

Before the decline in the major agricultural exports set in around 1820, crown revenues had grown substantially. The government in Rio collected export as well as import duties, and levied a 10 percent tax on the gross production of the land. Various taxes were levied on goods in transit by land between the royal city of Rio de Janeiro and other parts of Brazil. The crown collected excise taxes on items of necessity as well as on luxury goods, while municipal governments levied property taxes on real estate and slaves and remitted a portion of the proceeds to the royal treasury. Licensing fees and payments for monopoly concessions were collected on both levels of government. The crown retained and directly administered monopolies of diamond mining and tobacco distribution in Brazil. During the years of Dom João's rule in Brazil, crown revenue from almost all major sources increased; only the diamond monopoly and the 20 percent severance tax on minerals registered decreasing yields. But the income of the royal government consistently lagged behind its expenses. Costs incurred in the relocation of the court in Rio, the renovation of the city, the war in Uruguay, and the suppression of the rebellion in Pernambuco kept crown expenses ahead of crown revenues throughout the period.[11]

The crown tried to cover this deficit by making money. During the gold mining boom of the eighteenth century, gold coins were minted in Brazil and were exchanged for silver at a rate of one to sixteen. As in the United States and the rest of the Western Hemisphere, the Spanish *peso*, or silver dollar, was the monetary standard; it circulated with a value equivalent to 750 Portuguese *réis*. (*Réis* is the plural of *real*; a thousand réis make a *milréis*, and a million, a *conto*.) In 1814 the Rio mint melted down the royal treasury's stock of silver dollars and restamped them with a face value of 960 réis. The trick enabled the crown to evade a portion of its financial obligations, but it was not long before foreign and domestic moneymen adjusted their calculations to reflect the devaluation; it soon took 960 réis to make a dollar.[12]

The introduction of the printing press in 1808 provided another means for financing the government debt. The Bank of Brazil was chartered that year and was granted the power to issue legal-tender bank notes on its authorized capital of 1,200 contos, which was raised by private subscription, mainly from wealthy Cariocas. The royal government became one of the bank's principal borrowers, taking out loans secured by liens on certain sources of government revenue, like the sumptuary tax on two- and four-wheeled vehicles. Sometimes the government received cash advances on no security. The stockholders of the Bank of Brazil were little worried; their monopoly of commercial banking and their exclusive right to print money brought them regular annual dividends in the 11–23 percent range. Between 1814, when the treasury devalued the coinage, and 1820, the Bank of Brazil added more than 8,500 contos to the money supply. Inflation resulted and consumer prices rose. Then, in 1821 departing Portuguese withdrew their deposits in specie and exchanged their bank notes for coin, severely depleting the bank's bullion reserves. Many of the crown jewels that Dom Pedro had insisted on turning over to the bank as collateral for earlier advances disappeared with his relatives in April 1821. Brazilian depositers and holders of bank notes soon perceived the situation and conducted their own run on the bank, which was forced to suspend payments in July 1821.[13] Thus, the new regency of Dom Pedro faced a financial crisis as well as a downturn in traditional areas of Brazil's export economy.

"My husband, God help us, loves the new ideas," Dona Leopoldina wrote to her father in June 1821. In the weeks following the departure of the Portuguese court, Dom Pedro issued a series of decrees cutting taxes, reducing government spending and guaranteeing the civil liberties and property rights of the citizens of Brazil. If the substance of the decrees was welcomed, their motivation was questioned; a cloud hung over the new government, which, after all, had come to power by suppressing a popular assembly, bayonetting elected representatives of the people, and hustling the kindly king on board ship under cover of darkness. Those unsettling events had left the Carioca populace in a sullen mood. Signs appeared on the commercial exchange building, identifying it as the "Royal Butchershop." The army, which had cast itself as the champion of constitutionalism, was

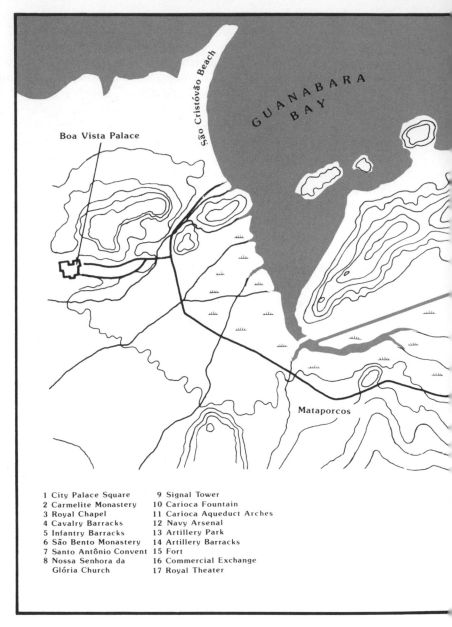

1 City Palace Square
2 Carmelite Monastery
3 Royal Chapel
4 Cavalry Barracks
5 Infantry Barracks
6 São Bento Monastery
7 Santo Antônio Convent
8 Nossa Senhora da
   Glória Church

9 Signal Tower
10 Carioca Fountain
11 Carioca Aqueduct Arches
12 Navy Arsenal
13 Artillery Park
14 Artillery Barracks
15 Fort
16 Commercial Exchange
17 Royal Theater

Rio de Janeiro in the year of Brazilian Independence: 1822

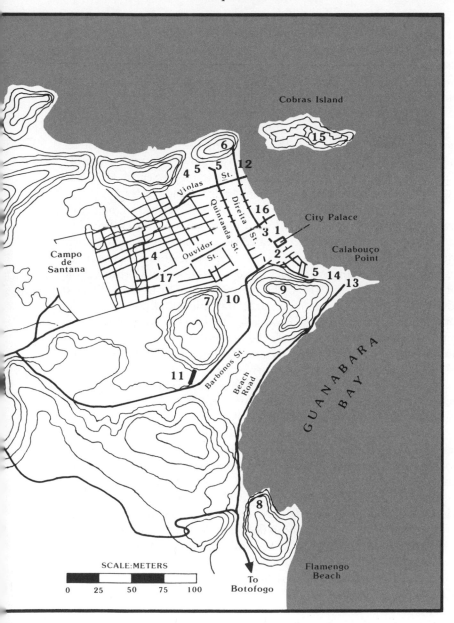

Cobras Island

15

6

4 5 5 St.
12

Violas

Direita St.

Quitanda St.

16

City Palace

3 1

2

Ouvidor

St.

Campo
de
Santana

4

17

Calabouço
Point

5 14

13

7 10

9

Barbonos St.

Beach
Road

11

G U A N A B A R A

B A Y

8

SCALE:METERS

0   25   50   75   100

To
Botofogo

Flamengo
Beach

rent by recriminations over its contradictory actions on the night of 21
April and the unseemly behavior, variously bloodthirsty and cowardly,
alleged of certain officers. Dom Pedro moved quickly to close the
books on the Easter events and to recover the popularity he had lost in
the streets and in the barracks. A royal investigation was hastily concluded and virtually everyone was either exonerated or pardoned; only
Macamboa and Duprat spent more than a few days in jail, and within
three months they were free and on their way back to Portugal, where
the younger man went to law school and embarked on a brilliant career
as an attorney. The district electors chosen by the defunct assembly
were duly recognized and the deputies that they selected were dispatched to Lisbon to represent Rio de Janeiro in the Cortes.[14]

Economic and financial problems preoccupied the young prince
regent. To stimulate the production of hides and jerked beef, he eliminated the royal salt tax. He removed an onerous burden from domestic
commerce by lifting the 2 percent cabotage tax. To make up for the
lost revenue, he cut his own salary, gave up his house with the flagpole
on top and moved into the main palace at Boa Vista, concentrated
government offices in the city palace, and sold off all but 156 of the
royal family's 1,290 horses and mules. The slaves at Santa Cruz were
put to work producing forage for the remaining animals and washing
clothes for Dom Pedro, his family, and his employees. With the salaries
of soldiers and arsenal workers in arrears, the royal treasury could not
be expected to pay the prince's laundry bill. "There is no greater
shame," Dom Pedro lamented, "than wanting to do well and fix everything and not having the wherewithal."[15]

While Dom Pedro's liberal tax policy reduced government revenues in the short term, other reforms announced by the prince bore no
price tag, but were calculated to pay immediate political dividends by
anticipating guarantees that would be written into the Portuguese
constitution. Private property was declared secure from arbitrary
seizure. A written warrant from a judge was now required for the
arrest of any free person, except in flagrante delicto; no citizen could be
held for more than forty-eight hours without formal charges and without knowing the identity of his accuser. Secret trials were prohibited
and defendents were guaranteed the means to conduct their defense.
Torture and the pretrial use of chains, manacles, shackles, and other
such irons was forbidden.[16] The prince professed liberal principles and
acted on them. The harsh measures employed on Easter morning had

been necessary, he maintained, to preserve the order without which liberty was impossible. When order was restored, those who had been deprived of their liberty were released. Dom Pedro had not interfered in the legitimate work of the assembly of parish electors, he could argue; the district electors and Cortes deputies had been duly chosen and he had accepted them. Still, the prince regent's constitutionalism was suspect. One reason was the count of Arcos.

The prince's mentor and cabinet chief had never sworn to uphold the forthcoming Portuguese constitution. He had not joined the parade of dignitaries who took the oath at the Royal Theater on 26 February, and he had managed to avoid all subsequent oath taking. In the last weeks of Dom João's stay in Rio, the count of Arcos had spent most of his time at home, indisposed, but receiving visits from the crown prince. The troops, influenced by both Portuguese and Brazilian constitutionalist agitators, began to suspect that Arcos, by manipulating the crown prince, had tricked them into striking the first violent blow against a constitution that the count refused to accept. Dom Pedro's close friendship with the count was open and obvious to everyone; what was not so apparent at that time was that the prince was insusceptible to manipulation. His actions were determined by his own will, shaped by his own instincts and, to a lesser degree, reasoning. Before his father left, Dom Pedro suggested, only half-jokingly, that he and his friend would not be able to work together in the government because he would not take orders from the count. But Arcos, though strong willed and direct in his personal relationships, did not try to give his royal friend orders under any guise. The count understood royalty in general, and recognized the particular regal attributes of his protegé. He spoke as frankly to the prince as he did to Dom João, and both admired him for it. This eighth count of Arcos—his father, the seventh count, died in a bullfight—was bred to the kind of easy familiarity with royalty that distinguished his first cousin, the marquis of Marialva.[17] Their shared grandfather was one of the few Portuguese grandees to escape the 1759 purge of the nobility by King José I's minister of state, the parvenu who became the marquis of Pombal. For twenty-six years, until the death of his royal patron, Pombal had been dictator of Portugal; some could picture Arcos as Brazil's Pombal, with Dom Pedro as his Dom José. But Dom Pedro, unlike his great-grandfather, would not be content with the pleasures of women and horses; he would insist on running the government as well.

In thought and action, the count of Arcos was in the tradition of the marquis of Pombal and the enlightened despotism of the eighteenth century. He would rule by reason and with the assistance of reasonable men; for the sake of order, the institutions of the past would be preserved—so long as they did not obstruct progress. New ideas and the spread of knowledge would be encouraged—insofar as they did not undermine the essential structure of order, the sine qua non of progress. This structure was strengthened by increasing the security of the productive elements of society. Thus Arcos approved of, and probably composed, Dom Pedro's decrees guaranteeing the property rights and personal security of Brazilian citizens. But Arcos was not one to welcome citizen participation in government. Himself a great administrator, he would rather deal with a king than with representatives of the people. Arcos's despotic propensities, however enlightened, did not commend him to constitutionalists, of either Portuguese or Brazilian origin. Portuguese constitutionalists, who predominated among the military in Rio, further distrusted the count for his long association with Brazil. Arcos had lived in Brazil since 1803, when he left Portugal to become governor of the Amazonian province of Pará, at the age of thirty-two. The last viceroy of Brazil, from 1806 to 1808, the count subsequently served as governor of Bahia and minister of the navy in Rio. In 1821 he was once again in a position to claim power over all of Brazil, this time in the name of the young prince regent. Arcos, the military believed, was capable of repudiating not only the Portuguese constitution but Portugal itself in his drive for power in Brazil.[18]

But with no concrete evidence of treasonous intent, the constitutionalist zealots were unable to rally the troops against Arcos and the regency. Then, towards the end of May 1821 the news from Portugal provided an excuse for action. The constitution was still unfinished, but the Cortes had adopted a set of "bases" for it, which was published in the Lisbon press. The Cortes required no action in Brazil on this preliminary legislation; in fact, the bases clearly stated that no constitutional provisions would go into effect in Brazil before the Brazilian deputies had taken their seats in the Cortes and had a chance to debate and vote on them. So Dom Pedro and his council of ministers did nothing about the bases. In the barracks the rumor spread that the count of Arcos had prevailed upon Dom Pedro to ignore the bases rather than proclaim this fundamental charter and swear to uphold it, as he should have done. It was now the military's duty, the zealots argued, to remove Arcos from power, to compel the prince to take an oath on the bases, and to establish a junta of government to insure that Brazil would henceforth be governed in accordance with the will of the Portuguese people, as expressed by the Cortes. Dom Pedro knew that something was afoot in the barracks, but on 4 June he went hunting anyway, at Santa Cruz. At five o'clock the next morning, on his way home to Boa Vista, he detoured by the barracks of the Portuguese Third Light Infantry Battalion to see what was going on.[19]

The prince was met at the portal of the barracks by a Portuguese captain who claimed that he had just gotten up, that most of the troops were still sleeping, that nothing was going on. Dom Pedro sensed that the officer was lying and intimated as much; the prince said he knew the captain to be the author of subversive proclamations, a mutineer, and a disturber of the peace, and told him to watch his step. That said, Dom Pedro left the barracks and headed for Boa Vista. The warning, instead of deterring the mutineers, apparently spurred them to action. When the prince was told at Boa Vista that the Third Battalion was in a rapid march toward the barracks of the Eleventh Battalion, he asked for the resignation of their division commander, General Jorge de Avilez. But the general ignored the request and put himself at the head of the Portuguese battalions as they assembled on the square in front of the Royal Theater. Dom Pedro soon appeared at the square on horseback; he rode up to a group of officers and inquired, "Who's the spokesman here?"[20]

The officers were taken aback; no one answered.

"Who speaks?" the prince demanded.

"I do, for the troops," General Avilez finally replied.

"What do they want?"

"For us to swear to the bases of the Portuguese constitution."

"I've no doubt," Dom Pedro responded. "What I regret is that there are men who feel that my word is no good, politically or religiously, seeing that I've already taken a sacred oath, voluntarily and *in totum*, to the constitution however the Cortes makes it."

Dom Pedro's customary bravura and Latin phraseology could not make the rebellious troops disappear. So the prince invited their officers into the vestibule of the theater to discuss the situation. "I'm not going to swear without knowing the will of the people that I govern," Dom Pedro insisted inside the theater. The troops were only part of the nation; he wanted to know the will of the rest of the people. The prince proposed to summon to the theater the people's representatives:

the Rio city council and the Rio district electors. Avilez and his officers agreed and for five hours Dom Pedro remained in the theater—calm and composed, conversing easily with those present—while the councilmen and electors were being rounded up. Meanwhile the count of Arcos was at his house adjacent to the Campo de Santana, trying to figure out a way to save his government. He conferred with old General Curado, who after his humiliation of 22 April had been wanting to do something to restore his reputation and return himself to royal favor. Eventually, Arcos came to the conclusion that neither he, Curado, nor anyone else would be able to rally the faction-ridden Brazilian army units effectively against the Portuguese on the theater square. So the count sent a letter of resignation to Dom Pedro at the theater, asking to be relieved immediately of his ministerial duties so he could prepare to accompany his daughter to Portugal on the packet boat leaving 10 June.[21]

Several dozen electors and councilmen assembled at the Royal Theater, with clear memories of the unfortunate events at the commercial exchange and no desire to offend the troops drawn up outside. They agreed with Avilez and his officers that everyone, including the prince, should swear to the constitutional bases, and everyone did so. They agreed that Arcos should leave the government, and accepted Dom Pedro's choice for his successor, Pedro Alvares Diniz, a respected Portuguese-born magistrate. They accepted the military's proposal that a junta of government be established to supervise the work of the ministry, and with army representatives voting, elected its nine members, who included army officers, clergymen, magistrates, and merchants, Brazilians and Portuguese, none of whom had been involved in the political agitation. They were supposed to insure that the constitution and laws of the Portuguese Cortes would be fully implemented in Rio de Janeiro.[22]

Dom Pedro had lost on almost every point. He was reduced to titular head of a caretaker provincial government. Avilez now wielded power in Rio; the prince's illusion of popularity with the troops was shattered. Even if somehow he should regain power in Rio, he could have little hope of extending his control to other areas of Brazil without the help of the count of Arcos. The loss of Arcos was potentially devastating. Dom Pedro was now completely alone in the political arena; he would have to find allies or withdraw. He was not optimistic, but he put on his best face and went back into the theater that night with Dona Leopoldina for a performance of Rossini's *L'Inganno Felice*.

A special attraction of the evening was the opera company's rendition of the "Hymn to the Constitution," a new composition with words and music by Dom Pedro. The prince was pleased with the applause his work received, and cheerfully acknowledged the usual *vivas* that greeted his appearance in the royal box.[23] He was, however, neither happy nor deceived.

Dom Pedro did his best to repair his relations with General Avilez and the Portuguese division after 5 June. He made frequent comradely visits to the barracks, treated the troops to his earthy humor and got himself invited to a series of dinners given by the officers of the division. Dona Leopoldina accompanied him to some of these affairs and struck up a friendship with the general's lovely wife, Joaquina de Avilez, who also received a lot of attention from Dom Pedro. The royal couple attended a European-style ball that the Portuguese officers gave at the Royal Theater on the first anniversary of the revolution in Portugal, and they danced quadrilles until six o'clock in the morning. But the social whirl provided Dom Pedro only temporary relief from a dismal state of affairs. He continued to preside over the council of ministers; contrary to expectations, the new junta of government did not interfere in the work of the cabinet. The junta seemed content to stand aside and let Dom Pedro's ministers grapple with the daunting problems of the city and the kingdom. Revenues from the provinces virtually ceased with the dissemination in Brazil of a Cortes decree instructing provincial governments to withhold tax payments to Rio. The royal treasury was empty, military pay was in arrears, and the Bank of Brazil was unable to redeem its bank notes. The paper Brazilian milréis for the first time traded for less than a dollar. On 28 July the bank formally suspended redemptions at par and began exchanging bank notes for 15 percent of their face value in silver, 10 percent in copper, and 75 percent in inconvertible paper. For Dom Pedro the problems of the Brazilian regency were too great and the rewards too few; he was ready to return to Portugal, he reiterated in letters to his father. "I beg Your Majesty, by all that is most sacred in the world," the prince wrote on 21 September, "to please relieve me of this job, that surely is going to kill me with the constant scenes of horror, some already in view and others much worse to come, that I have always before my eyes." Dom Pedro implored Dom João to let him go to Portugal and have the pleasure of kissing his father's hand and taking his place "at the foot of Your Majesty."[24]

Between May and July 1821 Cortes deputies were chosen, and the remaining royal governors were replaced by, or made to share power with, juntas of government in most of the provinces of the kingdom of Brazil. In the occupied province of Uruguay the military governor, Portuguese General Carlos Frederico Lecor, called a meeting in Montevideo of representatives of the four principal Uruguayan cities and persuaded the delegates to vote for annexation by the kingdom of Brazil. Portuguese army officers dominated the government in Uruguay as they did those in Rio, Bahia, and Pernambuco. But in other provinces of Brazil where few, if any, Portuguese troops were stationed, the new juntas of government were controlled by native Brazilians. This was the case in São Paulo, where three Brazilian brothers, the Andradas, took the lead in establishing the provincial junta. The royal governor was designated junta president, but real power in the new paulista government lay with the vice-president, José Bonifácio de Andrada, and the treasury secretary, Martin Francisco de Andrada. The third brother, Antônio Carlos de Andrada, was named to head the São Paulo delegation to the Portuguese Cortes.[25]

The Andradas were sons of a wealthy and well-connected merchant of the São Paulo port of Santos. All three were sent to Portugal for their education and earned degrees at the University of Coimbra: Martin Francisco in mathematics and José Bonifácio and Antônio Carlos in jurisprudence and natural philosophy. Martin Francisco, the youngest, was forty-six years old in 1821 and had been a director of mines and forests in the province of São Paulo; he explored for minerals in the Brazilian interior and wrote accounts of his expeditions and the Indians he encountered in the wilderness. Like his brothers, he urged humane treatment of the aboriginal Americans and was opposed to black slavery. Famous for his inflexible honesty and personal integrity, he was also said to be vain, bombastic, stubborn, and vengeful—traits also attributed to his brothers. Martin Francisco was thin and dark, but his brothers were lean and fair. José Bonifácio was the oldest at fifty-eight; he had spent thirty-six of those years in Europe.[26]

After graduating from law school at Coimbra, José Bonifácio de Andrada was denounced to the Inquisition in 1789 for denying the existence of God. Influential friends and relatives got him off the hook and arranged a government grant for him to travel and study in the intellectually more hospitable climes of northern Europe. He was in Paris during the revolutionary years of 1790 and 1791, taking courses in chemistry and geology. In 1792 he went on to the University of Freiburg and specialized in mineralogy and metallurgy. During the ten years he spent in France, Germany, and Scandinavia, José Bonifácio became a friend of Alexander von Humboldt and associated with Volta, Priestley, and Lavoisier. In Sweden he discovered and named four species of minerals and eight subspecies, and contributed articles to scientific journals. His interests extended to agriculture, forestry, general economics, and social organization; he was a member of scientific and learned societies in Berlin, Jena, Paris, and London. Returning to Portugal in 1800, during the enlightened regency of Dom João, the Brazilian savant accepted a full professorship in metallurgy at the University of Coimbra and a concurrent appointment as royal intendant general of mines and metals, and married Narcisa Emília O'Leary, whose parents were Irish. When the French invaded Portugal, Professor Andrada raised a battalion of students and led them against the invaders. After the victory in the Peninsular Campaign, José Bonifácio returned to teaching and his other government duties. Finally, in 1819 the king allowed him to resign his positions and return to São Paulo, accompanied by his wife, a teenaged daughter, and an illegitimate infant daughter, to whom the accommodating Narcisa gave her own name. The legitimate daughter, Gabriela, was betrothed to her middle-aged uncle, Martin Francisco. The other Andrada brother at this time was in jail.[27]

Antônio Carlos de Andrada had embarked on a judicial career after graduating in law from Coimbra. By 1805 he was crown-appointed magistrate in his hometown of Santos and, by 1817 he was a royal district judge in Pernambuco. A Freemason, like his brothers, and a closet republican, Antônio Carlos joined the Pernambucan revolt of 1817, and was captured when the movement collapsed. It was perhaps José Bonifácio's influence that saved him from the count of Arcos's firing squad. Antônio Carlos remained in prison in Bahia, teaching law and politics to fellow inmates and developing his rhetorical skills, until the Bahian constitutionalist uprising of February 1821 set him free. Returning to São Paulo, he helped his brothers establish the paulista junta of government, which, unlike the Bahian junta, declared its loyalty to the kingdom of Brazil and to the prince regent, Dom Pedro. Antônio Carlos had discarded his republicanism and now believed, like his brothers, that a liberal regime in Brazil could best be achieved under royal auspices. The Andradas were committed both to liberalism and to the preservation of Brazilian autonomy under the United Kingdom arrangement. Their program was embodied in the instructions given to the São Paulo delegation to the Cortes, a copy of which was personally presented to Dom Pedro on 9 November by Antônio Carlos, who was in Rio en route to Lisbon. The prince was impressed by Antônio Carlos and the document he carried. Dom Pedro wrote to Dom João that the Cortes should wait to hear from Antônio Carlos and his delegation before voting on Brazilian matters.[28] But by this time the Cortes had already enacted legislation to dismantle the kingdom of Brazil.

When the king and his court arrived in Lisbon in July, the leaders of the Cortes were sorely disappointed to find Dom Pedro missing. They had expected the entire royal family to return to Portugal, leaving power in Brazil in the hands of the various provincial juntas. Then the delegation from Bahia, six Portuguese-born deputies and only three Brazilians, arrived expressing fear that Dom Pedro and the count of Arcos were planning to attack their province, and asking for military reinforcements. The Cortes responded by ordering more Portuguese troops to Bahia and placing all Brazilian forces under Portuguese command. When Arcos showed up in Lisbon in August, he was thrown in jail for conspiring against the Cortes, and was left there for several months. In September—with only 46 of 72 authorized Brazilian deputies present, but with virtually all the other 109 seats filled —the Cortes voted to abolish the kingdom of Brazil. All crown agencies, departments, and courts of law that had been established in Brazil after 1807 were eliminated; instead of reconstructing the viceregal government in Rio, the Cortes made the provinces of Brazil directly subordinate to Lisbon. Military governors, appointed by the Cortes, were to exercise executive power in the provinces, independent of the local juntas. The crown prince had no business in Rio and was ordered to embark for Europe. But the Cortes decided that it did not want Dom Pedro in Portugal: he was to make an incognito tour through England, France, and Spain to further his education. These orders were dispatched to Brazil in October; the troops and warships to enforce them sailed later for Rio via Pernambuco, where Dom João had established a high court of justice. The Cortes decrees would make instant Brazilian patriots of countless judges, lawyers, clerks and bureaucrats.[29]

These measures were not unanticipated in Brazil. Even as they were being debated in Lisbon, anonymous posters were appearing on walls in Rio calling for the independence of Brazil under a liberal regime, with Dom Pedro as emperor. The crown prince publicly disowned and condemned this idea and reaffirmed his loyalty to the Cortes. The episode led to some ministerial changes in October —including the ouster of the timid cabinet chief, Pedro Alvares Diniz —with the approval of General Avilez. Dom Pedro gave the Portuguese military little grounds for complaint in the way he conducted the government: although the regency resorted to paper-money loans from the Bank of Brazil to meet other expenses, it continued to pay the officers in specie and the troops in copper. To all appearances, the prince's devotion to their welfare and to other Portuguese interests was beyond reproach. When the decree ordering Dom Pedro to leave arrived on 9 December, the prince promptly declared that he would obey it and had it published, along with the decree suppressing the tribunals, in the *Gazeta* on 11 December. Up to this time, despite the posters and the increasingly enthusiastic cheers he was getting at the theater in the streets, Dom Pedro had perceived little effective support for his remaining in Brazil. The Portuguese army division was in command of Rio and insisted that he obey the Cortes. The soldiers were backed up by Portuguese merchants and their employees who, discounting the Cortes' liberal rhetoric, looked forward to the reestablishment of the colonial system and the return of their commercial monopoly. Foreign and Brazilian merchants, along with native producers and consumers, dreaded this prospect, but the more prominent of them had been reluctant to adopt the Portuguese-born prince as their champion. The situation changed soon after publication of the Cortes legislation abolishing the central government of the kingdom of Brazil and ordering the prince to leave.[30]

New posters, pamphlets, and a newspaper named for a hot red pepper—*A Malagueta*—appeared in Rio urging the prince to defy the Cortes and stay in Brazil. But the most powerful document came from São Paulo; it was a petition to Dom Pedro, written by José Bonifácio and signed by all the members of the provincial junta, that the prince received on 1 January 1822. Paulista hearts, it declared, were fired by "noble indignation" at the brazen attempt by the Cortes to impress upon Brazil "a system of anarchy and slavery." The "enemies of order" in the Cortes aimed to "disunite us, weaken us, . . . leave us as miserable orphans by tearing from the bosom of the great family of Brazil the only common parent remaining to us after they had robbed Brazil of the beneficent founder of the kingdom, Your Royal Highness's august father." In perpetrating this great injustice, the Portuguese Cortes deputies had violated the constitutional bases to which they had all sworn, by not consulting Brazil's representatives: "How dare those deputies of Portugal, without waiting for those of Brazil, legislate concerning the most sacred interest of each province, and of an entire kingdom?" The "vast and rich kingdom of Brazil," the principal component of the "Portuguese nation," was to be divided into "miserable fragments" by the representatives of a minute fraction of the nation, who proposed to "annihilate by a stroke of the pen all the tribunals and establishments necessary to the existence and future prosperity" of Brazil. "Where now shall the unfortunate people resort in behalf of their civil and judicial interests? Must they now again, after being for twelve years accustomed to prompt recourse, go and suffer like contemptible colonists the delays and chicanery of the tribunals of Lisbon, across two thousand leagues of ocean, where the sighs of the oppressed lose all life and all hope?"[31]

It was inconceivable, the paulistas declared, that the "vast kingdom of Brazil" should be without a seat of government, and be deprived of a command center for the "direction of our troops, . . . to defend the state against any unforeseen attack of external enemies, or against internal disorders and factions, which might threaten public safety or the union of the provinces." Honest Brazilians "who pride themselves on being men, particularly the paulistas," could never tolerate "such absurdity and such despotism." They urged Dom Pedro to defy the Cortes and stay in Brazil, "to confide boldly in the love and fidelity of your Brazilians, and especially of your paulistas, who are all ready to shed the last drop of their blood, and to sacrifice all their possessions, rather than to lose the adored prince in whom they have placed their well-founded hopes of national happiness and honor."[32]

Like-minded Cariocas had been waiting for the paulistas to commit themselves. Members of the Rio city council rushed the collection of signatures on a petition that they planned to present to Dom Pedro on 9 January. Dom Pedro facilitated their work by publishing the paulista manifesto in the *Gazeta* on 8 January. In the meantime, resolutions calling on the prince to stay came in from two cities in Minas Gerais. This outpouring of support indicated that should Dom Pedro decide to remain he would have a good chance of prevailing in the inevitable confrontation with General Avilez and the Portuguese Division. And in José Bonifácio, with his decisiveness, knowledge, experience, and total dedication, the prince had the collaborator he would need in governing Brazil. Dom Pedro was no longer alone in the arena, and the elements for success were accumulating. He would announce his decision after receiving the petition of the Rio city council on 9 January. When General Avilez expressed his outrage, the prince reminded him that the constitutional bases guaranteed the right to petition; he would hear what the supplicants had to say. The prince regent's ministers, their positions already abolished by the Cortes, submitted their resignations in deference to Avilez.[33]

The president of the Rio city council, José Clemente Pereira —born in Portugal and bayonetted on the floor of the commercial exchange—presented the petition to Dom Pedro in a ceremony inside the city palace at noon on 9 January 1822. In his presentation speech José Clemente asserted that it was necessary for the prince to remain in Brazil to prevent its separation from Portugal. His departure and the destruction of the central government so wisely fashioned by his father would encourage separatist and republican groups, like those only temporarily overcome in Pernambuco in 1817, and which existed in many, if not all, Brazilian provinces. Without a liberal central government in Brazil, the provinces would go their separate ways and sever ties with the Bragança monarch and with the Portuguese nation. The prince should delay his departure until the Cortes could be informed of the true situation in Brazil. The petition that José Clemente handed to Dom Pedro bore 8,000 signatures.[34]

To José Clemente and the other councilmen and dignitaries present, Dom Pedro declared himself convinced that his presence in Brazil was in the interest of the Portuguese on both sides of the Atlantic. "Since it is for the good of all and the general happiness of the nation, I am ready; tell the people that I am staying." After José Clemente had relayed the decision to the multitude assembled outside the palace, Dom Pedro appeared on a balcony and received a rousing ovation.[35] The Portuguese for "I am staying," *fico,* galvanized the prince's supporters and would come to signify the beginning of the final phase of Brazil's march to independence. After he had made this momentous pronouncement at the city palace, Dom Pedro called for a horse to ride home to Boa Vista. Those around him urged him to take a carriage instead, but the prince refused, knowing that they wanted to pull the vehicle themselves, as people had drawn Dom João's coach on the day of the king's oath to the constitution. The thought of people, of whatever race or condition of servitude, carrying others around as if they were holy images disgusted Dom Pedro. "It grieves me to see my fellow humans giving a man tributes appropriate for the divinity," Dom Pedro told his admirers that afternoon; "I know that my blood is the same color as that of the Negroes." The prince was as proud of that statement as he was of the fico.[36]

The Portuguese Division stationed in Rio was not a division in the modern sense. It consisted of three battalions of chasseurs, or light infantry, and a battalion of field artillery: a total of fewer than 2,700 officers and men. They occupied barracks at the Campo de Santana and three sites near the waterfront, between Point Calabouço and the Morro do Castelo. The division commander, Lieutenant-General Jorge de Avilez, was also officially commandant of all armed forces in the Rio area, but Brazilian troops manned the harbor forts. In January 1822, as in the preceding April, they took orders from their aged countryman, Lieutenant-General Joaquim Xavier Curado. The forts joined the celebration on the afternoon of 9 January 1822, firing their cannon in salute to Dom Pedro and the fico. The Carioca jubilation carried into the evening, with the illumination of houses and public buildings. From the deck of the frigate HMS *Doris*, anchored in Rio harbor, the scene on shore was admired by the Scottish wife of the ship's captain. "The numerous forts at the entrance to the harbour, on the islands, and in the town," Maria Dundas Graham wrote in her diary, "have each their walls traced in light, so they are like fairy fire-castles; and the scattered lights of the city and villages connect them by a hundred little brilliant chains."[37]

Dom Pedro and Dona Leopoldina received a rousing welcome at the Royal Theater on the night of the fico, and the audience joined in singing the prince's "Hymn to the Constitution." Local orators addressed Dom Pedro and the audience between acts and distributed printed handouts extolling the idea of a free and autonomous Brazil. The nativist exuberance exacerbated the growing tension between the Brazilian populace and Avilez's Portuguese soldiers. The general and his officers seemed at a loss as to what to do—other than insult Brazilians and march their troops up and down the cobblestone streets of Rio, where unintimidated Cariocas mocked their heavy tread and called them "leadfeet." They could not agree on a plan to arrest Dom Pedro and ship him off to Portugal. The officers of the Third Battalion, at the Campo de Santana, lost their nerve as they perceived the strength of the Brazilian militia units that began forming nearby. Dom Pedro made no move against Avilez before the afternoon of 11 January, when the general claimed he received notice that the prince regent had fired him as armed forces commandant of Rio and ordered him back to Portugal. The prince later denied that he had dismissed Avilez; he did accept the resignation of the minister of war and other members of the pre-fico cabinet, and sent a message to São Paulo for José Bonifácio to come at once to Rio. After the showdown with Avilez, Dom Pedro would name José Bonifácio as the head of a new council of ministers.[38]

Dom Pedro appeared at the theater on the night of 11 January, accompanied by Dona Leopoldina, who was seven months pregnant. After receiving the cheers of the audience, the prince made his usual plea for tranquility and union between the Brazilians and Portuguese. But Avilez was not in his box and few of his officers were present to hear the conciliatory words. About eleven o'clock word spread through the audience that Portuguese troops were on a rampage in the streets, breaking windows, putting out lights, and committing other depredations. Dom Pedro, from the royal box, addressed the people in the theater, asking them to stay calm and be assured that they would be protected by his personal guard—almost all Brazilians—stationed outside. They should not go into the streets and add to the confusion; Dom Pedro had issued orders that would restore order to the city. In the meantime, the audience should remain with him in the theater and enjoy the rest of the opera. As the show went on, the prince received messages, consulted with military aides, made plans, and issued orders from the royal box. The men of the Eleventh and Fifteenth Battalions, he learned, were leaving the streets and concentrating on the Morro do Castelo, where they were being joined by the Portuguese field artillery. Officers of the Third Battalion informed Dom Pedro that they had not joined the mutiny and would not move from their barracks at the Campo de Santana except on his orders; however, they would be reluctant to take up arms against their Portuguese comrades. So the prince ordered the quasi-loyal Third Battalion to Boa Vista to guard the palace—but not to guard his family. When the opera was over Dom Pedro accompanied Dona Leopoldina home to Boa Vista and after a brief, stormy meeting there with Avilez at two o'clock in the morning, during which he berated the general for the indiscipline of his troops and declared that he was going to throw them out of Rio, the prince sent his wife and children off to Santa Cruz, eighty kilometers away, where they would be safe from the fighting. Dom Pedro took the extra precaution of asking Captain Graham of HMS *Doris* for asylum for his family and himself, should he lose the showdown with the Portuguese.[39] The prince was determined not to surrender to Avilez and suffer a repetition of his humiliation of 5 June.

In the predawn hours of 12 January, as Avilez asserted his command over the Portuguese mutineers and ordered them into position on the Morro do Castelo, Dom Pedro and the seventy-nine-year-old General Curado dispatched Brazilian forces to secure the Carioca waterworks, the gunpowder factory and artillery park at the Royal Botanical Gardens, the Naval Arsenal, and the munitions depot on Cobras Island. Native regulars and first-line militia denied these resources to the leadfeet, while second-line militia from Rio and the outlying area assembled on the Campo de Santana, along with the Brazilian artillery. There were friars on horseback, men and boys of all ages and colors—armed with pistols, knives, pikes, and a variety of fowling pieces and ancient blunderbusses—and black slaves bearing horse feed and drinking water. They numbered more than 4,000 when the tropical dawn broke over the Campo de Santana. By this time Dona Leopoldina and her children, the almost-three-year-old Dona Maria da Gloria and the ten-month-old Dom João Carlos, and their servants were well on their way down the bumpy wagon road to Santa Cruz. The summer heat was almost unbearable and Dom João Carlos began to suffer the effects of what his mother took to be an inflammation of the liver.[40]

General Avilez realized the hopelessness of his position when the Brazilian troops began to surround the base of the Morro do Castelo. He was stuck on the hilltop without water or other provisions. His troops could probably fight their way out of the encirclement, but without reinforcements they could not subdue the Brazilians, who by mid-morning had some 8,000 men under arms. He knew that reinforcements were on their way from Portugal; he had to withdraw to some place where his troops could be supplied while they awaited them. At eleven o'clock on the morning of 12 January General Avilez came down from the Morro to parlay with Dom Pedro at the city palace. The prince went through the motions of firing Avilez as military commandant of Rio and ordering him out of the country. The general agreed to leave, if he could take his troops and their arms with him. He proposed that they cross the bay to Niterói to wait there for the ships that were on their way from Portugal, bringing replacements; they would make the return voyage on those ships. Since Dom Pedro did not have his own ships ready to transport the leadfeet across the ocean, and since he wanted them out of Rio immediately, he consented to the temporary move to Niterói. The prince ordered immediate payment from the royal treasury of a month's salary to the troops, and agreed to the payment of two months' salary in advance as soon as they were all aboard ship and ready to sail. He insisted, however, that any Portuguese soldier who wished to remain in Brazil be separated from the division and allowed to stay. Avilez would not consent to this, but was unable to prevent the desertion of several hundred of his men to the Brazilian side. On the afternoon of 12 January and the morning of the 13th, the 2,000 remaining leadfeet were ferried across the bay to the military training camp at Niterói. In the aftermath of the leadfeet's withdrawal the prince regent published a proclamation to the people of Rio, hailing this victory for "union and tranquility," and decided on a new council of ministers, to be headed by José Bonifácio. The decision was relayed immediately to Dona Leopoldina at Santa Cruz, since it was expected that José Bonifácio would pass through there on his way from São Paulo to Rio.[41]

Dom João had extended the wagon road west from Rio to Santa Cruz, but from there to São Paulo the trail remained impassable to wheeled vehicles. The best way from São Paulo to Rio, for someone José Bonifácio's age, was by boat from the paulista port of Santos east along the coast to the mouth of the Itaguaí river, to the port of Sepetiba, near Santa Cruz, and from there by coach to Rio. This was the route taken by the illustrious paulista and four companions in January 1822. Dona Leopoldina ordered a coach and horses sent to Sepetiba to await the travelers; when she was informed that their boat had been sighted she summoned her own carriage and drove toward the river. She met the paulistas' vehicle on the road and gave José Bonifácio the news that he had been officially appointed to head her husband's government. She insisted that the new minister of the kingdom and foreign affairs join her in her carriage for the drive to the royal villa, where she wanted to introduce him to her children; then he could resume the journey to Rio. José Bonifácio could not refuse, nor did he want to. He and the princess conversed in French on the road, and in German at the former Jesuit dormitory that had been converted into a summer palace. The Brazilian scientist-statesman mispronounced a lot of German words, but he spoke the language rapidly, as he did French and his native Portuguese. José Bonifácio was a fast talker who tended to dominate conversations; but at Santa Cruz he deferred to royalty, and the princess found him charming.[42]

José Bonifácio was very short and slightly stooped. He had a full mane of long gray hair and small, impish eyes. Even in his late fifties, he was still dancing lundus and fathering illegitimate children. "Women," he would reflect, "have been the bane of my existence. I love them, but I don't esteem them. Give a woman a mirror and some bonbons and she's happy, Byron used to say."[43] Clearly Dona Leopoldina, who disdained mirrors and all instruments of feminine vanity, did not fit the stereotype. Perhaps she overindulged in bonbons —each pregnancy left her incrementally heavier—but sweets were hardly the source of whatever happiness she experienced. Like José Bonifácio, she enjoyed children, science, and the life of the mind. She was delighted to be in the presence of a great thinker—never minding that he was a libertine, a reputed atheist, and a proponent of the "new ideas" that she had consistently bemoaned in her letters to her father. She was changing; her husband's emotional commitment to political liberalism had left her duty bound to seek religious and scientific justification for the new creed. The priests in Rio disgusted her father's diplomatic representative, Baron von Marschall, with their bent for preaching "the sovereignty of the people instead of the gospel of Jesus Christ," for "citing from the pulpit William Tell and Washington instead of the evangelists,"[44] but they probably helped Dona Leopoldina reconcile her religion with the ideology of the emerging Brazilian nation. José Bonifácio would assure her of the scientific validity of the new ideas. He would become not only her mentor, but her surrogate father and grandfather to her children, filling the void created by the departure of Dom João. She presented Dona Maria da Gloria and Dom João Carlos—who was not well—to José Bonifácio, saying, "These two Brazilians are your compatriots and I beg you to treat them with paternal love." The old man was profoundly touched.[45]

After a few hours at Santa Cruz, José Bonifácio and his party resumed their journey to Rio, where they arrived early in the evening of the next day, 18 January. Dom Pedro insisted on seeing them immediately, and they were ushered into his presence at Boa Vista palace at nine-thirty that night. Tired and dirty from their many hours on the road, the paulistas were cordially received by the prince, whose handsome appearance, composure, and easy, friendly manner impressed them all. José Bonifácio spoke frankly to Dom Pedro: he would not accept the appointment to be minister of the kingdom and foreign affairs; although he would gladly serve the prince in any other capacity, he could not head his government. But Dom Pedro could not accept the refusal; he had to have José Bonifácio for the top job and politely asked him to state his conditions for taking it. The venerable paulista would not lay down conditions then and there, but after some prodding, he indicated that he and the prince might come to a "man-to-man" understanding that would allow him to take the position. Excusing themselves from the others, Dom Pedro and José Bonifácio went into private conference and reached the necessary agreement.[46]

José Bonifácio demanded and received personal assurances from Dom Pedro that the prince would not leave Brazil—no matter what might happen. The fico would be permanent, not temporary as suggested in the 9 January speech of José Clemente Pereira, who called for Dom Pedro to stay only while the Cortes reconsidered its actions toward Brazil. Any reconciliation with Portugal would not be at the expense of the autonomous, liberal government that José Bonifácio envisioned for Brazil, for which the continued presence in Rio of the prince regent was essential. The paulista probably did not know of Dom Pedro's inquiry about possible asylum on a British warship, but he must have suspected that the prince had some such contingency plan. On this matter, both parties were influenced by the events of 5 June: Dom Pedro was determined to avoid being captured and humiliated by Avilez, and José Bonifácio was determined to avoid the fate of the count of Arcos. Neither the prince nor his new mentor would be degraded or deported in the next confrontation with the leadfeet; they pledged to stand together and fight to the death, if necessary, for their autonomous liberal government. But it was victory, not martyrdom, that they sought, and José Bonifácio knew that success depended largely on the expulsion of Avilez from Niterói before more troops arrived from Portugal. Before taking office José Bonifácio made Dom Pedro promise to undertake military and naval operations to force the Portuguese out of Niterói as soon as possible.[47]

Dom Pedro's commitment to get tough with the leadfeet was reinforced by the return to Boa Vista of Dona Leopoldina and the children on 19 January. Dom João Carlos was now seriously ill, a condition his parents blamed on the Portuguese soldiers, whose mutiny had forced the family to make the arduous journey to safety at Santa Cruz. When a delegation of officers from Avilez's division arrived at Boa Vista on 22 January to pay their respects to Dona Leopoldina on her birthday, she and Dom Pedro refused to receive them. This incident and the various measures taken by the new José Bonifácio ministry pointed to an imminent showdown between the forces of Portugal and those of Brazil—provoked this time by the latter. Brazilian militia units were summoned from São Paulo and Minas Gerais and work was rushed on five ships in Rio harbor, to outfit them for transporting the leadfeet back to Portugal. On 21 January the ministry ordered that no law enacted in Portugal be enforced in Brazil unless approved by the prince regent. On 30 January instructions went out to all the Brazilian provincial juntas to take the necessary steps to subject themselves to the regency of His Royal Highness in Rio. On that same day, Dom Pedro ordered the Portuguese troops to begin loading onto the ships, which were now ready for the ocean voyage. General Avilez and his officers protested vigorously, declaring that they intended to remain until relieved by troops from Portugal. In the exchange of notes, Dom Pedro condemned the Portuguese officers for their insolence and warned them that if they were not all aboard ship by 5 February he would cut off their food and water. Brazilian troops under General Curado moved into positions that sealed off the Portuguese beachhead by land, and local civilians were ordered to stop trading with the division on 1 February. The leadfeet, however, had several small vessels that they used to bring in supplies from Rio; Dom Pedro ordered up the frigate *União*, the corvette *Liberal*, three gunboats, and the steamboat *Bragança*, for use in intercepting this traffic if the leadfeet were not embarked by the 5 February deadline.[48]

On 3 February the Portuguese division still had not begun to embark. José Bonifácio was monitoring developments from the city palace—on the waterfront, facing Niterói, four kilometers across the bay—when he received a message from Dom Pedro at Boa Vista. The prince regent could not join the minister in the city, he explained, "crying as I write this," because "my beloved son is taking his last breaths." Dom Pedro wanted to be on hand to "give him the last kiss and lay him to rest with the final paternal blessing." Later, José Bonifácio received a second dispatch from the prince, enclosing an epitaph for

Dom João Carlos and asking the minister ("My José") to "amend it if it is not good."[49] The child died on 4 February after a convulsive epileptic seizure that lasted twenty-eight hours. Dona Leopoldina confided in a letter to her father that she was able to survive the wrenching experience only because of her religious faith. Dom Pedro, in informing Dom João of the sad event, declared that the suffering and death of Dom João Carlos was "the fruit of the insubordination and crimes" of the Portuguese Division. The division, he emphasized, "was the murderer of my son, the grandson of Your Majesty." The inhabitants of Rio shared his grief, he said, and had not forgiven the mutineers for their depredations on the night of 11 January. Their hatred had grown: the people "will never allow the entrance of another Portuguese troop" into the city.[50]

There were still some Portuguese merchants in Rio who sympathized with the plight of their countrymen in Niterói. After Dom Pedro's government stopped provisioning the division and imposed the blockade on 5 February, Joaquina de Avilez, the general's wife, was seen in Rio arranging clandestine shipments of food to Niterói. It was said that the beautiful Joaquina sold her jewelry to raise money to feed her husband's men. General Avilez continued to play for time, sending notes to the Brazilians promising to complete the embarkation by 8 February if Dom Pedro would lift the blockade and provide additional ocean transports. The prince regent detailed two more ships for the ocean voyage and pulled back his blockaders from Niterói on 6 February. Great activity was observed among the leadfeet and their flotilla of small boats that day; a rumor swept Rio that the Portuguese were about to invade the city. The urban militia was called to arms and José Bonifácio appeared on the city palace square in uniform and on horseback. The invasion did not materialize, but neither did the Portuguese begin the promised evacuation to the oceangoing vessels. Dom Pedro tightened his blockade while making one last concession to the leadfeet on 8 February: he would give them three, instead of two, months' pay when they were all embarked. This produced no movement toward the transports, so Dom Pedro went aboard the frigate *União* to personally direct his forces in action against the Portuguese.[51]

Before launching the attack, the prince regent had the *União* heave in close to the leadfoot beachhead on 9 February and sent an officer ashore with a warning: unless the Portuguese troops began the embarkation by dawn the next day, Dom Pedro would regard them as enemies and give them no quarter. The note brought Avilez and most of his officers out to the *União* to protest and offer excuses. The prince regent would hear none of it; he had given the orders: either the Portuguese would be boarding the ships at dawn, or he would open fire. Vastly outnumbered by General Curado's forces on the ground, outgunned by the Brazilian naval squadron, and with no news of the long-awaited reinforcements, the leadfeet had no choice but to capitulate. The embarkation began early on 10 February and was completed the next afternoon. The division's officers were then permitted to go ashore in Rio to wind up their personal affairs, and on 15 February the transports sailed, escorted out into the ocean by the Brazilian corvettes *Liberal* and *Maria da Gloria*.[52]

Two days later the ministry issued orders forbidding the landing of any Portuguese forces in Brazil. When the expedition that Avilez had been waiting for—and that was supposed to bring Dom Pedro back to Portugal—finally appeared off Rio on 5 March, Brazilian forts barred its entrance into the harbor. While their vessels—one ship-of-the-line, one frigate, two corvettes, and two transports—rode precariously at anchor in the ocean, the expedition's officers were permitted to come ashore and state their business to Brazilian authorities. An agreement was reached whereby the frigate was turned over to the Brazilian regency, the expedition's remaining ships were allowed to refit in Rio for the return trip to Portugal, and the Portuguese soldiers were given the choice of returning to their homeland or remaining in Brazil as members of Dom Pedro's army. About 400 soldiers, plus some of the crew of the frigate *Real Carolina*, stayed to serve the prince regent when the expedition sailed from Rio on 23 March.[53] Thus Dom Pedro, with the indispensable guidance and resolute support of José Bonifácio, banished Portuguese military power from the Brazilian capital forever. Not one shot had been fired nor a single casualty inflicted in the protracted armed confrontation.

Dona Leopoldina began to experience labor pains at two o'clock on the morning of 11 March 1822. At three-thirty she called Dom Pedro and they were walking about the palace at five o'clock when the birth began. The princess wrapped her arms around her husband's neck and, with her feet planted on the floor, gave birth to a healthy baby girl. It was an occasion of "immense happiness," Dom Pedro wrote his father, but in a letter to Dom Miguel he did not conceal his disappointment that "God took João away from me and gave me another daughter who will be named Januária." He now believed that he would not leave a male heir, and that his older daughter, Dona Maria da Glória, would be his successor to the throne of the united kingdom of Portugal and Brazil. To secure her rights—and perhaps also to eliminate a potential threat to his own rights—on 14 March 1822 Dom Pedro proposed that his brother return to Brazil and marry Dona Maria da Gloria, with Dom João's permission. Dom Miguel would have a decade more to wait for his fiancée to reach puberty, but Dom Pedro would do everything possible to make his life in Brazil pleasant. It would be far better than living in Portugal under the thumb of the Cortes, Dom Pedro suggested. By coming to Brazil and marrying his niece, Dom Miguel not only would be helping his brother, but also serving the nation and his father, according to Dom Pedro.[54]

The life of the royal family in Portugal under the new regime was indeed difficult. But its more assertive members, Dom Miguel and his mother, Dona Carlota, were busy exploiting the factionalism within the Cortes and plotting with outside reactionaries to overthrow the parliamentary government. Although their objective was the restoration of royal absolutism, they were not working in the interests of Dom João—which the king fully realized. Because of government interception of his correspondence, Dom João had difficulty informing Dom Pedro of the situation in Portugal. By mid-1822 Dom Pedro knew that some of his enemies in the Cortes were conspiring to replace him as crown prince with Dom Miguel. "Your mother is for Miguel," Dom João wrote, "and I, who love you, can do nothing against the carbonari who don't like you."[55] That the reactionary Dona Carlota should be making common cause with revolutionaries—carbonari —was ironic, but not unprecedented. Once the Cortes made Dom Miguel crown prince, his mother could be expected to exploit his prestige and invite Portuguese absolutists to rally around him and overthrow the liberal regime. If successful, she certainly would not restore power to Dom João; probably she would have her hated husband pronounced mentally incompetent, and her beloved son, Dom Miguel, declared prince regent of Portugal and its overseas colonies.

Apprised of his mother's machinations against him and his father, Dom Pedro, who was genuinely fond of his younger brother, redoubled his efforts to get Dom Miguel out of Portugal, and out of Dona Carlota's influence. On 19 June he wrote to the king asking permission for Dom Miguel to come to Brazil and marry, in due time, Dona Maria da Glória. The same day he wrote to Dom Miguel, in language they both understood. "There'll be no shortage of people who tell you not to leave," Dom Pedro wrote. "Tell them to eat shit. And they'll say that with Brazil seceding you're going to be the King of Portugal: Tell them to do it again." Dom Miguel needed to get away from those enemies who surrounded him, who aimed to deceive and betray him, and come to Brazil, where the people would respect him and where he could "court my daughter at close range and marry her in due time. . . . Come, come, come—because Brazil will receive you with open arms, and you'll be happy having everything very secure without it costing you anything." It was not safe over there, Dom Pedro warned his brother; he was in danger of suffering the fate of "the Dauphin of France, and our father that of Louis XVI."[56] The prince regent of Brazil should have known better than to try to attract his brother with an offer of safety. Dom Miguel was more likely to seek danger than to flee from it. The brothers would remain in their respective hemispheres pursuing their separate interests, neither much concerned with personal security.

In Brazil, Dom Pedro took his first step toward creating a representative national government by summoning delegates from the provinces to Rio to form a council of procurators. Procurators were apportioned according to representation in the Portuguese Cortes: roughly, for every four deputies a province was entitled to send to Lisbon, it could send one procurator to Rio. The Rio council, which was scheduled to convene on 2 June, was not, however, a legislative body. Its function was strictly advisory: the procurators were to act as a council of state, to be consulted by the prince regent as he proceeded with the establishment of an autonomous constitutional regime in Brazil. There would be a constitution; the question was, would it be fashioned by Dom Pedro and submitted to the people's representatives for ratification, or would these roles be reversed? Some provinces that favored a constitutional convention, like Pernambuco, refused to send procurators to Rio. Others, like Rio de Janeiro, selected procurators who would pressure Dom Pedro to call such a convention and grant it full constituent and legislative powers. Bahia was still under Portuguese military control when Dom Pedro issued the decree establishing the council of procurators on 16 February. The next day the Bahians rose in revolt against the Portuguese, but, after four days of hard fighting, the patriots were forced to evacuate the capital city and take up positions in the countryside. Dom Pedro hailed the Bahian movement and issued a decree ordering all Portuguese forces out of that province and the rest of Brazil, if they did not submit to his authority.[57]

Closer to Rio, Minas Gerais posed a problem for Dom Pedro. There were no hostile Portuguese forces in that province, and most of its cities had rallied to the prince at the time of the fico, but the junta of government in the provincial capital of Ouro Prêto refused to submit to the authority of the regency in Rio—partly due to local antimonarchist feelings dating back to an abortive conspiracy against the crown in 1789. Dom Pedro realized that he had to bring Minas fully under his control before he could hope to extend his authority to the more distant provinces. On 25 March 1822 with four companions, three servants, and three soldiers, he left Rio on horseback for Minas Gerais to take his appeal directly to the people. It was the prince's first trip into the interior of Brazil beyond the province of Rio de Janeiro. It was an adventure of long, hard rides, sleeping on the ground with a saddle for a pillow, eating beans and manioc meal. The complete lack of pomp, the absence of military force, the prince's ready smile and down-to-earth manners won over the republican-inclined mineiros. Dom Pedro was greeted enthusiastically by the people of the villages, towns, and cities through which he passed on his way to Ouro Prêto. Civilian leaders and militia officers pledged allegiance to the prince and support for him in the event of a conflict with the junta in the provincial capital. Dom Pedro had been warned by José Bonifácio not to take at face value anything a mineiro might tell him—the stereotype of the mineiro as dissimulator was well in place by 1822—but he sensed that the pledges of support that he received were genuine, and felt that he had the power at his disposal to overcome the junta in Ouro Prêto. He halted outside the capital city and issued a proclamation demanding that the authorities there submit unequivocably to his rule. The junta complied and Dom Pedro entered Ouro Prêto in triumph. He spent a week and a half there, appointing a new military governor, ordering elections, hearing complaints, firing venal functionaries, pardoning prisoners, and issuing decrees on local and provincial matters.[58]

Dom Pedro left Ouro Prêto on 21 April, after receiving a letter from José Bonifácio informing him that the minister had uncovered a pro-Portuguese plot to install a "provisional junta" in Rio. The trouble in Rio supposedly was over, but the prince decided to return to his capital as quickly as possible. He covered the 530 kilometers between Ouro Prêto and Rio in the almost-incredible time of four and a half days, arriving in the Brazilian capital in time to appear at the theater on the night of 25 April and announce that all was tranquil in Minas Gerais. For three days, Rio celebrated the prince regent's epic feats of horsemanship and peacemaking. The excursion into the interior completed the Brazilianization of Dom Pedro; thereafter he made a point of referring to himself as a Brazilian in letters to his father. On 13 May 1822, his father's birthday, the prince assumed the title of "perpetual defender of Brazil" to the acclaim of the Carioca multitudes. A week later the Rio city council petitioned the perpetual defender to call a constitutional convention, and Dom Pedro replied that he would refer the matter to the council of procurators when that body met for the first time on 2 June. Only a small fraction of the procurators showed up for the first session of the council. They voted unanimously for a constitutional convention, and the next day, 3 June, Dom Pedro issued a decree convoking the desired constituent assembly, which would meet the following year.[59]

Freemasons, like the Rio city council president, José Clemente Pereira, were in the forefront of those who were pushing Dom Pedro toward a parliamentary system and an early declaration of Brazilian independence. Masonic lodges had existed in Brazil and Portugal during the reign of Dom João, and their membership, far from being confined to political liberals, had included some of the king's more conservative ministers and councillors of state, and even his valet. But the prominence of Freemasons in the revolt in Pernambuco and the conspiracy in Lisbon in 1817 prompted Dom João to proscribe the secret societies. They reemerged after 1820 with the constitutionalist victories in Portugal and Brazil. In Rio, the Commerce and Arts Lodge was resurrected in 1821. To accommodate a flood of new members, it chartered another lodge in the city and one across the bay in Niterói. Rather than reaffiliate with the matrix Great Orient Lodge of Portugal, the Rio area Freemasons decided to create a Great Orient of Brazil. This was done at a general meeting in Rio on 28 May 1822 that was attended by representatives of lodges in Bahia and Pernambuco. The Masonic brothers dedicated themselves to the unity and independence of Brazil and elected José Bonifácio as their grand master. José Bonifácio, who was not at the meeting—and was at the time engaged in organizing his own pseudo-Masonic secret society, the Apostolate—eventually accepted the Great Orient position and was inaugurated on 24 June. Soon, virtually every politically or socially ambitious male in Rio applied to join the fraternity. Some, like Francisco Gomes da Silva, the Chalaça, were rejected. But Chalaça's friend, Dom Pedro, already a member of the Apostolate, was proposed for membership in the Great Orient by Grand Master José Bonifácio and was accepted unanimously. The prince was initiated as a Freemason in Rio on the night of 2 August, under the pseudonym Cuauhtémoc, the name of the last emperor of the Aztecs.[60]

Dom Pedro and José Bonifácio were aware of the opportunity that lodge membership offered for keeping tabs on the political activists of Rio. They also perceived the utility of Masonic ties for binding the provincial leadership to the central government. Pernambuco, a stronghold of Freemasonry, did not subordinate itself to Rio until nearly six months after the fico. The Pernambucans retained some antimonarchist sentiment from the 1817 revolt, and they were mindful that in their province, unlike in Rio, blood had been shed in 1821 prior to the withdrawal of Portuguese troops. In November 1821 the Portuguese garrison in the capital city of Recife had been forced to embark, and three months later, the expedition from Portugal, which also was supposed to relieve Avilez in Rio, had been prevented from landing troops in Pernambuco. Although there were no Portuguese forces in Pernambuco in mid-1822, in Bahia the provincial capital was held by about 2,400 leadfoot regulars and some 2,000 Lusophile militia, who were locked in a vicious civil war with a larger, but less-disciplined force of patriot militia based in the adjacent countryside. On 14 July Dom Pedro dispatched Pierre Labatut, French veteran of various military campaigns and recent initiate of the Great Orient, to Bahia at the head of an expedition of 274 officers and men to assist the local patriots.[61]

Early in the next month, Dom Pedro issued manifestos calling home the Brazilian deputies from the Cortes in Lisbon, declaring war on the Portuguese army in Brazil, asking foreign powers to deal directly with his government in Rio, and denouncing 300 years of Portuguese tyranny and oppression of Brazil. Then, on 14 August the prince set out on horseback for São Paulo, accompanied by a secretary, two servants, the paulista Lieutenant Francisco de Castro Canto e Melo, and the Chalaça. The trip was prompted by a rift in the provincial government: the acerbic Martim Francisco de Andrada, provincial finance secretary, had been expelled from the junta by a group of his colleagues led by the junta president. José Bonifácio, with the prince's approval, gave his brother a new job as treasury minister in Rio, and fired the paulista junta president. Although the latter accepted his dismissal, Dom Pedro needed additional assurances of the loyalty of the important province of São Paulo, so he decided to go there personally to install a new military commandant and supervise elections for a new junta. Prior to leaving Rio, the prince designated his wife as provisional regent of Brazil during his absence from the capital.[62]

The city of São Paulo was about 630 kilometers from Rio, via Santa Cruz and the Paráiba Valley trail. The prince was received with great jubilation in the valley towns through which he passed. At each place there were local horsemen who wanted to join his party; before he reached the city of São Paulo, Dom Pedro had collected an "honor guard" of more than two dozen well-mounted volunteers. The roads they traveled were muddy and slippery in the southern Brazilian winter; it was chilly, and the Paráiba and its tributaries were swollen by seasonal rains. The hyperactive Dom Pedro, unwilling to wait while his party loaded onto a raft at one crossing, impetuously spurred his horse into the water and crossed the river on the back of the swimming animal. But his clothes were soaked from the waist down, and the prince would neither endure the cold discomfort nor further delay the trip by searching for a dry pair of pants in his baggage. He simply exchanged pants with a member of his party who crossed on the raft; and the volunteer, who had the misfortune of being Dom Pedro's size, was stuck with the prince's wet trousers. For all the comraderie, Dom Pedro never let his companions forget that he was the prince; not only would his orders be obeyed, but his personal needs would be met, even at their expense. Clothes, horses, women: if he desired them, he felt entitled to them. As a "liberal" he seldom demanded outright what belonged to others, but he expected his loyal subjects to offer him whatever they had that he showed an interest in. He acquired horses that way; compliments to the owner on the fine qualities of an animal usually won Dom Pedro possession of it as a gift. The prince, however, did not always get what he wanted. In the paulista town of Santos he spotted a beautiful young mulata and impulsively grabbed her and kissed her; she slapped his face and ran away. She turned out to be the treasured house slave of a prominent local family, who refused to part with her even when the normally tightfisted Dom Pedro offered to buy her.[63]

Dom Pedro was warmly received in the capital city of São Paulo. There was a Te Deum mass in the cathedral and a hand-kissing ceremony at the City Hall. The prince refused his hand to two men whom he recognized as instigators of the ouster of Martim Francisco; Dom Pedro ordered them to go to Rio and report to José Bonifácio, and they went away quietly. The only other discordant note was Dom Pedro's thoughtless reaction to the sight of an old gentleman who had journeyed from an interior town to the provincial capital to pay his respects to the prince. A captain major of militia since 1779, he appeared wearing a uniform from about that year, complete with scarlet jacket, ruffled shirt, powdered wig, and kneebritches. Beholding this eighteenth-century apparition, Dom Pedro could not contain his laughter; his companions joined in the merriment at the expense of the elderly captain major, who went away mortified. Soon realizing his mistake, the prince summoned the old man and apologized to him. The apology was accepted and the anachronistic captain major remained a staunch supporter of Dom Pedro, who in the years to come would furnish new decorations for his ancient uniform. The original offense was unintentional—something to be expected of a high-spirited youth who lacked self-control.[64]

Generally, Dom Pedro's business in São Paulo went smoothly. The provincial electors cast their ballots in the prince's presence, and while ratifying Dom Pedro's choice for president, elected to the junta some members of the anti-Andrada faction. The prince accepted the elections and went on to attend to other matters, like outfitting his honor guard as dragoons, with gilded helmets. He also got to know the sister of his traveling companion, Lieutenant Francisco de Castro Canto e Melo. The comely Domitila de Castro was the twenty-four-year-old estranged wife of a militia officer from Minas Gerais, and before the end of August she and Dom Pedro were lovers. On 5 September the perpetual defender of Brazil took leave of his new mistress to make an excursion to the port of Santos; he wanted to inspect the forts there and to visit some of José Bonifácio's relatives. Dom Pedro enjoyed the hospitality of the people of Santos, but he picked up a bad case of diarrhea there. He and his honor guard left town on the morning of 7 September, but his affliction necessitated numerous rest stops and they fell behind schedule on the return trip to São Paulo. In the meantime, a courier from Rio had arrived in the paulista capital with urgent mail for Dom Pedro. After waiting a while in São Paulo, the messenger rode off with a paulista escort down the Santos trail to find the overdue prince; they spotted some members of his honor guard stopped on a hill above a stream called the Ipiranga. Dom Pedro was down by the water, answering the call of nature. The mail was delivered to him as he was buttoning up and straightening his uniform. The prince gave some of the letters to a priest to read, while he read others.[65]

The dispatches included letters from Dona Leopoldina and José Bonifácio in Rio, and some official notices from the Cortes in Lisbon. Dom Pedro was informed that his regency was purely honorific and existed in Rio only at the sufferance of the Cortes, that his ministers were to be replaced by new ones appointed in Lisbon, and that legislation previously enacted by the Brazilian regency was voided by act of the Cortes. Although the Lisbon government did not reissue its earlier demand that the prince leave Brazil and return to Europe, it indicated that it would deal harshly with those who had collaborated in the fico; José Bonifácio and the other signers of the paulista manifesto were notified that they would be tried for treason. Except for backing down on the matter of Dom Pedro's remaining in Brazil, the Cortes was taking a hard line; the commander of the expedition that had returned to Portugal without landing troops in either Pernambuco or Rio was in jail in Lisbon for dereliction of duty. A new force of fourteen battalions—7,100 men—was being readied in Portugal for shipment to Bahia; this was in addition to 600 leadfoot reinforcements who had recently landed in that province. Clearly, Portugal intended to fight for Brazil. There was no hope now that the mother country would give in and recognize Brazilian independence under some face-saving dual kingdom arrangement. "The die is cast," José Bonifácio wrote, "from Portugal we have nothing to expect but slavery and horrors." Dona Leopoldina was similarly indignant about the actions of the Cortes, and she was fearful of their consequences; she begged her husband to return immediately to Rio and save their "beloved Brazil" from ruin. José Bonifácio urged Dom Pedro to decide on Brazil's future relationship with Portugal "as soon as possible, because irresolution and lukewarm measures . . . are worthless and each moment lost is a disgrace."[66]

The prince and the priest, who was José Bonifácio's nephew, made a few comments on the letters, explained their contents to Chalaça, Canto e Melo, and some others who had gathered around. After a moment of reflection, Dom Pedro declared: "The time has come. Independence or death! We're separated from Portugal!" Then he mounted his pretty bay mare, rode to the top of the hill and addressed his honor guard: "Friends, the Cortes persecutes us and wants to enslave us. From this day forward our relations are broken." He tore the blue and white insignia of Portugal from his uniform and his soldiers followed suit, shouting vivas for independence and for Dom Pedro. The prince drew his sword and swore: "By my blood, by my honor, and by God: I will make Brazil free." After everyone had taken the same oath, Dom Pedro stood up in his stirrups, looked in all directions, and announced, "Brazilians, from this day forward our motto will be—Independence or Death." Then he took off at a gallop toward São Paulo. It was four-thirty in the afternoon.[67]

On the one-hour ride from Ipiranga into São Paulo, the prince was unusually pensive and uncommunicative. Dom Pedro was not thinking about the diarrhea, which apparently had left him; he was composing Brazil's national anthem. He went to the São Paulo city hall, wrote down the music, and sent it to the orchestra at the local opera house, to rehearse for that evening's performance. The news of the declaration of independence spread rapidly through the city and the small theater was packed that night. At nine o'clock Dom Pedro appeared at the opera house and made a speech from his box recounting the events of the afternoon and repeating the oath of independence. The audience cheered and everybody in the theater took the oath. Then the orchestra struck up Dom Pedro's music and the prince sang his song. The audience joined in the chorus,

> For thee our country
> Our blood we shall give;
> In glory we can only
> Triumph or die.[68]

When the music stopped, there were cheers for independence and for Dom Pedro, king of Brazil. A local poet recited his own composition alluding to the hero as Brazil's "first emperor," the title Dom Pedro preferred. There were more cries of "Independence or Death" and more vivas to Dom Pedro, and finally the drama scheduled for that night was presented: *The Guest of Stone*, by an author since forgotten.[69]

The music of Dom Pedro's anthem was better than the words, which were replaced by others—written by Evaristo da Veiga, the young manager of a popular bookstore and intellectual hangout in Rio—before the work was published as the "Brazilian Constitutional Hymn." Besides the anthem, Dom Pedro gave the new nation its colors: green, the traditional color of the Bragança family, and gold, representing the wealth of a land that he believed to be as rich as it was big. The prince's honor guard became the Dragoons of Independence, with the motto "Independence or Death" emblazoned on their white uniforms in green and gold. The dragoons were impressive, but they could not keep up with their commander on the ride back to Rio, which Dom Pedro completed in only five days. Chalaça, now a dragoon, was proud of finishing second in the race, arriving in the capital eight hours behind his friend, who, four weeks later, was acclaimed emperor of Brazil.[70]

5 Constitutional Emperor

The liberal deviseth liberal things;
and by liberal things shall he stand.
Isaiah 32:8

Unaware of Brazil's declaration of independence, the Cortes in Lisbon on 23 September 1822 finally promulgated a constitution for the Portuguese nation—the charter that Dom Pedro had sworn so many times to uphold before it existed. Except for their objections to the elimination of the central government in Rio, most Brazilian deputies to the Cortes favored this basically liberal constitution, and half of them signed the final draft. The constitution did not reduce Brazil to colonial status; it did not revoke Dom João's decrees of 1808 opening Brazilian ports to world trade and permitting manufacturing in Brazil. Although there were proposals before the Cortes for a protective tariff, which would have favored the established industries of Portugal, and for the exclusion of foreign carriers from "interprovincial" trade—i.e., between Portugal and the Brazilian provinces—consideration of these matters was postponed until after the adoption of the constitution. Had Brazilian deputies not begun withdrawing from the Cortes early in October 1822, these measures could have been defeated. Brazil's delegation to the Cortes was not as large as Portugal's, but it was a sizable minority and it had great potential bargaining power within the parliamentary system. Population figures for the period are inexact, but if slaves are excluded from the calculations, Brazil probably was not much, if at all, underrepresented in the Cortes.[1] The Brazilian deputies who voted for the suppression of the costly and often corrupt tribunals in Brazil claimed that they were doing their countrymen a favor—and they probably were. Brazilian independence, contrary to what Dom Pedro would have had his father believe, was not caused by the "oppression" of the Portuguese Cortes.[2]

There were people in Brazil who wanted a central government in Rio because they felt it would better serve their needs. Dom Pedro wanted to be emperor, José Bonifácio wanted to be prime minister, and thousands of lawyers, planters, and merchants in the Rio–São Paulo–Minas Gerais area preferred a government within their reach to one across the ocean. The rich and politically active of more distant provinces, however, did not necessarily identify their interests with Rio; in the far North, in Maranhão and Pará, the ties were stronger with Lisbon, which in the age of sailing ships was closer to the northern cities than was Rio. But everywhere there was a contest, with Rio and Lisbon bidding for the support of the provincial elite. As the contention became violent, appeals were made to the masses, who were needed to do the fighting. Those who favored independence had to work hard to convince the people that they were Brazilians; most had never thought of themselves as such. But neither was their Portuguese identity very strong, except along the frontier with Spanish America. Even in the 1820s, a sizable minority of "Christians" in Brazil had not learned the Portuguese language: they still spoke the *lingua geral*, the lingua franca of the colonial period that was derived from the languages of the Tupi-Guarani Indians. Whites, Indians, mestizos, even black slaves spoke the lingua geral.[3] Ethnic, racial and linguistic differences were exploited by both sides in Brazil's war for independence.

History and geography were on the side of the Brazilian patriots. When Dom Pedro declared Brazil's independence in September 1822, Mexico, Central America, and most of Spanish South America already were free of European rule. Even Brazilians with a strong sentimental attachment to Portugal realized that Brazil's destiny lay in the Western Hemisphere, and that their little mother country was unlikely to succeed when Spain, and Britain earlier, had failed, in holding on to a huge mainland empire. The incentives of Lusophiles and of those who simply distrusted the emerging government in Rio to commit their lives and fortunes to the preservation of the transatlantic union diminished with the march of liberation across neighboring Spanish America. Brazil would be free of Portugal. The questions were: Would it survive independence in one piece? And if so, what kind of government would it have?

José Bonifácio favored a representative government. He wanted a national legislature made up of deputies elected for a limited term; the deputies would represent the people for that time, the present. The emperor figured in José Bonifácio's scheme as the representative of the continuing interests of the nation, of the past and the future. He was not to be merely the symbol of the nation, but a participant in government, coequal in power with the legislature. Having observed the runaway National Assembly in Paris in 1790–91, José Bonifácio felt the need to balance the power of the legislature with that of a strong independent executive. Also, on a more practical level, José Bonifácio had a program for economic and social development, which included the gradual abolition of slavery, something any elected Brazilian legislature was unlikely to accept unless subjected to strong outside pressure.[4] José Bonifácio wanted to preserve the power of the emperor because he counted on his support in the likely event of conflict with a future parliamentary majority.

Those in Rio who disliked José Bonifácio's policies, his domineering personality, or both, tended to espouse parliamentary supremacy and looked for ways to separate Dom Pedro from the head of his government. Foremost among the minister's opponents were José Clemente Pereira, president of the Rio city council, and Joaquim Gonçalves Ledo, secretary of the council of procurators, or council of state. José Clemente and Ledo—both former students at the University of Coimbra and veterans of José Bonifácio's Academic Battalion—moved against their exprofessor in the Great Orient Lodge in late August 1822, while Dom Pedro was in São Paulo. They engineered the election of Dom Pedro as grand master, with José Bonifácio as his first vigilante. Since this reflected their relationship within the government, which the lodge was sworn to uphold, José Bonifácio could not openly object to the maneuver. The Masonic brothers also passed a resolution calling for the early acclamation of Dom Pedro as emperor of Brazil under the constitution that the Brazilian Constituent Assembly, which was to convene in 1823, was going to make. Once again, Dom Pedro was to be asked to swear to a constitution before it existed, and, implicitly, to acknowledge the supremacy of an elected body. Perhaps guessing that this would anger the prince, and that he would be able to use the resolution later to destroy José Clemente and Ledo, José Bonifácio did not immediately oppose it. Also, he had to play along with José Clemente and Ledo for the time being, because he needed their help in orchestrating the acclamation, set for 12 October, Dom Pedro's twenty-fourth birthday.[5]

The perpetual defender of Brazil returned to Rio from São Paulo on 14 September and immediately assented to the acclamation project, although he did not accept the grand master position until 7 October, perhaps because he was miffed by the prior-oath provision. But he was pleased enough with the work of José Clemente and Ledo that on 23 September he acceded to a request by the latter, risking the anger of José Bonifácio and his brother, and dismissed all charges against those who had ousted Martim Francisco from the São Paulo junta. In the meantime, the Masons had gone to work for Dom Pedro: Ledo got up a circular that was distributed through Masonic channels, and José Clemente, as president of the Rio city council, issued a manifesto on 17 September calling on the municipal governments of Brazil to pass resolutions asking the prince to become their constitutional emperor. The petitions were essential because the position of emperor, unlike that of king, traditionally required election; one could not claim title to an empire by right of inheritance alone. The new constitutional emperor of Brazil would be elected by the country's town and city councils. Three days before the projected acclamation, with favorable results coming in from the provinces, Dom Pedro and José Bonifácio dealt with the prior-oath problem. The Rio city council, which was to present all the municipal petitions, was scheduled to adopt its own resolution on 10 October. The day before, Dom Pedro told Ledo and José Clemente that he wanted no mention of a prior oath in the Rio resolution, or in José Clemente's presentation speech at the acclamation. José Bonifácio warned José Clemente that he would throw him in jail if he did not comply with Dom Pedro's wishes. The weak-kneed Ledo reportedly fell at Dom Pedro's feet, and José Clemente capitulated in less dramatic fashion. The resolution that was passed the next day by the Rio city council did not ask Dom Pedro to swear to uphold the constitution as produced by the future Constituent Assembly; nor did José Clemente mention a prior oath in his speech on 12 October, when he formally petitioned Dom Pedro, in the name of the people of Brazil, to become their constitutional emperor as well as their perpetual defender.[6]

Heavy rains during the period could not dampen the enthusiasm of the people of Rio de Janeiro for the acclamation of Dom Pedro. Wherever he appeared after his return from São Paulo, he was received as a conquering hero. The Cariocas looked forward to the acclamation of Dom Pedro as their emperor on 12 October, and to his coronation in a far more elaborate ceremony a few weeks later. Shortly after ten o'clock on the morning of 12 October, the acclamation took place at the Campo de Santana on the balcony of a house that once served as the royal box overlooking the bullring, a structure that had been dismantled during the anti-Portuguese turmoil following the fico. José Clemente made a flowery speech, invoking "Holy Liberalism" and begging the perpetual defender to bow to the will of the people, as expressed in numerous municipal resolutions, and consent to be their constitutional emperor. "I accept the title of constitutional emperor," Dom Pedro replied, "because I have heard from my Council of State and General Procurators, and have examined the petitions of the municipal councils of the various provinces." The new emperor acknowledged that many municipalities had not been heard from, but he said that he was convinced that the reports at hand represented "the general will of all the others, which only because of lack of time have not yet arrived."[7] A wave of rejoicing swept the dignitaries on the balcony and the crowd standing in the rain on the Campo de Santana as the Brazilian artillery fired a 101-gun imperial salute. There was a Te Deum mass that afternoon at the city palace chapel, and that night there was a special performance of *The Independence of Scotland* at the Royal (now Imperial) Theater.[8]

The acclamation went off well, but José Bonifácio would not rest until he had disposed of José Clemente and Ledo. Those two, he warned the emperor, were conspiring with carbonari and republicans to overthrow the regime. As evidence of republican subversion, José Bonifácio pointed to a 19 October newspaper editorial dripping with fulsome praise for the emperor: "Dom Pedro the First, without a Second. . . . A pure democrat." There would not be a second emperor, the editorial inferred, because the democratic Dom Pedro I would bow to the people's desire for a republic. José Bonifácio wanted Dom Pedro to allow him to close the newspaper and exile its editor, and he urged the emperor to use his powers as Masonic grand master to disband the Great Orient and its affiliate lodges, which, the minister claimed, were dominated by subversives—i.e., followers of Ledo and José Clemente. Reluctantly, the emperor, who professed to believe in freedom of the press, consented to the closing of the newspaper and the deportation of the editor; and on 21 October Pedro Cuauhtémoc sent Ledo a friendly note declaring a temporary suspension of Masonic activities. Four days later the emperor told Ledo that he was lifting the suspension and called a meeting of the lodge for the next week. About the same time, the emperor reversed himself on the newspaper and its editor; the editor was to be allowed to stay in Rio and continue publishing his journal. José Bonifácio was outraged; he and his brother, Martim Francisco, resigned from the emperor's council of ministers on 27 October. As their price for returning to the government, the Andrada brothers demanded the arrest and deportation of Ledo, José Clemente, and two of their associates. Dom Pedro at the time could not do without the able José Bonifácio; and Martim Francisco, who as treasury minister had made remarkable progress in rehabilitating government finances, was equally indispensable. Ledo, José Clemente, and their Masonic clique, on the other hand, were expendable. Furthermore, the emperor had not forgotten their attempt to undermine his authority with the prior-oath resolution in the Great Orient; a period of banishment might teach them a valuable lesson. Arrest warrants were issued for Ledo, José Clemente, and two others; and José Bonifácio and Martim Francisco returned to their cabinet posts on 30 October amid the rejoicing of the Carioca multitudes. Ledo evaded capture and went to Buenos Aires; José Clemente was arrested, put aboard a French ship, and sent to Le Havre. The Masonic lodges remained closed for the rest of Dom Pedro's reign as emperor.[9]

Arrangements for the emperor's coronation were the responsibility of a committee of four, headed by José Bonifácio and including Friar Antônio de Arrábida, Dom Pedro's confessor and former tutor. Much of the ceremony would be in the Latin language beloved by both the Friar and his exstudent. The ritual was to be based on the traditions of the Holy Roman Empire, with some elements borrowed from Napoleon's coronation. It would reflect the strong religious convictions of Arrábida and Dom Pedro: the Brazilian Emperor, unlike Napoleon, would leave no doubt as to his subordination to God. The coronation was held at noon on Sunday, 1 December, a day of brilliant sunshine, at the city palace chapel. It was preceded by military parades through the city and much fanfare.[10]

Dom Pedro and his minister of justice knelt before the altar upon which the crown was placed. It was made of twenty-two-carat gold, inlaid with diamonds, and it weighed nearly three kilos. The imperial throne and the bishop's throne were to the side of the main altar, on the same level. Dom Pedro repeated the oath in Latin that was read to him by the minister of justice: "I, Pedro I, by the grace of God and the unanimous vote of the people, emperor and perpetual defender of Brazil, swear to observe and maintain the Apostolic Roman Catho-

José Bonifácio de Andrada e Silva
From Tobias Monteiro, *Historia do imperio: O primeiro reinado,* I (Rio de Janeiro, 1939).

Dom Pedro I, Emperor of Brazil: Painting by Simplício Rodrigues de Sá
From Octávio Tarquínio de Sousa, *A vida de Dom Pedro I* (Rio de
Janeiro, 1972).
Reprinted by permission of Livraria José Olympio Editora S. A.

lic religion. I swear to constitutionally observe and enforce the laws of the empire. I swear to defend and preserve its integrity with all my strength." Placing his hand on a Bible, he concluded, "So help me God, and these Holy Gospels."[11]

After prayers, the bishop presented the imperial sword to Dom Pedro, who sheathed it after making a symbolic cut in the air. Kneeling once more before the altar, Dom Pedro received the crown, which the bishop, intoning the words *"accipe coronam imperii,"* placed on his head. The bishop then presented the scepter, and the emperor, now invested with the symbols of his high office, rose and took his seat on the throne to the chanting of *"Te Deum Laudemus."* After a sermon by one of Brazil's best sacred orators and the partaking of Holy Communion, the ceremony ended with the master of arms crying out from a chapel balcony facing the plaza, "Imperial! Imperial! Imperial! By our most high and powerful Lord and Emperor Dom Pedro I!" The people cheered, church bells rang, bands played, and ships and forts fired their guns in salute. From the chapel the emperor proceeded to the city palace, and from a window, addressed the multitude in the square. "I swear," he said, "to defend the constitution that is going to be made, if it turns out to be worthy of Brazil and of me." That night there were fireworks, and at the Imperial Theater, a special performance of Rossini's opera, *Elisabetta, regina d'Inghilterra.*[12]

Carlos Frederico Lecor, the Portuguese commanding general in Uruguay, was afraid that the Cortes in Lisbon would trade his Uruguayan conquest to Spain for the miniscule Iberian municipality of Olivenza. He engineered the annexation of Uruguay to the kingdom of Brazil in hopes of forestalling this. The Cortes was displeased and disowned the annexation. Lecor supported Dom Pedro's fico and the Cortes tried to remove him from his command. Officers loyal to Portugal formed a military council in Montevideo, encouraged the local city council to rescind its annexation resolution, and forced Lecor to flee to the interior town of Canelones in September 1822. There Lecor rallied his Brazilian troops and some Uruguayans led by Fructuoso Rivera against the Portuguese forces in Montevideo.[13] The ensuing military standoff in Uruguay lasted more than a year, but involved a total of fewer than 8,000 combatants on both sides; it was only a sideshow in the Brazilian war for independence. The main arena of conflict was the province of Bahia.

Brigadier General Pierre Labatut, who sailed north from Rio with a handful of soldiers and a large quantity of arms and ammunition in July 1822, was unable to land in Bahia and link up with local patriots due to Portuguese naval superiority. He disembarked his troops and supplies in Alagoas and appealed for help from Pernambuco before moving into Bahia by land. Labatut, with headquarters in the town of Cachoeira, took command of all patriot forces in Bahia, and by the end of October, he controlled the shores of the bay except for the peninsula on which the capital city was located. But the Portuguese were dominant on the waters of the bay and they continued to receive supplies and reinforcements from Portugal by sea. Early in November, 1,300 leadfoot soldiers disembarked from six transports that had been escorted across the Atlantic by a corvette, a frigate, and the ship-of-the-line *Dom João VI*, now mounting seventy-four guns, the most powerful warship in Brazilian waters.[14]

With his strength increasing, Portuguese General Inácio Luís Madeira made waterborne forays against the Brazilians in the bay area and probed the patriot line across the peninsula north of the capital. More disconcerting to the Brazilians were Portuguese offers of freedom to slaves who deserted their patriot masters to fight for the mother country. This tactic came naturally to the Portuguese—a seafaring, mercantile, bullfighting, brawling people who had long been accustomed to disparaging their sedentary, slave-dependent Brazilian cousins. Although they were quite willing to feed the Brazilian addiction —hauling slaves from Africa to Bahia in hellish voyages during which the mortality rate among crewmen was as high as it was among the human cargo—the Portuguese would not tolerate slavery in their homeland, where it had been abolished in 1773, nearly a generation before the institution was outlawed in England. Hundreds of runaway slaves were bearing arms for Portugal when General Madeira launched a major assault on the Brazilian line at Pirajá. The leadfeet were thrown back with more than 80 killed by a Brazilian counterattack on 8 November. Eleven days later about 200 fugitive slaves in Portuguese service attacked near Pirajá; 70 were captured and 50 of them, all of the males, were executed by firing squad on the following day. But the patriots also took positive steps in dealing with their huge servile population. Bahian plutocrats who chose the patriot cause often preferred to send their slaves to do the fighting, rather than going themselves or enlisting their sons. But Brazilian slaves, who had been known to seize opportunities to escape their bondage by committing suicide, could not be expected to make good soldiers—especially against an enemy that offered them freedom—so the slaves were emancipated as they were inducted into the army, and formed into a Battalion of Freedmen.[15] In the meantime, more white soldiers were on their way from Portugal to the capital of Bahia; the government of the mother country seemed determined to hold that port and make it the staging area for the reconquest of Brazil.

For Dom Pedro's government to meet the Portuguese challenge without bankrupting the empire would take the financial genius of Martim Francisco, plus a little luck. In Bahia, General Labatut found caches of gold and silver, totaling 143 contos, buried on two Portuguese-owned plantations that his troops occupied. The confiscation of Portuguese property was one of the measures adopted by the imperial government to finance the war. Treasury Minister Martim Francisco rejected offers of loans from foreign sources and instead floated a domestic bond issue that raised 171 contos, mostly from the Rio de Janeiro area. The Bank of Brazil was considered a lender of last resort, as Dom Pedro's government already owed it some 6,000 contos by the beginning of 1823, and Martim Francisco earnestly sought to avoid the issuance of new bank notes and the further depreciation of the paper currency. The public was encouraged to make outright gifts to the war effort, and a fund drive for the navy raised 64 contos in 1823. Aside from these special collections, only the usual revenues from the province of Rio de Janeiro, including customs receipts, were available to the imperial government. The other provinces contributed practically nothing to the central government; Rio assumed much of the financial burden of supporting troops in Uruguay and Bahia, and had to meet virtually all the expenses of the Imperial Navy. By far the largest single source of imperial government revenue was the 15 percent import tariff on British goods entering through the port of Rio de Janeiro, which yielded 571 contos in 1822; next came the 10 percent production tax on coffee and goods for domestic consumption, 273 contos; varying import tariffs on slaves, 241 contos; and the 24 percent duty on all other imports, 210 contos. Total revenues in 1822 were 2,246 contos, against expenses of 3,907 contos. The next year, despite the extraordinary expenses of war, the deficit grew by only 15 percent, thanks to Martim Francisco's stern and efficient management of imperial finances.[16]

The navy was by far the biggest expense, and it was absolutely indispensable for the establishment and preservation of the Brazilian empire. Bahia and the northernmost provinces of Maranhão and Pará, where some local anti-Portuguese forces were forming by the end of 1822, might eventually have ousted the leadfeet without help from Rio; but then they would have had little cause to submit to the authority of Dom Pedro's government. The United States consul in Rio was sure that the Portuguese were finished in Brazil, but he was also sure that after they were gone the distant provinces, which had no more affinity for Rio than for Lisbon, would go their separate ways.[17] It was the Imperial Navy that proved him wrong. Dom Pedro's warships would project the power of the empire from Rio to the mouth of the Amazon, establishing the northern boundary and guaranteeing the survival of South America's greatest nation. Credit for this monumental achievement is due, in almost equal shares, to four men whose vision, determination, and rare abilities literally changed the course of history: the emperor, Dom Pedro; his chief minister, José Bonifácio; his treasury minister, Martim Francisco; and his Scottish admiral, Thomas, Lord Cochrane.

At the time of independence, the Brazilian navy had only two seaworthy frigates: the *União*, soon to be renamed *Ipiranga*, and the *Real Carolina*, which was out of service for lack of a crew. Construction of a third frigate, the *Niterói*, was suspended for want of funds. Laid up at the Naval Arsenal in need of extensive repairs was the ship-of-the-line *Martim de Freitas*; when recommissioned as the *Pedro Primeiro*, she would need a crew of 600, few of whom could be recruited in Brazil. The empire, lacking a pool of experienced officers and able seamen, was hard-pressed to man its one active frigate and three corvettes. José Bonifácio and Dom Pedro realized that their new Brazilian navy would have to employ large numbers of foreigners, and that it would need a competent and bold fleet commander, who would have to move quickly to eliminate Portuguese power and establish the authority of the central government throughout the empire, before Brazil disintegrated into a welter of Latin American republics. José Bonifácio—on the advice of the Brazilian diplomatic agent in London, Felisberto Caldeira Brant Pontes, and with the approval of Dom Pedro —offered the job to Lord Cochrane, then commanding admiral of the navy of Chile. Taking leave of his Chilean position, the admiral arrived in Rio on 13 March 1823 to discuss the Brazilian offer.[18]

Thomas, Lord Cochrane was the eldest son of the ninth earl of Dundonald, who had lost his Scottish estates and fled his creditors to France. At the age of seventy-five, three times a widower, the ninth earl lived in Paris with his mistress in alcoholic squalor. Although Lord Cochrane would eventually inherit his father's title, the ninth earl had disowned him for spurning a financially advantageous arranged marriage and eloping, at the age of thirty-seven, with sixteen-year-old Kitty Barnes in 1812. As the legality—as well as the propriety—of their civil wedding in Scotland was questioned, Lord and Lady Cochrane were married in the Church of England in 1818, after the birth of a son; later they would have a third wedding in the Church of Scotland. Lovely and spirited, Kitty had accompanied her husband to Chile and soon would follow him to Brazil.[19]

As a young man, Lord Cochrane had sought his fortune in the British Royal Navy. During the French Revolution and Napoleonic Wars he rose from midshipman to captain, earning a reputation as the most brilliant commander of a single ship in the British navy—perhaps in any navy, at any time. In numerous encounters Cochrane destroyed or captured heavily armed merchantmen or warships with many times the firepower of his own corvette or frigate. Aside from sheer audacity, the main ingredients of Cochrane's success were meticulous planning, highly disciplined and well-drilled crews, and, above all, deception. Cochrane habitually sailed under false colors and often went to great lengths to disguise his vessel and make it appear friendly to an intended victim. Once in position, he would run up the Union Jack and launch a furious assault, which usually would end after a few minutes, with stunned and confused French or Spanish seamen yielding another prize to the ravenous Scotsman whom Napoleon dubbed *le loup des mers*. The triumphs of the "Seawolf," according to one biographer, "were half the result of tactical genius, and half the outcome of a practical joke played on his enemies." They were certainly profitable: Lord Cochrane got rich in the British navy, as the vessels he captured were sold by prize courts and the proceeds distributed at various levels, from the captain's superiors to the seamen under his command. Cochrane's share of the prize money from one ten-week cruise off the Azores in 1805 was said to have amounted to 360,000 silver dollars. Lord Cochrane, however, never received as much as he thought he deserved; he was constantly haggling with the admiralty over the distribution of prize money and honors. The hero had "an embarrassing quickness to resent injury either to his reputation or his purse," which, along with his regular denunciations of graft in defense contracting, hindered his advancement in the Royal Navy.[20]

Without resigning his navy commission, the Seawolf went into politics, standing for Parliament in a notorious "rotten burrough." He ran as a reformer, refused to pay the standard bribe demanded by the electors, and lost overwhelmingly. But after the election—in which, like those in Brazil, there was no secrecy, with votes openly cast and recorded—Cochrane paid double the winner's bribe to each of the few electors who had voted for him. In the next election campaign the voters winked at the hero's insistence that he did not pay bribes and elected him by a large majority. When they went to the winner for payment, Cochrane disappointed them: he reiterated that he did not pay bribes. After much importuning he finally agreed to give his supporters a banquet, but when he received the bill he refused to pay it. Having no hope of reelection by that constituency, and having built for himself an antiestablishment reputation in Parliament, he ran next in the "democratic" district of Westminster as an independent radical and won handily.

Lord Cochrane lost his seat in Parliament, and his navy commission as a result of the notorious "stock exchange fraud" of February 1814. This was an elaborate hoax involving the arrival in London of a supposed official messenger from France, just as the stock exchange was opening, with news of the death of Napoleon and the Allied occupation of Paris. Lord Cochrane and some friends and relatives were speculating in British government securities, which soared when the bogus news reached the trading floor. The speculators took their profits before the hoax was discovered, but unfortunately for them the fake messenger failed to make his getaway and was apprehended wearing clothes supplied by Lord Cochrane. The naval hero and radical politician stoutly proclaimed his innocence and attributed his prosecution to a corrupt and vengeful Tory establishment. He was convicted nonetheless, expelled from Parliament, the Royal Navy, and the Order of the Bath, and sentenced to a year in jail. After escaping from jail, he appeared in the House of Commons to claim parliamentary immunity; his Westminster constituents had elected him to fill the vacancy created by his own expulsion. He was rearrested and returned to prison to complete his sentence, which expired on 20 June 1815.

By this time, Napoleon had been defeated, the Tories seemed

firmly in control of the government in London, and Lord Cochrane was tiring of British politics. While in jail he had invented an efficient oil street light, which was adopted by the city of London and used for a brief period until all such fixtures were replaced by gas lighting. Cochrane's most ambitious invention, a system for launching gas warfare, was rejected by the defense establishment. Eventually his thoughts turned to the defeated enemy whose great talents were wasting away on Saint Helena; he conceived the idea of rescuing Napoleon from his island prison and helping him set up a new empire in South America. The leaders of the independence movement in the Spanish colony of Chile, José de San Martín and Bernardo O'Higgins, were of a monarchist bent, and when they offered Cochrane command of the Chilean patriot navy in 1818, with the rank and salary of an admiral, he accepted, imagining this as the first step in the founding of a new Napoleonic empire. But while the Seawolf was destroying the Spanish navy in the southeast Pacific—making optimum use of his tactics of deception—Napoleon died, ending the admiral's imperial dream. Cochrane then became profoundly irritated by what he considered San Martín's weak leadership in the 1820–21 invasion of Peru, and there was also a quarrel between Cochrane and San Martín about the Scotsman's remuneration. Disputes over prize money and salary also marred the admiral's relationship with the O'Higgins government in Chile. Resigning from the Chilean navy in January 1823, Cochrane and a few of his mercenary colleagues chartered a "dirty little brig" in Valparaiso and set sail for Rio de Janeiro.[21]

In person, Lord Cochrane was only slightly more impressive than the vessel that brought him to Rio. He was very tall, but slightly stooped and heavy around the midsection. At age forty-eight his mop of red hair was still thick, but turning gray. His bent-over posture and great beak of a nose gave him something of the configuration of a vulture. He spoke English in the slow, economical manner of the Scottish lowlander, and his French and Spanish were limited. "His exterior and all his manners," a German-Russian naval officer in Rio noted, "are rather repugnant; in ordinary conversation he talks only in monosyllables, and it is difficult to see in him an educated and intelligent man."[22] But Cochrane was canny and shrewd, a hard bargainer.

Dom Pedro hurried from Boa Vista to the city when he learned that Lord Cochrane's brig had arrived. The emperor and the admiral met on the afternoon of 13 March at José Bonifácio's house on the theater square, and conferred until late that night. The next day, one of heavy rains, Lord Cochrane discussed his proposed duties with José Bonifácio and the imperial navy minister; on 15 March the admiral was personally escorted on an inspection tour of the Brazilian squadron by Dom Pedro. The two got along well together. Cochrane, whose principles forbade his serving a reactionary, satisfied himself that Dom Pedro was a liberal—although he was surprised by the hand kissing at the constitutional emperor's palace. The Seawolf noted that the monarch submitted to the osculatory desires of his subjects with "good humour and affability." The admiral was favorably impressed by Dom Pedro's grasp of the strategic situation and his strong commitment to his navy. Repair work on the imperial warships was proceeding at a rapid pace, and 450 officers and seamen from Britain and Ireland, plus scores from other foreign lands, had been attracted to Rio to man them. Still, the majority of the crewmen would consist of inexperienced and undisciplined Brazilians and possibly unreliable Portuguese. More disturbing to Lord Cochrane was the idea, held by Dom Pedro and José Bonifácio, that he would serve in the northern expedition under the overall command of a Brazilian officer. Remembering the unpleasantness with San Martín, Cochrane insisted that he have total control over the operation and be given the highest rank in the Brazilian navy. Dom Pedro, an almost infallible judge of character—or of what particular talents were required at a given moment—assented and authorized the appointment of Lord Cochrane as first admiral of Brazil.[23]

Money was a more difficult matter, and José Bonifácio, uncharacteristically, suffered the Seawolf's insolent pecuniary demands. Cochrane had been offered a position "in no way inferior" to the one he held in Chile, but the Brazilian government was trying to foist on him the salary of a Portuguese admiral, which did not meet the Chilean standard of 8,000 dollars a year plus bonuses. Also, the Scotsman reminded the Brazilians that their coinage was debased and did not have the exchange value they claimed; he wanted his money in silver dollars or their honest equivalent. He also demanded larger salaries than proposed for his officers and crew, virtually unlimited authority to seize enemy property, and guarantees of its disposal for the benefit of himself and his men. José Bonifácio could condone piracy in exceptional times, but his brother, the treasury minister, was hard-pressed to find the start-up funds. The Seawolf demanded twenty contos up front, in gold or silver, or he would not join the Brazilian navy and lead it against the Portuguese. Martim Francisco scrambled to scrape up the money. When he could find only four contos in the imperial treasury, he went to a wealthy friend, laid his own personal credit on the line, and came away with the needed sixteen contos. After a week of haggling, Lord Cochrane accepted the commission of first admiral of Brazil, and on 21 March ran up his flag on the *Pedro Primeiro*.[24]

The training of sailors and marines and the outfitting of war-ships proceeded urgently but confidently under the direction of Admiral Cochrane. Dom Pedro was swept up in the excitement and so was Dona Leopoldina, who recently had given birth to their third daughter, Dona Paula Mariana, on 17 February. The emperor would appear on shipboard at six o'clock in the morning and often spend the entire day, involving himself in the details of repair work and drills. He paid particular attention to the *Pedro Primeiro*; he and the empress came aboard the flagship at daybreak on 31 March, when some Brazilian officers were faced with the problem of what to do about some British sailors who had gone on a drunken spree the day before. The alcoholic abandon of these Celtic and Nordic seamen was something new to most Cariocas, but not to Dona Leopoldina: "Oh, 'tis the custom of the North, where brave men come from," she explained to the officers. "The sailors are under my protection; I spread my mantle over them." The seamen presumably went unpunished, and the squadron sailed at dawn the next day to battle the Portuguese for possession of Bahia.[25]

With one ship-of-the-line, three frigates, two corvettes, and four smaller vessels, Cochrane was outgunned by the Portuguese squadron that included a ship-of-the-line and five frigates. His first encounter with the Portuguese, who came out from Bahia to meet him in line of battle, was a near disaster for the Seawolf; the performance of his sailing and gun crews reflected their general lack of experience and the brevity of their training; the *Pedro Primeiro* found herself alone among hostile vessels after breaking through the enemy line, and for a while she was in danger of being captured or sunk. But she escaped and the engagement seemed to unnerve the Portuguese more than it did Cochrane's men. When the Portuguese did not come out again to fight, the Brazilian squadron put the port under a tight blockade. Meanwhile the patriot army, now numbering more than 10,000, tightened its grip on the land approach to the city. By this time, the Portuguese garrison in Bahia had been beefed up to perhaps 9,000 men, but they were demoralized and confused by recent news from Portugal—in fact, the liberal regime there was overthrown on 3 June by a counterrevolution begun in February and backed by Dona Carlota and Dom Miguel. Portuguese civilians in Bahia, their property condemned to confiscation by the Brazilian empire, wanted to get out with whatever goods they could take with them. General Madeira decided to evacuate the city, load his troops and civilian supporters on 60 or more transports, and trust the Portuguese squadron to escort them safely past Cochrane's blockaders to Maranhão, where the natives were still friendly.[26]

When the Portuguese came out of Bahia on 3 July, most of the Brazilian blockaders gave wide berth to the seventy-four-gun *Dom João VI* and escorting frigates, and fell on the booty-laden transports. Cochrane's *Pedro Primeiro*, aboard which the admiral had concentrated his best sailors and marines, attacked and captured a Portuguese troop transport, where he found documents containing secret signals and instructions for the voyage to Maranhão. After appropriating flags and uniforms from the captured transport, Cochrane broke off contact with the enemy and made a dash for Maranhão. The *Pedro Primeiro* entered the harbor at São Luís, Maranhão, flying Portuguese colors. When the official welcoming party came on board, Cochrane showed his true colors and demanded the surrender of the city; he exaggerated the number of marines he had aboard, and claimed that hordes of less-disciplined Brazilian troops were following in a fleet of transports and likely would ravish the city if committed to action. The trick worked: the provincial junta renounced its allegiance to Portugal and proclaimed the Brazilian empire. Meanwhile Cochrane graciously allowed the troops of the Portuguese garrison to board their transports and sail for the mother country, to avoid surrendering to the oncoming Brazilians. When the *Dom João VI* and the remnants of the convoy out of Bahia reached São Luís a few days later, they found their expected haven in enemy hands, and had to turn about and head out into the ocean for their ultimate refuge in Portugal.[27]

Cochrane dispatched one of his officers, Captain John P. Grenfell, and a party of marines to the last Portuguese stronghold in the north, Belém do Pará, on a brig that had been captured in Maranhão. Grenfell used his master's tactics to induce the pro-Portuguese junta there to switch to the empire. He convinced the Lusophiles that he represented the advance guard of Lord Cochrane's imperial armada, soon to appear on the horizon. But Grenfell's puny force had difficulty dominating the situation in Pará, where the government switch set off a provincial power struggle. A new junta was installed and several hundred adherents of a losing faction, variously identified as Lusophiles or republicans, were arrested; 5 were executed and 253 were thrown into the hold of an improvised prison ship, where all but 4 died of suffocation in October 1823. It was the worst atrocity of Brazil's war of independence, exceeding in number of victims the slaughter of the black prisoners in Bahia. The Brazilian struggle against Portugal was far from bloodless, but it ended on a civilized note in Uruguay, where an agreement was reached allowing the Montevideo garrison, the last Portuguese force in South America, to embark peacefully for Europe in November 1823.[28]

Members of the Brazilian Constituent and Legislative Assembly were chosen in the same way as were deputies to the Portuguese Cortes: by parish electors meeting on the district level. Elections were held at various times in the different provinces, and delegates began gathering in Rio in February 1823. By April they had a quorum, and the first organizational sessions were held that month. There were ninety delegates seated in the assembly: forty-five were lawyers, including twenty-two magistrates; sixteen were clergymen; seven, military officers. Planters, ranchers, merchants, medical doctors, and other professionals accounted for the rest, although the categories overlapped and combinations like priest–lawyer–planter were possible. Some were former deputies of the Portuguese Cortes, like Antônio Carlos de Andrada, who was elected to the Constituent Assembly from São Paulo, along with his brother, José Bonifácio. Martim Francisco was elected from Rio de Janeiro. Although the bishop of Rio was chosen to be the first president of the assembly, Antônio Carlos became its dominant figure; he vigorously propounded on the convention floor the ideas he shared with his two brothers, who continued to devote most of their energy to their ministerial duties.[29]

The assembly met in the old jail, the structure that had been remodeled in 1808 by the count of Arcos to serve as an annex to the adjacent city palace. It was decided that the emperor would officially open the assembly on 3 May. The formalities to be observed on that occasion were heatedly debated in the preliminary sessions of the assembly. One group of delegates wanted the assembly president's chair to be on the podium on the same level as the imperial throne, to indicate that the assembly was at least equal to the emperor in the national government, but this concept was opposed by the Andrada brothers. "How can there be parity between the hereditary representative of the entire nation and temporary representatives?" Antônio Carlos exclaimed. There was no "parallel between the monarch in whose being is concentrated a complete sovereign delegation, and the president of an assembly that collectively comprises another sovereign delegation," but is still subject to the first. "How," he asked, in a long series of rhetorical questions, was it possible, "to equate the inspirational power that regulates all the other political powers with a member of one of the regulated powers?"[30] Many delegates who on reflection might not have accepted Antônio Carlos's premises, apparently were overcome by his oratory and voted with the majority to seat the emperor on a higher plane than their president—who, as the representative of God at Dom Pedro's coronation, had sat on the same level with the monarch.

Dom Pedro arrived at the assembly hall, the old jail building, on 3 May in the imperial carriage pulled by eight fine mules. He delivered his speech from the throne bareheaded—the crown and scepter were laid on a table—wearing a green uniform and a cape made of yellow feathers. After summarizing recent history and reciting the accomplishments of his provisional government, the emperor addressed the principal problem facing the assembly, that of devising a constitution for the Brazilian nation. He reminded the delegates that on the day of his coronation he had pledged to "defend with my sword the fatherland, the nation, and the constitution, if it turns out to be worthy of Brazil and of me." He reaffirmed that promise and urged the delegates to help him fulfill it by framing a constitution that is "wise, just, adequate, and practicable, dictated by reason and not by caprice." He alluded to the "three powers" of government, presumably Montesquieu's executive-legislative-judicial formulation, and asked them "to give true liberty to the people, and sufficient strength to the executive power." The emperor wanted a constitution in which "the three powers shall be clearly delimited," and which "shall impose insuperable barriers to despotism, whether royal or democratic." Experience had shown, he cautioned, that all constitutions based on the French models of 1791 and 1792 are "totally theoretical and metaphysical, and therefore, impractical, as proved by France, Spain, and, most recently, Portugal." Instead of promoting general happiness, such constitutions fostered licentious liberty leading to the tyranny of the many, and ultimately to the despotism of one. Dom Pedro was sure that the delegates were aware of the "horrors of anarchy," and he expected "that the constitution you are going to frame will merit my Imperial acceptance, being sufficiently wise, just, and appropriate for the locality and civilization of the Brazilian people."[31]

An issue that Dom Pedro did not raise at the opening of the Constituent Assembly, but that was weighing on his mind at the time, was slavery. Evidence in the Imperial Archives indicates that the young emperor devoted more time and thought in April and May 1823 to writing an antislavery article than in composing the assembly speech, much of which was the work of José Bonifácio. The minister also undoubtedly provided Dom Pedro some guidance in organizing his thoughts for the antislavery article, but "every sentiment, every word," José Bonifácio acknowledged to the British consul, was the emperor's. It was one of the longest prose works that Dom Pedro had yet produced, some 1,600 words, and perhaps the emperor originally had intended to present it in a speech to the Constituent Assembly and later changed his mind—or was dissuaded by José Bonifácio. The minister was preparing his own antislavery treatise for delivery in the assembly at a later date; in May 1823 with the delegates just beginning their deliberations on the fundamental questions of allocating power, it probably seemed best not to distract them, and alienate many, by prematurely raising the slavery issue in the assembly. The emperor's article was published in a Rio newspaper on 30 May as a letter to the editor from a reader identified only as "The Philanthropist."[32]

"Slavery is the cancer that is gnawing away at Brazil," the Philanthropist wrote, "and it must be eradicated." The backwardness, "the immense and incalculable harm," that slavery inflicts on Brazil is just recompense for "our arrogating to ourselves a right to which we are not entitled, because I don't believe that men have any right at all to enslave one another." The existence of slaves obstructs constitutional rule by making their owners cruel and despotic. "Every slave master, from the time he was a child, has looked upon his fellow man with scorn, accustoming himself to act on his own will, unrestrained by any law." Because of slavery "we cease to be industrious" and "make no invention at all." The Philanthropist offered figures to show that slave labor is inefficient and retards Brazil's economic development, which requires an influx of free workers. The essential voluntary immigration would flow to Brazil, he believed, once the traffic with Africa was halted—as had been the case in English America.

Dom Pedro, writing as the Philanthropist, offered a plan to end the slave trade within two years, to promote free immigration, and gradually to abolish slavery in Brazil without disrupting the country's economy. The "merchants of human flesh" would receive public assistance in converting their slaving vessels to carriers of voluntary immigrants. The author suggested an imperial bond issue, like the one for the navy, to finance the conversion of the slaving fleet. The various provinces would be expected to earmark funds to subsidize, if necessary, the ocean passage of immigrants. The imperial government might pay the passage of those who agreed "to serve the State for a certain number of years"—presumably in the armed forces. Two years after the adoption of the plan, not only would the importation of slaves from Africa be banned, but all buying and selling of slaves in Brazil would be forbidden; those who had slaves could keep them, but could not acquire more, except through natural reproduction—which would encourage masters to treat more humanely the slaves they had. Dom Pedro did not advocate a free-birth law, perhaps because this would lead to neglect and mistreatment of pregnant slaves; an owner with little or no financial interest in an unborn child would regard a pregnancy as something to be overcome, an obstacle to the full exploitation of his property in the mother. The suppression of all commerce in slaves was Dom Pedro's way to insure the eventual demise of the nefarious institution: "Little by little," the Philanthropist wrote, "the cancer that is gnawing on Brazil" would be cured.

Although Dom Pedro's gradualism was faster than José Bonifácio was willing to go—José Bonifácio called for a four- or five-year delay before ending the African trade, and did not propose to ban all domestic commerce in slaves—the emperor and his chief minister basically were in accord on the slavery issue. They also generally agreed on constitutional theory. The main issue that divided Dom Pedro and José Bonifácio was the Andrada brothers' fierce persecution of their political opponents. After 30 October 1822, when they returned to the cabinet after forcing Dom Pedro to agree to the deportation of José Clemente and Ledo, José Bonifácio and Martim Francisco used their restored power to jail, exile, investigate, and harass their numerous enemies in Rio, São Paulo, and other provinces. "Measures that might seem too strong," Dom Pedro told the Constituent Assembly in his opening speech on 3 May, had been required in a time of great peril; in the weeks that followed, the emperor and many assembly delegates came to agree that the time for such harsh measures had passed. A general amnesty bill was brought up for a vote on 22 May, but Antônio Carlos rallied the Andrada forces in the assembly to defeat it, thirty-five to seventeen.[33] Although José Clemente, Ledo, and the others would remain in exile, the Andradas were put on notice that they would face significant opposition in the assembly if they attempted further deportations or newspaper closings.

A major thorn in the side of the chief minister was the newspaper *A Malagueta*, whose erratic editor, the Portuguese-born Luís Augusto May, was regarded as a "madman" by José Bonifácio. The day after the 5 June publication of a *Malagueta* editorial that roundly denounced the Andradas and their constitutional proposals and took some swipes at Dom Pedro as well, four masked men wielding sticks and swords invaded May's home and gave the editor a severe drubbing. The attack could have been instigated by either José Bonifácio or Dom Pedro, or both. The minister had a long record of intimidating newspapers, and the emperor, though an avid reader and sometime anonymous contributor to the Rio press, had a quick temper and might have reacted impulsively and violently to the disagreeable editorial. In any case, the beating of May produced a wave of indignation in the assembly; this did not, however, diminish the Andradas' drive to punish their enemies. On 20 June Antônio Carlos threw his support to a bill that would authorize the government to deport all Portuguese-born persons whom it suspected of not supporting Brazilian independence. After heated debate, in which Antônio Carlos, trying to justify an admittedly "odious" measure, got carried away and suggested that all native Portuguese—even the emperor—were potential enemies of Brazil, the bill was tabled on 26 June. In pushing this repressive legislation, the Andradas had gone too far for most assembly delegates, and for the emperor.[34]

Before Dom Pedro could come to grips with the problems posed by the Andradas, he had a bad accident. He fell from his horse and broke two ribs as he approached Boa Vista about sundown on 30 June. The fact that he was riding alone gave rise to the question of where he had been that afternoon. By this time, Domitila de Castro, Dom Pedro's mistress from São Paulo, had moved to the Rio suburb of Mataporcos, and the emperor might have been returning from a visit with her. But few people knew of that affair, which Dom Pedro was taking great pains to keep secret. The fall was said to have been caused by a loose or broken girth: as the saddle shifted, the horse bolted and the rider tried to jump clear, but landed badly on the hard ground, suffering various contusions, a dislocated collarbone, and some damage to the sciatic nerve, in addition to the broken ribs. In considerable pain, the emperor managed to hobble the short distance to the Boa Vista guard post, where he found help. For the next two weeks Dom Pedro was laid up at Boa Vista in a body brace devised by an orthopedic specialist; he was bled three times by nineteen leeches prescribed by the palace physician to reduce the swelling on the patient's left hip. José Bonifácio might have objected to this treatment, but he made no big issue of it. The minister reportedly was an early devotee of the medical heresy of homeopathy, which, because of the mildness of its prescriptions, did less harm to patients than did orthodox medicine. It acquired a large following in nineteenth-century Brazil.[35]

The emperor received a steady stream of visitors in his sickroom at Boa Vista palace. All but three of the Constituent Assembly delegates came by to see him at least once. The restless Dom Pedro, immobilized for the first time in his life, was eager to talk, ask questions, and hear answers. He spent hours with people he would otherwise see for only a few minutes on official occasions; the intimacy of the visits to the incapacitated monarch's bedchamber dispelled the inhibitions of the callers, who spoke frankly of their concern about the political situation. Freedom of the press had disappeared; José Clemente, Ledo, and others who had rendered valuable service to the cause of independence were banished from the country; many others were political prisoners in Brazil. The persecution was the work of the Andrada brothers, and it was worse in their home province of São Paulo, where charges of sedition faced some of the emperor's most loyal citizen-subjects. The vengeful investigations launched by José Bonifácio had never been justified, many visitors maintained, and were especially inappropriate now that the Portuguese had evacuated Bahia and the war was virtually over. The emperor was urged to halt the persecution and heal the wounds of the country. Dom Pedro obliged them, and without consulting his chief minister, ordered decrees drawn up that would free political prisoners in Rio and in the provinces, annul previous deportation orders, discontinue the sedition inquiry in São Paulo, and grant amnesty to all those who had been under investigation there.[36]

The documents were ready on 15 July and Dom Pedro showed them to José Bonifácio that night in the imperial bedchamber. The minister tried to talk the emperor out of issuing the decrees, but Dom Pedro was adamant. The exchange became heated, with José Bonifácio declaring that he was quitting the government, and Dom Pedro, in his rage, rising up in bed and breaking the bone-setting apparatus. He was ready to get out of it anyway, and twenty-four hours later he was back in the saddle riding through the rain with a handful of companions to the meeting place of the Apostolate; they officially closed that secret society, which Dom Pedro nominally headed, and seized its records to prevent it from becoming a focus of Andrada plotting against the emperor. Earlier that day, 16 July, José Bonifácio had sent in his written resignation, and Martim Francisco appeared personally before the monarch to present his, in his usual arrogant manner. Thus, Dom Pedro lost the services of two difficult but exceptionally competent men. Rigidly honest themselves, the Andradas never doubted that those who opposed them were scoundrels, if not traitors, who posed a real threat to the nascent Brazilian state. Typically, they questioned the emperor's motives for ending the persecution, and suggested that he granted the amnesty to please his mistress and members of her family in São Paulo, who allegedly had been bribed by the accused to use their influence at the imperial court in their behalf.[37] But later the Andradas —like Avilez, José Clemente, and other honorable men who fell out with Dom Pedro—would testify to his character by returning to his service.

In his proclamation to the Brazilian people announcing the end of the repression, Dom Pedro said that he "detested despotism and arbitrary acts." He lamented that he had only recently learned of the tyranny to which his people had been subjected. "Monarchs rarely hear the truth, and if they do not seek it, it never appears to them." Now that he had discovered the truth, with God's help, he would act on it, and restore the rights of the people. "Even though we do not yet have a constitution," reason dictated that the government respect the "sacred rights of security for the individual's person and property, and the inviolability of the citizen's home." These rights, which had been "attacked and violated," would "from this day forward" be "religiously upheld." Brazilians now could "live happily, secure in the bosom of your families, in the arms of your tender wives and surrounded by your beloved children." They could count on the emperor, just as he counted on them; together they would see "democracy and despotism restrained by reasonable liberty."[38]

Dom Pedro equated "democracy" with mob rule, with demagoguery; it was as bad as despotism, into which it inevitably evolved. Liberty, he believed, could not survive without safeguards: representative institutions must be constrained by time, compulsory reflection, and deliberation. He well remembered those hours of madness at the commercial exchange, when an assembly of respectable men came under the sway of a pair of gifted demagogues and the masses they commanded, and in a single evening dictated laws, and even a constitution, for the kingdom of Brazil. José Bonifácio, with his firsthand knowledge of the excesses of the French Revolution, was similarly opposed to "democracy," even after he left Dom Pedro's cabinet and took an active role in the Constituent Assembly. The ex–chief minister was named to the committee, chaired by his brother, Antônio Carlos, that was assigned the task of producing a draft constitution, which, when complete, would be submitted for the consideration of the entire assembly. The 272-article document that the committee presented was largely the work of Antônio Carlos, although José Bonifácio obviously contributed to it. A strong, independent executive, which both brothers had long favored, was provided for in the draft. The executive power was entrusted to the crown; the cabinet ministers were appointed by the emperor and responsible to him, not to the national legislature, or parliament. The emperor, in the Andrada committee proposal, which was submitted to the assembly on 1 September, wielded the executive power, but did not have what Antônio Carlos wanted to give him four months earlier: the power to regulate the other powers. The new Andrada thinking was to make the emperor, as the executive, coequal with the legislature and with the judiciary. The emperor could not dissolve parliament, and his veto could be overridden; his position would be like that of the president of the United States, except that his tenure was for life. The Andradas, sensitive to charges that they disregarded civil liberties, included a prohibition of extraordinary judicial proceedings in their draft constitution, along with guarantees of personal security and property rights, trial by jury, and freedom of the press.[39]

There was much in the draft constitution that pleased Dom Pedro. Never one to bear a grudge for long, he would not reject the proposal, if the assembly approved it, simply to punish its authors.

Assembly approval, however, was no foregone conclusion, and this worried José Bonifácio. Debate on the Andrada draft was scheduled to begin on 15 September and José Bonifácio wanted to avoid this; using the Austrian diplomatic representative as an intermediary, the ex-minister on 11 September proposed to the emperor that the constitution be adopted by acclamation. José Bonifácio would have Dom Pedro come before the assembly, declare the country in urgent need of a constitution, and order his new chief minister, José Joaquim Carneiro de Campos, a native of Bahia and delegate from Rio, to support an Andrada motion to adopt the committee draft without discussion, after which it would be immediately promulgated by the emperor. But Dom Pedro would not countenance the unparliamentary strong-arm maneuver; he said he wanted a full examination of the draft constitution and unrestricted consideration of all its 272 articles by the elected representatives of the people.[40] Debate began on schedule and relations between Dom Pedro and the Andradas resumed their decline.

The Andradas helped poison the political atmosphere in Rio with their Portuguese baiting. Developments in Portugal and Bahia had put Portuguese residents of Brazil in a difficult position about the time that José Bonifácio and Martim Francisco resigned from the imperial cabinet. The destruction of Portugal's military power in northern Brazil produced a patriotic frenzy in the capital and other parts of the country, where people clamored to complete the job of liberation by expelling the Portuguese who dwelt among them and by confiscating their property. No matter how often and how fervently a native of Portugal might profess his allegiance to Brazil, he could not escape suspicion of disloyalty. The suspicion touched the emperor himself, especially now that the Cortes had been suppressed and power restored to the king in Portugal. Dom Pedro, who remained the heir to the Portuguese throne despite the scheming of Dona Carlota and Dom Miguel, was suspected of having an agreement with his father to reunite Brazil with Portugal upon the death of Dom João, if not before. Even more credence was given to charges that Dom Pedro intended to suffocate Brazilian independence when early in August the emperor ordered that Portuguese prisoners of war in Bahia be sent to Rio, where they would be allowed to enlist in the Brazilian army. This order was roundly denounced in the first issue of *O Tamoyo*, a newspaper that the Andradas and two of their close associates launched on 12 August. *O Tamoyo* and another pro-Andrada newspaper, *A Sentinela da Liberdade* ("The Sentinel of Liberty") viewed with alarm what they perceived as growing Portuguese influence in the army in Rio.[41]

The name of *O Tamoyo* left no doubt about the newspaper's orientation. The Tamoyos were an extinct tribe of Indians who had fought to the death against the Portuguese occupation of Rio de Janeiro. The newspaper avoided direct attacks on the emperor, concentrating its fire instead on the "Portuguese party" that allegedly surrounded him. *O Tamoyo* and its sister publication, the *Sentinela*, defined imperial politics as a struggle between a small group of highly placed subversives, the Portuguese party, and the great body of patriotic citizens, the "Brazilian party." The appeal was to ethnic prejudice and had nothing to do with ideology. The Portuguese party included radical democrats and reactionary absolutists, united only as victims of Andrada vituperation. The most attractive target for the Brazilian party, however, was the stereotypical boorish Portuguese tavern fighter, O Chalaça, who had no politics other than staunch loyalty to his friend, the emperor. If Dom Pedro had any ideas about strangling the infant Brazilian nation, he did not get them from the Chalaça or any other member of the Portuguese party. But such notions seemed far from his mind, and the emperor quickly demonstrated his commitment to Brazilian independence whenever given the opportunity to do so. On 7 September a Portuguese brig appeared in Rio under a flag of truce, bearing an emissary from the restoration government in Lisbon, and Dom Pedro refused to receive him. A few days later, a Portuguese corvette bringing another emissary and mail from Lisbon sailed into Rio harbor without raising a white flag; the emperor ordered her seized as a prize of war, sent the emissary home on a packet boat, and made a show of refusing to open personal letters to him from members of the royal family of Portugal. Dom Pedro declared that he would not deal with Portugal until the mother country recognized the independence of Brazil.[42]

The emperor's position on relations with Portugal seemed to satisfy most Constituent Assembly delegates, who took time out from their debates on the constitution to consider such matters of immediate concern. But there were those who were disposed to snipe at Dom Pedro on any pretext—like his conferring the title of marquis of Maranhão on Lord Cochrane. It was argued that titles of nobility in a constitutional monarchy required the approval of the legislative branch. But it was not until the assembly was drawn into the newspaper campaign against Portuguese in the military that relations between the constitutional convention and the emperor reached the breaking point. The incident that sunk the assembly into the maelstrom of nativist agitation was the caning of an apothecary on the night of 5 November 1823. Two Portuguese-born army officers entered the victim's drugstore near the Carioca Fountain and one of them proceeded to hit the pharmacist at least two times with a walking stick. The intruders were reacting to an especially nasty diatribe against Portuguese-born officers that was published anonymously in the *Sentinela da Liberdade*. The druggist who received the blows — by mistake, for he was not the author of the article — was persuaded by some militants of the Brazilian party to take his complaint to the Constituent Assembly. His petition was referred to the committee on legislation, which ruled that it was a matter for the police: "The suppliant should resort to the ordinary remedies prescribed by law."[43] But Antônio Carlos and Martim Francisco would not let the matter go at that: they would make it an issue for the Constituent Assembly.

If José Bonifácio had some misgivings about his younger brothers' plans, he did not openly state them. The galleries at the converted jail building were packed for the morning session of 10 November, and visitors were allowed on the floor of the assembly, to stand behind the chairs of the delegates. When some delegates demurred, they were jeered by the invaders, and Antônio Carlos rose to defend the mob he had invited in and to chastise those who objected. "What amazes me," he exclaimed "is so much fear of the people and so little fear of the troops! In the midst of the Brazilian people we can never go wrong." Despite the prohibition in his own constitutional proposal of extraordinary judicial procedures, Antônio Carlos wanted a bill of attainder against the Portuguese officers, to deport them, at least. Martim Francisco would go to any lengths to avenge the assault on the patriotic Brazilian apothecary (who, in fact, was born in the Azores). "Great God!" he thundered, the Portuguese consider it "a crime to love Brazil, to be born here, and to struggle for her independence and her laws!" Referring to the assailants, and to all Portuguese by implication, Martim Francisco shouted: "They still live! We still tolerate such savage beasts in our midst!"[44] The crowd knew that the youngest Andrada would not shrink from hanging them; when he was a member of the São Paulo junta, he had personally supervised the execution of a mutinous soldier, persisting despite cries for mercy from spectators when the rope broke on the first attempt. At the Constituent Assembly the crowd roared its approval of Martim Francisco's speech, and the presiding officer, a moderate, called in vain for order. Finally, he declared the session adjourned at one o'clock in the afternoon, and Martim Francisco and Antônio Carlos were carried from the old jail on the shoulders of the people. From an upstairs window in the adjacent city palace, the emperor watched the spectacle.[45]

To Dom Pedro it must have looked like a replay of the episode at the commercial exchange—except that the assembly delegates had gone into recess for the rest of the day and the night, which gave him more time than he had had on the earlier occasion to determine his course of action. The military would help him decide: native officers joined their Portuguese-born colleagues in denouncing the demagoguery in the assembly and in the latest edition of the *Sentinela*, also 10 November, which declared that Brazil's happiness required that "the Lusitanians go to Lusitania." The *Tamoyo* stepped up its nativist rabble-rousing with a special edition the next day, giving full coverage to the incendiary speeches of Antônio Carlos and Martim Francisco in the assembly. With indignation rising in the barracks, the emperor ordered General Joaquim Xavier Curado, the military commandant of the Rio area, to concentrate his troops—regulars and first-line militia—at Boa Vista.[46] General Curado had learned his lesson about runaway popular assemblies at the commercial exchange nineteen months before; now older and wiser at the age of eighty, he was prepared to use force to end the foolishness in the old jail building. And he did not bear the stigma of Portuguese birth, for he was born in the heart of Brazil, in Goiás.

As the troops gathered near his palace, the emperor installed a new cabinet, replacing the moderate Carneiro de Campos as chief minister with the hard-line Francisco Vilela Barbosa, a military engineer and native of Rio de Janeiro. One of the new minister's first official acts was to send a message to the assembly on the morning of 11 November. The message explained that the troops were offended by the irresponsible actions of certain delegates and certain newspapers, and were being kept at Boa Vista for the safety of all concerned. The assembly delegates, in a sober mood, with spectators now barred from the floor, formulated a respectful reply: they regretted the events of the previous day, thanked the ministry for its concern about their safety, requested the names of the offending newspapers, asked what the government would have them do about the matter, and announced that they would remain in session until the crisis was resolved. Vilela Barbosa responded shortly after midnight on 12 November: the emperor had informed him that the offending periodicals were the *Tamoyo* and the *Sentinela*, which were controlled or influenced by the three Andrada brothers; it was up to the assembly to decide what to do about them. By this time José Bonifácio had gone home to get some sleep, but his two brothers were on hand to prevent the assembly from making any concessions to the emperor at their expense. Antônio Carlos and Martim Francisco argued that the assembly should refuse to take up the matter of press responsibility until the troops had been sent at least forty kilometers from the city. Unable to agree on a reply to Vilela Barbosa's second message, the delegates invited the minister to appear before the assembly at ten o'clock that morning.[47]

Vilela Barbosa's appearance before the assembly on the morning of 12 November was unproductive. The delegates would not consider any measures to punish the Andradas or to prevent future abuses of press freedom unless the emperor sent his troops forty kilometers away. Dom Pedro could not do this; he would not allow the assembly to usurp his powers as head of the executive branch and perpetual defender of Brazil. He had asked the Constituent and Legislative Assembly to legislate, and it refused to do so; as hereditary representative of the nation, he had no choice but to dissolve the assembly—or so the emperor theorized. On the practical level, the assembly's excursion into nativist rabble-rousing and the deadlock it produced demonstrated the need for a regulatory power in the new constitution; the emperor should have the authority to dissolve parliament and call elections for a new one. This was not provided for in the draft constitution under consideration by the assembly, and it was unlikely to be added in the course of its deliberations. After two months of debates the original proposal was little changed—only 24 of the 272 articles had been voted on—and the process promised to drag on for many more months, if not years, bringing no improvements and providing a continuing forum for purveyors of ethnic hatred. The emperor decided that Brazil would be better off without this Constituent and Legislative Assembly. In his decree dissolving the assembly, Dom Pedro promised to give the people a workable constitution "twice as liberal" as the one the assembly would have produced.[48]

The decree was dictated by the emperor to his private secretary, the Chalaça, and given to the commander of Dom Pedro's mounted honor guard to deliver to the president of the assembly. Chalaça, as a lieutenant in the guard, joined his outfit for the ride to the city palace square, where the dragoons arrived around one o'clock on the afternoon of 12 November. The emperor accompanied General Curado's infantry and artillery from Boa Vista to the Campo de Santana, where he remained after two columns of troops were detached and sent to converge on the old jail from opposite directions. Each of the perhaps 2,000 officers and men who took part in the operations that day wore a sprig of coffee leaves on his hat. Before all the troops were in place, the honor guard commander marched into the old jail and handed the emperor's decree to the assembly president, who read it and declared the body dissolved. There was grumbling, but no resistance; with the military buildup going on in full view outside, even the most recalcitrant delegates were persuaded to evacuate the building. Antônio Carlos, Martim Francisco, and several of their closest associates were taken into custody at the old jail, while an honor guard detail was dispatched to José Bonifácio's house to arrest the oldest Andrada. Dom Pedro, wearing the coffee-leaf cockade, appeared on horseback at the city palace square at about two-thirty P.M., after his orders had been carried out. There were cheers from onlookers, but it was not a time for rejoicing; the emperor rode south along the beach to the little Church of Our Lady of Glory, where he thanked God that there had been no bloodshed and prayed for guidance. The Andrada brothers and three other former delegates were held in military prisons while a captured Portuguese merchant ship was outfitted to take them and their families to exile in France. Dom Pedro did not visit the deportees before they sailed on 20 November, but he provided each with a yearly pension of 1,250 dollars from the imperial treasury.[49]

Lord Cochrane arrived in Rio from Maranhão on 9 November 1823, three days before Dom Pedro dissolved the Constituent Assembly. The admiral was welcomed by the emperor, who went aboard the *Pedro Primeiro* to greet him, and by Lady Cochrane, who was reunited with her husband after a separation of more than a year. The Seawolf apparently played no part in the political and military maneuvers of 10–12 November, but he was glad that Dom Pedro dissolved the Constituent Assembly. He was miffed by criticism in that body of the emperor's awarding him the title marquis of Maranhão, and by the assembly's refusal to approve a land grant to go with the marquisate.

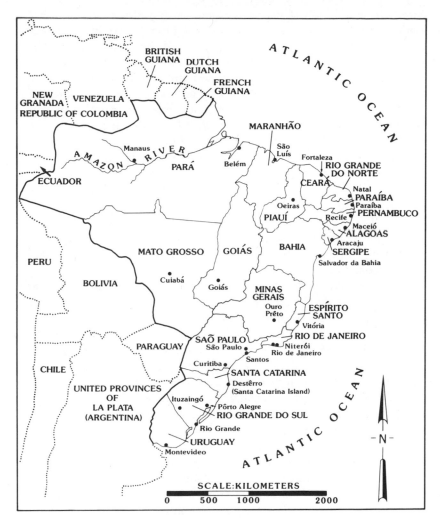

The Empire of Brazil: 1824
All international boundaries approximate and in dispute

After the dissolution, Cochrane urged Dom Pedro to reassure the world of his liberal principles by announcing that he would give Brazil a constitution based on those of England and the United States. The admiral noted that the monarch saw fit to adopt his advice in part.[50]

On 13 November Dom Pedro appointed a council of state and gave it the task of drafting a constitution for the empire. The council of procurators, which had served as a council of state prior to the convening of the Constituent Assembly, had been disbanded after the inauguration of the larger representative body. The new council of state, unlike its predecessor, was composed of imperial appointees, not elected representatives apportioned among the nineteen provinces. The new council of state had only ten members, all native Brazilians: five from Bahia, three from Minas Gerais, and two from Rio de Janeiro. Seven of the councillors had been delegates to the Constituent Assembly, including José Joaquim Carneiro de Campos, who played a major role in drafting the constitution, along with Dom Pedro, who presided over the council sessions.[51]

Some councillors of state were also members of the cabinet, or council of ministers, where there was much instability in the days after the dissolution of the assembly, reflecting conditions in Rio generally. Although the council of state did not change, ministers were appointed and dismissed, and portfolios shuffled, until the emperor got the cabinet he wanted. The cabinet members were all natives of Brazil and Dom Pedro depended on them to reassure the people that he remained firm in his commitment to Brazilian independence. The ministry issued arrest warrants for the officers involved in the caning of the apothecary; and captured documents, revealing Portugal's strategy for possible reunification talks with Brazil, were immediately published and denounced by the government. But militants of the Brazilian party were not easily appeased; a Portuguese-born citizen was assaulted on one of Rio's usually well-policed streets, and some imperial posters were pulled down or defaced on 14 November. The next day, Saint Leopold's Day, there was a hand-kissing ceremony at the city palace in honor of the empress's patron saint, and the United States consul reported "an observable absence of Brazileans."[52]

Lord Cochrane suggested that the emperor might improve his relations with native Brazilians by sending some of the more notorious members of the Portuguese party to well-paying positions abroad. At this time, November 1823, battle lines were being drawn between

Lord Cochrane and the Portuguese party, which the admiral would accuse of treason and larceny; he claimed that the Portuguese party was trying to deprive him and his men of their rightful spoils of war. The Seawolf estimated that he and his men were due about two million dollars in prize money; they had sent scores of captured merchant vessels back to Rio to be adjudicated by the imperial prize court, which Cochrane accused of being pro-Portuguese and in sympathy with the enemy shipowners. The court ruled that many of the captured vessels were not legitimate prizes, and it disallowed Cochrane's claim to the provincial treasury and customs house receipts of Maranhão, which the admiral had seized and still kept in an iron trunk under guard on the *Pedro Primeiro*. Cochrane argued that Maranhão had been an enemy province until he conquered it, and that the government property he confiscated there was enemy property, subject to disposal as a prize of war under the terms of his contract as first admiral of Brazil. He would not give up the funds in the iron trunk until the court ruled favorably on the captured vessels he and his men had brought into Rio.[53]

While the first admiral was occupied with these matters, the emperor and his private secretary, the Chalaça, were poring over copies of various constitutions from the files of the late Constituent Assembly, searching for provisions applicable to Brazil. They examined, among others, the Portuguese constitution of 1822 and the French and Norwegian constitutions of 1814; when Dom Pedro found an article he liked, he would write in the necessary changes and have the Chalaça copy the revised passage for presentation in the council of state. As the council of state in Rio worked on a constitutional draft to be submitted to a new Constituent Assembly, there was adverse reaction in the provinces to the dissolution of the old one; the city council of Bahia, after some stormy sessions, adopted a resolution on 18 December that expressed "profound grief" over the dissolution and expressed the hope that the council of state's proposed constitution would appear without delay. In fact, it was published in Rio two days later. The proposal was well received in the imperial capital, where the city council petitioned the emperor to dispense with a new Constituent Assembly and to promulgate the council of state proposal as the constitution of the empire. This was what Dom Pedro wanted to hear—he realized that he had made a mistake in promising a new Constituent Assembly. On 26 December, acting on the advice of the Rio city council, the government suspended elections for the new assembly while the town and city councils of the empire were consulted on the proposed constitution. The elections were never held; after half of Brazil's municipal governments had accepted the council of state draft, it was proclaimed by the emperor as the constitution of Brazil, on 25 March 1824. Brazil's next nationwide elections would be for the first parliament under the constitution of 1824.[54]

Dom Pedro had promised Brazil a constitution "twice as liberal" as the one the Constituent Assembly was going to make. He did, in fact, provide a unique charter under which Brazil for sixty-five years safeguarded the basic rights of citizens—not perfectly, but better than any other Western Hemisphere nation during that time, with the possible exception of the United States—while its Latin American neighbors, under innumerable constitutions differing only in detail from the assembly draft, all fell victim to prolonged periods of dictatorship and arbitrary rule. In practice, Dom Pedro's constitution was more than twice as liberal as those of the Constituent Assembly genre. In theory, it was more liberal than the assembly proposal in some areas, like religion: congregations of Jews and other non-Christians were allowed to maintain houses of worship under Dom Pedro's constitution. It was certainly more specific in defining "inviolable" personal and property rights; it listed thirty-four as opposed to only six in the assembly proposal. But Dom Pedro's constitution was theoretically less liberal in its concentration of power in the hands of a hereditary chief of state. Both documents called for the establishment of Roman Catholicism as the religion of the empire, with the emperor as patron of the Church in Brazil.[55]

The Brazilian constitution of 1824 created a centralized national government of four branches, or powers—legislative, executive, judicial, and moderating. The legislative power was wielded by a General Assembly, or parliament, consisting of a Chamber of Deputies elected for a four-year term, and a Senate, whose members served for life. Suffrage was extended to free adult males with an annual income of at least 100 dollars, but elections were indirect. Local voters chose electors who cast their ballots on the provincial level for deputies and senators; in the case of the latter, three nominees were named for each vacancy, and the final choice was the emperor's. Representation in both houses was based on population, including slaves; for every two deputies there was one senator. Provincial governors, called presidents, were appointed by the national executive in the imperial capital; they were advised by elected provincial councils. Constitutional amendments were fairly easy to effect, requiring the approval of two successive parliaments.[56]

The emperor was the "chief of the executive power," which was delegated to a cabinet, or council of ministers. The ministers were appointed by the emperor and served at his pleasure; they were not responsible to the legislature, as they would have been in a parliamentary system. The executive branch enforced the laws enacted by the General Assembly, ran the administrative departments and the armed forces, and conducted the foreign relations of the empire. Treaties were sanctioned by the emperor and did not require ratification by the legislative branch. To allay fears that the emperor might sign away the country's independence, the constitution specifically prohibited the union of Brazil with any other nation.[57]

The judicial branch was to consist of a Supreme Court and such lower courts as established by law. The option of trial by jury in both criminal and civil cases was to be offered as soon as practicable—Brazil had no experience with the jury system—but was available immediately in cases involving freedom of the press, which the constitution guaranteed, although citizens could be held accountable for "abuses," as defined by law. Press freedom and personal security rights could be temporarily suspended in cases of rebellion formally declared by the emperor with the approval of the General Assembly, or by the monarch alone when parliament was not sitting.[58] Slaves were not citizens and had no rights under the constitution; Dom Pedro, in hopes of winning quick acceptance of the charter, sacrificed his strong feelings on this matter. Unlike the 1787 Constitution of the United States, the Brazilian constitution of 1824 did not indicate a date for the termination of the African slave trade. But the emperor provided himself with treaty-making powers that he would use in attempting to end the traffic.

The fourth power, the moderating power, Dom Pedro's constitution stated, in a direct translation from Benjamin Constant, "is the key to all political organization." As the moderator, or arbiter of the political process, the emperor and perpetual defender of Brazil was allocated certain clearly defined powers, to enable him to break deadlocks and to ensure the functioning of the government in accordance with the constitution and in the permanent interests of the nation. Some of these powers could be found in three-branch schemes, usually allotted to the executive—e.g., the authority to pardon convicts and reduce (but not increase) sentences, and to veto legislation. The emperor's veto was in theory suspensory, but because the votes of three successive parliaments were required to override, it was practically absolute. Most important, the monarch could dissolve the Chamber of Deputies at his discretion, before its four-year term was up, and convoke elections for a new parliament.[59] The emperor could not make laws, but he could exert considerable pressure on the parliament to legislate in what he determined to be the perpetual interests of Brazil.

As a devotee of Benjamin Constant, Dom Pedro realized that a system of separation of powers required an arbiter. If not assigned in the constitution, the moderating power would be appropriated extraconstitutionally. In the three-branch republics of Spanish America, the moderating power was seized by the armed forces; in the United States, by the Supreme Court. The justices of the United States —appointed for life and responsible only to God and the Constitution —were establishing themselves as the arbiter of their country's political system at the time that Dom Pedro was wrestling with the problems of constitutional organization in Brazil. The justices of the North American republic were several (seven in 1824), while the South American emperor was a single individual; to assist the monarch in defending the past and future against present excesses of passion or lethargy, the Brazilian constitution established the council of state, composed of ten members appointed for life, which the emperor was required to consult on a regular basis, and prior to any exercise of the moderating power. The ten-man council that had helped him frame the constitution became, with the same personnel, the constitutional council of state. Secure in their lifetime tenure, the councillors were obligated to speak freely and offer their opinions on all questions brought before them; but the final decision on every matter was the emperor's.[60]

The powers granted to the emperor smacked of royal absolutism to many Brazilians, and a number of city councils hesitated or refused to ratify the constitution. Nevertheless, a majority of Brazil's municipal governments had indicated their acceptance by 25 March 1824, when Dom Pedro promulgated the constitution after a pontifical mass at the Rio cathedral. The ceremony included a reading of the entire text of the document, followed by oath taking by the emperor, the empress, the bishop, and all the high officials of state. That night there was the usual—for such occasions—gala at the Imperial Theater. After the performance as the imperial couple were returning to Boa Vista, a great fire lit up the sky behind them. In a matter of two hours, the Imperial Theater was almost completely consumed by flames; only some exterior walls of weakened masonry remained standing, precariously.[61] In the North of Brazil, in Ceará and Pernambuco, the fires of revolution were being kindled.

One town council in Ceará not only refused to ratify Dom Pedro's constitution, but declared the emperor dethroned for dissolving the Constituent Assembly. The principal municipal governments in Pernambuco, the councils of Olinda and Recife, rejected the provincial president appointed by Dom Pedro, along with the constitution, although they continued to profess loyalty to the emperor. Dom Pedro was willing to compromise: he withdrew his original appointment and named to the presidency José Carlos Mayrink, a Brazilian of Dutch descent, whom he hoped would be acceptable to the councils of Recife and Olinda. But the two municipalities insisted on their original choice, Manuel de Carvalho. The emperor could not allow the city councils to select the provincial president; the constitution assigned that authority to the central government in Rio. Dom Pedro had no choice but to enforce his constitution. Captain John Taylor with two Imperial Navy frigates arrived in Pernambuco at the end of March, under orders to blockade Recife, if necessary, to persuade the local authorities to accept the emperor's appointee as their provincial president. The Pernambucans, inspired by the words of a local journalist and Carmelite Friar, Joaquim do Amor Divino Caneca, held firm in their insistence on Carvalho. It was Mayrink who was intimidated by the Pernambucan resistance to his appointment, and he resigned at the end of May. With no one to install as provincial president, Taylor was ordered to lift his blockade of Recife and return to Rio. When the frigates were gone, Carvalho, emboldened by the signs of imperial weakness and egged on by Friar Caneca, proclaimed the independence of Pernambuco on 2 July and called on the provinces of northeastern Brazil to form a new nation, the Confederation of the Equator.[62]

After months of temporizing, Dom Pedro responded vigorously to the challenge in the Northeast. "What did the insults from Pernambuco require?" the emperor asked rhetorically in a 27 July proclamation. "Surely a punishment, and such a punishment that it will serve as an example for the future." An indispensable instrument of this chastisement was Lord Cochrane, who for all those months had been locked in bitter controversy with the imperial navy minister and the prize court over the spoils of his last campaign. The admiral and his foreign crews would not sail against the rebels in Pernambuco until they received satisfactory remuneration for their earlier efforts in behalf of the empire. Dom Pedro, who at one time was on the verge of sending troops aboard the *Pedro Primeiro* to seize the admiral's specie-laden iron trunk, relented and authorized the distribution of 200,000 dollars to Cochrane and his men pending the settlement of the court claims. Thus mollified, the Seawolf set sail on the *Pedro Primeiro* on 2 August, accompanied by a corvette, a brig, and two transports carrying 1,200 soldiers under the command of Brigadier Francisco de Lima e Silva. Three frigates would follow later in the month. To facilitate the suppression of the rebellion and ensure the punishment of its instigators, the emperor suspended constitutional guarantees in the province of Pernambuco. Later, after a rebel government was proclaimed in Fortaleza, capital of Ceará, civil liberties were suspended in that province as well.[63]

Brigadier Lima e Silva's troops were disembarked south of Recife, in the province of Alagoas, and began to march from there to the Pernambucan capital, linking up with loyalist militia along the way. Cochrane sailed on to Recife, blockaded the port, and invited Carvalho to parlay; the rebel leader tried to bribe the admiral to join the revolution, and the latter tried to persuade the former to give up and transfer the provincial treasury to the *Pedro Primeiro*. This was not done, and Carvalho fled to safety on a British vessel as imperial troops closed in on the city and the warships began their bombardment. The revolution in Pernambuco collapsed quickly on 17 September 1824, leaving only Friar Caneca and a few stalwart souls to fight their way through the backlands to join their comrades in Ceará. Cochrane sailed to Fortaleza, the capital of Ceará, where he landed a small force of marines and secured the city for the empire on 17 October. Some rebels fought on in the interior of Ceará until they were finally overcome by imperial troops a few weeks later. Sixteen captured rebel leaders, including Friar Caneca, were hanged or shot after being convicted of insurrection by military tribunals. When the sentences, which Dom Pedro refused to commute, had been carried out, constitutional guarantees were restored in Pernambuco and Ceará. Though criticized at the time and later, the punishment effectively deterred secessionist movements in that part of

Brazil for the rest of Dom Pedro's reign, and in the context of the times it was hardly excessive: fifty black men had been executed by the patriots in Bahia in one day in 1823.[64] The number of executions approved by Dom Pedro was small indeed when compared with the total ordered by almost any other liberator in Latin America.

Lord Cochrane's contribution to the preservation of Brazil's territorial integrity was enormous, and the admiral felt he was ill compensated for it. After occupying Fortaleza he went on to São Luís, Maranhão, where he spent several months mediating a conflict between rival supporters of the emperor. When the situation stabilized in Maranhão, Cochrane requisitioned 106,000 dollars from the provincial treasury for his squadron payroll, transferred his flag to the frigate *Ipiranga*, and sent the *Pedro Primeiro* back to Rio. The Seawolf then took a cruise into northern waters "for his health." The *Ipiranga* wound up in England, were Cochrane turned her over to the Brazilian consulate, along with his resignation and a bill for services rendered to the empire. His next adventure was in the Mediterranean, where he fought for the independence of Greece from Turkey.[65]

6 Misfortunes of Love and War

So very difficult a matter is it to trace and find out
the truth of anything by history.
Plutarch, *Lives: Pericles*.

"My duties bind me to my husband," Dona Leopoldina wrote to her sister in June 1823, "but unfortunately I cannot place my faith in him."[1] Dona Leopoldina was not of a suspicious nature and for years had ignored or discounted evidence of Dom Pedro's infidelities. When a servant told her in 1821 that Dom Pedro had taken sexual advantage of a pa' ːaid, Dona Leopoldina went directly to her husband, who indignantly denied the servant's allegation, fired him, and shipped him off to Portugal. Dona Leopoldina apparently was convinced that Dom Pedro was innocent, and, in this case, he probably was. He generally sought sexual adventures beyond the palace grounds and among women unknown to his wife. An exception was Joaquina de Avilez, wife of the Portuguese general; Dona Leopoldina probably suspected Dom Pedro of having an affair with Joaquina in 1821, but did not pursue the matter.[2] Anyway, Joaquina was gone with her husband and his troops in February 1822. Six months later Dom Pedro met Domitila de Castro.

Domitila was the sister of a Brazilian lieutenant who accompanied Dom Pedro on his trip to São Paulo in August 1822. The lady was separated from her husband, Felício Pinto Coelho de Mendonça, a militia officer and sometime planter and merchant. Accused of infidelity, she abandoned him in 1819; he pursued her and attacked her with a knife, inflicting two wounds that would leave scars on her body. After the attack Domitila and her three children found refuge with her father, Colonel João de Castro. The colonel, a native of the Azores, was retired from the Portuguese regular army and was the proprietor of a general store and livery stable in São Paulo. He apparently felt that his son-in-law had cause for attacking Domitila, for he took no action against him. In any event, he was not a particularly powerful or influential man. He had arrived in Brazil as a twenty-one-year-old lieutenant in 1775, fought in the 1776–77 colonial war against Spain, and spent the rest of his military career guarding the frontiers of Portuguese America. He married the daughter of an old and respected paulista family, of mixed Portuguese and American Indian ancestry, and settled in the city of São Paulo upon retiring from the army. His son, Francisco de Castro Canto e Melo, pursued an army career and was on hand in Rio in August 1822 to escort Dom Pedro to São Paulo and introduce him to his father and sisters. Dom Pedro, who had a predilection for old soldiers, became quite fond of Colonel João de Castro.[3]

Domitila de Castro became the great love of Dom Pedro's life. Twenty-four years old when they met in 1822, she was almost a year older than her lover. She was an attractive light-skinned woman with chestnut-colored hair; dark, greenish eyes; a delicate, slightly hooked nose; and a mouthful of straight, pearly white teeth. Domitila was taller than average, well built, with ample bosom and hips, and arms and neck that seemed shaped by a sculptor—having no visible bones or muscle. She carried herself with extraordinary grace, and dressed to accentuate her best features.[4] When Dom Pedro saw her, he had to have her. Domitila was more than willing to give herself to him, seeing in this royal suitor a way out of her miserable provincial existence. Once Dom Pedro was hers, she devoted her considerable talents to keeping him, to making the romance endure.

Though intelligent and witty, Domitila lacked education. Her writing was poor, as deficient in spelling and syntax as that of her royal lover. In great contrast to the erudite Dona Leopoldina, Domitila had no schooling in any scientific or humanistic discipline. But she knew better than the empress how to please the man they both loved. Domitila was a sensuous Luso-Brazilian, a product of the mingling of races, native of the hot climate; Dona Leopoldina was a cerebral, unwashed Middle European, daughter of the Germanic caesars, who could no more adapt physically and mentally to the tropical environment than she could eliminate inappropriate exclamation points from her writing in Portuguese. Aside from her cultural disadvantage, Dona Leopoldina lacked "the intelligence of self love;" she would not enhance her appearance with cosmetics or flattering clothes. She ate compulsively and became quite fat. But she never actually repelled Dom Pedro, who would continue to admire her for her many fine qualities, and father her children, who arrived regularly, one each year, from her first successful pregnancy until her death. After an initial miscarriage, Domitila fell into the same pattern in 1824; she produced a child a year for the emperor until their separation in 1828. For Dom Pedro it was not a question of either Domitila or Dona Leopoldina: he wanted them both, and others as well. One of the others was Domitila's older, married sister, Maria Bendita, who bore the emperor a son, Rodrigo, in November 1823. While hiding his relationship with Domitila from his wife, Dom Pedro was also concealing from his principal mistress his affair with her sister.[5]

Dom Pedro arranged for Domitila, Maria Bendita, Colonel João, and other members of the Castro family to move from São Paulo to the Rio area. Domitila was set up in a house at Mataporcos, about halfway between Boa Vista and the city palace. Maria Bendita went with her husband to the royal family estate at Santa Cruz, where he was given the job of general administrator. A place at Santa Cruz was even found for Domitila's estranged husband, Felício, who became manager of the estate's main trading post. For this and other inducements, Felício agreed not to contest Domitila's divorce proceedings against him. The petition for divorce cleared the church tribunal in forty-eight hours; the grounds were cruelty and adultery, evidenced, respectively, by the scars on Domitila's body and affidavits by Felício recognizing two of his own illegitimate children. Civil court proceedings took a while longer, and the final decree in Domitila's favor was handed down on 21 May 1824. Felício, while cooperative in the divorce suit, still bore a grudge against his ex-wife. He sent her an insulting letter that threw Dom Pedro into a rage when she showed it to him; the emperor mounted his horse and rode eighty kilometers through a dark and rainy night to the trading post at Santa Cruz where he beat Felício with a whip and forced him to sign a paper promising never to bother Domitila again.[6]

At the time the divorce was granted, which was two days before Domitila gave birth to her first child by Dom Pedro, the emperor was dallying with Adèle de Bonpland, wife of the French naturalist, Aimé Bonpland, who had strayed into the republic of Paraguay, where he was being held prisoner by that country's xenophobic dictator, Dr. Francia. Madame Bonpland came to Rio with hopes of enlisting Dom

Pedro's help in bringing pressure on Dr. Francia to free her husband. The emperor, who had enough trouble with the rebels in Pernambuco, was not inclined to stir up more on Brazil's border with Paraguay. However, he was quite happy to entertain Adèle de Bonpland, "a beautiful young Frenchwoman who could have passed for Spanish, so delicate were her hands, so long and shiny her tresses."[7] From the emperor, Adèle learned of a plan concocted in the council of ministers to search Lord Cochrane's flagship while the admiral was detained at a military review in Niterói, scheduled for 4 June 1824. Dom Pedro had been led to believe that Cochrane had stashed away on the *Pedro Primeiro* far more than the 40,000 dollars that he acknowledged holding as security for prize money. Adèle, since she was getting nowhere politically with Dom Pedro, took the story to Lord Cochrane at his house in Rio late on the night before the planned review and search. The outraged admiral jumped on a horse, galloped out to Boa Vista, pushed his way past the palace guards, got the emperor out of bed, and told him that he would defend his ship if anyone attempted to search it without his authorization. The Seawolf claimed he had nothing to hide, and would gladly conduct the emperor or anyone officially designated by him on a thorough inspection of the *Pedro Primeiro*, but he would not permit the underhanded, shameful, sneak attack on his honor planned for the next day. Dom Pedro, according to Cochrane, realized that he had been misled by his ministers. The review would be cancelled and there would be no search, because "I will be ill in the morning," the emperor said, "so go home, and think no more of the matter."[8]

Dom Pedro looked perfectly healthy to Lord Cochrane on the night of 4 June, so the Scotsman naturally thought the illness was a complete fabrication. But apparently the emperor had actually suffered an epileptic seizure earlier on the evening of the admiral's visit. The next morning the government newspaper, *Diário fluminense*, announced that "His majesty the emperor yesterday was menaced by one of his old attacks," requiring that he take great care, although his life was not in danger. According to the palace surgeon, it was the first seizure Dom Pedro had suffered in five years; it began around seven o'clock in the evening, lasted three to four minutes, and was not very violent, the official medical report stated. But the emperor told the French consul that the attack was "very strong and lasted many minutes."[9] Members of the diplomatic corps, the council of ministers, and the council of state went out to Boa Vista on 5 June to visit the stricken monarch—as did Lord Cochrane. "On catching my eye," the first admiral recalled, "His Majesty burst into a fit of uncontrollable laughter, in which I as heartily joined; the bystanders, from the gravity of their countenances, evidently considering that both had taken leave of their senses. The ministers looked astounded, but said nothing—His Majesty kept his secret, and I was silent."[10] If the whole affair was a hoax, it was one worthy of Lord Cochrane. But Dom Pedro was not in the admiral's class as a dissimulator; the joke was that he really had suffered an attack and the dour Seawolf thought he had faked it.

The emperor liked to laugh. "He treated everyone with familiarity," a contemporary wrote, "laughing, making jokes, always having anecdotes to tell about the private life of everybody." Sometimes he went too far, ridiculing people, humiliating them; and "with the same facility that he laughed, he would get angry." But "later he would give satisfaction, begging their pardon and embracing the people." Dom Pedro had a "noble spirit, a good heart," this normally critical source admitted, and was "incapable of vengeance." The emperor was the "friend of his friends, procuring their happiness, even in their domestic troubles. When he heard of some estrangement he would try to bring about a reconciliation," acting as a neutral mediator, taking the side of neither the husband nor the wife—even if the husband "happened to be his favorite."[11]

Dom Pedro's "favorite" was Francisco Gomes da Silva, the Chalaça, whose wife, Maria Antónia da Silva, does not appear in her husband's memoirs and is rarely mentioned in other records of the time. The Chalaça made maximum use of his limited schooling, which he received as a boy seminarian in his native Portugal. His handwriting was good and he had mastered the essentials of Portuguese spelling and grammar. With these skills, his ebullient personality, his total dedication to the emperor, and his lack of political ambition, the Chalaça was well suited to be Dom Pedro's private secretary. Another Portuguese of low birth and little education served the emperor well as palace treasurer and majordomo; this was Plácido de Abreu, a master of the art of barbering and the science of arithmetic. Plácido shaved Dom Pedro daily, cut his hair when required, supervised the palace staff, administered the payroll, and assigned vehicles and horses from the imperial stables. The majordomo was assisted by João Carvalho Raposo and João Carlota, former stableboys who had come to Brazil

Friar Antônio de Arrábida, Bishop of Anemúria
From Tobias Monteiro, *Historia do imperio: O primeiro reinado, I* (Rio
de Janeiro, 1939).

from Portugal at an early age. They were playmates from Dom Pedro's unsupervised childhood, of whom the emperor remained extremely fond. The manners and language of these Portuguese immigrants were coarse, but Dom Pedro enjoyed their company far more than he did that of his ministers and councillors of state, all native Brazilians in 1824, and most university graduates. Contrary to charges by militants of the Brazilian party, these palace servants were not conspiring to return Brazil to Portuguese sovereignty, or to overthrow the constitution and establish an absolutist regime in Rio; they simply did not concern themselves with such matters.[12]

Dom Pedro's most intimate Brazilian friend, Domitila de Castro, was involved in politics to the extent that she sought government favors for her paulista friends and relatives. Domitila's associates tended to be Brazilian and liberal, rather than Portuguese and absolutist —indeed, José Bonifácio and his followers believed her to be part of a republican conspiracy. Whatever her ideological orientation, as imperial mistress, she was not inclined to remove the crown from her lover's head. She accumulated considerable wealth in this position, much of which she spent—after Dom Pedro was gone—to support a liberal insurrection in São Paulo. If Domitila temporarily sacrificed radical principles for the sake of her relationship with Dom Pedro, her rival, Dona Leopoldina, suppressed her own inborn conservatism. From divine-right monarchy, she had made the mental transition to José Bonifácio's authoritarian constitutionalism by the time of the break between her husband and his chief minister. The split between Dom Pedro and José Bonifácio saddened and confused her; the latter's exile deprived her of a second surrogate father, after Dom João, and left her feeling very much alone at a time when evidence was accumulating of her husband's involvement with a new and special mistress whose identity she did not know and did not try to find out. But Dona Leopoldina was hardly abandoned; she was almost continually pregnant, and when she was physically able, she and Dom Pedro went walking or horseback riding together twice a day. She frequently accompanied him on inspections of government offices and defense installations.[13]

Dom Pedro was usually up by six o'clock each morning, inspecting the slaves and employees at Boa Vista. He was especially solicitous about their health and welfare, according to Maria Dundas Graham, widow of the late captain of the frigate HMS *Doris* and briefly governess to the Princess Dona Maria da Glória in 1824. The emperor would keep a busy pace throughout the day—except for an hour's nap after dinner, at midday—and late into the night. In his mid–twenties he retained his childhood curiosity about how things functioned, especially military and naval equipment, and he still liked to work with his hands. Mrs. Graham noted the great size of his hands. She and other Europeans were not impressed by his height, which was only about average by their standards. "He is a good looking man," a German visitor reported, "very robust, slightly marked by the small-pox, with a piercing eye and a quick understanding."[14] Except on official occasions, he dressed simply, often in white cotton trousers and a striped cotton jacket, with a bandana looped casually around his neck and a broad-brimmed straw hat on his head. Silver spurs would be attached to boots worn inside the pant legs and covered by white spats. He was always neat and clean.[15]

The emperor's appetite, Mrs. Graham recorded, was good, but "it certainly was not delicate." His main meal would consist of pork fatback and rice, "some kind of kale," potatoes, "cooked cucumbers, and, at times, a piece of roast beef, everything arranged separately on the same plate." The beef was "so tough that few knives could cut it." For indoor recreation, Dom Pedro and Dona Leopoldina had their music; he occasionally played billiards or chess and she liked backgammon. Mrs. Graham did not know if either played cards, of which she disapproved. The emperor may have flirted with Mrs. Graham, but he apparently made no serious passes at her. She lost her job as governess to Dona Maria da Glória due to the dissension she caused among other members of the palace staff by declining to wear a uniform —she did not consider herself a domestic servant—and by refusing to allow Majordomo Plácido and his cronies to play cards in the princess's antechamber. Like so many others who had felt Dom Pedro's wrath, Mrs. Graham bore the emperor no ill will. He was "subject to sudden explosions of violent passion," she wrote, "followed by a generous and frank civility, a readiness to do more than necessary to undo the ill that might have been done, or the pain that might have been caused in the moments of rage."[16]

Dom Pedro loved his children, enjoyed romping with them, and was concerned about their education: he wanted them to have better training than he had. Mrs. Graham, after leaving her position as governess to Dona Maria da Glória, was relieved to learn that the emperor had placed Friar Arrábida in charge of the education of the princesses. She, like virtually every other palace visitor, of whatever religion, had a very high opinion of the Portuguese-born Franciscan. Friar Arrábida was the only man to influence the thought and actions of the adult Dom Pedro for any length of time. The influence, however, only indirectly affected government policy; it was largely confined to the realm of religion and morals, and even there it had its limits. The emperor's confessor did not overstep the bounds of his relationship with the monarch; he did the best he could, cultivated the natural religious instincts of his communicant, bolstered his "noble spirit" and "good heart," and nudged him onto the path of righteousness whenever possible. The emperor went to church often. Early in the morning, on any day of the week, he might ride six kilometers across the hills from Boa Vista to hear mass at the little whitewashed church of Our Lady of Glory, perched on a promontory above Glória Beach. He also was accustomed to stopping off at the church on afternoons and at night, after adulterous adventures. The empress usually accompanied him on Sunday mornings to mass at this church, which was dedicated to the patron of their oldest child.[17]

The former Royal Chapel adjacent to the city palace fell on hard times after the coronation of Dom Pedro. Despite the emperor's love of music, the chapel orchestra and choir suffered the brunt of the government's economy drives. Von Neukomm and the Italian castrati returned to Europe, and chapel masters José Maurício and Marcos Portugal lived in disillusionment and near poverty on their reduced stipends. The choir shrank to a fraction of its former size, and the chapel orchestra all but disbanded during Dom Pedro's reign. Secular music suffered a blow with the burning of the Imperial Theater in March 1824. But opera was saved with the rebuilding of the theater the next year. The works of Rossini would completely dominate the new music scene. While the Imperial Theater was out of commission and professional companies could not be engaged in Rio, various amateur groups privately staged operas and plays in small, makeshift auditoriums. One of these was the Constitutional Little Theater of São Pedro, where admission was by invitation only. Domitila showed up for a performance in September 1824 without an invitation and was refused admittance. She informed her lover of the rebuff and he was furious; he ordered all the exclusive little theaters closed for violating an imperial decree of 1823 outlawing "secret societies."[18]

Dom Pedro rather often involved himself in matters that probably should have been left to his ministers or to the police. Enraged by reports that imperial troops were not being paid on time, he stormed into a treasury office with a horsewhip and physically chastised some clerks. In calmer moments he would pass through government offices jotting down the names of functionaries who were not at their desks and ordering disciplinary action against those whose absences were unexcused. On his rides through the city he would stop often to chat with people of all classes and hear their complaints. After learning that some fabric stores were giving short measure, he and an aide went from store to store with an official yardstick, confiscating measuring rods that did not meet the standard. He had "a taste for governing small things."[19]

On larger matters he was more likely to defer to his ministers. If he did not like the way business was being conducted at the highest level, he would change the responsible minister. But his rapport with his cabinet after November 1823 was such that this did not occur frequently; and when a minister was removed, he was often shifted to another post rather than dropped from the cabinet altogether. The emperor had a pool of about a dozen native Brazilians, most university graduates, from which he chose his ministers. Some of them were also lifetime members of the council of state. An able group—though lacking the brilliance of the Andrada brothers—they included Francisco Vilela Barbosa, minister of the navy, who also briefly held the army and empire portfolios; Finance Minister Mariano José Pereira da Fonseca; Foreign Minister Luís José de Carvalho e Melo; and, most distinguished of all, Minister of the Empire João Severiano Maciel da Costa, an outspoken opponent of the slave trade, former governor of occupied French Guiana and former president of the Constituent Assembly, who had cooperated with Dom Pedro in the dissolution of that body. Another capable and experienced statesman, José Clemente Pereira, was available for a cabinet post, but bore the stigma of having been born in Portugal. José Clemente and his liberal Masonic colleague, Joaquim Gonçalves Ledo, returned to Rio about the time that the Andradas, who had deported them, were themselves exiled. Rather than appoint José Clemente and Ledo to his cabinet in 1824, the emperor honored them with membership in the Order of the Cruzeiro.[20]

Membership in the Order of the Cruzeiro, a knighthood established at the time of Dom Pedro's coronation, was conferred by the monarch for meritorious service to the empire. The emperor, as patron of the Church in Brazil, also assumed the right to name members of the Order of Christ. Membership in these two orders was handed out rather liberally during the first two years of Dom Pedro's reign, but only one patent of nobility was granted—to Lord Cochrane, as marquis of Maranhão. As the second anniversary of his acclamation approached, Dom Pedro decided to reward João Severiano with the title of Viscount Queluz. As minister of the empire, the future viscount was responsible for promulgating the emperor's lists of induction into the orders of knighthood, and he had the bad judgment to slip two names, unapproved by Dom Pedro, onto the list for the Order of Christ. He became a viscount on 12 October 1824, and was fired as empire minister two days later. "Nobody regrets more than I having to dismiss João Severiano," the emperor wrote to his justice minister. But he had "invaded my imperial authority by putting on the list for the insignia of Christ two men whom I had not designated." After ordering the justice minister to prepare the decree dismissing João Severiano, and signing himself as "your master, and friend whom you have to defend, the emperor," Dom Pedro added, "P.S. This is how you are taught to be ministers."[21] As the United States consul in Rio emphasized on another occasion, the emperor *will have things in his own way.*"[22]

Dom Pedro, like Dom João before him, wanted to attract European colonists to Brazil. The first non-Portuguese colonists, a few hundred German Swiss, were settled in the mountains near Rio at Nova Friburgo in 1815. A second contingent, 334 Rhinelanders recruited on Dom Pedro's orders, joined the Nova Friburgo colony in 1823; more Germans arrived in the next year and were given land in the province of Rio Grande do Sul, at a place named São Leopoldo for the empress's patron saint, although most of the colonists were Lutherans. The recruiting agent was Dr. Georg Anton Ritter von Schäffer, a German physician, resident of Rio since 1818, and confidant of Dona Leopoldina. Early in 1824 Foreign Minister Carvalho e Melo felt that the Brazilian government could not afford to underwrite the immigration, and he instructed Schäffer to suspend his operations. The emperor, however, overruled his minister and ordered the doctor to continue his efforts, but instead of recruiting married men with families to enlist single males who could serve in the army—up to 3,000 of them. The men were to pay for their passage with military service, after which they would receive Brazilian land grants and be free to bring over brides from the old country or intermarry with the natives. A similar order for 3,000 soldier-colonists was given to Felisberto Caldeira Brant Pontes, who in April 1824 began his second stint as Dom Pedro's diplomatic representative in London.[23]

Felisberto Caldeira Brant Pontes was the grandson of a famous diamond contractor in Minas Gerais. In 1788, at the age of 16, Felisberto was sent to Portugal for his education; he graduated with distinction from the College of Nobles and the Royal Naval Academy and received commissions in both the Portuguese army and navy. As an army officer he was stationed in Angola, and later in Bahia, where he married the daughter of a wealthy family in 1801, and began amassing a huge personal fortune. In the provincial capital he acquired a large commercial house that dealt in sugar and slaves, and in the countryside he accumulated vast agricultural estates, while simultaneously commanding a regiment of regular infantry. He happened to be in Lisbon when the French invaded Portugal in 1807, and he returned to Bahia with the squadron that brought Dom João and his court to Brazil. He soon was promoted to general and made commander of the Bahia military district. In 1815, after his troops had put down a disturbance on one plantation, Brant concluded that there was a widespread conspiracy among blacks to raise the province's slaves in a general insurrection. Without the approval of the governor—the count of Arcos, who despised slavery and was trying earnestly to improve the conditions of the province's nonwhite population—the general launched a violent campaign of repression against Bahian blacks, in which "a great many forfeited their lives" and many more suffered severe corporal punishment. Appalled by Brant's excesses, Arcos expelled the general from the province, and when he returned, he ordered his arrest and imprisonment. But Dom João sided with Brant, whose reinstatement Arcos was compelled to accept.[24]

A chubby, clean-shaven, baby-faced man, Brant was accustomed to writing long letters to monarchs and ministers to offer advice on a variety of subjects. He was undeniably intelligent: while his military colleagues fought the French in the Peninsular Campaign and Artigas's gauchos in Uruguay, General Brant remained in Bahia and got richer and richer. His interests extended to modern technology, and he was responsible for launching the first steamboat in Brazilian waters in 1819. Two years earlier, he had cooperated with his former adversary, the count of Arcos, in mobilizing Bahia's forces against the rebels in Pernambuco; fortunately for the general, the insurrection collapsed before he was required personally to take the field. Brant's next military experience was not so happy: when, after much procrastination, he marched against the supporters of the Portuguese Cortes in Bahia in February 1821, his horse was shot out from under him and he was compelled to surrender to the Lusophile liberals. The new Bahian constitutionalist junta forced him to flee to Rio, where the king granted the general's request for a furlough to go to London to take care of some personal business.[25]

General Brant left Rio for England in April 1821, shortly before Dom João departed for Portugal. With the break between Dom Pedro and the Lisbon Cortes in 1822, Brant offered his services to the Brazilian government as its diplomatic agent in London. Duly commissioned, Brant maneuvered with considerable skill in attempting to negotiate British recognition of Brazilian independence in 1822–23. Perceiving the strength of Foreign Minister George Canning's commitment to end the Atlantic slave trade, the general indicated that his government would be willing to accept this in return for diplomatic recognition and the opening of the highly protected British market to Brazilian sugar. Brant and his sugar-producing compatriots wanted continued access to African slave labor, but even more, in those depression years, they wanted markets for their produce: it was a reasonable trade-off. But at that time Great Britain could not bring itself to abandon its own West Indian sugar producers by opening its market, or to abandon its ancient ally, Portugal, by recognizing Brazilian independence—so Brant's deal did not go through.[26]

While Brant was negotiating in London, the Brazilian war for independence devastated much of the Bahian sugar country. Patriot forces requisitioned the property of the absent general, and the Portuguese looted and burned his plantations and freed his slaves. "The Lusitanians, because of hatred, and the national army, because of necessity," Brant lamented, "did away with half of my fortune."[27] The Bahian electors gave the general some consolation by choosing him as one of their delegates to the Constituent Assembly. He left London in August 1823 and took his seat in the assembly in Rio a few weeks before its dissolution by Dom Pedro in November. With the emperor no longer constrained by the assembly, and Dom João back in possession of his royal powers in Lisbon, chances for a peace treaty between

Brazil and Portugal had greatly improved. Early in 1824 Dom Pedro sent Brant back to London to begin peace talks with Portuguese representatives in the British capital. The general was given various other missions as well, like recruiting soldier-colonists, negotiating a loan for the Brazilian government from English bankers, arranging the purchase of a steam-powered frigate for the Brazilian navy, and buying thoroughbred horses for the emperor's stables.[28]

Felisberto Caldeira Brant Pontes, later marquis of Barbacena, was one of the eminent figures of Dom Pedro's reign as emperor of Brazil. In contrast to other Brazilian-born statesmen who served Dom Pedro, mostly lawyers, scientists, or engineers—from the Andrada brothers to Vilela Barbosa and João Severiano—Brant was closely identified with large plantation, slaveholding interests. The major worry of the sugar planters of Bahia and the Northeast was Cuban competition; to survive the challenge they believed that they needed at least the same access to cheap labor as had the Spanish island, which was importing large numbers of slaves from Africa in the early 1820s. The coffee planters of the Rio–Minas Gerais–São Paulo area, on the other hand, faced no serious international competition, but the burgeoning demand for their product prompted them to greatly expand their operations, creating a labor shortage, which, most of them felt, could only be remedied by a large-scale importation of slaves from Africa. A few had hopes for the immigration of free labor from Europe; but the process was slow and almost as expensive initially as the importation of slaves. And once in Brazil, the free immigrants showed a marked reluctance to take jobs on coffee plantations and work side by side with slaves. So the slave trade with Africa continued, and increased in the South of Brazil, with Rio far outdistancing Bahia by 1824 as an entrepôt for the infamous traffic. General Brant and his planter associates realized that the international community, backed by the power of the British navy, would not allow the Atlantic slave trade to continue indefinitely. What they asked for was a ten-to-twenty-year grace period during which Britain would permit them to continue importing slaves from Africa while they began to shift to a system of free labor, provided by European immigrants.[29] Dom Pedro, writing in 1823 as the Philanthropist, had proposed a two-year period; political reality would force him to accept a term twice that long.

With his willingness to end the slave trade, Dom Pedro won favor with the British, whose other concerns included negotiating a treaty that would preserve the trading privileges they had acquired under the Strangford Treaties of 1810. Independent Brazil might choose not to honor the British–Portuguese treaties, which, in any case, would expire in 1825 unless renewed. The British government wanted to negotiate these matters, but could not properly deal with Brazil as a sovereign nation until Britain's ally, Portugal, acknowledged the independence of its former colony. So Britain, as Dom Pedro expected, brought pressure on Portugal to come to terms with Brazil and recognize its independence. Austria, under Dona Leopoldina's father, Emperor Franz I, and his chancellor, Prince Metternich, also offered Brazil its good offices to facilitate a recognition agreement with Portugal. But family ties alone were insufficient to explain why the leading light of absolutist legitimacy in Europe should look kindly upon a breakaway constitutional state in South America. The Austrians and their partners in the Holy Alliance, Dom Pedro learned, had some misconceptions: they attributed his break with Portugal to the liberalism of the Lisbon Cortes and believed that his subjects had forced him against his will to promise them a constitution. Once the situation in Brazil had stabilized, the European absolutists evidently expected, Dom Pedro would follow the examples of his father, Dom João, and his Spanish cousin, Don Fernando VII, and dispense with the constitution. Dom Pedro instructed his representatives in Vienna to disabuse the Hapsburg monarchy of those notions. The European sovereigns, Dom Pedro wrote in February 1824, had to be made to realize that the constitution then being acclaimed in the city councils of Brazil was not forced on him, but was entirely his idea. The Viennese court was to be informed that Dom Pedro was "intimately convinced that an emperor who does not cherish the freedom of his country and does not give to the people the just liberty that guarantees the security of their property and persons . . . is unworthy of being an emperor and must belong to the genre of wild beasts." The Brazilian monarch would rule with honor over hearts that were brave and free: "I love liberty, and if I find myself obligated to govern without a constitution, immediately I will give up being emperor."[30]

Dom Pedro's liberal protestations hardly pleased the Hapsburg court, but Metternich continued to view the Brazilian monarchy favorably—as a bulwark against the republicanism that was rampaging across Spanish South America. Austria joined Britain in sponsoring peace talks in London between Brazil and Portugal, and Vienna gave refuge to Dom Miguel, who was deported from Lisbon in May 1824 for attempting to overthrow his father in the *Abrilada*, or April coup. For nine days beginning on 30 April Dom Miguel and his absolutist followers imposed on the Portuguese capital a reign of terror —actually directed by his mother, the queen, Dona Carlota. The prince's troops kept Dom João bottled up in his palace, pressuring him to abdicate in favor of Dom Miguel. But the Lisbon diplomatic corps rallied to the cause of the king and escorted him to safety on a British warship; Dom João then summoned Dom Miguel to the ship, where in the presence of his benign father the ferocious prince unexpectedly capitulated, to the great disgust of his mother. The aging queen was confined to Queluz palace as her favorite son made his way to exile in Vienna, a usually hospitable environment for absolutists. Nevertheless, the Hapsburg emperor, while accepting Dom Miguel as a refugee, made clear his sympathy for Portugal's legitimate monarch; Franz wrote Dom João that he was greatly pleased that God had protected the king's rights during the Abrilada.[31] Thus Austria cultivated the goodwill of both conservative and reactionary absolutists in Portugal, as well as that of the constitutional government of Brazil.

The Abrilada brought Dom João a letter of sympathy from Dom Pedro, who condemned the "treason" of his younger brother. Dom Pedro warned the king to beware of "enemies" still lurking at the Lisbon court, and urged him to end the lamentable state of war between their two countries by recognizing Brazilian independence. But the wily Dom João, supported by an equally astute French ambassador in Lisbon, held out for Brazilian concessions on matters of sovereignty and reparations. British Foreign Minister Canning, who thought he would be able to dictate to Dom João after the Abrilada, was greatly disappointed. The French ambassador, who had played at least as important a role as that of his British colleague in frustrating Dom Miguel's coup, recognized his own country's interest in delaying Portugal's acknowledgment of Brazilian independence. As long as Brazil was claimed as a colony by Portugal, Britain could not negotiate with Dom Pedro's government for a new commercial agreement; the old one was due to expire in February 1825, and after that, the goods of Britain would lose their tariff advantage over those of France and every other nation in the Brazilian market. The Portuguese representatives at the London talks, which began in July 1824, made impossible demands, and the negotiations got nowhere. They were broken off in February

1825, with Brant, however, promising Canning that Brazil would honor the old commercial agreement at least until June. In the meantime, the British took direct action in Lisbon: they threatened to disregard their alliance with Portugal and to recognize Brazilian independence without further ado. This forced Dom João to dismiss his pro-French cabinet chief, to ask Paris to recall its ambassador, and to appoint a British subject, Sir Charles Stuart, as his minister plenipotentiary to go to Rio and negotiate for Portugal a treaty of recognition with Brazil.[32]

Arriving in Rio on 18 July 1825, Sir Charles Stuart, as the agent of Dom João, met with the negotiators designated by Dom Pedro: Foreign Minister Carvalho e Melo, Navy Minister Vilela Barbosa, and Councillor of State José Egídio Alvares de Almeida. It took them six weeks to produce a treaty, which they signed on 29 August and Dom Pedro ratified the next day. The treaty went into effect with Dom João's ratification on 15 November; Portugal's recognition of Brazilian independence was followed quickly by the establishment of formal diplomatic relations with Rio by London and the courts of continental Europe. The United States had officially recognized Brazil the year before—after the Monroe Doctrine was enthusiastically received in Rio—but most of the Spanish American republics remained hostile toward the Brazilian empire, seeing it as the stalking horse of the Holy Alliance, as a tool of European monarchies committed to assisting Spain in the reconquest of its former colonies.[33]

In negotiating the treaty of recognition for Portugal, Sir Charles Stuart did a good job of protecting Dom João's interests. Although there would be no dual kingdom, as the king had hoped, Dom João was given the right to call himself emperor of Brazil, as well as king of Portugal, for the rest of his life. Under the treaty, Dom João, as king of Portugal and Brazil, recognized the independence of Brazil; Brazil then recognized Dom João as its emperor, and he, in turn, bestowed the title on Dom Pedro, retaining simultaneous use of it during his lifetime, but without any sovereign power in Brazil—this had been conferred exclusively on Dom Pedro "by unanimous acclamation of the people." Thus, the treaty embodied the concept that the Brazilian people had won their independence from Portugal, not from the Bragança monarchy, and that Dom João recognized the fact and appointed his son to rule over them, with their consent. After the king's death, the treaty made clear, there would be only one emperor of Brazil—Dom Pedro or one of his descendents—but the sticky question of who would rule Portugal after Dom João was avoided.[34] This was the way Dom João wanted it; a formal renunciation of the Portuguese throne by Dom Pedro would have left Dom Miguel as the king's heir. After the unpleasantness of the Abrilada, Dom João more than ever wanted to leave open the possibility of Dom Pedro's succeeding him in Portugal—even though the Brazilian constitution seemed to prohibit the emperor from wearing two crowns.

The treaty committed Brazil to pay compensation for Portuguese government and private property confiscated during the war for independence. A mixed commission composed of Brazilian, Portuguese, and supposedly neutral British members was to ajudicate claims. However, this provision was rendered moot by a secret codicil attached to the treaty that required Brazil to take over payments on a loan of 1,400,000 pounds sterling that Portugal had contracted with English bankers, and, in addition, to pay 600,000 pounds directly into the Portuguese treasury within one year of ratification. Payment of this total of 2,000,000 pounds, about 9,500,000 silver dollars, would discharge all of Brazil's financial obligations to Portugal. It was a high price, but one Dom Pedro was ready to pay for recognition and the goodwill of the great powers. He had hopes of gaining their cooperation in promoting immigration and the economic and social development of the empire. Another commitment to Portugal was Brazil's promise to reject any petition for annexation by any Portuguese colony —meaning Portugal's African possessions. This too was in line with the desires of Dom Pedro, who wanted to halt the flow of slaves into Brazil as soon as possible. Brazilian planters, however, would deplore the concession, for they had envisioned the annexation of Angola or Mozambique as a means of assuring themselves a continuing supply of slaves by making the traffic a domestic matter, thus circumventing the anticipated international agreements against the trade. Less controversial were the commercial provisions of the treaty: Brazil and Portugal granted each other most-favored-nation status, with import duties set at 15 percent ad valorem.[35]

After signing this treaty for Portugal, Sir Charles Stuart next negotiated a commercial agreement with Brazil for Great Britain. Canning had authorized him to arrange a two-year extension of the 1810 Strangford Treaties, but Sir Charles felt he had the authority to negotiate new treaties on commerce and the slave trade, and he proceeded to do so. The Stuart commercial treaties provided for reciprocal most-favored-nation treatment, which gave British goods the same 15 percent tariff rate of the earlier convention. The slave-trade treaty provided for the complete abolition of the traffic between Africa and Brazil within four years of ratification. The Stuart treaties did not continue the extraterritorial privileges conceded to British subjects in Brazil in 1810. Dom Pedro had reason to be pleased with the new British treaties; he ratified them on 18 October 1825 and had them published the next month. Foreign Minister Canning, however, was appalled by these agreements, which would have put British subjects on the same legal footing as the natives in Brazil. The British government refused to ratify the treaties; they would have to be renegotiated.[36]

Indirect elections for members of the Chamber of Deputies and nominees for the Senate were held in the provinces of Brazil towards the end of 1824. The emperor carefully scrutinized the lists of Senate nominees and appointed those most likely to support him. But Dom Pedro could not control the composition of the Chamber of Deputies, which, he realized, would include members hostile to him—like Luís Augusto May, editor of the Rio newspaper *Malagueta*, who was elected from Minas Gerais. But the emperor avoided convening the newly elected parliament for more than a year: unrest in two provinces provided excuses for the delay. In Bahia some troops rose up and killed their unpopular commanding general; and although the mutiny had no apparent political significance, the emperor decided to take no chances and proceeded to suspend constitutional guarantees in the province in November 1824, while military tribunals meted out summary justice to the mutineers. Five months later a much more serious situation developed in the province of Uruguay: a small force of Uruguayan exiles from Buenos Aires, led by Juan Lavalleja, landed on their native soil and raised much of the Spanish-speaking population of the countryside against the imperial government. The emperor's cause suffered a severe blow on 29 April 1825, ten days after the revolt began, when Fructuoso Rivera, commander of the Uruguayan militia, defected to Lavalleja's rebels, whose objective was to detach Uruguay from Brazil and join it to the Spanish-speaking United Provinces of La Plata, then in the process of organizing a national government in Buenos Aires.[37]

Dom Pedro's government suspended constitutional guarantees in Uruguay and dispatched reinforcements to General Lecor, president and military commandant of the province, in Montevideo. By mid-1825 a stalemate had developed, with Lecor holding Montevideo and some other coastal towns and the rebels controlling most of the Uruguayan countryside. As soon as Lecor had sufficient troop strength, he was expected to move into the interior and launch a pacification campaign like the successful one he had conducted against Artigas's gauchos in 1816–20. The emperor, while awaiting favorable developments on the Uruguayan front, turned his attention to other matters in Rio. In April 1825 he persuaded Dona Leopoldina to choose Domitila as one of her ladies-in-waiting; the innocent empress thought the appointment was a reward for services rendered her husband by the lady's father, Colonel João de Castro. About the same time, Dom Pedro honored his friend and secretary, the Chalaça, by naming him chief of the emperor's *Gabinete Particular,* or private cabinet. Apparently Chalaça was the sole member of this "cabinet," which was created on paper to give the private secretary the added dignity of heading an imperial agency. Other associates of Dom Pedro were flattered with titles of nobility, thirty-nine of which were handed out on the emperor's birthday, the third anniversary of his acclamation, 12 October 1825. Among the seventeen viscounts and viscountesses—ranked between one count and twenty-one barons—was the viscountess of Santos, Domitila de Castro. About this time Dona Leopoldina realized that Domitila was her husband's mistress. The empress bore the unwelcome knowledge with fortitude at a time when she was in the advanced stages of pregnancy. On 2 December, to the great joy of her husband, she gave birth to a son—the male heir he had despaired of, the future Emperor Dom Pedro II.[38]

The news from Uruguay was not so good. General Lecor, having received reinforcements from Rio Grande do Sul, sent a column of 1,580 men out of Montevideo to find and destroy the enemy. Instead the imperial troops were routed by a superior force of Uruguayan rebels at the Battle of Sarandí on 12 October 1825. Two weeks later, the government in Buenos Aires formally accepted a petition from the Uruguayan patriots for the readmission of their province into the Argentine union, with Lavalleja as governor. The government in Buenos Aires was headed by Bernadino Rivadavia, who was trying to transform a loose confederation of Spanish-speaking provinces into a centralized Argentine republic. The Uruguayan conflict gave Rivadavia the opportunity to rally the Argentine provinces under his leadership for a nationalistic crusade to free their compatriots in Uruguay from the Luso-Brazilian imperialists. Troops from Buenos Aires and the other Argentine provinces were sent to Uruguay to reinforce Lavalleja. Dom Pedro, determined to defend the empire against the foreign invasion, declared war on the Argentine Republic on 10 December 1825. He ordered the Brazilian navy to blockade Buenos Aires, and instructed his minister of war to proceed with a buildup of the Brazilian army.[39]

The minister of war was João Vieira de Carvalho, who, on taking office in August 1824, became the first native of Portugal to serve in the cabinet since the dissolution of the Constituent Assembly. In the army for which he was responsible nearly half the officers were similarly of Portuguese birth. The great majority of enlisted men, however, were Brazilian natives, most of whom were conscripts. The Brazilian conscription law of 1822, based on earlier Portuguese statutes, made every able-bodied free male liable for compulsory military service, unless he was married, a member of the clergy, or his family's sole surviving son. Forcible conscription to fill vacancies in regular or active militia units could begin thirty days after the issuance of a call for volunteers. The advantages of volunteering included higher pay and a shorter maximum term of enlistment—eight as opposed to sixteen years—than accorded to conscripts. Local military command-ers had wide discretion in accepting volunteers and applying the con-scription law; they filled the ranks of their units with men who were very poor, unemployed, or who lacked the personal or family connec-tions necessary to avoid the draft. As soldiers, their social status was of the lowest order of free persons; their pay was meager and their living and working conditions were harsh, little better than those of slaves.[40] But in the context of the times, the conditions and recruitment prac-tices of the Brazilian army were not unusual; they were hardly worse than those of the British navy.

The Brazilian army did have some pampered regular units: the emperor's Guard Battalion and four battalions of foreign mercenaries. The first foreign units were organized in 1823 and manned by recruits sent from Europe by Dr. Schäffer. Apparently, in signing up agricul-tural colonists in Germany, Schäffer neglected to inform some of the single men of the military obligation they incurred under Brazil's con-scription law. When they landed in Rio, those unmarried males whose passage had been paid by the Brazilian government were inducted into the army. Whether or not they were volunteers, all were treated as such: their pay was set well above that of native soldiers of comparable status, and they were housed in new barracks constructed at Vermelha Beach, at the foot of the Sugar Loaf. The length of their enlistment was not specified, although under Brazilian law they could be retained for eight years. Complaints about the uncertain length of service, alleged mistreatment of the immigrants in the Brazilian army, and Schäffer's misrepresentation of his mission as a military recruiter gave Brazil a bad name in Germany, where a number of states banned the solicitation of colonists by Brazilian agents and forbade the emigration of their citizens to Dom Pedro's empire.[41] This reaction virtually doomed the emperor's program for populating Brazil with hardworking foreigners who would demonstrate to the natives the superiority of free labor over slavery.

In the Brazilian army, the hoped-for salutary effects of the foreign presence were not evident. Native troops resented the preferential treatment given the foreigners, and fights between members of the two contingents became fairly frequent on the streets of Rio. The German soldiers, most of whom were Lutherans, tended to deprecate the Catholic religion and treat all Brazilians with contempt. Their officers also were mostly foreign—Italian, Danish, Scottish, and Irish, as well as German—and often shared the prejudices of the troops. Each battalion, however, had at least one Luso-Brazilian officer, a major, whose job was to ensure that the mercenaries remained loyal to Brazil and to the emperor. These officers were quite sensitive to indications of disrespect for themselves or their country by the hired warriors. The emperor also kept a close watch on the mercenaries, and sometimes spent whole days overseeing their training at Vermelha Beach. European officers were impressed by Dom Pedro's military knowledge and dexterity in performing the manual of arms, but were repelled by what they regarded as the emperor's excessive familiarity and lack of shame: he defecated in view of the troops and called his mother a "bitch."[42]

Dom Pedro's war plans for 1826 called for employing the Brazilian navy to sustain General Lecor at Montevideo, to interdict enemy supply lines across the Uruguay River and the Plata Estuary, and to cut off Argentine commerce with the outside world by blockading Buenos Aires, the republic's only ocean port. In the meantime, the Brazilian army would begin concentrating thousands of soldiers, including one 800-man German battalion, at Livramento on the border between Uruguay and Rio Grande do Sul to block any enemy movement to the north and to prepare for a sweep south into the rebel province. For a military undertaking of this magnitude, the emperor needed to be sure that he had his country behind him. He could not much longer delay the convening of the first parliament, which was finally scheduled to meet on 3 May 1826. Prior to this, Dom Pedro planned to make a visit to Bahia to sound out opinion and bolster his partisans in that vital province, which was presided over by the Viscount Queluz, ex–Minister of the Empire João Severiano. The emperor's stay in Bahia, 27 February–19 March, served its purpose of rallying the Bahians behind the war effort in the South,[43] but Dom Pedro's behavior on the trip there provided grist for Brazilian gossip mills for years to come, and contributed to undermining his rule.

The trip to Bahia was not like the hard-riding, sleeping-on-the-ground excursions that Dom Pedro made to Minas Gerais and São Paulo in 1822. This time the monarch was transported in imperial luxury aboard the flagship of the Brazilian navy, the *Pedro Primeiro*, along with his wife, his oldest daughter, his mistress, and seventy-eight other invited guests. The voyagers were not expected to subsist on Dom Pedro's usual fare of rice and fatback: before setting sail on 3 February 1826 the *Pedro Primeiro* was stocked with 800 chickens, 300 pullets, 200 ducks, 50 doves, 30 capons, 20 turkeys, 260 dozen eggs, 30 sheep, 15 lambs, 6 milk goats, 1,000 oranges, 600 lemons, and ample supplies of coffee, tea, chocolate, jelly, jam, biscuits, cake, raisins, cheese, liquor, and wine—including four cases of Margaux and six of Médoc. During the twenty-four-day voyage, Dona Leopoldina consumed her share of the provisions: "She dined alone, and often, because she was a lady and one of her greatest pleasures was eating." While the empress was served in her stateroom, the emperor would eat in the dining room with Dona Maria da Glória, a vivacious blond child of seven years, seated on his right, and Domitila on his left. Dom Pedro, his daughter, and his mistress also were seen strolling together about the ship and lounging on the quarterdeck. And the emperor was heard to address Domitila by her pet name, "Titília." These displays humiliated Dona Leopoldina, who would retire early to her stateroom to avoid them. After they landed in Bahia, Domitila stayed close to her lover; when the imperial family went on carriage rides in the countryside, Dom Pedro would drive the horses with Dona Leopoldina at his side, and Domitila and Dona Maria da Glória were seated behind them. Bahian officials treated Domitila as if she, not Dona Leopoldina, "were the true sovereign." The accommodations provided the imperial mistress at the governor's palace were equal, if not superior, to those assigned to the empress.[44]

The imperial party returned to Rio on 1 April with Dom Pedro and Domitila intending to continue their open relationship; a week later Domitila signed a contract to buy a house across the road from the main entrance to the imperial palace at Boa Vista. While Domitila was involved in moving her household to Boa Vista, Dom Pedro received the shocking news, on 24 April, of the death of his father — the king was fifty-nine years old and not known to be in bad health. But there was little time for grief, because with the death notice came the news that Dom Pedro had been proclaimed king of Portugal, thus reuniting Brazil with the mother country under the same monarch — a situation presumably prohibited by Brazil's constitution, and certain not to be tolerated by the Brazilian parliament that was scheduled to convene in ten days. Dom Pedro knew he had to divest himself of the Portuguese crown in order to keep the Brazilian one; but he could not pass up the opportunity to strike a blow for liberty in Portugal by giving the old country both a constitution and a constitutional monarch: his daughter, Dona Maria da Glória. But there was no certainty that Portugal would accept Dom Pedro's gifts. He had been acclaimed Dom Pedro IV, king of Portugal, by a regency headed by his sister, Dona Isabel Maria, in accordance with the wishes of his late father. If Dom Pedro abdicated the Portuguese throne, his legitimate successor would not be his daughter, but his infant son, whom the emperor was reserving for the Brazilian monarchy. There was likely to be significant resistance in Portugal, both to Dona Maria da Glória and to a constitution, from the absolutist followers of Dona Carlota and Dom Miguel, the rightful heir to the Portuguese throne if all the Brazilian Braganças were disqualified.[45]

To ensure acceptance of Dona Maria da Glória, Dom Pedro felt he had to make a dynastic deal with Dom Miguel, and issue to Portugal a constitution less liberal than Brazil's. Although the Brazilian emperor had not communicated directly with his brother since the Abrilada, he had reports from his ambassador in Vienna that indicated that Dom Miguel was sincerely sorry that he had tried to overthrow their father, and would welcome an opportunity to restore harmony in the family and, at the same time, improve his own claim to the throne. So Dom Pedro updated his 1822 offer: if Dom Miguel would promise to marry his brother's daughter and swear to his constitution, he could rule Portugal as regent during his fiancée's minority, and jointly with her as king after their wedding. Thus he could be assured that his descendants would succeed to the Portuguese throne thereafter. The constitution would be sent to Vienna with the marriage contract; Dom Pedro's abdication of the Portuguese throne would be announced the day before the Brazilian General Assembly convened on 3 May, though it would not take effect until after Dom Miguel signed the two documents.[46]

Faced with the May deadline, Dom Pedro and the Chalaça once again went to work devising a constitution, a job they would complete in less than five days, on 29 April. This time, they had their own Brazilian charter to use as a model; Chalaça went through one printed copy striking out "empire" and "Brazil" and substituting "kingdom" and "Portugal" while Dom Pedro pondered more involved changes. Essentially, the changes amounted to giving a role in government to the hereditary nobility in the Portuguese constitution, and to assigning more power to the crown and less to the legislature than in the Brazilian charter. In Portugal, the monarch's veto of legislation would be absolute, instead of suspensory, as in Brazil. In the New World, where a true hereditary nobility did not exist, it was feasible for senators to be nominated by electors and appointed for life by the crown. But in Portugal it was necessary, Dom Pedro concluded, to allocate one house of parliament to the nobility, as in England; he apparently felt that the lords would be less dangerous to the new regime as legislators than as conspirators. As a liberal, Dom Pedro recognized the inevitability and desirability of change; he had reason to believe that political institutions would evolve toward more freedom if provided the proper framework for constitutional order. This he tried to do for Portugal with the constitution of 1826, copies of which were dispatched in May to Lisbon and to Vienna, where in October Dom Miguel swore allegiance to it and accepted the marriage contract. Under the constitution he could not become regent until he attained the age of twenty-five the following October. In the meantime, Dona Isabel Maria would continue as regent of Portugal.[47]

In Brazil, the convening of the General Assembly on 3 May 1826 marked the end of thirty months of quasi-autocratic rule by the nation's "constitutional emperor and perpetual defender." Although the constitution of 1824 theoretically was in effect during most of the period, it was officially suspended in several provinces at various times; revolts were suppressed, accused rebels tried by special tribunals and executed, without benefit of the judicial procedure so meticulously spelled out in the constitution. Even in the imperial capital the constitution was, at best, imperfectly observed. Freedom of the press disappeared in Rio; the pro-Andrada newspapers folded as their patrons were arrested and deported at the end of 1823; the *Malagueta* ceased publication in July 1824, when its editor found it advisable to retire temporarily from journalism, leaving only the official press to inform Carioca readers until 1826. Early that year a recently arrived Frenchman, a "citizen of the world," published a pamphlet critical of Brazil's treaty of recognition with Portugal; he was deported in April in Dom Pedro's last serious transgression against freedom of the press. But during the generally illiberal period, elections were held that probably were as open and honest as those conducted in most districts or burroughs of the United States or Great Britain at the time. Certainly some outspoken critics of the emperor's government were elected to the Chamber of Deputies, including the editor of the defunct *Malagueta*. In 1826 with the convening of the General Assembly, a new independent newspaper, the *Astréa* (Star of Justice), appeared in Rio, and soon would be joined by many more—including a revived *Malagueta*. A vigorous free press would characterize the remaining five years of Dom Pedro's reign as emperor of Brazil.[48]

The two houses of the Brazilian parliament, after separate organizing sessions, assembled in a joint meeting on 6 May 1826 in the Senate building, formerly the count of Arcos's mansion on the Campo de Santana, to hear the emperor's speech from the throne. The ritual was similar to that of the opening of the Constituent Assembly three years before. In his speech Dom Pedro pointedly reminded the legislators of the fate of that earlier body, and then presented his assessment of the state of the empire in mid-1826. Peace and order had been restored in all the provinces except Uruguay, where "ungrateful men" were sustained in arms by the Argentine government, with which Brazil was at war. The "national honor" demanded that Uruguay be preserved as a province of the empire. Dom Pedro then recounted the diplomatic accomplishments of his government in securing recognition from Portugal and other nations, and spoke of his abdication of the Portuguese throne as a sacrifice that he had made for Brazil. He asked the legislators to give particular attention to "the education of

193

the youth of both sexes" and to public finances, as well as to the revision of existing laws to bring them in line with the constitution.[49]

In the area of education, the General Assembly authorized the creation of two national law schools, one in São Paulo and one in Pernambuco. The war effort in Uruguay evoked little enthusiasm. Members of the Chamber of Deputies complained bitterly of the grave social and economic consequences of conscription in their provinces, and the harsh treatment received by recruits; one deputy estimated that nearly 1,000 recruits had died in transit to the war zone. Aside from being a personal calamity for many of the 26,000 men in the army, and for their families, the war portended disaster for imperial finances. With Brazil undertaking to pay two million pounds sterling to Portugal and Britain—a fact that was received with shock and consternation by members of the Chamber of Deputies when it was revealed to them during the 1826 session—the nation could ill afford the army buildup or the cost of maintaining some sixty warships on blockade station off Buenos Aires. Although English bankers were willing to lend money to the empire, their price was high. Felisberto Caldeira Brant Pontes in 1824 had negotiated Brazil's first foreign loan: 3,686,200 pounds sterling from Nathan Rothschild and other London bankers at 5 percent annual interest and an initial discount of 18.33 percent. The proceeds of this loan were expended by 1826 and the treasury had resorted to an issue of copper coins with a nominal value of 2,400 contos, four times their intrinsic worth. With gold and silver driven from circulation in accordance with Gresham's Law, the treasury borrowed 4,000 contos from the insolvent Bank of Brazil and added the inconvertible bank notes to the money supply.[50]

Members of the Chamber of Deputies sought to draft legislation to regulate the currency and establish a budgetary system, but they got little help from Dom Pedro's finance minister. The emperor recognized the need for such laws, but was reluctant to concede to the deputies the right to summon his ministers to appear before them. None of his ministers in 1826 were deputies—most were Senators —and the emperor wanted to avoid any appearance of ministerial responsibility to the lower house. Eventually, however, Dom Pedro came to realize that legislative efficiency required that his department heads cooperate readily with the Chamber of Deputies. This was pointed out by Bernardo Pereira de Vasconcelos, deputy from Minas Gerais, in offering a bill for "ministerial responsibility." Vasconcelos said he was not trying to establish a system like that of Britain, where the cabinet was the agent of the House of Commons; in Brazil, the ministers should remain responsible to the emperor, the mineiro conceded in 1826, but they also should be required to respond to requests for information or testimony by the Chamber of Deputies, unless they could formally state compelling reasons for not doing so. Dom Pedro accepted this definition of ministerial responsibility and signed Vasconcelos's bill into law in 1827, after the General Assembly had reached the end of its constitutionally prescribed four-month session in 1826 without approving a budget or enacting much legislation in other areas of concern to the emperor.[51]

By the end of the 1826 session Bernardo Pereira de Vasconcelos had emerged as the leading figure of the Chamber of Deputies. Organized political parties did not exist, but Vasconcelos, eloquent advocate of parliamentary power and staunch defender of slaveholding interests, came to speak for the majority in the Chamber of Deputies. The question of the slave trade seemed to preoccupy most deputies; although many were pleased with the absence of extraterritorial concessions to the British in the Stuart treaties of 1825, they were distressed that the emperor had agreed to halt all importation of slaves within four years of ratification. When the news arrived during the 1826 session that Britain had definitely rejected the treaties, Vasconcelos and his colleagues were given new hope. Bills were introduced in the Chamber of Deputies calling for the continuation of the slave trade for six to fourteen more years, but were not brought to a vote before the recess.[52]

The General Assembly adjourned in September, and the next month, a British emissary arrived in Rio to reopen negotiations on commercial relations and the slave trade. The commercial question, which included the issue of extraterritoriality, was separated from that of the slave trade, which the new British minister plenipotentiary, Robert Gordon, decided to take up first, despite his instructions to the contrary. Gordon sensed that long and hard negotiations would be required to overcome the resistance of Dom Pedro's government to the granting of extraterritorial privileges to British subjects, but that they could reach an agreement on the slave trade rather quickly, especially now that the General Assembly was in recess. Negotiations began on 31 October; the emperor's representatives held out a while for British compensation for lost revenue from slave import duties, but dropped this demand and gave in to Gordon on all other points on 22 November.

The next day the treaty was signed and ratified by the emperor; it went into effect with ratification in London on 13 March 1827. It provided for the complete cessation of all commerce in slaves between Africa and Brazil within three years of ratification. At the end of that period the British navy would be empowered to search and seize in international waters Brazilian flag vessels suspected of slaving; accused slavers would be tried before mixed British-Brazilian tribunals to be established in Brazil and on British territory in Africa.[53]

When the Chamber of Deputies met for the 1827 session, it was presented with a *fait accompli*. The dominant proslavery faction, however, could not refrain from denouncing the action taken by the emperor's government to halt the inhuman traffic. The case against the slave-trade treaty was summed up by Raimundo José da Cunha Matos, deputy from Goiás. The treaty was "derogatory to the honor, interests, dignity, independence and sovereignty of the Brazilian nation," according to Cunha Matos, because, "(1) It strikes at the fundamental law of the Brazilian Empire. . . . (2) Injures national commerce enormously. . . . (3) Ruins the principal agriculture vital to the existence of the people. . . . (4) Annihilates navigation. . . . (5) Delivers a cruel blow to the revenues of the state. . . . (6) Because it is premature" and "(7) Finally, because it is extemporaneous." Elaborating on the last point, Cunha Matos claimed that the treaty infringed on the right of the General Assembly to legislate for Brazil, and made Brazilians subject to British courts and judges, "incompetent justices and tribunals that none of us are familiar with." He concluded with the hoary proposition that Christians who bought slaves actually "rescued" them from death or some fate worse than slavery. (Apologists over the centuries have mentioned cannibalism, idolatry, homosexuality, and other horrors.) Ending the slave trade, according to Cunha Matos, would mean "depriving . . . Brazilians of the liberty to rescue or deal in black slaves" in African ports.[54] The emperor and his critics in the Chamber of Deputies had rather different conceptions of the word "liberty."

Dom Pedro's second child by Domitila, a boy, died in Rio while the emperor and his mistress were visiting Bahia. The surviving child of the illicit union, Isabel, celebrated her second birthday on 23 May 1826, and in honor of the occasion the emperor formally recognized her as his daughter and raised her to the highest rank in the Brazilian nobility, giving her the title "duchess of Goiás" and decreeing that she

Domitila de Castro, Marchioness of Santos
Painting attributed to Francisco Pedro do Amaral, Museu Histórico
Nacional, Rio de Janeiro

Dom Pedro I, Emperor of Brazil: Painting by Manuel de Araújo
Porto-Alegre
From Octávio Tarquínio de Sousa, *A vida de Dom Pedro I* (Rio de
Janeiro, 1972).
Reprinted by permission of Livraria José Olympio Editora S. A.

be addressed as "Your Highness." A gala birthday party for the duchess was held at her mother's home and was attended by the emperor and various nobles of the realm. The official press praised the monarch for his "honesty" in revealing that he was "human," while independent journalists ignored the story to concentrate on the more weighty matters under discussion in the General Assembly. The recognition of the young duchess and her frequent appearances at Boa Vista palace greatly upset Dona Leopoldina: "I can endure anything," the empress confided to some attendants, "except seeing that little girl on the same level with my children; and I tremble with anger when I see her; it is the greatest of sacrifices for me to receive her." But Dona Leopoldina continued to suppress her anger and make sacrifices, receiving both the duchess and her mother with smiles and kisses.[55]

Financial problems added to the distress of the empress, as her normally frugal husband spent an ever larger share of their income on the upkeep of his mistress. The Chamber of Deputies, though unable to decide on a national budget, agreed to an increase in the emperor's annual stipend from 200 to 400 contos; but the inflation resulting from the debasement of the currency cancelled out much of the raise, and the real costs of the emperor's affair were rising. Domitila, determined never to return to a threadbare middle-class existence, was accumulating assets as insurance against the uncertainties of the future. Her lover, no less businesslike, squeezed the palace budget—leaving his kind-hearted wife almost nothing to distribute to the needy people who regularly sought her assistance—and he strove to put the imperial estate at Santa Cruz on a paying basis. Slaves whom Dom Pedro wanted to free were kept working in his cane fields, grinding mill, and distillery, producing cachaça for several retail outlets in Rio that were owned by the emperor. Dom Pedro apparently did not sell titles of nobility or other honors, but some honorees recommended by Domitila almost certainly had secured her endorsement in exchange for money. Domitila herself, already a viscountess, was among twenty-three marquises and marchionesses created on 12 October 1826. Her sister, Maria Bendita, and Maria Bendita's husband became the baron and baroness of Sorocaba, and her father, Colonel João, became Viscount Castro. Marquisates were handed out to most cabinet ministers and councillors of state, including João Severiano, who was raised from viscount to marquis of Queluz. Another viscount who rose a notch in the nobility in 1826 was Felisberto Caldeira Brant Pontes, now the marquis of Barbacena. General Brant also was named by Dom Pedro to replace General Lecor, Viscount Laguna, as commander-in-chief of imperial forces in the Uruguayan war.[56]

The war was not going well. Lecor in Montevideo in 1826 faced a situation far different from that of ten years before, when he commanded an army of mostly Portuguese regulars, veterans of the Peninsular Campaign, against a smaller force of native gauchos whom the government in Buenos Aires wanted eliminated as much as he did. Lecor no longer had an army of regulars: most of the Portuguese veterans had gone home in 1823 and 1824, and Lecor's Brazilian garrison in Montevideo was of indifferent quality. Furthermore, his forces were vastly outnumbered by the enemy in the countryside, who had the active support of the Argentine republic. The buildup at Livramento continued through the first half of 1826, but Lecor could make little use of this mostly conscript force. Their morale plunged with the onset of winter in June, as hungry, shoeless, cotton-clad Pernambucans and Bahians shivered in weather so cold that, to their amazement and despair, water turned solid. Their comrades in the Brazilian navy, many of whom were foreigners, were better prepared to withstand the southern winter, but the vessels off Buenos Aires were insufficient to establish an effective blockade. The European powers and the United States refused to recognize the blockade, and the seizure of their merchantmen by Brazilian warships produced angry protests and threats of armed intervention. To make matters worse, the Argentine government issued letters of marque to foreign privateers, who began ravaging Brazilian shipping from Maranhão to Rio Grande do Sul in "beautiful Baltimore built schooners, and brigs from one to twelve guns, manned by adventurers of all nations."[57] The war threatened to do as much damage to the commerce of Brazil as to that of Argentina. Dom Pedro was determined to end the conflict with an offensive in the summer of 1826–27; the emperor would go to Rio Grande do Sul to raise the morale of the troops, who were to be led into battle by General Brant, the marquis of Barbacena—a new commander who could not be blamed for past mismanagement and the failure to provide the soldiers with adequate food, clothing, and supplies for the winter in Livramento. The marquis of Barbacena was a lieutenant general of the empire, planter, slavocrat, entrepreneur, diplomat, financier, and irrepressible commentator on military affairs; he had, however, never been in a war.

The marquis left Rio for the front on 3 November 1826, but the emperor did not leave the capital city until near the end of the month. Dom Pedro was occupied with the slave-trade negotiations and with personal problems. At the beginning of the month his good friend Colonel João, Viscount Castro, lay dying, and the emperor was almost constantly at his bedside, for six days and nights, until the old soldier expired on 2 November. Returning to the palace looking bedraggled and mournful, Dom Pedro finally provoked an outburst of anger from his long-suffering wife, who rebuked him for neglecting her and his family to attend to an uneducated old man who had contributed to her humiliation. Heated words were exchanged, apparently in the presence of the late viscount's daughter, Domitila, and the empress was severely wounded. She was in the third month of a difficult pregnancy, and was already afflicted by a variety of physical ailments and in a state of deep depression. Insult was added to injury as Dom Pedro charged Dona Leopoldina with spending too much on food and reduced by half the palace kitchen budget; the emperor's well-nourished mistress would suffer no such indignities. In her despair, Dona Leopoldina considered leaving the palace for a convent and living there until her father could send a ship to take her back to Europe. But she still loved her husband and could not leave him. She could forgive him, but not the "monstrous seductress" who, she informed her sister, was the cause of her being "reduced to a state of the worst slavery and totally forgotten by my adored Pedro."[58] On the night before his departure for Rio Grande do Sul, which he postponed for three days due to his concern for her health, Dona Leopoldina gave Dom Pedro a ring with two small diamonds and the inscription, inside the band, of their names on two hearts. She wept as she showed it to him. "I'm dying," she said. "When you return from Rio Grande, I'll no longer be here. Those who are separated in life will be united after death." He embraced her and they both cried. Then she said, "May everyone forgive you, and no one bear you any rancor."[59]

Dom Pedro sailed from Rio on 24 November aboard the *Pedro Primeiro*, which, along with nine other warships and transports, was carrying to the war zone the 800 officers and men of the mercenary Twenty-seventh Light Infantry Battalion. After five days at sea the emperor disembarked in Santa Catarina, and before departing overland for Rio Grande do Sul, sent two almost identical letters back to Rio: one to Dona Leopoldina and one to Domitila. They recounted the same events of the voyage in the same words. One recipient, the marchioness, was addressed as "my dear girl and friend of my heart," and the other was "my dear wife of my heart." The writer had "severe heartaches" for one, Dona Leopoldina, while absence from the other tore apart his heart. But the passion, in closing, was exclusively Domitila's: "I'm yours no matter what, whether it's in heaven or hell or I don't know where."[60] Dom Pedro spent most of the next week in the saddle, riding with the Chalaça, a few other companions, and a military escort, from São José, on the coast of Santa Catarina, to Porto Alegre, the capital of Rio Grande do Sul, a distance of more than 400 kilometers. When he arrived in Porto Alegre at dusk on 7 December, the emperor soon learned that the condition of the Imperial Army and militia in the province was far worse than he had been led to believe. He reacted with his customary energy: he issued a flurry of orders, fired reputed grafters and incompetents, fraternized with the troops, and generally shook up military and civilian administration. The marquis of Barbacena, himself only recently arrived in Rio Grande do Sul, had not expected Dom Pedro to appear there so soon. He assured the emperor that he was working diligently to clean up the mess and soon would have the army in shape to take the offensive against the Uruguayans and Argentines, who at the time were raiding deep into Rio Grande do Sul and threatening to overrun the entire province west of Livramento. In fact, the efforts of Barbacena and the emperor did much to lift morale in the province, and more *riograndenses* volunteered for the army and fewer deserted.[61]

Dom Pedro's visit to the war zone was cut short by news of the death of Dona Leopoldina. The letters reached him at the town of Rio Grande. "My pen, even, refuses to write the words," one from Friar Arrábida began. "The virtuous Empress Leopoldina is no longer of this world!" Other letters and the messenger informed the shaken Dom Pedro of the sequence of events leading to the death of his wife. Suffering headaches and rheumatic pains following her husband's departure on 24 November, the empress cancelled court appearances for the first two days in December, and, on the third, miscarried a male fetus. In the week that followed she suffered violent convulsions alternating with "nervous attacks," and despite the best efforts of her physicians to save her—they prescribed "dusting powders, massages, leeches, baths, laxatives, antispasmodics, emetics"[62]—she died at 10:15 on the morning of 11 December. The council of ministers offered the emperor their condolences, and in a report dated the day of his wife's death, went on to say that they felt it their duty "to communicate to Your Imperial Majesty that the empress . . . in her delirium, pronouncing words that indicated the reasons for her distress, left the impression that some moral causes occupied her imagination, and that objects of distaste and resentment had largely taken over her spirit and, having reached the knowledge of the public, from which nothing can be concealed in such circumstances, incited the public to much backbiting with threats of vengeance." The object of the crowd's wrath was presumably Domitila, who complained in a letter to her lover of the treatment she had received from the ministers and from Friar Arrábida, who barred her from entering Dona Leopoldina's bedchamber to pay her respects to the dying empress.[63]

The emperor returned quickly to Santa Catarina, boarded the *Pedro Primeiro*, and after an exasperating eleven-day voyage of unfavorable winds and short rations, arrived in Rio on 15 January 1827. He grieved for Dona Leopoldina, but was also angry with his ministers and Friar Arrábida for their attitude toward Domitila. The friar and most of the ministers, headed by the stern Vilela Barbosa, marquis of Paranaguá, stood their ground when confronted by the emperor: his affair with the marchioness was a grave error and should be terminated for the good of the country. The enraged monarch proceeded to fire four of his six ministers, retaining only the minister of the empire, José Feliciano Fernandes Pinheiro, Viscount São Leopoldo; and the sole Portuguese-born member of the cabinet, João Vieira de Carvalho, count of Lajes, the minister of war—who, in view of the mess in which Dom Pedro found the army in Rio Grande do Sul, was the one who truly deserved to be dismissed. In this complete reversal of good sense, symptomatic of the emperor's passion for Domitila, even the faithful Friar Arrábida was banished from the palace. But, as the ill-advised affair continued, that indispensable cleric was soon reinstated as the emperor's confessor. And the dismissed ministers were replaced by others of comparable ability, including João Severiano, marquis of Queluz, who returned to the cabinet in the double role of minister of foreign affairs and of finance.[64]

The new cabinet was put to the test by the rapid march of events in the South. The Argentine squadron, under the Irish Admiral William Brown, came out of Buenos Aires and destroyed the Brazilian naval detachment on the lower Uruguay River on 10 February. Ten days later General Brant, the marquis of Barbacena, led his revitalized Brazilian army of 6,000 men into an Argentine ambush at Ituzaingó in Rio Grande do Sul. The imperial cavalry disintegrated under the gaucho attack, but the square of German infantry held, and Barbacena was able to regroup his forces and withdraw toward Porto Alegre. The Argentines, who had suffered almost as many casualties as the Brazilians, did not pursue; instead they returned to Uruguay, which allowed Barbacena to claim that although he had not won the battle, he had not lost it. Four weeks later Brazil suffered an incontestable defeat when an Imperial Navy expedition was totally destroyed in Argentine Patagonia, near the mouth of the Río Negro, in an attack on a privateer base. The corsairs would continue to ravage Brazilian commerce in the South Atlantic. But when Admiral Brown led the regular Argentine navy into deep water, he was decisively defeated on 8 April by the Brazilian division of Commodore James Norton and was driven back to Buenos Aires. As the war intensified and losses mounted on both sides, Great Britain urged the belligerents to negotiate an end to the conflict. President Rivadavia, faced with a federalist revolt in the Argentine provinces, decided to try to make peace with Brazil, and on 19 April he dispatched an envoy to Rio on a British warship.[65]

Argentine Minister Plenipotentiary Manuel García was instructed to negotiate on the basis of Uruguayan independence: both Brazil and Argentina would give up their claims to the province, which would become an independent republic. But Dom Pedro and the marquis of Queluz rejected the compromise and García felt that he had no choice but to accept peace on Brazilian terms. The treaty he signed on 24 May recognized Uruguay as an integral part of the Brazilian empire, provided for the immediate withdrawal of all Argentine troops from the province, and provided for the payment of an indemnity to Brazil for the damage done to its commerce by privateers. President Rivadavia could not accept such a one-sided treaty, and the fact that his agent had signed it contributed to the overthrow of his centralist regime shortly afterward. The Argentine republic reverted to a loose confederation of provinces, and the war dragged on for another year in Uruguay, where the patriot army of Lavalleja and Rivera was divided on the question of independence or integration into the United Provinces of La Plata. The disarray among the enemy seemed to bode well for the Fabian tactics of General Lecor, Viscount Laguna, who was reinstated as supreme commander in southern Brazil after Barbacena's debacle at

Ituzaingó. Even if Lecor were to fail to defeat Lavalleja in battle, he should be able to bribe him into submission to the empire, Dom Pedro's ministers reasoned, especially now that the Uruguayan's patron had disappeared from the scene in Buenos Aires.[66]

But the emperor's efforts to retain Uruguay received little support in the General Assembly, which convened for its second session in May 1827. The plantation, slaveholding interests that controlled the Chamber of Deputies were not inclined to fight for Uruguay, a land unsuited for the cultivation of sugarcane or coffee, and where slaves were few. The retention of Uruguay by the empire presented a threat to their vital interests: the danger was that the southernmost province, like the northernmost states of the United States, would provide a geographical focus of economic and political power hostile to slavery. The planters of the Rio–São Paulo–Minas Gerais area were bound more firmly than ever to the forced-labor system; slave imports to Rio soared in tandem with coffee exports from the same port. Annual coffee shipments from Rio rose from 13,286 metric tonnes in 1825 to 18,869 in 1826; by 1828 they would be 26,703 tonnes. Meanwhile, between 1825 and 1828 annual slave imports to Rio increased from 26,254 to 43,555. The wartime privateering had not greatly affected the export of coffee, most of which was hauled in foreign bottoms, nor the import of slaves, for the corsairs did not consider the perishable human cargoes attractive prizes. But the British navy was going to target for seizure every slave shipment bound for Brazil at the end of the three-year period specified in the slave-trade treaty. The proslavery majority in the Chamber of Deputies was furious at the emperor's government for not negotiating a longer grace period. João Severiano, the marquis of Queluz—native of Minas Gerais, magistrate expelled from Rio as an ultra-liberal in the time of Dom João, and author of an 1821 pamphlet condemning the slave trade—was called upon as the emperor's foreign minister to defend the government before the Chamber of Deputies; he was unconvincing in arguing that Brazil had been "forced" to give in to Britain's demand for the three-year period.[67]

The marquis of Queluz had not been in the cabinet when the slave-trade agreement was made in Rio in 1826, but as foreign minister in 1827 he had been directly involved in negotiations for a commercial treaty, and had experienced British pressure at first hand. These negotiations finally ended with the signing of a treaty on 18 August 1827. The major sticking point was the issue of extraterritoriality; in the end,

British subjects got their special courts in Brazil, but the treaty recognized that the arrangement was temporary, and theoretically could be terminated before the end of the seventeen-year term of the treaty. Since the Brazilian parliament had not yet enacted legislation setting up a system of courts in accordance with the constitution, Dom Pedro had some excuse for making the concession. The treaty specifically acknowledged that the constitution of the empire of Brazil had "abolished all special jurisdictions" and that extraterritoriality for British subjects should continue "only until some satisfactory substitute" should be "established, capable of providing, in an equal degree, for the protection of the persons and property of His [Britannic] Majesty's subjects." Members of the Chamber of Deputies denounced this provision as heartily as they had the one in the slave-trade treaty that subjected Brazilians accused of slaving to tribunals that included British judges.[68] Men who were eager to abandon to the Argentine confederation a province that their ancestors had colonized in 1680 and had fertilized with their blood for nearly a century and a half, were nevertheless not indisposed to take the emperor to task for surrendering Brazilian rights to foreigners.

Dom Pedro had various reasons for giving in, however reluctantly, to the British demand for extraterritoriality. One such reason had little to do with the interests of Brazil: he needed continued British support for the constitutional regime he had proclaimed for Portugal, and for the rights of his daughter, Dona Maria da Glória, as queen. Early in 1827 British troops had landed in Portugal at his request to prop up the constitutionalist regime and discourage the absolutists, whose favorite, Dom Miguel, had still not appeared in Rio to claim the fiancée he had accepted in October 1826. A withdrawal of British troops from Portugal or any other sign of a weakening of Britain's commitment to the Portuguese constitution and queen could only encourage Dom Miguel to welsh on his deal with Dom Pedro and cast his lot with those who wanted him to be their absolute monarch. A wary Dom Pedro made a show of confidence in Dom Miguel in July 1827 by officially recognizing him as regent of Portugal, although he was still in Vienna. Dom Pedro needed British help to keep his brother in line in Portugal, but he also wanted Britain's good offices for a negotiated peace between Brazil and the Argentine confederation, or failing that, London's acquiescence to his recruitment in Ireland of mercenaries with which to continue the war. With immigration from

Germany virtually halted due to bad publicity and German government action, Ireland seemed to be Brazil's most promising source of colonists and soldiers. Shortly after learning of Buenos Aires's rejection of the peace treaty signed in Rio, Dom Pedro sent Colonel William Cotter to Ireland "for the purpose of engaging colonists on the same principles as those on which the Germans, who had been drafted into the army, had already been engaged."[69]

The recruiting practices of Colonel Cotter, a native Irishman, were similar to those used in Germany by the unscrupulous Dr. Schäffer. Advertisements in Irish newspapers promised free passage to Brazil for able-bodied men and their families, plus free clothes, guaranteed wages, and forty-acre grants of land. Apparently nothing was said in the advertisements about military service, but at least some of the males who signed up did so realizing that they had acquired an obligation to train as militiamen to defend their settlements, and others "whose idle habits led them to prefer a military life," freely volunteered for the army.[70] Brazilian newspapers and parliamentary deputies opposed to the Uruguayan war were fully aware of the military destination of the Irishmen, and they poisoned the atmosphere in Rio against the immigrants. In January 1828 about 2,400 arrived in Rio from southern Ireland, mostly from counties Waterford and Cork. "Mothers with their infants at the breast, young girls approaching womanhood, and athletic labourers in the prime of life," an Englishman recorded, "were all landed in a state of almost utter nudity." From the quays they were marched off to barracks on Barbonos Street, near the aqueduct, "amid the taunts of the populace, and the jeers of multitudes of negroes, shouting and clapping their hands at the unexpected apparition of the 'white slaves,' as they were pleased to denominate the unfortunate Irish."[71]

The housing and what little food and clothing was provided to the Irish on Barbonos Street fell far short of the promises made by Colonel Cotter. The immigrants complained about this, and about attempts to force all their men into the Brazilian army, to British Minister Robert Gordon. The minister—an "ill mannered and obstinate Scot," in Dom Pedro's view[72]—secured better provisions for his king's Irish subjects, together with the Brazilian government's acknowledgment that they were not subject to the military draft. Those who chose to volunteer received contracts specifying a four-year term of enlistment with pay considerably higher than that provided to the

Germans. Even so, fewer than 400 Irishmen were induced to enlist, not enough to form a separate battalion; most of them were assigned to the German Third Grenadiers, stationed at the Campo de Santana. There was considerable friction between the Irish and the Germans, but the main trouble was between Irishmen and Brazilians. Antigovernment newspapers fanned the flames of ethnic hatred, complaining about the bodies of drunken Irishmen littering the streets of Rio. Carioca blacks were encouraged to attack the Irish, who were not above provoking fights themselves. Gangs of off-duty Irish soldiers roamed the city at night beating up blacks and mulattoes, while knife-wielding capoeiras stalked the hated "white slaves" in darkened streets. In daylight, insults were traded that occasionally led to melees, as when an officer made the mistake of trying to march a detachment of unarmed Irishmen past the Carioca fountain, where the brawniest black water carriers congregated.[73]

It was among the Germans, however, that the spark was struck that set off the great mercenary mutiny of 1828. The 500-man Second Grenadier Battalion, almost exclusively German, was quartered in a converted monastery near the boat landing at São Cristóvão Beach, less than a kilometer from Boa Vista palace. On the morning of 9 June the troops were assembled to witness the punishment of a German soldier who had failed to salute the unit's disciplinary officer, a Brazilian major, the night before. The soldier, who was to receive 150 lashes, refused to take off his jacket, protested his innocence, and claimed that he had not recognized the officer, who was wearing civilian clothes at the time of the incident. This infuriated the major, who, from his horse, ordered the man bound to a stake and the number of lashes increased to 250. After 230 had been applied, the onlooking soldiers broke ranks and charged the mounted officer, threatening his life. The major managed to break away and gallop ahead of the pursuing mob to his beach house, where he disguised himself and escaped through a back window as the mutineers were battering down the front door. The enraged Germans smashed his furniture and totally wrecked his house, even tearing down the walls. Then they proceeded in a more-or-less orderly fashion to Boa Vista, where they respectfully laid their grievances before the emperor: the Germans wanted the major punished, assurances of better treatment for themselves, and written contracts like those given the Irish, which specified a four-year term of enlistment. Dom Pedro said he would consider their requests and give them an answer within eight days; in the meantime, they should go back to their barracks and obey their officers.[74]

The German soldiers returned to the old monastery at São Cristóvão, but instead of submitting to their officers, they beat them up—those they could lay their hands on—and elected their own leaders. Then they armed themselves and prepared for action. The next day was a standoff; the commanding general of the Rio military district appeared outside the old monastery to urge the mutineers to lay down their arms and resubmit to authority. On the morning of 11 June a party of fourteen German mutineers set out from São Cristóvão for Rio to capture their hated interim commander, a Brazilian major. They spotted him, but he eluded them and took refuge inside a Brazilian police station. When the Germans assaulted and overran the station, their quarry once again escaped on a fast horse. By this time the Germans had attracted the attention of the Irish, seventy or eighty of whom joined the fourteen mutineers from the Second Grenadiers in taking out their frustrations on the civilians of Rio. Terrified Cariocas fled the streets and barricaded themselves in their houses as the Germans and the Irish looted taverns and stores, got drunk on liberated wine and cachaça, and went on a rampage of robbery, vandalism, and murder. The enlisted men of the Third Grenadier Battalion at the Campo de Santana joined the mutiny that day, with the Irish taking the lead; they expelled Colonel Cotter and the rest of their officers, attacked a nearby post of the Brazilian police, whom they hated, and killed six policemen before turning their fury on the general population. Irish civilians, including women, joined the grenadiers in the bloody orgy in downtown Rio; they demolished more than fifty houses and killed or maimed many of the occupants. At Praia Vermelha, Colonel MacGregor managed to retain control of his Twenty-Eighth Light Infantry Battalion, which was composed of Irishmen and Germans shorter than the grenadiers, who were supposed to be six feet tall. Although some of his men took advantage of the situation to kill an unpopular Italian officer, MacGregor kept his battalion out of the general uprising. The men of the Twenty-Eighth were at best, however, neutralized; they were of no use in putting down the mutiny.[75]

Through the streets of Rio reverberated shouts of "Death to the Brazilians!" and "Death to the Portuguese!"—the mutineers being unable to distinguish between the two. The challenge was met by the emperor's Brazilian-born minister of war, Bento Barroso Pereira, who had replaced the Portuguese João Vieira de Carvalho seven months earlier in a move to appease the nativists. "Kill them all," the minister instructed his Brazilian troop commander. "Give no quarter to anyone; kill those foreigners."[76] But the Brazilian regular and militia forces immediately available were deemed inadequate for the task, so Barroso Pereira called for civilian volunteers and ordered the distribution of arms to all, including slaves. Rio blacks entered the fight with gusto; capoeiras, for the first time, practiced their art openly and with the approval of the authorities. A day and a night of combat left dozens of horribly mutilated bodies in the streets. The surviving Germans and Irish retreated to their barracks as marines from British and French warships in the harbor landed at the request of the emperor and secured the army arsenal and the artillery park between the Morro do Castelo and Point Calabouças, which freed Brazilian forces to pursue the mutineers. The barracks at the Campo de Santana was surrounded by Brazilians who offered the mercenaries the opportunity to surrender on 12 June; many did so, but others held out and the barracks had to be taken by assault. The scene was repeated the next day at São Cristóvão. These final actions took the lives of about 150 mercenaries and many more Brazilians. Captured mutineers suffered the taunts and insults of the Carioca populace, especially the blacks, as they were marched through the streets of Rio on their way to prison ships in the harbor.[77]

The mutiny of the mercenaries ruined Dom Pedro's plans for populating Brazil with immigrants from Ireland. At British Minister Gordon's insistence, 1,400 of the 2,400 Irish men, women, and children who had arrived in January were shipped back to Ireland in July, at the Brazilian government's expense. And the mutiny, which virtually destroyed two of what were supposed to be the best units of his army and closed the door to further recruitment in Brazil or abroad, dashed the emperor's hopes for victory in the war to retain Uruguay. The costly futility of that struggle was underscored in July when a French navy task force—a ship-of-the-line and two frigates—sailed into Rio harbor and demanded immediate restoration of all French vessels taken in the blockade of Buenos Aires, plus compensation for lost cargoes and other damages. Dom Pedro was in no position to wage war against France: he settled with the French on their terms. And he conceded the loss of Uruguay by concluding a peace treaty with the United Provinces of La Plata that recognized the contested province as an independent nation. The treaty was negotiated in Rio and ratified by the emperor on 28 August 1828. The Brazilian navy was withdrawn from the Río de la Plata and imperial troops from Montevideo shortly thereafter. The three-year war had cost Brazil more than 30 million dollars and about 8,000 men.[78]

The Brazilian army was reduced to fewer than 15,000 officers and men, half its former size, during the remaining three years of Dom Pedro's reign. The mercenaries were withdrawn from Rio after the mutiny and most of them were mustered out of the service in Santa Catarina or Rio Grande do Sul. The punishments they received were generally light. Dom Pedro allowed the execution of only one convicted mutineer, a young German from the Second Grenadiers, who died bravely before a firing squad at the São Cristóvão barracks. The emperor was concerned that the man, believed to be a Protestant, receive the ministrations of his faith in his last hour. There being no Lutheran pastor available, Dom Pedro dispatched an Anglican clergyman—the British legation chaplain—and a Catholic priest to the place of execution. The condemned man, however, accepted the services of neither; the Catholic priest "he dismissed . . . at once, telling him to go and reform his master, who more wanted it."[79] The emperor was, in fact, taking steps at that time to put his own life in order.

Dom Pedro's blatant affair with Domitila, the marchioness of Santos, was unrestrained even during the period of mourning for the late empress, who had been beloved by the people for her virtue and generosity. Well before the mutiny of the mercenaries, this affair had sent the emperor's popularity to an all-time low. The military and diplomatic reverses of 1827–28, ably exploited by proslavery elements in parliament and in the press, reduced it even further. During 1827 Dom Pedro decided to remarry, both to provide his children with a mother and to improve his standing with the people. But his reputation was not good among the royal families of Europe, and the chances of winning a suitable bride were slim—absolutely nonexistent as long as he maintained his liaison with the marchioness of Santos. Eventually his sense of duty to his empire, to his legitimate children, and to the memory of his late wife led him to break with Domitila. One night Domitila discovered him weeping and embracing Dona Leopoldina's portrait. In May 1828 the emperor explained to his mistress that reasons of state required that they part; he asked her to leave Rio before the end of June and to return to São Paulo. But she remained in her house across from the palace throughout June and July as well. Domitila could not believe that Dom Pedro would choose the empire over her, and she concluded that her sister, Maria Bendita, baroness of Sorocaba, had stolen her lover. On the night of 15 August a shot was fired at Maria Bendita's carriage; although it missed the baroness, one of the marchioness's servants was caught with the smoking gun. Dom Pedro ordered Domitila out of Rio without further delay and she was gone by the end of the month.[80]

7 Abdication

I will do everything for the people, but nothing by the people.
Dom Pedro I.

Brazilian history in the second quarter of the nineteenth century is essentially the economic fact of coffee and the social fact of slavery. The ascendant coffee economy breathed new life into the institution that had dominated Luso–Brazilian society since its inception in the mid–sixteenth century: slavery would continue to subjugate the great majority of Brazilians, in body or mind, until the middle of the nineteenth century. The liberalism that penetrated Brazilian culture early in the century did not alter this sad fact; indeed, the generous "ideas of the century" were appropriated by conservatives who twisted them and used them to preserve the slave society. Brazil's coffee planters were conservative men who chose old means to exploit the new opportunities that were thrust upon them after 1808 — when the colonial system suddenly collapsed, world markets beckoned, and the king appeared in their midst, distributing land grants and coffee seedlings from his Botanical Garden. Planter resistance to the new crop weakened as coffee pioneers flaunted impressive profits; and it evaporated in the 1820s as the old crop, sugar, was battered in world markets by Cuban competition.[1] Traditional production methods were adapted to the new crop; they required the maintenance of the forced-labor system, and the continuing importation of new slaves from Africa.

The slavocrats encountered little resistance in Brazilian society, which was conservative to the core. A few intellectuals who had studied abroad — like José Bonifácio and João Severiano, marquis of Queluz — wrote against slavery, but their publications on the subject, bearing foreign imprints, were not well received by the native intelligentsia. The man in the street was even less susceptible to liberal notions about free labor; if he was not a slaveowner, he aspired to be one. The Brazilian dream — shared by the most destitute of free persons, and sometimes realized — was to own a slave or two, whose labor could be hired out at a return sufficient to free the dreamer forever of the necessity of working. Labor conferred no dignity in Brazil's slave-oriented society; it was better to beg than to work. Even beggers owned slaves: to the suggestion from a French visitor that a panhandler sell his two slaves, the Brazilian curtly replied that he had asked the foreigner for money, not advice. Forcigners, including Portuguese, tended to be critical of Brazilian society, and this was fiercely resented by natives of all free classes. Brazilians referred disparagingly to their Lusitanian cousins as *marinheiros* ("sailors") as if plying the trade that Portugal taught to the world was somehow shameful. Few Brazilians were attracted to the seafaring life, which was why the ships of Dom Pedro's navy were manned mostly by foreigners; the call for naval volunteers in 1823 was answered in Rio by prospective seamen who insisted that they be accompanied during their enlistment by their personal slaves.[2]

Dom Pedro hoped to transform Brazilian society by offering alternatives to slave labor, and by demonstrating the material as well as the moral superiority of the liberal principles of free labor and individual enterprise. The emperor put his principles into practice by granting homesites and subsistence plots to the exslaves whom he freed on his estate at Santa Cruz. "Property rights," a French resident noted, "motivated the dedication of those new citizens, who undertook various types of useful activity" at the behest of their imperial patron.[3] Freedmen and European immigrants, Dom Pedro believed, could provide Brazil with the manpower and the inspiration it needed to break with the past and establish a progressive, innovative, truly liberal society. Like other liberals in hostile environments, the emperor tried to appeal to the self-interest of his audience, though the examples he set seemed to have been prompted as much by humanitarian impulses as by economic considerations. The existence of slavery in Rio Grande do Sul—a sparsely settled, temperate-zone province that he hoped to colonize with free immigrants—especially offended Dom Pedro, who managed to persuade local owners to free at least two of the slaves he encountered on his trip to the south in 1826–27.[4]

Wherever he went, the emperor affronted the values of the slavocracy. In Rio and Bahia, where the rich went about in sedan chairs and anyone who could afford two slaves was apt to be carried through the streets in a hammock slung under a pole, Dom Pedro rode on horseback or in a carriage drawn by a team of horses or mules that he drove himself. He would not permit his subjects to render him the traditional homage of pulling him in his carriage on special occasions.

("My blood is the same color as that of the Negroes," he said in refusing the honor at the time of the fico.[5]) He was not ashamed to work with his hands; in fact, he was proud of his skills as a wrangler, blacksmith, and cabinetmaker, and would have liked to have been a sailor. Believing that no person had the right to own another, the emperor had a plan for the gradual abolition of slavery,[6] but could not implement it because the liberal constitution he gave Brazil delegated all law-making power to the General Assembly, which came under the control of intransigent slavocrats. Using his treaty-making powers he was able to set the date for the termination of the African slave trade, but the enforcement of this commitment would depend on a Brazilian judicial system that, under the constitution, was to be devised by parliament. Other constitutional provisions that would affect the emperor's ability to promote social and economic change included the legislative branch's control over the raising of revenue and the appropriation of government funds, its power to set military and naval force levels, and its power to authorize or disallow the employment of foreigners in the Brazilian armed services.

Not long after the convening of the General Assembly in 1826, the outline of a conservative agenda began to emerge. The first order of business was to establish a judicial system in which the judges of the first instance would be selected by the local slaveholders, not appointed by the crown. To help them keep the servile population in a state of terrorized submission, the judges would need a criminal code that would provide harsh penalties for slave rebellion. The conservatives aimed to deprive the emperor of the means of enforcing the slave-trade treaty he had made with Great Britain: this included cutting military spending and reducing the size of the army and navy—especially by expelling the foreigners, who had no ties to the slavocracy. The conservatives would resist the emperor's plans to encourage immigration and promote economic diversification. But Brazil's slavocrats, like their counterparts in the southern United States, took some liberal positions: they favored low tariffs and the liquidation of the national bank, both measures that would serve the established agricultural export interests of the slavocracy by denying the central government the instruments for stimulating a rival finance-industrial capitalism. Planter-exporters opposed tariffs that inordinately raised the prices of the goods they consumed, and they feared the huge accumulation of capital in the monopolistic Bank of Brazil. Aside from being a major supplier of funds to a government the slavocrats distrusted, the bank was the country's principal source of private business credit.[7] The conservatives would not settle for merely cutting the ties between the bank and Dom Pedro's government, for the bank would retain the potential for financing development inimical to the established economic and social order; the bank had to be liquidated.

By 1827 Brazil's conservative slavocrats had formulated their legislative program and had chosen their leader: Bernardo Pereira de Vasconcelos. A lawyer trained in Portugal, Vasconcelos represented his native province, Minas Gerais, in the Chamber of Deputies. Vasconcelos's province was the empire's most populous and wealthiest—if its huge slave population were counted as both people and property. By the 1820s the surplus of slaves in Minas Gerais, which was left over from the mining era at the beginning of the century, had disappeared; both capital and servile labor were increasingly allocated to the production of coffee. The mineiro parliamentary delegation was the chamber's largest, including seventeen of the total of fewer than one hundred deputies; and its potential for serving its slavocratic constituency was boosted beyond the power of its numbers by the persuasive eloquence of Vasconcelos. He was only thirty-two in 1827, but he looked at least twelve years older. Short, "rather corpulent," he had a "sallow complexion, dark eyes, projecting underlip," and a "profusion of black hair curling about his face."[8]

Vasconcelos suffered from "a series of maladies, attributed by his enemies to profligate indulgence"—he apparently had syphilis —which gave him "the decrepid [sic] appearance and demeanor of a sexagenarian" while he was still in his thirties. "His skin withered, his eyes sank, his hair began to turn grey, his step lost its firmness, his respiration became impeded, and a spinal complaint . . . became to him a source of the most excruciating tortures." While he was "undergoing his premature wreck of the physical frame," Vasconcelos, a "crude and abrupt orator" in 1826, honed his forensic skills, and within two years "obtained a command of language, a facility of sarcasm, and a development of argumentative talent, unpossessed by any other member" of the chamber. "When, heated by enthusiasm, or roused by indignation, he gave vent to his emotions, his decrepid and curved figure rose like that of some presiding spirit to its full height; his eyes again became animated with all their pristine lustre, and every feature of his wrinkled and cadaverous countenance became as if it were for the instant illumined with renewed youth and intelligence."[9]

The ire of the great orator was aroused by suggestions like those made by Dom Pedro and José Bonifácio that slavery was a "cancer" that was consuming the moral fiber of Brazil. "It has not been demonstrated that slavery demoralizes a nation," Vasconcelos insisted. "A comparison of Brazil with nations who have not slaves, will put this beyond doubt." Vasconcelos defended Brazil's slavocracy by attacking its foreign critics, especially the British. Although he was gracious toward individual foreign visitors, his public position tended to be xenophobic and shortsighted. In the 1820s he opposed granting concessions to European companies to revive his province's decadent mining industry; Brazil, he believed, would suffer, not profit, from the infusion of foreign capital and technology.[9] Two decades later, when railroads were stretching out across Europe, North America, and Cuba, Vasconcelos vociferously opposed their introduction into Brazil; "rust will destroy them," he argued.[10]

Vasconcelos's conservatism dominated the first Brazilian parliament, but there were among the deputies some notable liberals —generous and progressive men who would welcome to Brazil new ideas, new technology, foreign capital, and free immigrants. One was the Portuguese-born deputy from São Paulo, Nicolau de Campos Vergueiro, a lawyer and planter. Vergueiro wanted to replace slaves on Brazilian plantations with free immigrant labor, but, ever conscious of the stigma of his own birth, he had to trim his proposals to suit the nativist slavocrats. Vergueiro's immigrant labor bill, which finally passed the General Assembly in 1830, set up "a complicated system of contracts which in their essence were little more than disguised slavery," and which defeated the author's purpose of attracting foreign workers to Brazil. Nevertheless, Dom Pedro admired Vergueiro for his progressive views, and in 1828 he selected him to fill a Senate vacancy in the Minas Gerais delegation.[11]

Other liberals were found among the twenty-three priests elected to the first Chamber of Deputies. Father Diogo Antônio Feijó, landowner and sometime parish priest from São Paulo, former deputy to the Portuguese Cortes, was a man of strong character, austere habits, and enlightened ideas. But Feijó seldom spoke in the Brazilian parliament, and when he did it was usually on Church matters. The illegitimate son of a priest, Feijó made reform of the clergy his main project in the late 1820s: specifically, he wanted to abolish clerical celibacy in the established Roman Catholic Church of Brazil. His campaign against clerical celibacy involved him in sterile polemics with the primate of the Church in Brazil, and deputy from Pará, Romualdo Antônio de Seixas. Born in an Amazonian river town in 1787, Dom Romualdo was bishop of Pará when Dom Pedro nominated him to be archbishop of Bahia in 1826. The following year the Pope confirmed him in this position, the pinnacle of the Brazilian Church hierarchy. Like José Bonifácio, whom he greatly admired, Dom Romualdo favored the peaceful integration of the Indians of the interior into Brazilian society as free workers. In the Chamber of Deputies the archbishop also spoke out in favor of European immigration, calling for "a liberal system of colonization." In the 1827 debate on the slave-trade treaty, Dom Romualdo was the only deputy to take an unequivocal stand against the infamous traffic. With speaker after speaker denouncing the treaty and predicting dire economic consequences for Brazil if the trade were not extended beyond the three-year grace period, Dom Romualdo called for an immediate end to the traffic, arguing that the sooner Brazil got started building a free society, the better it would be for everyone.[12] Dom Romualdo was not reelected to the 1830 parliament, nor was his protegé and fellow deputy from Pará, José Tomás Nabuco de Araújo, who was consoled with a crown appointment as president of the province of Paraíba.[13] Nabuco did not play a conspicuous role in the 1826–29 General Assembly, but his son and grandson would be the most prominent abolitionist statesmen of their respective generations.

The outstanding spokesman for liberalism in the late 1820s was not a member of the first parliament. This liberal spokesman was instead a young poet and bookstore proprietor, Evaristo da Veiga, who brought out the first issue of his influential newspaper, the *Aurora fluminense* ("Rio Sunrise") on 21 December 1827. Evaristo's *Aurora fluminense* had an elegant style and editorial consistency that were lacking in other independent journals, like the *Astréa*, which had two publishers and opened its columns to writers of diverse talents and points of view, and the *Malagueta*, mouthpiece of the proslavery and erratic Luís Augusto May. Evaristo was not a provincial cleric like Feijó or Dom Romualdo, or a planter-liberal like Vergueiro (who came from a farming family in Portugal), but a city-bred, middle-class intellectual, the classic bourgeois liberal. Born in Rio in 1799, the son of a Portuguese bookseller and schoolteacher, Evaristo was a voracious reader and earnest assimilator of enlightened disquisitions. Curly haired, plump, and light skinned, the studious Evaristo had shied away from political activism in the years before he launched his newspaper, which immediately made him a public figure. His new celebrity and the scent of power apparently led him to downplay his liberal aversion to forced labor and to emphasize the points in which his doctrine coincided with that of the slavocrats—like lowering tariffs, cutting government spending, stabilizing the currency, liquidating the national bank, reducing the armed forces, and ending the war in Uruguay.[14]

A bill providing for an elected local judiciary, dear to the hearts of the slaveholders, had already been passed by the General Assembly and reluctantly signed into law by Dom Pedro when the *Aurora fluminense* commenced publication late in 1827. Fiscal matters and the Uruguayan war received the most attention in Evaristo's newspaper in the first half of 1828. The *Aurora* railed against the "destructive war devouring the wealth of the citizens"[15] and denounced the emperor's government—but not the emperor—for hiring foreign mercenaries. Evaristo waged his antiwar campaign on all fronts, and though he personally favored immigration, his journal mercilessly attacked the poor Irish soldier-colonists. Members of the British community in Rio blamed the *Aurora* for inciting Brazilians to the acts of violence against the Irish that led to the mercenary mutiny of June 1828. Evaristo, for all his liberalism, stereotypically regarded the Irish as congenital alcoholics and the blacks as "a rude and stupid race."[16] The disturbances that he helped provoke in 1828 probably confirmed his bourgeois prejudices. Those events certainly assured the success of his crusade to end the war and get Brazil out of Uruguay. The long-term consequences of the victory of Evaristo and the other antiwar activists were not happy ones for Brazil. The independent republic of Uruguay would be not a buffer state, but a vortex that would draw Brazil into two wars that would consume six times as many Brazilian lives as had been lost in the 1825–28 conflict. Brazilians of the next generation would regard Uruguay as their California.[17] But Brazil's destiny was not manifest: the earlier failure of national will had forever removed the prize from the empire's grasp.

It was rather late in the war before Dom Pedro decided to cultivate the good will of the Chamber of Deputies. After the 1827 session, which the emperor extended beyond its regular four-month term to allow the deputies and senators to complete work on such measures as the judiciary and ministerial responsibility bills, on 20 November 1827 Dom Pedro appointed a new cabinet in which the war minister, for the first time since the war began, was Brazilian born; the empire, justice, and finance portfolios, for the first time, were held by members of the Chamber of Deputies, all natives; the navy and foreign ministers were Portuguese born. The deputies who were named to the cabinet were required by a curious provision of the constitution to be reelected in order to continue serving in the chamber. All were, so when the General Assembly reconvened, three members of the government were sitting in the chamber, available to their legislative colleagues and committed to the implementation of the ministerial responsibility act. But the emperor's hopes for improved relations with the chamber were shattered by the mercenary mutiny of June 1828. Dom Pedro was outraged by the "kill all the foreigners" order of his war minister, Bento Barroso Pereira, and by his truckling to the nativist demagogues, whom the emperor blamed for provoking his foreign troops. Dom Pedro fired the war minister, which prompted the other Brazilian-born members of the cabinet to resign in solidarity with their dismissed colleague.[18]

In attempting to resolve the cabinet crisis of June 1828, the emperor once again reached out to the Chamber of Deputies. He offered the ministry of justice to Vasconcelos, but the great orator refused it. It was filled on an interim basis by José Clemente Pereira, deputy from Rio de Janeiro, who accepted a regular appointment as minister of the empire, or internal affairs. Thus the Portuguese-born José Clemente, ultra-liberal of 1821–22—who had been bayonetted on the floor of the commercial exchange, who as president of the Rio city council had rallied the Cariocas behind Dom Pedro prior to the fico, who had outmaneuvered José Bonifácio in the Great Orient Lodge and had tried to make the emperor subordinate to the Constituent Assembly, who had been deported by the Andradas—finally returned to power on 15 June 1828 as the head of Dom Pedro's council of ministers. For eighteen months he would champion the emperor's cause; he struggled valiantly, but futilely, in the Chamber of Deputies to maintain a strong army and navy, to keep the mercenaries, to secure adequate funding for the executive departments, and to save the Bank of Brazil. Eventually, three members of the former cabinet were induced to serve with José Clemente, including Deputy Miguel Calmon, a Bahian and close associate of the marquis of Barbacena, as finance minister. Another holdover was the foreign minister, the Portuguese-born Senator João Carlos de Oeyenhausen, marquis of Aracati. Oeyenhausen had served with José Bonifácio and Martim Francisco on the 1821 São Paulo junta that drew up the famous memorial urging Dom Pedro to remain in Brazil; but the following year Oeyenhausen, as junta president, had played a major role in expelling Martim Francisco from the paulista government. The combination of José Clemente and Oeyenhausen was anathema to the Andradas—two of whom, Antônio Carlos and Martim Francisco, returned to Brazil three weeks after the new cabinet took office.[19] While battling the powerful slavocrat-liberal-nativist coalition, José Clemente also had to contend with the Andradas, whose thirst for vengeance overcame any sympathy they might have felt for his position on important issues, like saving the Bank of Brazil. When the patriarch, José Bonifácio, returned to Brazil the next year, José Clemente's days in power were numbered.

The power of Bernardo Pereira de Vasconcelos, unlike that of José Clemente, was firmly rooted in the social, economic, and political reality of Brazil in the late 1820s. His legislative triumphs in 1827 included the ministerial responsibility act, which the emperor favored, and the elected judiciary act, which Dom Pedro opposed, but did not veto; he would reserve that instrument for use only in extraordinary cases. By the end of 1827 Vasconcelos had completed the draft of a criminal code for the elected judges to apply: it provided the death penalty for slave insurrection, but practically exempted the nonslave population from capital punishment, and made it virtually impossible to convict a free person of treason or rebellion. This comforted crypto-republicans, secessionists, and other would-be revolutionists who habitually flew liberal colors and made up an important segment of the dominant coalition in the Chamber of Deputies. Dom Pedro was naive to think that Vasconcelos might accept the post of minister of justice, for this would have cost him the real power that he had attained as leader of the "opposition" in parliament. The emperor and his ministers were the real opposition in the Brazilian political system: they could "make no way, nor do anything of importance," without the cooperation of the elected Chamber of Deputies; as an English observer noted, "the opposition were the Government." "In England," John Armitage wrote, "many members of the Parliament were nominated by the Peerage, and, in France, under the Bourbons, where the double vote of the grand Colleges, and the small number of electoral capacities, maintained a factitious representation of the country, it became possible for a Ministry to have a majority in the House, without having it in the nation. But in Brazil, where the base of the elective system was more ample, and where nearly all of the free population were entitled to the privilege of voting, this was impossible."[20]

The emperor was being reduced to impotence by the political system he had decreed. The free vote of a slave-oriented society threatened to shrink to insignificance the number of Dom Pedro's supporters in the next Chamber of Deputies. The emperor's dreams of a liberal empire were being dashed. The weakening of the armed forces and the removal of penalties against rebellion, Dom Pedro feared, would encourage secessionist movements—especially in those distant and economically depressed provinces that were untouched by the coffee boom. The loss of Uruguay might have been only the first act in a long tragedy of imperial disintegration, and the victory over the slave trade could prove illusory in the absence of means to enforce the prohibition—an independent judiciary and a strong navy. The emperor was greatly troubled by these prospects at the beginning of 1829, when a disturbance occurred in Pernambuco that involved some revolutionary posters and a few dozen mutinous soldiers and civilian rioters. Although the situation was easily dominated by local authorities early in February, Dom Pedro's council of state recommended the suspension of constitutional guarantees in the province, and the emperor contemplated still more drastic action. In a memo circulated to a few of his most trusted advisers, including Friar Arrábida and Vilela Barbosa, marquis of Paranaguá, Dom Pedro asked for assessments of the extent and causes of "revolutionary ferment" in the empire, and for opinions on the advisability of his overthrowing the parliamentary regime with the support of troops solicited from friendly European monarchies, and "giving [Brazil] a new constitution that would be truly monarchical."[21]

There was some revolutionary ferment in Brazil, Friar Arrábida replied, but this was inevitable in a society faced with change, with "the harsh customs, the cruel habits of a population of masters and slaves confronting an unfamiliar civilization." The remedy consisted of "unity and firmness in the executive branch. Precise implementation of the law. Organization and discipline in the armed forces. Vigilance in the moderating power and good faith and harmony among all the branches" of government. The emperor should not try to amend the constitution, much less impose a new one. As for the idea of calling in foreign troops: "My emperor, my lord, my friend," the Franciscan effused, "I would be a vile traitor, an ingrate, a coward, if I concealed from Your Imperial Majesty the horror that the design of this query caused me." The country would be bathed in blood if Dom Pedro brought European forces to Brazil for the unworthy purpose of depriving his subjects of their constitution. "Burn it, Sire, burn the paper that contains this question, the very thought of which will be considered a crime."[22]

Vilela Barbosa, marquis of Paranaguá, was similarly forthright in expressing his opinion. He did not fear political "ferment," which he saw as natural among a people "divided into only two classes —slaves, who begrudge their slightest act of obedience as coerced and unjust—and masters jealous, through pride in their station, of every kind of superiority." The remedy prescribed by the Rio-born military engineer was "to govern, that is, to obey the laws and have them obeyed; to reform at the same time public habits and reestablish public morality through the good example of those who should set it; to nourish honor and probity; to utilize and reward only virtue and merit." The emperor should keep his hands off the constitution, Vilela counseled, and give it more time to work before suggesting amendments. "Only the Genius of Evil, not someone who loves Your Majesty both from the heart and out of duty" would advise him to invite foreign troops to Brazil to intimidate his subjects. It would mean "the return of absolutism and violence"; it would be "European influence sustained against liberal principles by cannon and bayonets." Through his "perspicacity" Dom Pedro could not fail to perceive "all the horror of such a project," the marquis wrote; "Divine providence cannot permit the realization of a plan of such malignity." Vilela exhorted his sovereign to "sustain the great work" that had earned him recognition as "Man of the century *par excellence*, as political philosopher prince."[23]

Dom Pedro heeded the words of his two faithful counselors. He would respect the liberal system he had given Brazil, even if it facilitated control of the country by conservatives, or the destruction of the empire by revolutionaries. He would try to use what little power he retained to advance the cause of freedom, but mostly he would have to stand aside and hope for the best. On 1 October 1829, in anticipation of the 13 March 1830 effective date of the slave-trade prohibition, the emperor's navy minister announced that no slavers would be allowed to sail for Africa from Brazilian ports after 15 November 1829.[24] But the slavocrats who controlled the Chamber of Deputies would not provide the means to enforce the order.

Having decided to remarry, Dom Pedro sent the marquis of Barbacena to Europe to select a bride for him. The marquis, alias General Brant, had demonstrated military ineptitude at the Battle of Ituzaingó, but his reputation as a diplomat was good. He had represented Brazil well in London during 1822–25, mixing easily with ministers, bankers, foreign diplomats, and nobles of the realm. The great optimism the marquis exuded in embarking on his nuptial mission in August 1827 was, in view of his record, certainly more justified than his boast of a few months earlier that he would raise the Brazilian flag over Buenos Aires. "Agreeable in conversation, and polished in his manners," Barbacena "was a sagacious and talented courtier; possessed of considerable tact . . . and of great self-conceit." He also had experience handling large sums of money, having negotiated Brazil's first foreign loan, 3,686,200 pounds sterling from Rothschild and other London bankers in 1824. The search for an imperial bride was sure to be expensive, and the costs were to be borne entirely by Dom Pedro personally, although Barbacena was given access to the funds and credit of the Brazilian legation in London, the famous "magic cashbox." The emperor would have to reimburse the Brazilian treasury from his personal allowance for funds drawn in his name by Barbacena; nevertheless, Dom Pedro gave him a blank check, with instructions to spend whatever might be necessary to win him a suitable wife.[25] A decade earlier, the super-aristocratic marquis of Marialva had spent a great deal of his own money in arranging Dom Pedro's first marriage; with the super-acquisitive marquis of Barbacena the cash might be expected to flow the other way.

The search for a second wife for Dom Pedro became involved with the question of the Portuguese succession, and Emperor Franz I and his chancellor, Prince Metternich had a hand in both matters. The Hapsburg emperor wanted his grandchildren in Brazil to have a proper stepmother. A man almost inured to personal tragedy—he had buried three wives and was married for the fourth time—Franz seemed to bear Dom Pedro no ill will on account of Dona Leopoldina. He was willing to make initial inquiries on behalf of his ex-son-in-law to the various royal houses of Europe, and even before Barbacena departed Rio, had informed Dom Pedro of two prospective brides in Bavaria. At that time, mid-1827, Dom Miguel, fiancé of Franz's granddaughter, Dona Maria da Gloria, now Queen Maria II of Portugal, was still in Vienna under the protection of the Austrian emperor and chancellor, who did not want him to go to Brazil to pick up his fiancée prior to going to Lisbon to assume the Portuguese regency; presumably, they wanted to keep the regent-designate as far removed as possible from the liberal constitutionalist influence of his older brother. Earlier in the year, Dom Pedro had sent a palace confidant—João da Rocha Pinto, Portuguese-born former customhouse clerk, friend and kindred spirit of the Chalaça—to Lisbon and Vienna to make arrangements for Dom Miguel's return to Portugal via Brazil. When Rocha Pinto was unable to induce the Portuguese prince to make the trip, Dom Pedro accepted British advice that he excuse his brother from going to Brazil, and instruct him to proceed instead via London to Lisbon, to assume the position of constitutional regent of Portugal without further delay. Barbacena was to impress upon Dom Miguel the importance of his consulting with Prime Minister George Canning's government in London, and going on to Lisbon as soon as possible.[26]

Dom Miguel was enroute from Vienna to London and Barbacena was traveling in the opposite direction when the two met in Paris in December. Barbacena was greatly impressed by Dom Miguel, whose "political creed," the marquis reported to Dom Pedro, "is reduced to carrying out the orders of Your Imperial Majesty." After enthusiastically certifying the loyalty of Dom Miguel, Barbacena resumed his journey to Vienna, where he was cordially received by the Hapsburg monarch. Franz I told Barbacena that he had advised Dom Pedro to send Dom Miguel's bride-to-be, the ten-year-old Queen Maria II, to Vienna, where he, her grandfather, would arrange for her education and upkeep until she reached a marriageable age. On the matter of a bride for Dom Pedro, Franz appeared cooperative: "The most important thing," he told Barbacena, "is that she be pretty and spirited, to make my son-in-law happy—not timid and negligent as my daughter was."[27] Franz pledged that he would "not cease my efforts until there is found a most perfect bride for my son-in-law and a loving mother for my grandchildren." But the prospects to whom he referred Barbacena —princesses from Bavaria, Sardinia, Wurtemburg, and Sweden—one after another, rejected the formal proposals of marriage that the marquis made on behalf of the emperor of Brazil. Reports of Dom Pedro's scandalous behavior during his marriage to Dona Leopoldina and speculation that he was responsible for her death filled countless European newspaper columns and were sources of court gossip in many lands. Barbacena had not realized how difficult it would be to sell Dom Pedro to the royal houses of Europe, even with the help of the Hapsburg emperor. Rather than blaming his own overconfidence and mismanagement, Barbacena suggested to Dom Pedro that Franz and Metternich had betrayed them: Franz, the marquis suspected, had named candidates likely to reject his proposal, and Metternich was working behind the scenes to make sure that they would.[28] Barbacena gave the impression that he had been set up, led into a diplomatic Ituzaingó.

Dom Pedro did not believe that Franz and Metternich had betrayed him, and when Barbacena returned to Brazil empty-handed in May 1828, he did not press the point. Dom Pedro decided to send Queen Maria II to Vienna and place her under the protection of her grandfather, as requested. Barbacena agreed to undertake this mission for the Portuguese crown, and to resume his search, on behalf of the Brazilian emperor, for an imperial bride. As temporary custodian of the Brazilian-born Portuguese queen, Barbacena had at his disposal the money that Brazil had owed to Portugal under the independence settlement at the time of Dom João's death: 350,000 pounds sterling, which Dom Pedro claimed as king of Portugal and had transferred to his daughter when he abdicated in her favor. (Dom Pedro formally declared that his abdication was "complete" on 3 March 1828, after receiving Barbacena's assurances of Dom Miguel's loyalty.) Dona Maria was recognized as queen of Portugal by all the European powers, including Great Britain, which provided a ship-of-the-line to join two Brazilian frigates in escorting the young monarch across the Atlantic and the Mediterranean to Genoa. When the ships called at Gibraltar on 2 September Barbacena learned that Dom Miguel had suppressed the constitution and had been acclaimed king of Portugal by an absolutist assembly in Lisbon. Supporters of the constitution had held out for a while in the liberal city of Oporto, but had since surrendered or embarked for exile in England, or the Azores, where the island of Terceira remained under constitutionalist control. In view of the changed circumstances, Barbacena decided not to deliver the young constitutionalist queen to her absolutist grandfather, but to retain control of Dona Maria and her treasury, and proceed to London to treat with her exiled subjects.[29]

In Britain the situation had changed since the death of George Canning at the beginning of 1828. The new prime minister, the ultra-conservative duke of Wellington, was less inclined than his predecessor had been to support constitutional rule in Portugal. In fact, Wellington's withdrawal of British troops from Portugal in April had undoubtedly encouraged the absolutist movement that culminated in Dom Miguel's acclamation as king in June. Although Wellington welcomed Dona Maria to England and continued to recognize her as queen of Portugal, his government refused to allow her liberal Portuguese partisans, led by the marquis of Palmela, to use British territory as a base of military operations against Dom Miguel's regime. Constitutionalist forces that arrived in England after the fall of Oporto were prevented by the British navy from sailing for any Portuguese territory, including the Azores. Wellington agreed with his Austrian colleague, Metternich, on a solution to the Portuguese problem: the wedding contract between Dom Miguel and Dona Maria should be observed—permitting them to share Portugal's throne as king and queen—but Dom Pedro's Portuguese constitution should be ignored. To go to Rio and try to persuade Dom Pedro to accept this solution, the Iron Duke picked an old Luso-Brazilian hand, the Anglo-Irish Viscount Strangford. But by the time Lord Strangford arrived in Rio at the end of 1828, Dom Pedro had declared Dom Miguel a traitor and resolved that he would never allow his daughter to marry such a scoundrel. The Hibernian spent several months in the Brazilian capital in the company of the Austrian ambassador, baron von Marschall, trying to induce the emperor to relent. They finally gave up after Dom Pedro mocked and insulted them at a reception in April 1829. Other diplomats reported hearing the emperor say something like: "Those two sons of bitches thought they were going to take me to the cleaners, but I told them to get lost."[30]

Dom Pedro sent orders to Barbacena in London to wind up the wife hunt and bring his daughter back to Brazil as soon as possible. The emperor's requirements for a mate were somewhat flexible: she was to be distinguished by birth, beauty, virtue, and education, but Barbacena could compromise on the first and fourth qualities if the candidate were strong in the second and third, which were absolutely essential. The marquis reported finding some willing princesses in Denmark, but they were too ugly. In the meantime in Rio the emperor was keeping company with various commoners. One was Clémence

Saisset, whose husband, the French proprietor of a fashionable dress shop on Ouvidor Street, exploited her relationship with the monarch for business purposes. When Clémence began to show signs of pregnancy for which, everyone acknowledged, Dom Pedro was responsible, she and M. Saisset were packed off to France with a hefty indemnity from the emperor in December 1828. With Clémence gone and his hopes for the success of Barbacena's mission dwindling, Dom Pedro's thoughts turned increasingly to his old love, Domitila de Castro, the marchioness of Santos. He was constantly reminded of her by the presence of their daughter, the four-year-old duchess of Goiás. When the imperial mistress had departed for São Paulo in August 1828, she had left the child and her sister, the infant duchess of Ceará, to be raised at the palace with the emperor's legitimate children. The duchess of Ceará died of meningitis in October 1828, her death contributing to the burden of woes that Dom Pedro carried into the next year. Finally, he sent for Domitila and she moved back into her mansion across the road from the main entrance to Boa Vista palace in April 1829.[31]

The General Assembly met in special session that month to deal with financial matters, especially the impending expiration of the charter of the Bank of Brazil. Consideration of the bank question carried over into the regular session in May, when the emperor, in his opening speech, called for legislation to promote immigration, reported on the disturbances in Pernambuco, and noted that freedom of the press was being widely abused in the empire. The "freedom" granted the press in the 1824 Constitution meant, at minimum, exemption from prior censorship. The fact that jury trials were required for all cases of "abuses of press freedom" demonstrated that the constitutional freedom to publish was not absolute. In establishing Roman Catholicism as the state religion and in declaring the person of the emperor "inviolable," the constitution precluded, in the opinion of most Brazilian politicians and journalists, direct attacks on the Church or the monarch. That the constitutional system itself should not be criticized in print was a strongly held belief among liberals: when one senator, the marquis of Queluz, tried to include in the printed record of the Senate a treatise of his authorship that questioned the appropriateness of elected representative government in "countries where the communications are difficult," the liberal Senator Vergueiro led a successful fight to prevent its publication.[32]

From time to time liberals demanded the suppression of "absolutist" newspapers, but these, if they existed at all in Brazil, were few and ephemeral. Journals supporting the emperor's cabinet as well as those backing the parliamentary majority professed liberal principles. Newspapers speaking for the dominant slavocrat-liberal-nativist parliamentary coalition outnumbered those friendly to the José Clemente ministry by about five to one. (The total number of newspapers in the empire had grown to twenty-five in 1828, and would double in the next two years.) The press joined the Chamber of Deputies in demonstrating the truth of the assertion that in Dom Pedro's Brazil "the government [was] the opposition." The ministry had less control over the press than over the legislature; it was futile to threaten journalists with prosecution for abuses of press freedom, as they inevitably were acquitted by juries of their peers. The emperor's "inviolability" shifted the fire of the press to his ministers and close associates, like the Chalaça, who were attacked mercilessly in the columns of Rio newspapers, which were reprinted in the provinces. Some publications expressed their feelings about the monarch by consistently referring to him as "our dear emperor," using an adjective that can mean "expensive" as well as "beloved," or by identifying the target of their attacks as the *poder* ("power"), an anagram of "Pedro."[33]

Veiled criticism of the emperor intensified with his growing involvement in Portuguese affairs, and with the arrival in Brazil of hundreds of refugees from Dom Miguel's absolutist regime in Portugal. Some of these were destitute, and Dom Pedro's private secretary, the Chalaça, made himself more conspicuous than ever in soliciting private funds for their relief. In June Dom Pedro intervened directly in Portuguese affairs by issuing a decree, as the "tutor and natural protector" of Queen Maria II, naming a regency of three men, headed by the marquis of Palmela, to direct the constitutional government of Portugal established in the Azores. Many Portuguese constitutionalists wanted Dom Pedro to return to Portugal and personally lead them against the despotism of his brother—and so did other European liberals, including Benjamin Constant. The French-Swiss sage saw the struggle to free Portugal as the first campaign in a war against European absolutism, and he urged Dom Pedro to take command of the liberal war effort. The Brazilian emperor was gratified by the confidence expressed in him by his intellectual idol, but this did not prevent him from seeking help for his daughter from the king whom Benjamin

Constant was trying to overthrow, the despotic Charles X of France. It was not ideological affinity, but his perception of international power rivalries that pointed Dom Pedro toward Charles X's regime: with Britain and Austria pressuring him to accept Dom Miguel as joint ruler of Portugal and future husband of Queen Maria II, Dom Pedro thought he might be able to persuade France to support his daughter without Dom Miguel and with the constitution.[34] But Dom Pedro and the Portuguese constitutionalists would get no help from France until Charles X had been deposed and Benjamin Constant and other liberals were in power in Paris.

European politics were very much on the mind of the marquis of Barbacena as he continued his fruitless search for a bride for the Brazilian emperor. He was informed that the grand duke and duchess of Baden had three eligible daughters and might be amenable to a marriage proposal from the emperor of Brazil. This information was developed independently by two French citizens, one a veteran of Napoleon's army, who had personally discussed the matter with the grand duchess, a cousin of the Empress Josephine's first husband. The Napoleonic connection, though slight, was disagreeable to Barbacena. The parvenu marquis had affected a legitimatist disdain for *buonapartistes* and he advised Dom Pedro against trying to marry one, as that would offend "the Holy Alliance," which "proposed to exterminate the race." The Brazilian emperor, unconcerned about the Napoleonic stigma and fed up with the rejections from mainline royal families, ordered his emissary to pursue the Baden lead, and if it did not yield results to return to Brazil. By the time Barbacena received these instructions, the search had moved to Bavaria. The grand duchess of Baden liked the idea of one of her daughters marrying the emperor of Brazil, but her husband vetoed the proposed match. The grand duchess suggested to Colonel Antoine Fortuné de Brack, one of the free-lance marriage brokers, that he consider her niece, the beautiful seventeen-year-old daughter of the dowager duchess of Leuchtenberg. The duchess was a member of the legitimate Bavarian royal family, and her late husband was Napoleon's esteemed stepson, Prince Eugène de Beauharnais, son of the empress Josephine by her first husband. The young lady's name was Amelia Auguste Eugenie Napoleona von Leuchtenberg, and she and her mother readily agreed to the marriage. All that remained was for Barbacena to draw up a contract, sign it in Dom Pedro's name, and arrange for a proxy wedding in Munich—which he did with great dispatch.[35]

Dom Pedro received word of the successful conclusion of the marriage negotiations and a portrait of his bride late in June 1829. He was ecstatic. "You have no idea of our master's happiness," Chalaça wrote Barbacena. "He changed his way of life: He doesn't sleep away from home; he makes his visits always accompanied by an attendant." The emperor assigned to Chalaça, the devoted and indefatigable secretary who had handled the correspondence with Barbacena throughout the long search, the task of paying off Domitila and getting her out of Rio before his new wife arrived. Within a month Chalaça had closed the deal: the emperor bought back from his ex-mistress all the real estate he had given her, including the mansion across from Boa Vista palace, for 300 contos, payable in installments; her furniture was loaded aboard the brigantine *Happy Union* and shipped to Santos. The marchioness of Santos, three months pregnant, left Rio for São Paulo on 27 August 1829 and never saw Dom Pedro again.[36]

While the emperor prepared to receive his new wife, he had to deal with an increasingly recalcitrant parliament. It would not give him the immigration legislation he wanted, and rather than reform the Bank of Brazil, as he requested, it liquidated it, eliminating the country's principal source of business credit. The bank's outstanding notes amounted to 19,174 contos, a sum practically balanced by the government's debt to the bank, 18,301 contos. In the bank's vaults were reserves of more than 1,000 contos in specie, which were applied to redeem the balance and pay off the stockholders, who received 90 percent of their original investment. Thus, virtually all the bank notes were retained in circulation as imperial treasury instruments, along with a debased copper coinage; but the bank's accumulated capital, which had served as a magnet drawing private funds to the bank for reinvestment, was dispersed. The emperor had encouraged Martim Francisco and other developmentalists to speak out on the dire consequences for Brazil of such action,[37] but their warnings were unheeded by a parliament beholden to the vested interests of planter-exporters.

The most acrimonious exchanges between the emperor's ministers and members of the parliamentary majority were over the suspension of constitutional guarantees in Pernambuco in February 1829. The Chamber of Deputies not only refused to sanction the suspension, but tried to censure and force the dismissal of the minister of justice who decreed it and the minister of war who set up military tribunals to try suspected rebels. Although the disturbance in Pernambuco, as it

The Marquis of Barbacena
From Tobias Monteiro, *Historia do imperio: O primeiro reinado*, I (Rio de Janeiro, 1939).

Dona Amélia, Empress of Brazil
From Tobias Monteiro, *Historia do imperio: O primeiro reinado, II* (Rio
de Janeiro, 1946).

turned out, posed no real threat to the empire, the government was within its constitutional rights in suspending civil liberties in the province pending approval by the General Assembly. But the constitution did not provide for special tribunals, and government foes pursued the war minister who had established them (although no one was actually tried by them), while dropping their case against the justice minister. Dom Pedro, who prior to the convening of the first parliament had authorized military tribunals following serious revolts in the Northeast, felt that the prosecution of the war minister was really an attack on himself. It was also an attempt to force the emperor to remove a minister unacceptable to the Chamber of Deputies, and to extend the principle of ministerial responsibility one step closer to parliamentary supremacy. To demonstrate that he retained the power to appoint and dismiss ministers without the approval of the Chamber of Deputies, Dom Pedro would accept the resignation of the war minister only if the censure motion failed. The emperor personally lobbied the deputies, and convinced Ledo, Dom Romualdo, and other civil libertarians that a vote against censure would not be one in favor of military tribunals. The motion was barely defeated, thirty-two to thirty-nine, which gave Dom Pedro no cause for celebration. There was no praise and no thanks for the legislators in the emperor's speech that closed the last session of the first Brazilian parliament on 3 September. The entire speech consisted of the words, "August and most worthy gentlemen, representatives of the Brazilian nation: the session is closed."[38]

Dom Romualdo, archbishop of Bahia, who was not reelected to the second parliament, remained in Rio after the closing of the first to give the nuptial benediction to the wedding of Dom Pedro and Dona Amélia. Although a proxy wedding had been held in Munich, the bride's mother had made Barbacena promise that he would not turn her daughter over to Dom Pedro before the benediction. This suited the marquis fine, for it would give him maximum exposure in Rio as the guardian of the lovely and virtuous princess whom he had discovered and brought to Brazil to restore morality to the imperial palace. On the trip over, Barbacena undertook to coach his temporary ward on various matters. The bastard daughter that the bridegroom was keeping at the palace, the intelligent but initially pliable Dona Amélia, had to go. Some disreputable characters who surrounded the emperor would have to be removed in due course, Barbacena suggested, and he would do what he could to help bring this about.

The smooth-talking marquis was going to double-cross the Chalaça —the coarse and fun loving, yet honest and diligent, private secretary with whom he had maintained a frank and cordial correspondence for two years.[39]

The frigate *Imperatriz*, carrying the marquis of Barbacena, Empress Amélia, her nineteen-year-old brother, Prince Auguste, and Queen Maria II of Portugal, and escorted by the frigate *Isabel*, arrived at the entrance to Guanabara Bay on 16 October 1829. The emperor took a steamboat out to meet them, and on boarding the *Imperatriz*, first greeted his daughter, the queen, which impressed his bride with his fatherly devotion. Dom Pedro was not disappointed in Dona Amélia; a creature of "rare beauty" as Dom Romualdo noted, she was a little timid at first, but quickly regained her regal composure. She was tall, well proportioned, graceful, with an oval face, a profusion of honey-blond hair, and a modest smile that gave her the look of a Gainesborough portrait. Her body reminded the Brazilian ambassador in Vienna, the marquis of Resende, of a Correggio painting of the queen of Sheba. With her voluptuous good looks went a well-trained intelligence; at age seventeen she was, according to the *London Times*, one of Germany's best educated and "most complete" princesses. The new empress landed at the Naval Arsenal on 17 October under threatening skies, and rode in a carriage with Barbacena through triumphal arches and past throngs of Cariocas standing and cheering in the rain to the Imperial Chapel, where Dom Romualdo pronounced the nuptial benediction and what was left of the chapel choir and orchestra performed a mass composed for the occasion by Dom Pedro. In celebration of his second marriage, the emperor created the Order of the Rose, dedicated to love and fidelity. Among those inducted into the order was the marquis of Barbacena, whose oldest son the emperor made a viscount.[40] Dom Pedro was immoderately grateful to the marquis for delivering Dona Amélia to him and for saving his daughter from the clutches of Metternich and Dom Miguel.

For nearly a month the newlyweds were feted with receptions, dances, picnics, and operas by Rossini. The new empress did not lay eyes on the illegitimate duchess of Goiás, who was packed off to a convent school in France. Her eldest stepdaughter, the queen of Portugal, was installed in Domitila's former home, now site of the Portuguese court in exile. Across the road at Boa Vista palace, shortly after the conclusion of the wedding festivities, the emperor and empress received an important visitor: José Bonifácio de Andrada e Silva. Dom Pedro was delighted to see his old mentor, a recent widower, who had retired with his "adopted" daughter to the seclusion of the bay island of Paquetá after returning to Brazil in July. The emperor presented the patriarch to his wife as his "best friend," and the three conversed in French, with José Bonifácio, as usual, dominating the conversation. He urged the empress to reconcile her husband with his people, and she was as charmed by the old man as her predecessor had been.[41] Dom Pedro, in the glow of his new marriage, and bitten by nostalgia for the heroic days of 1822, would have given José Bonifácio anything he asked, had he asked for anything.

The marquis of Barbacena fully appreciated the restored influence of José Bonifácio at the imperial palace. He tried to persuade the patriarch to offer to form a new cabinet for the emperor, one that would include Barbacena. José Bonifácio was unwilling to return to government service himself, but, so much did he desire the removal of José Clemente and Oeyenhausen, that he agreed to support Barbacena as head of a new government. From his experience as foreign minister in 1822–23, José Bonifácio knew Barbacena to be an artful diplomat; perhaps his qualities were the ones required to save the Brazilian monarchy. But Barbacena intended to put himself forward as a financial genius, the man to rescue the country from the monetary chaos caused by the regionally fluctuating values of copper coins and unsecured paper. José Bonifácio and his associates thought it curious that the marquis, while claiming the finance portfolio for himself, would retain in his cabinet, as foreign minister, the ex–finance minister, Miguel Calmon. The one holdover from the despised José Clemente cabinet was to be "Brazil's greatest counterfeiter"—in the words of one Andradista—the man responsible for issuing 6,000 contos of copper coins at four times their intrinsic value.[42]

On the recommendation of José Bonifácio and Dona Amélia, on 4 December 1829 Dom Pedro named Barbacena head of a new cabinet that included Miguel Calmon. The marquis became, in effect, Brazil's first prime minister, choosing his cabinet colleagues and assigning their portfolios. Barbacena professed to regret that José Bonifácio would not accept a ministerial position. "The public good," he remarked to the patriarch, would best be served "if I had your talents or you had my guile."

"That's impossible," José Bonifácio replied, "because you wouldn't have your guile if you had my talents."[43]

On 7 December 1829 Dom Pedro was driving on Lavradio Street, returning to Boa Vista palace with his second wife, her brother, and his daughter, the queen of Portugal, when the tongue broke off his carriage, panicking the horses, who broke into a mad gallop. The emperor, with the sangfroid he usually displayed in such situations, applied all his strength to rein in the animals, but the reins came off in his hands, the traces snapped, and the horses ran free. The carriage careened off the road and turned over. Dom Pedro, who had been standing at the driver's seat, catapulted onto the ground and was knocked unconscious. All the passengers received some cuts or bruises in the spill, except the lovely Dona Amélia, and she was shaken and frightened. She was relieved when her new husband regained consciousness after five minutes, though he was in great pain. Judging his injuries to be serious, the empress directed that Dom Pedro be moved only as far as the nearby home of the marquis of Cantagalo. Palace physicians confirmed that the emperor had broken two ribs, and insisted on operating to remove a "tumor" caused by the accident. Throughout the ordeal, Dona Amélia remained at the side of her husband, proving herself to be his "most assiduous and intelligent" medical attendant. "The caresses and tenderness of this angelic princess" soothed the patient and promoted healing. He was well enough by 1 January 1830 to be moved to Boa Vista palace.[44]

During his convalescence Dom Pedro realized how valuable Dona Amélia was, and how much she had cost. He began adding up the bills from Barbacena's wife-hunting expeditions. His debt to the imperial treasury amounted to 182 contos, which he could not contest because it was incurred in his name by Barbacena, whom he had authorized to spend whatever he judged necessary to obtain for him a suitable wife. Nevertheless, Dom Pedro, tightfisted and with a passion for minutiae, wanted to know exactly where the money had gone; early in 1830 he began an examination of invoices, payment receipts, and exchange rates that would extend over several months and lead him to the conclusion that many of the goods and services for which he had been charged had never been received, or were grossly overvalued. In the meantime, more funds were spent on a grand ball held at the Senate Building on the night of 20 January. Dom Pedro had recovered enough from the accident to make an imperial entrance between rows of torch bearers, with fireworks exploding overhead and with the empress of Brazil on one arm and the queen of Portugal on the other. As they stepped into the building, the orchestra struck up the national anthem, composed by the emperor, which everyone began to sing. The first dance, a waltz, was danced by the empress and her handsome and personable brother, Prince Auguste. Other dances followed, including a new quadrille that was not on the program, but that the Chalaça had persuaded the dance master to introduce. According to the *Astréa*—a newspaper with Andradista connections, and friendly toward the Barbacena ministry—the emperor's secretary berated some musicians and insulted an army general. Chalaça's "shameless behavior, his hardly decent manners—if you can call them that," the *Astréa* reported, "offended all the sensible people there."[45] The campaign to deprive the emperor of his devoted servant, to render him ever more helpless to resist Barbacena's machinations, was shifting into high gear.

Dom Pedro, sunk in marital bliss, seemed oblivious to the intrigue. After the dance the emperor and his wife departed Rio for six weeks in the mountains, where he had purchased some land—the site of the present city of Petrópolis. The Chalaça, left in the capital, lashed back at his tormentors with an anonymous newspaper article attacking unnamed nativists who were trying to drive Portuguese-born Brazilians from their adopted homeland. When the emperor returned to Rio at the beginning of March, feelings against the Chalaça and his equally outspoken palace colleague, João da Rocha Pinto, were running so high that, according to Barbacena, it had become necessary for both to leave the country for their own good and for the good of the monarchy. Barbacena was posing as a friend not only of the emperor, but of the Chalaça as well, which helped him overcome Dom Pedro's great reluctance to part with his loyal secretary. The Chalaça, hardworking and conscientious, was willing to do whatever his master asked him to do—except take a job he knew he was not qualified for. Dom Pedro asked him to accept the post of Brazilian minister to the Bourbon court in Naples, but, being no diplomat, he refused, offering to go to Europe instead as the emperor's private secretary to handle his personal affairs in the Old World. Dom Pedro readily agreed and kept him on his personal payroll at a salary of 5,000 dollars a year. Rocha Pinto, at an annual salary of 4,000 dollars, was commissioned to "go to France to buy different things for the palaces and estates" of the imperial family.[46]

While Dom Pedro was helping Chalaça pack—personally

searching the palace for items his friend could use on the trip, making sure he had enough liquor for the long voyage—another traveler was being briefed by Barbacena and Calmon. He was their associate from Bahia, José Egídio Alvares de Almeida, marquis of Santo Amaro, ex–foreign minister, who was appointed special ambassador to the courts of London, Paris, and Vienna, with the mission of negotiating an agreement with the powers for a resolution of the Portuguese crisis that would free the Brazilian emperor of all involvement in the affairs of the mother country. Dom Pedro was weary of Brazilian criticism of his preoccupation with Portuguese problems; he would wash his hands of those matters if Dom Miguel would send an emissary to the court of Dona Maria in Rio recognizing her as queen and sole monarch of Portugal. Dom Pedro was willing to let the queen herself decide when she reached the age of eighteen, whether to marry Dom Miguel. The emperor still referred to Dom Miguel as a traitor, and sometimes as a murderer (of their father), but his feelings may have been tempered by an affectionate letter he received from his brother late in February 1830, which informed him of the death of their mother. In any case, the death of the intransigent Dona Carlota—whom Dom Pedro mourned for eight days, secluding himself at Boa Vista palace —removed one obstacle to a settlement that would exclude Dom Miguel from the throne except as the freely chosen consort of Dona Maria II. To win the support of the powers for such a settlement, Barbacena and Calmon came up with the idea of promising them Brazilian help in promoting the establishment of constitutional monarchies in the republics of Spanish America. Santo Amaro received his instructions on 21 April, and three days later sailed for Brest on a Brazilian frigate. The next day Chalaça and Rocha Pinto departed for Falmouth on a British packet.[47]

In domestic affairs the Barbacena cabinet made some changes; it replaced several unpopular provincial presidents appointed by the former government, and suppressed as an outlawed "secret society" the Columns of the Throne clubs that had been formed by friends of the emperor in Pernambuco and Ceará to combat republican subversion in those northeastern provinces. The cabinet, which had only one Portuguese-born member, the minister of war, at times seemed to pander to the nativists, which gave the emperor cause for concern. But Dom Pedro could count on at least one staunch friend in the cabinet —Navy Minister Vilela Barbosa, marquis of Paranaguá, who had the loyalty and financial integrity of the Chalaça, plus the virtues of political insight and a willingness to speak unpleasant truths to the emperor. Paranaguá, like José Bonifácio, had misgivings about Barbacena, but recommended that Dom Pedro support the prime minister as the best hope for building a bridge between the palace and the new parliament that was to convene in May 1830. Before it did, the emperor reaffirmed his commitment to Barbacena by appointing him to fill a vacancy on the council of state.[48]

One of the first acts of the new Chamber of Deputies was to offer the emperor a vote of thanks, delivered by Martim Francisco, freshman deputy from Minas Gerais, for dismissing the José Clemente–Oeyenhausen ministry, "which had lost public confidence through continuous violations of the constitution and the law." The chamber, however, did not compliment the emperor on his declaration, in his speech opening the session, that "the slave trade has ceased" and that "the government is determined to employ all the measures that good faith and humanity demand to prevent its continuation under any pretext whatever,"[49] although a few individual deputies welcomed (prematurely, as it turned out) the end of the traffic. Dr. Antônio Ferreira França from Bahia, brother of a deceased member of Dom Pedro's council of state and himself sometime personal physician to the emperor, had the temerity to introduce a bill for the total abolition of slavery in Brazil over a period of years; it got nowhere. Legislation enacted during the 1830 session, which was extended to 30 November, included Vasconcelos's criminal code—draconian in its repression of black folk aspiring to freedom, but relatively liberal in other areas —and Vergueiro's ineffectual immigration and colonization bill. The emperor was disappointed that the General Assembly did not resurrect the national bank, despite the best efforts of Martim Francisco, nor pass legislation to regulate the currency. The budget enacted in 1830 was austere, and appropriations and force levels set for the army and navy were below what the emperor desired, but he accepted them—as he did a law dismissing from the armed forces by the end of the year all foreigners who were not veterans of the war for independence.[50]

Dom Pedro, having turned his government over to a prime minister, assumed a more detached attitude toward the workings of parliament in 1830 than he had taken in previous years. And despite his protestations to the contrary, he was increasingly absorbed with European matters. As if he needed to be reminded of his Old World origins, his royal genetic heritage reasserted itself on 20 May, when he suffered his first grand mal seizure in six years. Regaining consciousness after ten minutes, he made light of the matter to visitors. But it slowed him down some, and must have made him more aware of his own mortality, more conscious of the fact that he did not have unlimited time in which to seat his daughter on the throne of his ancestors. Except for the epilepsy and a kidney stone problem, he seemed to be in good health at the age of thirty-one, but there were signs of physical decline that he could not ignore: most disturbing of all was a waning of his sexual powers, evident since April. Extramarital affairs, had he desired them, he confided to his intimate correspondent, the marquis of Resende, were no longer a physical possibility for him.[51] But his adventurous spirit was no less diminished than his sense of duty, and the news that Resende, Chalaça, and Rocha Pinto sent him from Europe in July fired his imagination and pointed his thoughts to exciting opportunities for fulfilling his obligations on that side of the Atlantic. The plans of Barbacena and Calmon for associating Brazil with the governments of the Tory Wellington, the reactionary Metternich, and the despotic Charles X, and for making the Holy Alliance the arbiter of Portugal's destiny, were dashed by the liberal revolution in Paris, which broke out one month after Santo Amaro arrived in the French capital. Charles X tried to change the French constitution and was deposed by the July revolution; in August, "Citizen King" Louis Philippe mounted the throne and named Benjamin Constant president of his council of state. "I had foreseen everything," a jubilant Dom Pedro wrote to Rocha Pinto in September; the revolution was "a necessary consequence of a despotism such as that practiced against the social pact that had been accepted under oath by Charles X and by the proud and freedom-loving French people. You see," the Brazilian emperor congratulated himself, "I do well in not changing from being constitutional." He was "still constitutional, the same as I have always been, not through fear," but out of conviction. "I am ever more convinced that the appropriate government for our Brazil, the one certainly worthy of good fortune, is the constitutional one."[52] What was appropriate for Brazil was indicated also for Portugal. Dom Pedro had established constitutional rule in one; it soon would be the turn of the other.

In the meantime, Dom Pedro undertook an audit of the financial accounts of the constitutional queen of Portugal, of whom he was the "tutor and natural defender." He asked Foreign Minister Miguel

Calmon, who had been Brazil's finance minister while the queen was in London in 1828 under the protection of Barbacena, for some documents dealing with the transfer to London of funds Brazil owed Portugal and their distribution to Barbacena through the Brazilian legation's "magic cashbox." Calmon was willing to explain the transactions orally, but he would not give the emperor anything in writing. After repeated evasions of his requests by Calmon, Dom Pedro verbally abused his foreign minister, prompting him to tender his resignation, which the emperor immediately accepted, on 26 September. The emperor then informed Barbacena that he intended to conduct a thorough audit of the finance ministry's records for 1828, and that because the transactions under investigation concerned him, he should give the finance portfolio to Paranaguá and move to the foreign ministry vacated by Calmon.[53]

But Barbacena refused to do the emperor's bidding. He had entered the cabinet, he said, at great personal sacrifice, and had accepted the finance portfolio purely as a favor to the monarch. He did not wish to be foreign minister; if the emperor no longer wanted him to be finance minister, he would leave the cabinet and retire to his sugar plantation in Bahia—but he asked Dom Pedro to keep him on as finance minister for at least eight more days. The emperor, already suspicious of Barbacena from auditing the wife-hunting accounts, was not going to give the marquis time to cook the finance ministry books. Accepting what he took to be Barbacena's resignation, Dom Pedro made it effective immediately, on 28 September. Three days later the ex-minister objected to the official announcement that he had been relieved at his own request: he had not resigned, but had been fired. The emperor then ordered a new decree drawn up, which was published on 5 October, stating that Barbacena had been dismissed because it was necessary to investigate the "great expenses" he had incurred in London in 1828 as the agent of the Brazilian emperor and the Portuguese queen.[54]

Barbacena countered the imputation of dishonesty by issuing a pamphlet detailing and attempting to justify his expenses, and containing copies of personal correspondence between him and Dom Pedro. The miffed marquis even published the emperor's requirements for a wife. Claiming credit for finding the lady who met them, Barbacena asserted that Dona Amélia was well worth what she had cost Dom Pedro. Avoiding a direct attack on the monarch, Barbacena suggested that his downfall was the work of Dom Pedro's "secret counselors," the first reference in print to what nativist journalists would call the "secret cabinet"—a cabal of Portuguese-born intimates of the emperor who were engaged in a conspiracy to "recolonize" Brazil. Barbacena, a palace insider, confirmed the fears of the xenophobes and gave the demagogues new leverage for raising the rabble against Rio's Portuguese community, now swollen by refugees from Dom Miguel's regime in Portugal. The liberal *Aurora fluminense* was not above belaboring the nonexistent secret cabinet, but the nativist attack was led by *O República*, a journal founded in Rio at the beginning of October by Antônio Borges da Fonseca, twenty-two years old, and recently arrived in the imperial capital from the economically depressed northeastern province of Paraíba. This intense young provincial was offended by the great number of Portuguese he encountered in the Brazilian metropolis and by their apparent domination of the city's commerce, and was ready to believe—or at least publish—the wildest Lusophobe rumors. Unfortunately for the conspiracy mongers, the man whom the public visualized as the chief of the secret cabinet, the Chalaça, had been gone from Brazil for six months. Borges da Fonseca and other nativists could only argue that the Chalaça was manipulating the emperor from abroad, and publish false reports of the Joker's imminent return to Brazil. It was popularly believed that Chalaça, from Europe, had precipitated Barbacena's fall by sending the emperor evidence that the marquis had embezzled a total of 400 contos from Dom Pedro and the Brazilian and Portuguese treasuries.[55]

The nativists welcomed Barbacena's revelations about the secret cabinet, but did not make the marquis their hero, and seemed mostly indifferent to his removal from office. The Chamber of Deputies took the dismissal of Barbacena and Calmon in stride and was gratified when the former was replaced as finance minister by a popular member of the lower house. Calmon, the only deputy in the Barbacena cabinet, was succeeded by a senator. A third vacancy in the cabinet, created by an earlier resignation for health reasons, was filled by a deputy, but he was a native of Portugal and a dissident member of the Minas Gerais delegation; his appointment greatly annoyed chamber kingpin Vasconcelos. The ministers of justice, war, and navy were held over from the Barbacena cabinet; in both governments the minister of war was a native of Portugal. Dom Pedro's ministerial changes did not prevent the General Assembly from closing on a positive note at the end of November, with the cabinet and the Senate deferring to the Chamber of Deputies to secure the enactment of essential legislation on the budget and the armed forces. In December most of the slavocrat legislators, including the marquis of Barbacena, returned to their plantations in the provinces, leaving the less fortunate journalists in Rio to suffer the summer heat and stir up trouble for Dom Pedro's government.[56]

Although all Rio newspapers hailed the July revolution in France, liberal-nativist journals professed to see special significance for Brazil in the French developments. They warned Dom Pedro, unnecessarily, that he would suffer the fate of Charles X if he tried to suppress his country's constitution. This gave rise to the qualified cheer, *Viva o Imperador, enquanto constitucional* ("Long live the emperor, as long as he's constitutional"), which understandably irritated Dom Pedro. Carioca nativists identified the hated Portuguese with the supposed movement, coordinated by the secret cabinet, to suppress the Brazilian constitution and proclaim Dom Pedro absolute ruler of a reunified Portugal and Brazil. Liberal-nativists like Rio's Evaristo da Veiga, who had been elected to the 1830 Chamber of Deputies from Vasconcelos's Minas Gerais, posed as defenders of the constitution against this imaginary threat, while their allies from the more distant provinces, like the Paraíban Borges da Fonseca, were plotting drastic changes in the constitutional regime, if not its overthrow. At the least they wanted a decentralized, federal monarchy, in which the provinces would enjoy a large measure of self-government and administrative autonomy. Evaristo, whose accommodation with the slavocrats had put him into parliament, was quite capable of making a temporary alliance with the federalists, whose doctrine was part of the liberal creed in some areas of the world. But Evaristo knew, as Dom Pedro knew, that federalism, if implemented in Brazil in the 1830s, would destroy the unity of the nation; he would resist it in the end as the emperor had resisted it from the beginning.[57]

The enthusiasm of Evaristo and Borges da Fonseca for the French July revolution was shared by their colleague in São Paulo, the editor of the newspaper *Observador constitucional*. A recent immigrant from Italy, the *Observador*'s editor had the Brazilianized name of João Batista Líbero Badaró. The editorials of this itinerant journalist encouraged some exuberant public celebrations of the Paris event in the streets of São Paulo, which led to the arrest of some law students for disorderly assembly. The *ouvidor* (district judge) who ordered the detention of the students was severely castigated in the columns of the *Observador*, and Badaró was approached on the night of 20 November by four men, one of whom pulled a pistol and shot Badaró in the stomach. Before dying the next day, the victim identified his assailants as Germans and speculated that they had been hired by the ouvidor to silence him. The district judge was arrested and sent to Rio for trial by a tribunal composed of his fellow ouvidores, who acquitted him for lack of evidence. The decision was denounced by newspapers in Rio, São Paulo, and throughout the empire. The involvement of Germans, presumably soon-to-be discharged mercenaries of the Imperial Army, stirred the nativist passions of Brazilian soldiers who had long resented their better-paid foreign comrades.[58]

The emperor was especially concerned about the situation in São Paulo in the wake of the Badaró murder, so he designated Brazilian-born General Francisco de Lima e Silva, who had led the imperial troops that crushed the Confederation of the Equator in 1824, to take command of the paulista military district in December 1830. General Lima e Silva was at the time commander of the Rio military district; one of his brothers, a brigadier, was commander of artillery in the imperial capital; and another, a colonel, commanded the emperor's Guard Battalion. The general's appointment was dated 9 December, but three weeks later, when Dom Pedro departed Rio on a trip to Minas Gerais, Lima e Silva still had not left to assume his new command. While the emperor was gone, the general, in a letter to the war minister, the count of Rio Pardo, declined the São Paulo appointment for "financial reasons." Although he could not make Lima e Silva go to São Paulo, the Portuguese-born Rio Pardo at least made him relinquish his Rio command. The insubordinate Brazilian-born general was lionized by nativist agitators and journalists in Rio in January 1831 while Dom Pedro and Dona Amélia were in Minas Gerais.[59]

The imperial couple's journey to Minas Gerais was a leisurely one, made for no compelling reason. The emperor hoped that his presence in the province might improve chances for the reelection to the Chamber of Deputies of his empire minister, José Antônio da Silva Maia, but, in the face of Vasconcelos's opposition, that cause was hopeless. Dom Pedro made no serious attempt at electioneering, and he took Silva Maia's defeat gracefully. Whatever the political tension beneath the surface, his tour was an easy-riding, ten-week excursion through the cool uplands, with extended stopovers, sight-seeing, bathing in hot springs, and pleasant receptions. The question of federalism came up in Ouro Prêto, the provincial capital, which prompted the emperor to issue in that city in February a proclamation interpreting the constitution as forbidding the consideration of federalist reforms. Many disagreed, including a jury in Rio that in January had absolved Borges da Fonseca of "abusing press freedom" by advocating federalism. But less weighty matters claimed most of the emperor's attention on the Minas Gerais tour. Finding five leased slaves employed in the maintenance of an imperial tax-collection station, Dom Pedro ordered them replaced by free workers; typically, Evaristo's *Aurora fluminense* criticized the emperor for disregarding the rights of the slaveowner. The imperial travelers quickened their pace on the return trip, and arrived back at Boa Vista palace almost a week earlier than expected, at three o'clock in the morning of 11 March.[60]

Dom Pedro was afraid that his arrival from Minas Gerais would set off a violent confrontation between his native and Portuguese-born subjects. His early return was probably designed to disrupt the plans of both sides. Members of the Portuguese community, subjected to rising levels of abuse during Dom Pedro's absence, increasingly saw the emperor as their deliverer from nativist bigotry; they were sure to be conspicuously present in any celebration of Dom Pedro's return, a prospect likely to prompt a boycott by Brazilians swayed or intimidated by the agitators—if not an actively hostile reaction to the festivities. In fact, word of the unscheduled arrival of the emperor and empress at Boa Vista on 11 March spread quickly among the Portuguese, who illuminated their houses and shops in their honor and hastily planned street dances and bonfires for the next two evenings. Most native Brazilians—including some who lived in predominantly Portuguese areas, like Evaristo da Veiga on Quintanda Street—refused to illuminate their houses and shunned the festivities on the night of 12 March. On the next night, however, a gang of young nativists led by *Repúblico* editor, Borges da Fonseca, appeared on the scene and put out several bonfires. The Portuguese, who for months had passively endured the insults of Borges and his crowd, finally struck back at the provocateurs with sticks, stones, and bottles. As streetfighters, the Portuguese —store clerks, tavern workers, warehousemen, sailors—had few equals, and they quickly routed their adversaries, severely beating many of them. Now unchallenged, the Portuguese paraded through the streets for hours shouting "Long live the emperor" and "Death to the editor of the *Repúblico*" and other slogans against republicans, federalists, and those who had not illuminated their houses. Borges and his partisans returned to the streets the next day with some young army officers whom they had recruited, and the chanting of slogans and intermittent fighting continued into the night, with the Portuguese still dominating the situation and the police standing by doing nothing. All this time Dom Pedro remained at Boa Vista and did not enter the city, for fear of aggravating matters.[61]

Finally, the emperor demanded that his Brazilian-born minister of justice and Portuguese-born minister of war do something to end the violence. The police moved in on the night of 15 March and arrested some rioters, including several nativist army officers—whose detention became a *cause célèbre* for Evaristo's *Aurora fluminense* as well as Borges's *Repúblico*. The twenty-two-year-old Borges apparently decided that it was within his power to destroy the monarchy and create a federal republic; the arrest of the army officers and their exploitation as martyrs by the *Repúblico* enhanced his ability to recruit among the military. Borges and the radical-nativists began organizing themselves into 100-man paramilitary companies, while Evaristo and his liberal colleagues began meeting to decide what position to take in the impending crisis. They would encourage Borges and his shock troops to put pressure on the emperor to make a deal with the Brazilian liberals to save his crown—for his five-year-old son, if not for himself. In the meantime, a semblance of order had been restored in Rio. On 17 March the emperor and empress entered the city for the first time since their Minas Gerais journey to attend a Te Deum mass at the Imperial Chapel thanking God for their safe return, and a hand-kissing ceremony at the city palace. Their carriage was accompanied through the streets by throngs of jubilant Portuguese, fifty on horseback, the sight of whom infuriated nativist onlookers who countered Portuguese cheers to the emperor with vivas to federation. Few prominent Brazilians attended the mass or the beija-mão; military officers were conspicuous by their scarcity.[62]

On the next day, 18 March, the justice minister received a petition addressed to the emperor and signed by Senator Vergueiro, Evaristo, and twenty-two other deputies who happened to be in Rio during the parliamentary recess. The petitioners called for the punishment of the "foreigners . . . who, on the nights of the 13th and 14th instant, insulted and assaulted our fellow-countrymen under the pretext that they were federalists; on account of a political question, the decision of which appertains solely to the legislative power, and not to the insensate and sanguinary fury of uneducated individuals, whose minds have been alienated by perfidious suggestions." The Portuguese-born planter-senator Vergueiro and his nativist collaborators criticized the arrests of Brazilian officers, alluded to "traitors who may surround the throne," declared that the people had "almost lost" confidence in the government, and inferred that there would be a revolution if the Portuguese went unpunished. The emperor responded to the petition by dismissing the justice minister, the Portuguese-born minister of war, and two other cabinet members, replacing them all with native Brazilians. The reorganized cabinet released the arrested Brazilian officers, restored General Lima e Silva to command of the Rio military district, and demanded that Dona Maria's minister to the Portuguese community in Rio call the queen's subjects to order. This he did: the Portuguese retreated to their homes, ships, and commercial establishments; after 19 March the nativists controlled the streets of Rio.[63]

March 25 was the seventh anniversary of Dom Pedro's promulgation of the constitution, and Borges da Fonseca organized a Te Deum mass in celebration of the occasion at the São Francisco de Paula Church, to which the emperor was not invited. Dom Pedro showed up anyway, on horseback; the few cheers he received as he dismounted and entered the church were conditional ones—"Long live the emperor, as long as he's constitutional"—but he heard an unqualified endorsement of his young son: "Viva Dom Pedro II!" An earnest bystander begged the emperor to obey the constitution. Dom Pedro reminded the man that he was the author of that document and had sworn to uphold it, a promise that he would never break. But the monarch was shaken by the total inversion of reality: he had done nothing to threaten the constitutional order, whereas Borges and the radicals were trying to force drastic changes, to convert the centralized empire into a federation, perhaps a republic; yet the revolutionaries were posing, and being accepted, as defenders of the constitution, whereas he was perceived as its imminent betrayer. Had he considered a coup against the constitution in 1831, as he had two years earlier, he would have no means of carrying one out. The Imperial Army in Rio was under the unreliable command of General Lima e Silva, many of whose troops had already defected to the nativist-radical cause. This was evident at a parade that the emperor attended that morning, at the Campo de Santana, where nativist spectators cheered the units they believed to be on their side.[64]

Borges da Fonseca and his comrades had entrée into most Rio barracks, and they stepped up their agitation among the soldiers towards the end of March. The first day of April was Good Friday. Dom Pedro was at the city palace reviewing religious processions, while Borges and his henchmen were at the nearby artillery barracks distributing free copies of a special edition of O *República* that falsely reported the assassination of various Brazilians. The crowds in the city palace square began to murmur against the emperor, religious marchers who passed beneath his balcony refused to doff their hats to him, and the artillerymen were on the verge of taking up arms to depose the monarch, when General Lima e Silva stepped in to calm the soldiers and persuade Dom Pedro to return to Boa Vista. The general snatched a revolutionary victory from Borges and briefly reversed the tide of mass hysteria that the young journalist had orchestrated on Good Friday, but O *República* was out again on Saturday, preaching the legality and "sacred duty" of resistance to "a tyrant." On Easter Sunday, Borges and his cadres were back in the streets near the city palace, leading mass demonstrations against the "tyranny," attacking isolated Portuguese homes and businesses, and assaulting persons suspected of loyalty to the emperor. The army and the police patrolled the boundaries of the Portuguese-dominated commercial districts—where the rioters feared to go—but did nothing to counter the disorders along Direita Street and around the artillery barracks.[65]

The disturbances continued through the night and the next day, Dona Maria's birthday, but the emperor insisted on going through with a scheduled reception at the queen's residence-in-exile, Domitila's former home, across the road from Boa Vista palace. Among the members of the diplomatic corps present at the affair were the envoys of the new liberal governments of France and Britain. Both recognized the gravity of the situation in Rio, and the British minister promised Dom Pedro asylum aboard one of his country's warships, should this be necessary. The emperor knew that Borges's radicals would not be satisfied with any concession that he could make: "I am liberal, the chief of the constitutionalists," Dom Pedro declared to the French minister, "but I'll never be the head of the revolutionaries." The emperor still felt that he might be able to rally enough military support behind the throne to disperse the revolutionary mobs. He pinned his hopes on a light infantry battalion from Santa Catarina that was due to land in Rio the next day.[66] But the emperor's cabinet had already given up; the ministers of justice and war informed the monarch that the police and army were incapable of putting down the disturbances. Dom Pedro fired them, and appointed an entirely new cabinet on the evening of 5 April.[67]

None of the new cabinet ministers were members of the Chamber of Deputies, and two were natives of Portugal. The appointment of the new cabinet gave Vergueiro, Evaristo, and their parliamentary colleagues a concrete goal, one less drastic than the overthrow of the monarchy, that would attract those soldiers and civilians touched by Borges's demogoguery but still hesitant about joining the revolutionary movement. News of the cabinet change, however, arrived too late for the 6 April edition of the *Aurora fluminense*, and its pudgy liberal editor, who lacked the radical Borges's taste for action, went into hiding while his liberal-nativist colleagues went about the city calling on the people to assemble at the Campo de Santana, a maneuver that shifted the focus of the demonstrations away from the radical-dominated city palace area. By one o'clock in the afternoon there were 600 people on the campo; the number of protesters there grew to 2,000 by three o'clock, and perhaps to as many as 4,000 two hours later. Soldiers and officers from the adjacent infantry barracks swelled the crowds after five o'clock; several prominent nativist-liberals joined with Borges da Fonseca and his cadres to organize the rally and maintain a precarious order. At the Campo de Santana the young radicals deferred to their distinguished liberal partners, who included José Joaquim Vieira Souto, parliamentary deputy and editor of the *Astréa*. The leaders of the rally agreed to send a delegation of parish judges to Boa Vista palace with a demand for the reinstatement of the dismissed cabinet. While the elected magistrates of the Rio area were being summoned to the Campo de Santana, General Lima e Silva, who was monitoring events there, dispatched a messenger to the palace to tell the emperor what was happening. After being briefed by the messenger, Dom Pedro told him that he would receive the delegation of parish magistrates, and sent him back to the campo with a proclamation to be read to the people. "Brazilians!" the emperor admonished his subjects, "Calm yourselves. I give you my imperial word of honor that I am constitutional from the heart, and that I will always uphold this constitution. Have confidence in me and in the cabinet." The imperial proclamation was torn to shreds after it was read, around six o'clock, and the crowd clamored for the delegation of parish judges to leave immediately for the palace, to demand the cabinet change.[68]

The emperor received the delegation of three parish judges at Boa Vista palace shortly after seven o'clock. He politely explained to them that the constitution gave him the power freely to select his ministers; he would violate his oath to uphold that charter if he allowed the people to dictate his choices, for then he would cease to be the representative of the permanent interests of the nation, and become another instrument of the present majority, which was already served by the Chamber of Deputies. "I will do anything for the people," Dom Pedro told the judges, "but nothing by the people." Those words, when relayed to the masses gathered at the Campo de Santana, evoked shouts of "Death to the tyrant!" By eleven o'clock almost every army unit in Rio—including the artillery commanded by one of General Lima e Silva's brothers, and the emperor's Guard Battalion, commanded by the other—had assembled on the Campo de Santana and joined the popular movement. General Lima e Silva, for the second time that day, sent his aide to the palace, this time shortly before midnight, to inform the emperor that the people's will could no longer be resisted, that the more he delayed in making the cabinet changes, the greater the risk of the radicals' taking over the movement and destroying the monarchy.[69]

Dom Pedro would make one last try to preserve at least a semblance of his imperial prerogative. He agreed to dismiss the cabinet, but instead of reinstating the former one, he would call on Senator Vergueiro to form a new government. A police officer was sent out to find Vergueiro and bring him to the palace while the emperor stoically waited in the company of his sobbing wife, his ministers, the diplomatic representatives of Britain and France, and General Lima e Silva's aide. Dom Pedro had little hope that Vergueiro would allow himself to be found; if the senator did not appear within a reasonable period of time, the emperor would give up his crown. "I prefer abdicating to accepting violent impositions that are contrary to the constitution and imposed by the people and a mutinous army," Dom Pedro told the French minister. The emperor perceived the problem as one of national origins. "All those who were born here are in the campo and against me," he acknowledged. "They don't want me as a ruler because I'm

Portuguese. No matter how they do it, they're determined to rid themselves of me. I expected this for some time. During the trip to Minas I predicted that my return to Rio would be the signal for the struggle between natives and Portuguese, provoking the present crisis. My son has the advantage over me of being Brazilian, and the Brazilians like him. He'll reign without difficulty and the constitution will guarantee his prerogatives. I'll descend from the throne with the glory of ending as I began, constitutionally."[70]

Around three o'clock in the morning the police officer returned to announce, as expected, that he could not find Senator Vergueiro. The emperor retired to his private study and returned a few minutes later with a piece of paper on which he had written:

> Using the right that the Constitution concedes to me, I declare that I have very voluntarily abdicated in favor of my very beloved and esteemed son, Senhor Dom Pedro de Alcântara. Boa Vista, April 7, 1831, Tenth Year of Independence and of the Empire.
>
> Pedro

Dom Pedro handed the paper to General Lima e Silva's aide. "Here you have my act of abdication," he said. "I'm returning to Europe and leaving a country that I loved very much, and still love."[71]

Dom Pedro was leaving not only his adopted country, but his only son and three of his daughters as well. There was only one person he could trust to take care of them. After Dom Pedro, Dona Amélia, and Queen Maria II of Portugal boarded a British warship at daybreak, the ex-emperor forwarded another document to General Lima e Silva, dated 6 April. "Using the right conceded me by the constitution," Dom Pedro wrote, "I appoint . . . as the tutor of my beloved and esteemed children the very upright, honorable, and patriotic citizen, José Bonifácio de Andrada e Silva, my true friend."[72] The patriarch of independence would carry out his new assignment with great courage and dedication, though controversy swirled about him and turmoil engulfed the empire.

The political system that Dom Pedro had fashioned for Brazil was shattered by Borges da Fonseca and the radicals. Evaristo and the liberals would pick up the pieces and make it whole again, and Vasconcelos and the conservatives would take it away from them. The planter-slavocrats held the preponderance of economic power at the time, and the liberal system had to accommodate them. But liberalism guaranteed economic and social change, and this eventually came about in a more orderly and peaceful manner in Brazil than in any other nation in the Western Hemisphere. Dom Pedro had served his adopted country well.

8 Dom Pedro versus Dom Miguel

*Every man must regret deeply
that those who are employed in disseminating liberty through the universe
are sometimes stained with vices and baseness.*
Colonel Charles Shaw, Commander,
Queen Maria's Scottish Fusiliers

Four longboats sent out by the British ship-of-the-line *Warspite* and the French frigate *Dryade* met Dom Pedro's party at the landing at São Cristóvão Beach as day was breaking on 7 April 1831. Some of the foreign sailors were armed and one of the British launches displayed a small cannon on a swivel mount. The ex-emperor refused to get into that boat; he was not going to leave his country under armed escort. In any case, there was no danger to Dom Pedro or his family. Evaristo appeared before the masses at the Campo de Santana at sunrise to help them celebrate their great victory and lead the cheering for the new Brazilian-born emperor, five-year-old Dom Pedro II. Evaristo and General Lima e Silva saw to it that there would be no march on the palace, no proclamation of a republic. The general, backed by his troops and most of the members of parliament who happened to be in Rio that morning, assumed the presidency of a temporary regency—composed of himself, Senator Vergueiro, and the marquis of Caravelas—which was to rule in the name of the young emperor until the full General Assembly could convene and name a regular regency in accordance with the constitution. The people accepted the dictation of Lima e Silva and no revolutionary mobs threatened the evacuation route from Boa Vista to São Cristóvão Beach.[1]

The greatest commotion was caused by dozens of slaves and servants from Boa Vista who ran behind their master's carriage to the landing, begging to be taken with him. But only a few members of the palace staff—including six slaves and João Carlota, the ever-faithful valet and stable master—could go with the ex-emperor; the rest would have to stay and serve his son, their new master. British and French sailors had to physically restrain some disappointed slaves from climbing into the boats. Aside from this unpleasantness, the drive from Boa Vista to the landing and the boat trip from there to the *Warspite* appeared more like a recreational outing than a flight from power. The ex-emperor seemed serene, even happy, offering lighthearted reassurance to a worried Dona Amélia. Dom Pedro wore a brown frock coat and a jaunty top hat, the kind of attire appropriate for a picnic excursion to the island of Paquetá. The ex-empress wore a bonnet and full-skirted dress, but without some essential undergarments—as her husband reminded her after they reached the *Warspite* and she approached the ladder to climb out of the boat and onto the deck of the ship. When she hesitated, the gallant Admiral Baker, who had descended into the boat to help her up, asked what was wrong, and Dom Pedro answered for her in French: *Mais elle n'a point de pantalon.* The ex-emperor requested that a chair-hoist be lowered for his wife, but as there was no such apparatus on board, the lovely Dona Amélia had to ascend the ladder, which she did gracefully, to the admiration of oarsmen below and officers and seamen above.[2]

Dom Pedro was leaving the country "voluntarily," he maintained; he was not leading an exodus of his partisans from Brazil. All of his children, except the queen of Portugal, and all of his ministers and councillors of state were to remain in Brazil; even his confessor, Friar Arrábida, now bishop of Anemuria *in partibus* was to stay, to help José Bonifácio educate the ex-emperor's children. Dona Maria and her miniscule Portuguese court-in-exile embarked on the *Warspite*, but there was no room for her subjects, who fearing a massacre by the nativists, rowed out to the British flagship in dozens of small boats, clamoring to get aboard. Among the few Portuguese who did embark were the ex-emperor's sister, Dona Ana de Jesus, and her husband, the marquis of Loulé. Dona Ana was the only sister of Dom Pedro to side with him against Dom Miguel; she and the marquis had only recently arrived in Brazil from exile in France. Another lady, the Chalaça's wife, was invited to make the trip, but she declined, saying that she would stay in Rio and await instructions from her husband. As his secretary on the trip to Europe, the ex-emperor took along M. Plasson, French editor of the court-subsidized newspaper *O Moderador*, which had no future after 7 April. To attend the ex-empress, who was two months pregnant, Dom Pedro selected the Brazilian mulatto physician, Dr.

João Fernandes Tavares. Dona Amélia's brother, Prince Auguste, had returned to Europe the year before. The combined entourage of the queen of Portugal and ex-emperor of Brazil, including family dependents and servants, amounted to perhaps 150 persons, all of whom initially were accommodated on the *Warspite*.[3]

Aboard the British warship lying in Rio harbor, Dom Pedro busied himself with personal financial matters. He worked furiously with his accountants and financial agents to inventory and liquidate as much of his property as possible before sailing—to sell his mortgages, real estate, furniture, carriages, harness, saddles, horses, mules, cattle, and slaves. His jewelry and silverware he would take with him, as they conveniently could be disposed of in Europe. Wary of Brazilian bank notes, he was delighted when one of his agents brought him a pouch of gold dust. The ex-emperor's preoccupation with such mundane matters amused the crew of the *Warspite*. One officer thought it ironic that the "legitimate Champion of the Constitutional Rights of Man —that Imperial Tom Paine," should be concerned about getting a good price for his slaves.[4] Secure in his British navy salary, the officer apparently did not stop to think that liberation costs money. But even had the British officers been sympathetic towards their guest's financial dealings, they could not allow him to carry them on for long: the ex-emperor's continued presence in Rio harbor was lending some credence to rumors fabricated by the radicals that the British and French were planning to land marines in Rio to join with resident Portuguese in a coup to restore Dom Pedro to the throne. On 12 April, with nativists threatening the Portuguese community with a holocaust, Admiral Baker announced that the ex-emperor would sail the next day, and Dom Pedro submitted to the press his farewell letter, expressing regret that he was unable to write personally to all his friends, asking forgiveness for any offense he might have given them, and concluding with "Goodbye fatherland, goodbye friends, and goodbye forever."[5] He would never return to Brazil, but would always consider himself a Brazilian.

Because there was still a possibility of a nativist attack on the Portuguese and other foreign nationals in Rio, Admiral Baker decided to remain there with his flagship and to transfer Dom Pedro and Dona Amélia to the frigate HMS *Volage*. The queen of Portugal and the marquis and marchioness of Loulé were shifted to the French frigate *La Seine*, which would stay in Rio for another week before following the *Volage* to France. At dawn on the morning of 13 April a steamboat towed the *Volage* out of Rio Harbor and into the Atlantic Ocean, where, bucking the Brazil current, she reached off for the southeast trade winds and then set a course due north for the Azores. For six weeks the sailing was smooth, until 27 May when a great storm blew up that caused Dona Amélia much discomfort, but fascinated her husband, who described it to his son in a letter that he illustrated with drawings. For the rest of his life Dom Pedro would correspond regularly with his son and daughters in Rio; his letters to Dom Pedro II often were written above the youngster's level of understanding, apparently to record the father's thoughts and actions and preserve them for the recipient's later contemplation.[6]

The storm carried the *Volage* almost to the harbor at Faial, in the Azores, where the frigate dropped anchor on 30 May. The warship remained there for only ten hours, long enough to take on provisions and for Dom Pedro to forward some communications to the Portuguese constitutional regency on the nearby island of Terceira. From Faial it was ten day's sailing to Falmouth, where the *Volage* put in for a few hours before resuming her voyage to France. The news given out at the English port was that the ex-emperor and empress of Brazil were enroute to Cherbourg, whence they would proceed overland to Munich to visit her mother. Among the letters Dom Pedro posted at Falmouth was one to Francisco Gomes da Silva in London; the Chalaça lost no time in taking a boat to Cherbourg for a joyful reunion with his master and friend. At Cherbourg the ex-emperor received a twenty-one-gun salute and all the honors due a reigning monarch; 5,000 men of the National Guard were drawn up for his inspection; a mansion was placed at his disposal by the municipal government; and he was hailed in welcoming speeches as a champion of liberty, a giver of constitutions, who had stepped down from his throne rather than violate Brazil's sacred charter. Dom Pedro decided to survey the European situation from Cherbourg before making his next move. He was soon joined there not only by the Chalaça from London, but by the marquis of Resende from Paris.[7]

António Teles da Silva, the marquis of Resende, was one of Dom Pedro's boyhood companions, a Portuguese-born confidant of the young emperor, eight years his junior. Dom Pedro had sent him to Vienna in 1823 to secure Austrian recognition of Brazilian independence. In mid-1829 Resende had moved from Vienna to Paris as Brazilian minister to France. On the eve of the July revolution he correctly sized up the situation: despite official recognition of Dona Maria as queen of Portugal by the government of Charles X, the Bourbon regime was conniving with Metternich to undermine her position and bolster that of Dom Miguel, who, his questionable legitimacy notwithstanding, was regarded as an indispensable bulwark of absolutism on the Iberian peninsula. The overthrow of Dom Miguel, the reactionaries of Paris and Vienna feared, would lead to a constitutionalist revolution in Spain. What the absolutists feared, Resende reported to Dom Pedro early in 1830, the French liberals devoutly desired; they were the real friends of Dona Maria, and they had come to power in Paris with the July revolution. Shortly before the revolution, when Barbacena and Calmon were directing Brazilian foreign affairs, Resende was reassigned to the court of the Russian czar in St. Petersburg —banished to the "North Pole," he complained—but he was recalled to Paris by Dom Pedro a few months later.[8]

The marquis of Resende moved easily among French liberals and Spanish exiles in Paris. The euphoria of his friends in mid-1830 had faded by the end of the year, before Resende returned from St. Petersburg. Aggressive liberals, those who wanted to promote freedom in other lands, were displaced in the government of King Louis Philippe by moderates, noninterventionists except where French economic interests clearly were at stake. The venerable marquis of Lafayette, doyen of international liberalism, was removed as commander of the National Guard in November; Benjamin Constant died in December. In foreign affairs, during the winter of 1830–31, the attention of the July monarchy was focused on nearby Belgium, and Louis Philippe moved from a policy of trying to extend French influence over that struggling new kingdom to one of seeking an accommodation with Britain to guarantee Belgian independence and neutrality. In more distant Portugal, the French government recognized the preponderance of British interests and consistently deferred to London. Although Portuguese despotism was equally distasteful to London and Paris, French residents of Portugal suffered more from Dom Miguel's arbitrary rule than did British nationals. But the French would not send a naval expedition to Lisbon to demand reparations until they were encouraged to do so by British Foreign Secretary Lord Palmerston in June 1831. The power that could put Dona Maria on the throne in Lisbon, Resende knew, was in London, not Paris. So he and Dom

Pedro and their friend, the Chalaça, left Cherbourg on 21 June for a visit to London.[9]

Dom Pedro checked in at London's Clarendon Hotel as the duke of Bragança, assuming an ancient Portuguese title and modifying its coat of arms by adding the words "perpetual defender of Brazil." The marquis of Resende traveled under that Brazilian title of recent origin, as chamberlain to the duke, having resigned as Brazil's minister to France. The day after their arrival in London they were cordially received by Lord Palmerston, and were presented to King William IV on 29 June. Prime Minister Earl Grey was less enthusiastic than was his foreign minister for the cause of Portuguese liberty, and the king was at best indifferent. Nevertheless, William IV gave a dinner at St. James palace for the duke of Bragança on 1 July. It was attended by all the British cabinet ministers and various members of the diplomatic corps. The French ambassador was the durable Prince Talleyrand, to whom Dom Pedro turned as it became clear that the British government could not be persuaded to intervene militarily in Portugal on behalf of Queen Maria II—at least not before the Belgian problem was solved.[10]

Although he promised Dom Pedro no direct assistance for the liberation of Portugal, Talleyrand assured him that he would be well received in Paris on the first anniversary of the July revolution. The duke of Bragança, after arranging for a state visit to England by Dona Maria, who had recently arrived from Brazil at Cherbourg, made a quick trip to Paris at the end of July. When Dom Pedro and Resende got to the latter's house in Paris on 26 July they found an invitation to dine with the king and queen that night. They arrived at the dinner party late, and the ex-emperor appeared embarrassed, although the king and queen received him graciously. All eyes were on him, and he was especially shy in responding to the ladies to whom he was introduced. Then he was presented to the marquis of Lafayette—nearly seventy-four years old, a bit stout, wearing a black wig, with the Cross of July decorating his dinner jacket. Dom Pedro could not contain his joy at meeting the original "hero of two worlds"; words of reverence, praise, obeisance gushed from the ex-emperor's lips. Dom Pedro expressed his feelings to Lafayette, an onlooker noted, with "an air of amicability, as if he had known him for a long time."[11] The marquis was not offended: he became one of Dom Pedro's staunchest supporters.

In the three days of parades and other public ceremonies commemorating the July revolution, Dom Pedro, in his green Brazilian uniform with gold epaulets, became a familiar figure to the people of Paris, who saw him standing, walking, and riding horseback at the side of the king. He would stop to banter with the Parisians and to explain to them the struggle for Portuguese freedom. He won many hearts with his verbal support for another liberal cause, shouting with the crowds "Vive la Pologne!," thus placing himself on the side of the Polish patriots in their desperate struggle against the Russian autocracy. Disappointed in their own king, militant French liberals reserved their cheers for Lafayette and for Dom Pedro. "Long live the constitutional emperor!" they cried, referring to the duke of Bragança; "Vive Dom Pedro!" The people were friendly, and so was the government; the king offered Dom Pedro the use of a chateau outside Paris, rent free, as a residence for his family. The duke would have preferred two Portuguese warships that the French navy had captured in its punitive expedition to Lisbon. At first, the French foreign minister said that the ships would be given to the Portuguese liberals, but he was overruled by the king, who insisted that France follow Britain's policy of no overt intervention in Portugal's internal affairs. About the only military assistance that Louis Philippe could provide Dom Pedro was the use of an island off the south coast of Brittany as a secret staging area for his forces.[12] The duke of Bragança would have to raise and equip these forces without the help—financial or otherwise—of the governments of Britain or France.

Having committed himself to bringing the Portuguese queen to England, Dom Pedro left Paris on 30 July, picked up Dona Amélia and Dona Maria in Cherbourg, and arrived with them in London on 2 August. They stayed at the Clarendon Hotel, where they were visited by the British royal family on 4 August. At the end of the following week Dom Pedro, Queen Maria II, and Dona Amélia were overnight guests of the king at Windsor Castle. In the meantime, the ex-emperor met with Lords Grey and Palmerston in the vain hope of arranging British government financing for his projected expedition to overthrow Dom Miguel. He was advised to seek private funding. Dom Pedro was able to open a 12,000-pounds-sterling line of credit for the Azores regency at the Rothschild Bank, but that institution later refused to honor it. Ultimately more productive was an agreement that Dom Pedro signed on 14 August with a group headed by the Spanish exile and financier, Juan Álvarez y Mendizábal, to broker a 2,000,000-pounds-sterling loan in the name of Portuguese Queen Maria II. But Dom

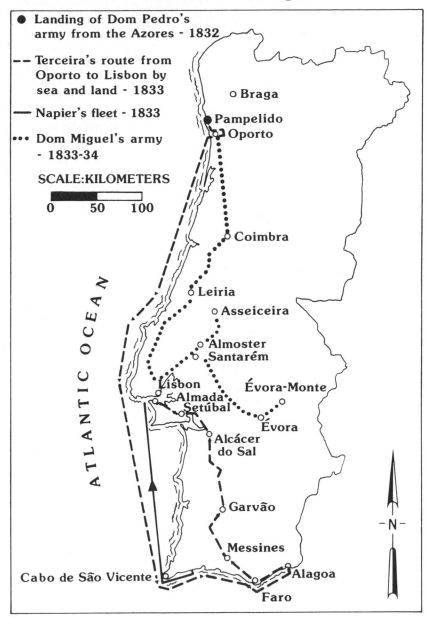

- ● Landing of Dom Pedro's army from the Azores - 1832
- – – Terceira's route from Oporto to Lisbon by sea and land - 1833
- —— Napier's fleet - 1833
- ••• Dom Miguel's army - 1833-34

SCALE:KILOMETERS

0   50   100

Braga

Pampelido
Oporto

ATLANTIC OCEAN

Coimbra

Leiria

Asseiceira

Almoster
Santarém

Lisbon
Almada
Setúbal

Évora-Monte

Évora

Alcácer
do Sal

Garvão

Messines

Cabo de São Vicente

Alagoa

Faro

- N -

Portugal: 1832–34. Dom Pedro versus Dom Miguel

Pedro, whose personal resources were dwindling rapidly, could not afford to remain in England while Mendizábal and his associates tried to raise the money for the queen; the duke of Bragança decided to sell his silver and jewels in London, pay his bill at the Clarendon Hotel, and move his household to Paris, accepting Louis Philippe's offer of free lodging. After summoning the marquis of Palmela from the Azores to London to take charge of the project of raising an expeditionary force in England to liberate Portugal, Dom Pedro escorted the Portuguese queen and Dona Amélia to France to take up residence at the Chateau Meudon outside Paris. The duke of Bragança departed London on 16 August, and Talleyrand noted, "he is not very pleased with his latest stay in England."[13]

Dom Pedro had hopes of securing private financing in France for the liberation of Portugal. The two most important promoters of the project in Paris were the marquis of Lafayette and General João Carlos Saldanha. The latter, a great favorite of Lafayette, was a Portuguese exile who also was popular among the numerous Spanish liberal refugees in France. Saldanha advocated the liberation of Portugal from Dom Miguel as a step toward the overthrow of Spain's despotic King Fernando VII and the creation of a liberal Iberian empire, embracing the peninsula's two kingdoms. Saldanha's candidate for emperor of Iberia was Dom Pedro, whom the general had admired since his days as a Portuguese officer in Brazil. A much-decorated veteran of Wellington's Peninsular Campaign, Saldanha had further distinguished himself in fighting Artigas's gauchos in Uruguay. Summoned back to Portugal shortly before Brazil's declaration of independence in 1822, Saldanha obeyed the order despite Dom Pedro's best efforts to persuade him to stay and enter Brazilian service. For his outspoken support of Dom Pedro's Portuguese constitution of 1826, Saldanha, a grandson of the marquis of Pombal, incurred the wrath of the kingdom's absolutists. When Dom Pedro made the mistake of naming Dom Miguel regent of Portugal in 1827, Saldanha decided to get out of the country. When Dom Miguel usurped the throne in 1828, Saldanha joined with Palmela, then in London as the ambassador of the deposed constitutional regime, in a bungled attempt to relieve the liberal forces holding out against the absolutists in Oporto. Each blamed the other for the fiasco, after which Saldanha went to France to pursue his Iberian empire schemes, and Palmela went to Terceira in the Azores to head the Portuguese regency named by Dom Pedro.[14]

Aside from their personal animosity, Palmela and Saldanha had strong policy disagreements. The marquis was afraid that Saldanha's association with Spanish liberals would alienate the British, who were trying to persuade Spain's King Fernando to withdraw his recognition of Dom Miguel as king of Portugal. Palmerston told Palmela that the British government would look the other way while he recruited mercenaries of any nationality—except Spanish. The British insisted, like their French allies, that the attack on the Portuguese usurper not appear as a threat to the legitimate Spanish regime, which, they hoped, would evolve along liberal and constitutional lines after the death of Don Fernando.[15] Palmerston seemed to think that the withdrawal of Spanish recognition—if Britain could bring this about—would do as much to persuade Dom Miguel to retire from Portugal as would an invasion of the country by liberal exiles and foreign mercenaries.

Except the Papacy, Spain was the only European power that recognized Dom Miguel as king of Portugal. The only other country that had diplomatic relations with Dom Miguel's regime was the United States. The populist administration of President Andrew Jackson recognized that Dom Miguel was enormously popular with the Portuguese people; the Anglophobe Old Hickory probably thought that anyone so hated by the British could not be all bad. The Portuguese peasants adored their bullfighting, horse-racing, deer-slaying young king, and he loved them. The tens of thousands who were driven into exile, the thousands who rotted in royal prisons without trials or the hope of obtaining them, the hundred or so who were executed, were not dirt farmers, fishermen, or herdsmen, but merchants, professionals, liberal clerics, and dissident noblemen—or, according to the retrograde priests and monks who infested the countryside, Freemasons, heretics, Jews, and foreigners. Crazed friars preached xenophobia and bigotry to a susceptible rural population. The Portuguese peasantry would defend their king against his enemies, who were also the enemies of their country and their religion: the French Freemasons who invaded their waters and assaulted their ships, the heretical English whose privileged presence within their cities was an insult to God, the king's faithless brother who had stolen Brazil from them. Liberalism held no appeal for Portugal's priest-ridden peasants; their meager possessions were not threatened with confiscation; they were secure, in body and soul, in their Holy Faith; they did not covet the property of the Church; they were free Christian men and women who did not aspire to read, write, or think blasphemous thoughts. On Good Friday 1831 Dom Miguel raised the religious fervor of his benighted subjects by presiding over a reenactment of the crucifixion, in which a life-sized image of Jesus was nailed to a cross.[16]

There was no shortage of brave and dedicated peasant soldiers ready to fight for Dom Miguel; what his regime lacked was competent military leadership. Army officers formed part of that professional class most attracted to liberal doctrines. Perhaps half the Portuguese officer corps—the more talented half—was liberal. Though nationalistic, Dom Miguel's conservative and capricious tyranny had difficulty retaining the loyalty of intelligent and ambitious—if not idealistic—military professionals. Opportunity lay on the liberal side, and that was where the best generals were. Besides Saldanha, there was the count of Vila Flor, who from the original constitutionalist base on Terceira conquered the other islands of the Azores, and overran the last absolutist stronghold, on São Miguel, early in August 1831. With the integration of Migelista prisoners into its ranks, the liberal army in the Azores numbered about 7,700 men. On the Portuguese mainland Dom Miguel had some 80,000 of his subjects under arms. Dom Pedro planned to make up part of this troop disparity with foreign mercenary soldiers. He also needed a naval force to transport the constitutionalist army to Portugal. Lord Cochrane offered his services—"I desire no recompense," he wrote, astonishingly, to Dom Pedro—but the ex-emperor chose a less flamboyant British veteran to command his daughter's navy, Captain George Rose Sartorius.[17]

The choice of Sartorius was supported by the marquis of Palmela, who arrived at Dom Pedro's Chateau Meudon from the Azores via London on 27 September. As head of the regency, Palmela vetoed the participation of General Saldanha in the coming expedition. However, the marquis was eager to step down from the three-man regency, which he believed should be dissolved and replaced by Dom Pedro as sole regent for the queen. In making arrangements for the liberation of Portugal, Dom Pedro had been acting on his ill-defined authority as "tutor and natural defender" of the young queen. The duke of Bragança preferred to remain a "private citizen" at least until after Dona Amélia gave birth to their first child, due near the end of November. He saw no need for him to abandon his wife precipitously in order to go to the Azores and assume sole responsibility for the Portuguese constitutional government. He was willing to lead the troops ashore in Portugal, but it would be many months before the invasion force would be ready. The purchasing of ships and the hiring of mercenary sailors and soldiers was just beginning, after the Mendizábal loan had been closed on 23 September.[18]

Dom Pedro became quite fond of Juan Álvarez y Mendizábal, the Spanish exile financier whom he had met in London in August. The gifted son of a family of Jewish clothiers and pawnbrokers of the port city of Cádiz, the tall, thin, hawk-nosed Mendizábal was a banker with the manners of an hidalgo, and he was a dedicated liberal. At the age of thirty he had pledged his first fortune to the Spanish liberal revolution that began in Cádiz in 1820. The French invasion and counterrevolution of 1823 forced him into exile in London, where he amassed a new fortune and continued to contribute his financial talents to the cause of Iberian freedom.[19] Mendizábal, like his friend, the Portuguese General Saldanha, visualized the overthrow of Dom Miguel in Portugal as the prelude to the liberation of Spain. But the Spanish banker also had reason to believe that Dom Miguel deserved dethronement on his own demerits. The usurper was summoning up from the murky depths of the Portuguese soul a dangerous fanaticism, reviving the mind-destroying bigotry that had produced the Inquisition, launched the persecution of the Jews, and had stopped Iberian progress in its tracks around the year 1500.

Mendizábal and his associate Saldanha had far more rapport with Dom Pedro than had Palmela, yet the ex-emperor allowed Palmela to bar Saldanha from participation in the expedition that was to be launched from the Azores. There remained, however, the possibility of Saldanha's leading a second strike, financed by Mendizábal, or perhaps by friends of the marquis of Lafayette. That ancient comrade of George Washington was a frequent visitor at the Chateau Meudon, where the marquis of Resende and the Chalaça were kept busy issuing appointments and regulating the steady stream of callers who had business with the duke of Bragança. The chateau, with its landscaped gardens and regal interior decorations—huge paintings, mirrors, medieval tapestries—was an appropriate location for the court of the Portuguese queen in exile. But it was very costly; although he paid no rent, Dom Pedro was responsible for the upkeep of the chateau, its grounds, and stables with twenty-five horses. The maintenance bill was enormous, and the parsimonious ex-emperor soon decided to move the Portuguese court to a rented townhouse in Paris. The queen, her father and tutor, her pregnant stepmother, and various attendants took up residence in October at 10 Rue de Courcelles.[20]

Joining Dom Pedro, Dona Amélia, and Dona Maria at their home on Courcelles Street was the seven-year-old duchess of Goiás — also known as "Bela" — the illegitimate daughter of the ex-emperor and the marchioness of Santos. Bela had been interned at the Sacred Heart convent school in Paris since 1829, when her father had sent her abroad from Rio to please his new wife, who, coached by the marquis of Barbacena, had declared that she wanted nothing to do with the little bastard. Perceiving her husband's great love for the child, and with her maternal instincts perhaps sharpened with the approach of her own motherhood, Dona Amélia took the motherless Bela into her home and heart. Another individual of irregular origin against whom Barbacena had poisoned Dona Amélia's mind, the Chalaça, also came to be appreciated by the ex-empress in Paris. After Dom Pedro's death, the Chalaça would serve Dona Amélia as honestly and faithfully as he had served her husband.[21]

From his city residence Dom Pedro regularly rode out to a firing range to practice his marksmanship. He also did a good deal of walking, strolling along the streets of Paris, enjoying the urban ambience. And he danced more while he was in Paris than ever before in his life. He and Dona Amélia were invited to the numerous grand balls of the autumn season, and because of her advancing pregnancy, the ex-emperor found himself with a multiplicity of ballroom partners; he took lessons to improve his technique, but never became a good dancer. An incurable music addict, Dom Pedro frequently appeared with Dona Amélia at the Paris Opera or the Théâtre Français, in King Louis Philippe's box. But the duke of Bragança was primarily attracted to Gioacchino Rossini's Théâtre Italien. Since his days as crown prince in Brazil, Dom Pedro had practically worshipped the works of Rossini, and the emotional impact of his meeting the great composer was perhaps second only to that of his presentation to the marquis of Lafayette. The burly Rossini — whose musical talents had been enlisted on the side of liberalism two years before, with the appearance of his opera *William Tell* — seemed to consider himself similarly honored in making the acquaintance of Dom Pedro. The maestro examined some of his new friend's musical manuscripts and asked permission to produce one composition, an "Ouverture à grand orchestre," at the Théâtre Italien. Rossini's orchestra played the piece in a concert on 30 October.

Some people in the audience did not care for Dom Pedro's overture and walked out during the performance, which prompted one critic to write that "Monsieur l'Empéreur would be more properly employed in chasing his bloodthirsty brother out of Portugal than in driving peaceful concert goers out of the theater."[22]

Among Dom Pedro's visitors in Paris in 1831 was José Inácio Abreu e Lima, native of Pernambuco and son of the revolutionary Padre Roma, who had been executed on orders of the count of Arcos in 1817. Escaping from prison in Brazil, Abreu e Lima joined the forces of Simón Bolívar in Venezuela in 1818 and served the Liberator until his death in 1830, attaining the rank of brigadier general in the Colombian army. At odds with the post-Bolivarian government of Colombia, Abreu e Lima went to the United States, where he heard the news of Dom Pedro's abdication. This he viewed as a potential disaster for his native Brazil, which Dom Pedro had managed to hold together during his nine-year reign while the lands that Bolívar had liberated flew apart, impelled by regional interests similar to those that pervaded the Brazilian empire. Abreu e Lima proceeded from the United States to France to offer his services to Dom Pedro in restoring him to the Brazilian throne. He established "very good relations" with the ex-emperor, who shared his opinions on important political and social questions—like the need to abolish slavery—but was committed to a European project and was not free to return to South America at that time. In any case, the groundwork had to be laid in Brazil for Dom Pedro's recall. General Abreu e Lima left Paris before the end of 1831 and went to Rio, where he joined the growing ranks of Brazilians who were working actively for the restoration of the exiled monarch.[23]

Brazil was on Dom Pedro's mind as Dona Amélia went into labor with their first child. The ex-emperor summoned the Brazilian minister to France to his house on Courcelles Street on 1 December 1831 to witness the birth—or at least the cutting of the umbilical cord—to certify the infant as a Brazilian citizen and a member of the imperial family. The baby, a girl, was delivered by the Brazilian mulatto Dr. Tavares, and was named Maria Amélia. The next day was the sixth birthday of Dom Pedro II, child emperor of Brazil, an event that was marked by a gala banquet at his father's house in Paris. As toasts were being drunk to each of the princesses who had remained in Brazil, Dom Pedro felt sick. He got up from the table and went to his room, complaining of nausea and dizziness. He was still indisposed the next day, but received a visit from King Louis Philippe and his family. Not until 5 December did Dom Pedro feel well enough to leave his house for a drive to the Tuileries palace. The trauma of exile, the onset of the Parisian winter, perhaps the rich French food, had affected his health; he suffered more frequently from kidney-stone attacks after his departure from Brazil, and he looked heavier in his Paris portraits than in earlier ones—an appearance that may have been due more to edema than to solid weight gain. Nevertheless, by 11 December he had sufficiently recovered from his attack of 2 December to attend mass at the church of St. Phillip of Roule, directly in front of his house. After church he was visited by George Rose Sartorius, now admiral of the Portuguese constitutionalist navy, who informed him that the expeditionary force was beginning to take shape. Some ships and their crews were already at Belle Isle, and the hiring of mercenary soldiers had begun in England in November.[24]

His ailments disappeared or were ignored as Dom Pedro prepared to go to war; he returned to the firing range for target practice, rode horseback, read books on military tactics and strategy, and drilled French troops at the invitation of King Louis Philippe. Palmela appeared on 26 December to report that his mission in London was accomplished: the ships had been purchased, the mercenaries hired, and all had left Britain for Belle Isle. The ships were to be armed at Belle Isle and outfitted there for a voyage to the Azores, where the mercenaries were to be taken to train with Portuguese constitutionalist troops and Dom Pedro was to be inaugurated as regent prior to the invasion of Portugal. On 8 January 1832 Mendizábal arrived in Paris from Belle Isle to tell Dom Pedro that the ships were ready, although some of the contracted mercenary soldiers had not yet reported to the staging area. The duke of Bragança confirmed that his departure was imminent at a dinner party given for him and his wife by the king and queen at the Tuileries on 12 January. The next day the marquis of Lafayette appeared at 10 Rue de Courcelles to give the coming crusade his liberal benediction; Lafayette's grandson, Lasteyrie, signed on as an officer with Dom Pedro's expedition. Lafayette and some 200 other well-wishers gathered at Dom Pedro's house early on the morning of 25 January for a farewell breakfast, after which the duke of Bragança embraced his wife, said goodbye to Dona Maria, and got into a coach with the marquises of Palmela and Loulé and rode off toward Belle Isle.[25]

Dr. Tavares followed in another vehicle, while the marquis of Resende and the Chalaça remained in Paris to look after Dom Pedro's family.

Dom Pedro and his party were met by Mendizábal in Nantes, where they attended some festivities given in the duke's honor by the municipal government. In Nantes, Dom Pedro went to church, confessed, and received communion from the bishop before boarding a steamboat for Belle Isle, where he arrived on 2 February. There he beheld the constitutionalist squadron: two aging merchantmen purchased from the East India Company that had been converted to "frigates" mounting forty-two and forty-six guns, a couple of smaller vessels denominated "corvettes," and two transports. The duke presided over the swearing in of the ships' crews and the ground troops —several hundred foreign mercenaries and Portuguese exiles, including the poets Almeida Garrett and Alexandre Herculano. More mercenaries were due on at least two more transports, but Dom Pedro decided not to wait for them. He sailed for the Azores on 10 February aboard Admiral Sartorius's flagship, the *Rainha de Portugal*, which was accompanied by two of the other three warships. The corvette *Dona Amélia* was left at Belle Isle to escort the transports, which finally set sail on 29 February with a battalion of soldiers. By that time the *Rainha de Portugal* had already anchored in the Azores, at Ponta Delgada on the island of São Miguel. Dom Pedro remained there a few days before going on to the seat of the constitutional government, Angra, on the island of Terceira, where, on 3 March he formally assumed the position of sole regent of Portugal, in the name of Queen Maria II.[26]

On the island of Terceira, Regent Dom Pedro appointed a council of ministers and proceeded to issue a series of liberal decrees. Taking advantage of a civil-war situation—as Abraham Lincoln would do three decades later—Dom Pedro dictated essential reforms that would have taken generations to bring about through the normal constitutional process. Dom Pedro's situation was the reverse of the one Lincoln would face, as slavery did not exist in rebel territory but was legal where the loyalists were. Backed by the overwhelming power of his liberal army, Dom Pedro abolished slavery in the Azores on 19 May 1832. Other reforms were aimed principally at the mother country, and could not be put into effect until Dom Pedro's forces occupied the Portuguese mainland. But their enunciation defined the movement Dom Pedro was leading: it was not just legitimist and constitutional, but also unequivocally liberal. It promoted individual freedom and condemned corporate privilege—even though the great majority of the Portuguese people probably felt quite happy and secure within the folds of their corporatist society, and cared nothing for the liberty that Dom Pedro wanted to foist on them. The liberal decrees—most of which were formulated by Finance and Justice Minister José Xavier Mousinho da Silveira, to the consternation of the more moderate Foreign and Interior Affairs Minister Palmela—guaranteed the security of private property while freeing most secular estates from entailment and making the holdings of religious orders liable to confiscation and sale. Most taxes, including the 10 percent gross income levy for support of the Church, were eliminated or reduced. Special courts and legal privileges for clergymen, the military, nobles, guildsmen, and other social or occupational groups were abolished, as were rights to tribute and other feudal extractions.[27] Unlike in Brazil—where similar changes, required by the constitution, were implemented over a period of years by parliamentary legislation—in Portugal the reforms were to be imposed immediately by an invading army. The decrees ensured that the invaders would be fiercely resisted.

Dom Pedro and his military chiefs underestimated the resistance their expedition would face in Portugal. Admiral Sartorius and General Count Vila Flor, army commander for the invasion, seemed to feel that just the appearance of Dom Pedro on the Portuguese mainland at the head of a spirited, well-trained and disciplined liberal force, would be enough to persuade the Miguelistas to lay down their arms. To produce a sufficiently impressive show of force, Queen Maria's army and navy were put through three months of fairly rigorous training under the eyes of Dom Pedro, beneath the subtropical, sometimes stormy, skies of the verdant, volcanic Azores. Foreign mercenaries were an essential part of Dom Pedro's military scheme, but the regent had to make do with less than half of the 1,200 he had hoped to enlist. Most of these belonged to the British Battalion commanded by Colonel Lloyd Hodges; there were smaller contingents of Frenchmen, Germans, Dutchmen, and Poles.[28]

As the Portuguese had come to expect, the British did a lot of drinking during their off-duty hours. In their pursuit of recreation, some were warmly received in the convents of Esperança and São Gonçalo, on the island of Terceira. "We amuse ourselves with the nuns," wrote Major Charles Shaw, a red-bearded Scot, second in command of the British Battalion. The sisters were "quite correct during the day," Shaw reported in a letter to his brother, but "keep open house when it is dark." The foreigners brought their own music to the nunnery: "We have astonished them by our band, and four of us danced a Scotch reel in the *parloir*, such doings were never heard of." The nuns, the major had to admit, were "very ugly, dirty and slipshod, and spit about abominably."[29] Presumably his commander in chief had the pick of the lot: Sister Ana Augusta of the Esperança convent, who was pregnant by Dom Pedro when the expedition sailed, was, according to Azorean folklore, "very beautiful."[30]

Far from a wife whom he truly loved, Dom Pedro reverted to his old womanizing habits. And before he left the Azores, the regent reclaimed another role that he had often played in Brazil: nemesis of shiftless bureaucrats. He appeared at the Terceira customhouse one morning around nine o'clock, an hour after it was supposed to open, and finding no functionaries on duty, he locked the door, put the key in his pocket, and walked home. That afternoon he issued a decree dismissing all the customs officers on the island of Terceira and appointing new ones.[31]

By the beginning of June Dom Pedro's forces were concentrated on the large, eastern island of São Miguel, but storms and unfavorable winds delayed their departure for the mainland until 27 June. The invasion fleet numbered more than fifty vessels, including two frigates, three steamers, and numerous smaller craft that would be useful in scouting the enemy coast. The fleet transported a landing force of about 7,500 men, organized as infantry and artillery; they brought sixteen field pieces, but no horses. The regent, who sailed on the corvette *Dona Amélia* under the blue and white flag of the liberal movement, had tentatively decided to land near Oporto, so the expedition headed for that area. Land was sighted on 7 July, and that night Admiral Sartorius made a personal reconnaissance of the shore. He reported his findings to Dom Pedro the next morning, and the landing began at two o'clock in the afternoon, at Pampelido Beach, twelve kilometers north of Oporto. The disembarkation was unopposed, as the absolutist commander in the vicinity grossly overestimated the size of the liberal forces and hastily withdrew to the south of the Douro River—a move that unhinged the Miguelistas in Oporto, who abandoned the city during the night. The long-suppressed liberals of Oporto rose up as the absolutists fled; they seized the government buildings, freed the political prisoners at the jail, killed Dom Miguel's local

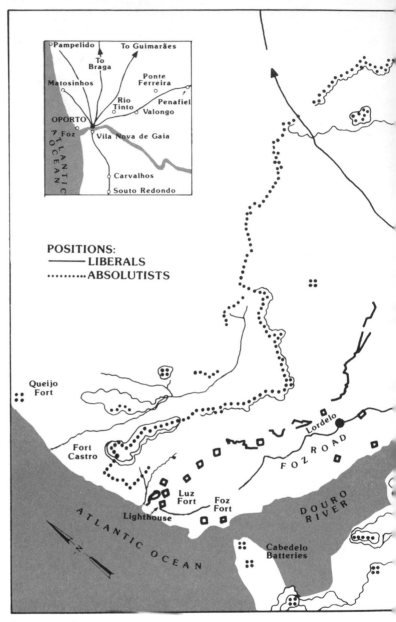

The Siege of Oporto: 1832–33

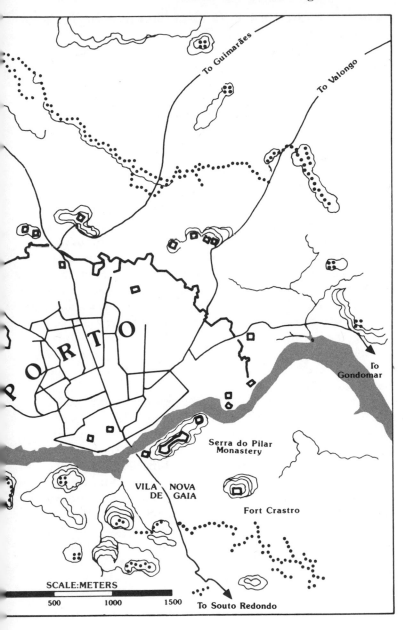

hangman, and welcomed Dom Pedro's troops into their city with great rejoicing on the morning of 9 July.[32]

The operation had gone just about as Dom Pedro had hoped it would. Most of his brother's forces were concentrated around Lisbon, where the invasion had been expected. The defenses of the North had been relatively neglected, though absolutist troops in and around Oporto numbered more than 13,000. Their commander, however, panicked at the sight of the liberal fleet arrayed on the horizon; he did not realize that many of the ships that he saw were really small vessels with fake superstructures to make them look like large men-of-war or troop transports. The rumor had been that Dom Pedro was on his way to Portugal with an army of 30,000; and that was the force that the absolutists assumed was descending on Oporto. Most peasants north of the city fled inland with their livestock as the unwelcome liberators landed, and the best horse that could be found for Dom Pedro to ride into Oporto was a small and altogether unimpressive work animal. He was preceded by liberal soldiers who strolled onto the Praça Nova with blue and white flowers stuck in the muzzles of their muskets and passed out copies of the "Hymn to the [Portuguese] Constitution," music (but not words) by Dom Pedro. The regent made his triumphal entrance at noon, the city masses hailing him with cheers and singing. The main disappointments were the hostility of the rural population and the near total absence of defections to his side by the officers and men of Dom Miguel's army.[33]

Most of the people of Oporto seemed genuinely enthusiastic about Queen Maria's constitutional government, now lodged in their city. The British community, composed mainly of port-wine exporters and their families, was particularly happy with the liberal occupation. About the only people in Oporto who appeared displeased were the regular clergy; it was in their monasteries that most of Dom Pedro's troops were quartered. Many men of the city began to grow beards to show solidarity with Dom Pedro and his officers, who had vowed not to shave until they had liberated Lisbon. The northern port yielded hundreds of volunteers for the constitutional army, and a few dozen horses. From Oporto the regent issued a proclamation to the Portuguese people, offering them "peace, reconciliation, and liberty," and urging them to "rally to the banners of your legitimate queen."[34] Copies of the document went south with Admiral Sartorius and part of his squadron, sent to blockade Lisbon; and north with a force of 400 constitutionalist soldiers, sent overland towards Braga to proclaim the cause of the queen in that direction. A similar-sized unit crossed the Douro and chased the absolutists out of Vila Nova da Gaia, where the headquarters and warehouses of the Portuguese government wine monopoly were located, directly across the river from Oporto. The absolutists fell back in good order to Oliveira de Azeméis, where they began a major buildup.[35]

On 18 July Dom Pedro launched a probe to the east of Oporto, sending a column of about 1,000 men, spearheaded by 40 mounted scouts and part of the British Battalion, toward Penafiel. They entered that city only after overcoming fierce resistance; they killed perhaps 200 Miguelistas and suffered dozens of casualties of their own. Learning that more absolutist troops were marching on Penafiel, the liberals sacked and burned two monasteries and retreated to Oporto, arriving on 20 July. The next day the expedition that had been sent towards Braga returned to Oporto with a similar tale of popular resistance to the constitutionalist cause. By this time, absolutist troops from Azeméis had crossed the Douro twenty kilometers upstream from Oporto and were threatening to encircle the city. On 22 July Dom Pedro sent his mounted scouts, the British and two other battalions, and four pieces of artillery eastward to find and fix the new enemy positions. They were drawn into an ambush just beyond Valongo, and were driven back with heavy losses to Rio Tinto. When word of the disaster reached Oporto, Dom Pedro and his army commander, the count of Vila Flor, reacted quickly and vigorously. The count marched on Rio Tinto with the troops that were immediately available in Oporto, and Dom Pedro rounded up the rest, called in the southern outposts, and led all these forces to Rio Tinto later in the night. He stationed a three-gunboat patrol on the Douro River to protect the constitutionalists' southern flank, and left a detachment of 200 to 300, mostly new recruits, with the Oporto military commandant to guard the city.[36] Everyone seemed to agree that the coming battle would decide whether the constitutionalist movement in Portugal would perish or survive.

The liberals launched a three-pronged attack on the absolutist positions at Ponte Ferreira, on the east side of Valongo, at eleven o'clock in the morning of 23 July. The Miguelistas had a great numerical advantage, 12,000 to 8,000, but were poorly organized. Befitting a reactionary army of noblemen and peasants, they were strong in cavalry and relatively weak in artillery; they had about the same number of pieces as had the liberals, but with inferior gunners. Their peasant infantrymen, however brave, were no match for the well-drilled constitutionalists, spearheaded by bayonet-wielding British and French mercenaries. The action seesawed through the afternoon, with liberal infantry taking absolutist positions only to be ejected by mounted counterattacks. The constitutionalists had difficulty bringing their artillery to bear on the elusive enemy cavalry and dragoons. Dom Pedro stayed close to the action, his telescope at his eye, as absorbed in the details of war as he had always been in those of peace, and seemingly oblivious to the incoming cannon and musket fire striking around him. At length, the count of Vila Flor and some others persuaded the indispensable symbol of Portuguese constitutionalism to move to the rear. At about six o'clock the absolutists launched a concentrated attack on a thinly held portion of the liberal line, but the day was saved for Dom Pedro by his artillery, which broke up the advancing enemy column with two perfectly placed rounds. The Miguelistas then abandoned the field to the liberals and withdrew to Penafiel. Dom Pedro's troops suffered 460 casualties, including dead and wounded, but the absolutists lost a greater number in the Battle of Ponte Ferreira.[37]

With no cavalry, Dom Pedro could not pursue the fleeing enemy, certainly not at night. He sent word of the great victory to Oporto, where it was celebrated with illuminations and the ringing of church bells, and remained with his army at Ponte Ferreira, where he and Vila Flor discussed plans for advancing on Penafiel the next day. But the next day brought news of panic in Oporto: the jubilation of the night had given way to terror in the morning as a rumor spread that the liberal army had been routed and Dom Pedro had embarked at a beach north of the city. The military commandant had ordered the city evacuated; his troops had fled to the beaches; documents had been burned; cabinet ministers scrambled aboard the vessels in the river; men shaved their beards; and women hid their blue-and-white dresses. All that was left to defend the city against an invasion by the thousands of Miguelista troops drawn up on the south bank of the Douro was a two-gun battery at the Praça Nova, manned by twenty-five resolute academics. Dom Pedro had no choice but to turn his army around and march it back to Oporto before the enemy rushed in. The panic in the city ended as the liberal troops approached with the regent at their head; the ladies of Oporto retrieved their blue-and-white dresses and gave Dom Pedro a warm welcome as he made his second triumphal entry into their city at five o'clock on the afternoon of 24 July. The regent dismissed the city's military commandant, appointed a new one, and ordered extra wine rations for the troops. On 25 July the officers and men of the Fifth Light Infantry Battalion were sleeping off the effects of the victory celebration at the Franciscan monastery when the friars apparently tried to incinerate them in their beds. At any rate, the monastery went up in flames before dawn, but the alarm was sounded among the soldiers soon enough for almost all to escape unharmed. The incident exacerbated the bad feelings between the constitutionalists and the regular clergy, who thereafter were forbidden to appear in public in their distinctive garb.[38]

The regent called his ministers and military chiefs together for a council of war on 26 July. With the enemy closing in on Oporto from all directions, should the liberals concentrate on the static defense of the city, or take the offensive? The question was put to a vote, with Dom Pedro agreeing to accept the majority decision. Offense won despite the arguments of a minority that the war could not effectively be carried into enemy territory without cavalry. They decided to send Palmela to London to buy horses and to hire more mercenaries. Communication between Oporto and the outside world were kept open by the constitutionalist naval squadron, which also gave the liberals an offensive capability along the coast that they did not have in the interior. The frigates that were stationed off Lisbon were recalled to Oporto, and the steamer *City of Edinburgh* was sent north with a landing force of 300 to Vila do Conde, to seize the absolutist arsenal there. They were unsuccessful and returned to Oporto on 1 August. A more ambitious operation began on the night of 6 August as Vila Flor crossed the Douro with 4,000 men and eight field pieces to attack the enemy troop concentration at Souto Redondo. He was thrown back to Oporto the next day, having lost more than 400 men and all his artillery. After the lifting of the blockade, the Miguelista naval squadron had come out from Lisbon. Admiral Sartorius engaged the enemy in an inconclusive battle on 10 August; the absolutist ship-of-the-line *Dom João VI* put in to Vila do Conde for repairs, but other warships remained at sea to threaten Dom Pedro's lifeline to London.[39]

In the British capital the marquis of Palmela received a letter from Dom Pedro informing him of the disaster at Souto Redondo and describing the near-hopeless situation of the liberal forces in Oporto. The regent asked Palmela to find out if the British would commit their

Dom Pedro, Duke of Bragança, at the time of the siege of Oporto
Painting by John Simpson, Museu Nacional "Soares dos Reis," Oporto

Dom Miguel as King of Portugal
Painting by João Baptista Ribeiro, Museu Nacional "Soares dos Reis,"
Oporto

navy to protecting the withdrawal of the constitutionalist army from Oporto to the Azores. Yes, Lord Palmerston told Palmela, the British would guarantee the evacuation; but as soon as Dom Pedro was gone, they would consider the Portuguese question resolved and recognize Dom Miguel as king. The other powers would certainly follow the British in establishing diplomatic relations with Dom Miguel's government, and all that would remain for the constitutionalists to do would be to negotiate the surrender of the Azores, as there could be no further hope of seating Dona Maria on the throne in Lisbon. Also, Mendizábal's lenders would lose all the money that they had advanced to the Portuguese constitutionalists. The evacuation idea was quickly abandoned; Dom Pedro told Palmela to forget that he had even mentioned it. Palmela and Mendizábal in London got busy raising the money to hire 3,000 more mercenaries and buy another frigate and 500 horses. In Oporto, Dom Pedro and his troops threw themselves into the task of fortifying the city and preparing for a long siege.[40]

"I am well," Dom Pedro wrote to his children in Rio on 12 August 1832, "although very tired from physical and moral travail; this population is fanaticized by the padres and has given no indications thus far of loving liberty." A devout Catholic accustomed to the sermons of liberal priests in Brazil, Dom Pedro was sorely disappointed that most of the ministers of the universal Church in Portugal favored special privilege over individual freedom. The difficulty of the task he faced perhaps led him to exaggerate its importance: "Upon this struggle in which I am engaged," he wrote to his son on 1 September, "depends the triumph of liberty; if we win, Europe will be free; if not, despotism will crush the people."[41] After a brief bout with despair following the disaster at Souto Redondo, Dom Pedro did not waver in his commitment to the liberation of Portugal. He was prepared to sacrifice for the cause not only his life, but his well-being. Actually, the desperateness of the effort to erect defenses against the absolutist hordes closing in on Oporto seemed to arrest the decline in his health, to renew his strength, and to restore his old vigor. For days on end, from before dawn until late at night, he maintained a frantic pace, supervising the work of fortification. "Many times," one of his officers reported, "we saw him with pick and shovel in hand," laboring in the trenches. He would eat his meals at the worksite "so as not to lose time."[42]

The absolutists had moved within artillery range of Oporto,

from the north and east, by 22 August, and were beginning to emplace their guns, employing more than 10,000 laborers. Sporadic shelling of the city began on 25 August. The liberals included in their defense perimeter Vila Nova da Gaia and the riverside monastery of Serra do Pilar, both south of the Douro, but the town fell to the Miguelistas on 8 September despite the brave resistance of its garrison; the fortified monastery, perched on a cliff above a narrow stretch of the river overlooking the center of the city, withstood the absolutist attack. Two days later, the systematic bombardment of Oporto began, with solid shot and explosive shell. The bursting of some shells, a witness recorded, "produced smoke, and suffocating and unbearable vapors." But the city of Oporto, situated on a granite ridge alternately swept by land and sea breezes, was a poor testing ground for gas warfare. The conventional shelling took a heavy toll in lives and property, even among British residents, for whose protection the frigate HMS *Orestes* was stationed in the river between Oporto and Vila Nova da Gaia. Although no place was really safe, and virtually every structure in Oporto sustained some damage, the people of the city learned to cope with the bombardment and minimize its effects on their daily lives. Citizens in the streets learned to recognize the whistle of incoming shells and throw themsleves on the ground, where they were safe from all but a direct hit, as the projectiles exploded upward on impact. Rounds that fell through the roofs of houses were the most destructive. The deep trenches and thick parapets constructed by Dom Pedro and his troops limited the harm that could be done to them by the shelling, which was costing the absolutists dearly—about 10 dollars for each mortar round.[43]

The Miguelistas tried to take Oporto by assault on 29 September, St. Michael's Day. Two columns of 5,000 men each emerged from the early morning fog and fell on the eastern sector of the liberal perimeter. Promised "plunder in this world and salvation in the next," and expecting the intervention of their king's patron, the Archangel Michael, the absolutist soldiers punched through Oporto's outer defenses, enveloped and captured several constitutionalist batteries, and penetrated into the city. However, they were stopped and eventually driven out of Oporto by a series of counterattacks over a period of eleven hours. They left 4,000 of their men—dead, wounded, or captured—on the battlefield. Among the defenders there were about 100 dead and 300 seriously wounded.[44] Palmela, who had returned from London in time to take part in the fighting on 29 September, wrote to his wife that Dom Pedro "conducted himself admirably, and he exposed himself to death more than once." Before closing he reiterated—about a man with whom he had had many personal and political quarrels, dating back to 1820, and did not really like—"The emperor comported himself perfectly, with much activity and presence of spirit, being extremely popular in the army and in the city."[45] A less-grudging admirer reported seeing Dom Pedro "under terrible fire, displaying the greatest coolness and courage, inspiring his subordinates." Officers fell dead at his side, but Dom Pedro "kept himself always under the thickest fire of artillery and musketry."[46]

The liberal victory on St. Michael's Day was due at least in part to the energy and bravery of Dom Pedro, and to his inspirational presence on the battlefield. The count of Vila Flor, a courageous and competent general whose reputation still suffered from his defeat at Souto Redondo, resigned as supreme military commander not long after this constitutionalist success, which, in the popular mind, was credited to Dom Pedro. The regent graciously accepted Vila Flor's resignation, personally assumed command of the liberal army in his stead, and elevated the count in the nobility, granting him the title duke of Terceira. Dom Pedro, who had no illusions about himself as a strategist or tactician, regarded his new position as temporary and transitional. To win the war, he realized, the liberals needed a great general, one whose plans would inspire confidence in the officers who would have to carry them out. Dom Pedro had his wife and friends in Paris looking for such an architect of victory, for a great general, preferably French, to whom he could turn over command of Queen Maria's army. In the meantime, the regent issued a call for all Portuguese emigrés—including General Saldanha—to come to Oporto and join the army of liberation. Palmela, however, would not have to endure the presence of his old enemy in Oporto, for he soon stepped down as foreign minister and returned to London as Portuguese constitutionalist emissary to Britain.[47]

For nearly two weeks after the attack of 29 September Oporto was subjected to only sporadic artillery fire. The Miguelistas recommenced their sustained bombardment on 11 October, the eve of Dom Pedro's birthday. Absolutist infantry, about 5,000 strong, repeatedly attacked the liberal stronghold south of the river, Serra do Pilar, on 14 October, but each time they were repelled with heavy losses. The war at sea remained a stand-off. Admiral Sartorius's flagship *Rainha de Portugal* put into Oporto on 20 October, heavily damaged from a fight with a Miguelista frigate. The enemy vessel was also injured, but had gotten away to Lisbon. This result greatly displeased Dom Pedro, who had expected Sartorius to capture Miguelista warships and add them to the liberal squadron. The strength of Dom Pedro's naval force, instead of increasing, had actually decreased. The squadron's lost firepower was soon restored with the addition of a frigate purchased in England, but the morale of the seamen was plummeting, partly because they had not been paid.[48] Dom Pedro was losing confidence in Sartorius; eventually he would have to find another admiral.

Despite its problems, the squadron kept the sea-lanes open, and by November 1832, men, horses, and equipment procured by Mendizábal in London were pouring into Oporto. Among the newly arrived mercenaries were 600 scruffy characters recruited from the slums of Glasgow, who were assigned to Charles Shaw, now promoted to colonel, and were denominated the Battalion of Scottish Fusiliers. Few of the Scots had any military experience, but they responded to Shaw's primitive training methods and acquired awesome proficiency with musket and bayonet. Three bagpipers helped keep their spirits high, and they professed great devotion to the rightful queen of Portugal, "Dony Maree," and stern determination to put an early end to "that damned John MacDougal," as they called Dom Miguel. No less ferocious were several hundred Irish who formed another infantry battalion under Colonel William Cotter, erstwhile commander of an ill-fated contingent of their countrymen in Brazil. The liberal army finally got a cavalry arm with the arrival of Colonel Anthony Bacon—an English aristocrat who had hunted foxes with the duke of Wellington during the Peninsular Campaign—and a few hundred horses. Colonel Bacon naturally became a great favorite of his fellow equine enthusiast, Dom Pedro, and his regiment of lancers included Portuguese horsemen and volunteers from half a dozen foreign lands. The army got a new supreme commander early in January 1833, with the arrival from France of Jean Baptiste Solignac, who had been a general under Napoleon. Dom Pedro promoted Solignac to marshal and turned over to him command of the army, which the regent had personally exercised during the two months following the resignation of the count of Vila Flor, who, as the duke of Terceira, was retained as a division commander.[49]

While Dom Pedro's army was being reorganized and its new recruits trained, the Miguelistas tightened their siege of Oporto. On 7 December they completed the emplacement of a battery on the sandspit at the mouth of the Douro, extending from the south bank, which effectively closed the entrance to the river. Thereafter, supplies bound for Oporto would have to be landed at Foz, on the ocean, and hauled into the city via a road on the river's north bank. The Foz road was subject not only to interdiction by Miguelista fire, but also to flooding by a tributary of the Douro that it had to cross. The strategy of the absolutists—whose war effort was managed by the duke of Cadaval, dean of the Portuguese nobility—was to starve the liberals into submission. Rather than launch another general assault on Oporto, they would probe the constitutionalist lines with limited attacks while concentrating on strengthening their own positions, and on preparing their troops to withstand any liberal attempt to break out of the encirclement. The morale of the Miguelistas was boosted by the arrival of their king at the front. Dom Miguel established his residence at Braga in November, and appeared among the soldiers besieging Oporto on various occasions thereafter.[50]

For the liberal army and the civilian population of Oporto, the situation grew desperate as food supplies dwindled—not only because of the increased difficulty of bringing the supplies into Oporto, but also because of the lack of money with which to purchase them. Food was scarce, but wine was plentiful, and drunken foreign soldiers, unpaid and on half rations, inflicted almost as much injury on the city and its civilian population as did Dom Miguel's artillery. Among the worst offenders were the Scottish Fusiliers, who eventually were transferred out of the city and stationed at Lordelo, on the road to Foz, a position that they held "for many months, although with the most murderous loss," as Miguelista infantry made repeated attempts to dislodge them during daytime and at night.[51]

Colonel Bacon and his lancers occasionally carried the war into enemy territory as they foraged for grain to feed to their horses. Wounded cavalry horses were butchered and eaten by the lancers, and other soldiers and civilians consumed the city's donkeys, dogs, and cats. Fuel was as scarce as food: during the siege nearly all the trees in Oporto were cut down, and many houses dismantled, for firewood. Almost any building damaged by the shelling might be pronounced uninhabitable by bystanders, who would proceed to strip it of its wooden furniture and fixtures. At the beginning of the siege Dom Pedro lived with his staff in a huge stone mansion atop the ridge directly across the river from the enemy batteries at Vila Nova da Gaia. An easy target for Miguelista gunners, the mansion was often hit and in October 1832 was abandoned by the regent, who moved to a more modest but less-exposed residence on Cedofeita Street. Dom Pedro's new house was poorly insulated, and with the shortage of firewood, afforded its occupants only a minimum of protection from an unusually severe winter.[52]

Weakened by hunger and cold, the people of Oporto were exposed to epidemic disease in January 1833 as the cholera bacillus appeared in the city with the entourage of Marshal Solignac. Of a population estimated at 70,000 at the beginning of the year, 3,621 reportedly died within six months. The bombardment, which intensified with the new year, was directly responsible for many civilian deaths. The largest gun employed by the absolutists was a 280-millimeter howitzer that hurled balls of solid stone as well as explosive projectiles. In all the Miguelistas had some 150 artillery pieces emplaced along a twenty-two-kilometer siege line. They fired into the city an average of five rounds per gun per day during the ten-month siege, Colonel Bacon calculated; one day he saw 16 cannon balls in the air at the same time. Another observer counted 150 projectiles falling on one neighborhood in one afternoon.[53]

The Miguelistas would usually intensify their shelling prior to launching an infantry assault on the constitutionalist lines. Dom Pedro, perceiving the enemy intention and determined to be on the ramparts with his troops during the battle, first would go to a church on Rainha Street to confess, hear mass, and receive absolution. Then, to the consternation of his generals, the regent would find his way to the most dangerous sector and joke about his narrow escapes from death. Dom Pedro's courage and coolness under fire were greatly admired by his soldiers and by foreign officers in his army. The cantankerous Colonel Shaw, otherwise one of the regent's severest critics—who continually imagined himself and his men to be victims of Portuguese perfidy, incompetence, and ingratitude—acknowledged that "there is not the least doubt" that Dom Pedro "was a brave man and a good officer."[54] The aristocratic Colonel Bacon found the regent to be "open, honest, courageous, possessed of great presence of mind, frugal and hardworking."[55] Another English officer of the lancers gave Dom Pedro credit for saving Oporto by discovering absolutist sabotage of the guns of a key liberal battery. The regent "adopted the judicious practice of prowling about at night, inspecting the posts and batteries when he was least expected," Alexander Tolmer reported. "The unwearied activity of Dom Pedro . . . astonished everyone. . . . By Dom Pedro's continued vigilance, the sentinels were kept to their duty."[56]

Another Englishman, Lieutenant-Colonel Lovell Badcock, military aide to Lord William Russell, British consul-general in Lisbon, visited Dom Pedro in Oporto on 8 January. Colonel Badcock, like his superior, was strongly anti-Miguelista and was predisposed toward Dom Pedro, whom he described as "of middling stature, upright and active: his complexion is not good, and does not bear the stamp of health: the great fatigue he has endured, and the harassing life he has led, do not conduce to good looks. His manners were good and conciliating: he was very abstemious, drinking nothing but water, and taking a glass of wine merely as a compliment to some stranger"—a courtesy he paid to Badcock. The Englishman visited Dom Pedro just before the cholera was identified in Oporto; most civilian deaths were being attributed to hunger. "Numbers of poor were starved to death," he noted. "People might be seen growing daily weaker and weaker until they dropped off." The men of the liberal army in Oporto were getting just enough food to stay alive, but more troops were deemed necessary to defend the city, and Dom Pedro—who for the most part subsisted on a soldier's rations—feared that he would be unable to feed a larger military population. The ever-helpful Colonel Badcock recommended that the regent send to New Zealand for Maori warriors, "as those people kill and eat their enemies, which would much simplify the defence."[57] Dom Pedro apparently took no action on the recommendation.

As the civilian and military death toll in Oporto mounted, Marshal Solignac, the new liberal army commander, developed plans to secure his supply lines by pushing the Miguelistas back from their positions around Foz. The plans were coordinated with Admiral Sartorius, who was supposed to bring his ships in close to support the operation with naval gunfire. But on the day of the attack, 24 January 1833, the squadron remained far out at sea and did not deliver the promised support. Although liberal ground troops managed to overrun the main absolutist position near Foz, the battery at Monte de Castro, they were unable to hold it. That day's action led to three-way recriminations among Solignac, Sartorius, and Dom Pedro. The regent would give the marshal another chance, but he was determined to replace the admiral. Dom Pedro tried to engage Lord Cochrane, who had offered his services in 1831, but learned that the Seawolf was no longer available. However, another famous Scottish seaman, Captain Charles Napier, expressed interest when approached in London by Palmela.[58] Money was the main stumbling block, which could be removed only by the financial genius of Mendizábal, assisted by the aristocratic connections of Palmela.

In the meantime, General João Carlos Saldanha arrived in Oporto on 28 January, and was given command of one of the three divisions of the liberal army; the other two being commanded by the duke of Terceira and Sir Thomas Stubbs. Saldanha immediately undertook a project to secure the Foz road and neutralize the Miguelista batteries near the beach. After working day and night for two and a half weeks, Saldanha and about 1,400 men had almost finished their fortifications when they were attacked on 4 March near Foz by 10,000 absolutists—whom they repelled with heavy losses. This liberal victory did much to raise the morale of the people of Oporto, although stormy weather prevented the landing of supplies at Foz for the next few weeks, and the famine continued. Sartorius and his squadron sought shelter from the storms in Spanish waters, in the Bay of Vigo, and refused to come out until Dom Pedro made up their back pay. In fact, they threatened to sell their ships in order to collect what was due them. Eventually, Mendizábal was able to raise the money to pay off the seamen, including Sartorius, who agreed to turn over his command to Dom Pedro's new admiral, Charles Napier. The latter insisted on collecting six months' pay in advance before sailing from Falmouth on 27 May with five steamers, 160 seamen, two battalions of mercenary soldiers, Palmela, and Mendizábal.[59]

Napier rendezvoused with Sartorius and the constitutionalist squadron off the Douro, and before dawn on 2 June the new admiral went ashore with Palmela and Mendizábal at Foz, where they were cordially greeted by General Saldanha, who provided them with mules for the ride into Oporto. The travelers proceeded to the house of the duke of Terceira (formerly the count of Vila Flor) for breakfast, and then appeared at Dom Pedro's residence on Cedofeita Street. Palmela went in first to see the regent, to prepare him for his meeting with Napier. Preparation was necessary because Napier's looks and manners were rather odd, and because the admiral had come with a plan that he insisted on implementing immediately. Dom Pedro had not been consulted about the plan and he apparently got the impression that Palmela—to whom he had recently offered a dukedom—was trying to push him around. Palmela put Dom Pedro in a foul mood to meet the stocky, dishevelled Napier, who appeared before him in a filthy sailor's uniform and with a dirty flannel rag wrapped around his head and tied under his chin to relieve the neuralgia from which he suffered. As Napier recalled the scene, he "was received at the door of the apartment by the Emperor, who stood with his hands behind him, looking very angry, and speaking as roughly as he looked." Dom Pedro would not discuss Napier's war plans; he told the admiral to take them to Marshal Solignac, "and dismissed me rather abruptly."[60]

  Napier's plans called for an immediate assault on Lisbon with the entire naval squadron and 6,000 ground troops from Oporto. A large-scale landing near the capital, he calculated, was then possible, but would not be after the absolutist squadron had put to sea. Dom Miguel's warships, which were being refitted at Lisbon, would soon come out of the Tagus and make any such operation by the liberals extremely difficult; now was the time to act, to win the war with one deft blow. But Marshal Solignac argued that Oporto's defenses would be fatally weakened by the withdrawal of so many troops, and Dom Pedro agreed; they wanted to make a major effort in the North, to break the encirclement and envelope part of the besieging army. Dom Pedro perceived two options: a major offensive in the North; or continued defensive operations around Oporto and a small expedition to the South. Although he favored the first option, Dom Pedro was willing to abide by the majority decision of his military chiefs. Solignac demurred; he saw no choice but to keep the liberal army intact and under his direct control. When his general officers voted to dispatch an expeditionary force of 2,500 men to the South, the marshal resigned his command. Napier, who had considered resigning after his brusque reception by Dom Pedro and the rejection of his 6,000-man plan, accepted the decision, and his relations with the regent developed into real friendship. With the departure of Solignac, Dom Pedro once again personally assumed command of the liberal army in Oporto, with Saldanha as his chief of staff. Command of the expeditionary force —which was to bypass Lisbon and land in the extreme South of the country, in the Algarve—was entrusted to the duke of Terceira, with the duke of Palmela designated civilian governor of whatever territory they liberated.[61] Mendizábal went along for the action.

The troops were loaded onto Napier's steamboats at Foz under cover of darkness and the squadron sailed on 20 June. The liberal warships passed close to Cape Roca, skirted the mouth of the Tagus, and rounded Cape São Vicente on the night of 23 June. The duke of Terceira and his troops landed the next night about forty kilometers east of Faro, the capital of the Algarve, and began their march on that city at daybreak. They met only light resistance, and on 28 June occupied Faro, where the duke of Palmela disembarked from Napier's flagship and organized a provisional government. The admiral then collected his vessels and headed back toward Cape São Vicente to engage the absolutist squadron that he knew would be coming out of Lisbon to meet him. The two forces sighted each other off the cape on 3 July. The Miguelista squadron consisted of two ships-of-the-line— the *Dom João VI* and the *Rainha*—two frigates, three corvettes, two brigs, and a xebec, mounting a total of 372 guns. Napier had only three frigates, one corvette, and two smaller sailing vessels, with a total of 176 guns, plus the five steamboats, which had no offensive armament, but which the admiral planned to use for towing his frigates into action. For two days Napier maneuvered about the enemy, waiting for a calm that would give him the advantage over the exclusively wind-powered enemy. A dead calm descended on the morning of 5 July, but the steamboat crews had second thoughts about the admiral's battle plan and deserted with their vessels. Deprived of his steampower, Napier was left to fight an old-fashioned naval battle.[62]

The Battle of Cape São Vicente was a complete victory for the liberal squadron. Both Miguelista ships-of-the-line were captured—the *Rainha* after boarding and a bloody fight on her decks—along with both frigates and one corvette. The constitutionalists also fared well on land that day, 5 July; the defenders of Oporto repelled with heavy losses the Miguelistas who, perceiving a liberal weakness with the subtraction of the expeditionaries, had mounted simultaneous assaults on the northern and eastern sectors. Dom Pedro gave Saldanha credit for the victory and promoted him to lieutenant-general. On the other side, a new commander for the Miguelista army disembarked at Vila do Conde on 10 July. He was Louis Auguste Victor Bourmont, marshal of France, conqueror of Algeria, confirmed absolutist who had refused to swear allegiance to Louis Philippe and had commanded the forces of the unsuccessful Vendée counterrevolution of 1832. The military contest at Oporto between Saldanha and Bourmont, the marquis of Lafayette noted, fairly epitomized the general struggle between liberty and oppression.[63] The lines were indeed well drawn in the internationalized Portuguese civil war; the additions of Bourmont and Napier —inventor, mercenary, eccentric, Whig politician—completed the picture.

To Bourmont, Napier's mastery of the sea underscored the urgency of closing Oporto's corridor to the ocean. He massed 12,000 absolutists on the coast north of Foz and sent them against the liberals in seven columns on the morning of 25 July. Dom Miguel was there to watch the battle, which raged for nine hours. The liberal line held at Foz, but to the east, two battalions of Miguelistas breeched Oporto's defenses and drove into the city. With no reserves to commit, Saldanha gathered about him eighteen mounted staff officers and twenty lancers and led them in a charge that turned back the enemy advance. At Lordelo the Scottish Fusiliers mounted a counterattack that carried the absolutist batteries in that sector; their success was announced by the wail produced by a piper marching back and forth atop the captured ramparts, the blue-and-white flag of liberty flying overhead, and Colonel Shaw screaming "Pipe, damn you, pipe!"[64] After that, the absolutists withdrew all along the line, having lost more than 4,000 men. The people of Oporto scarcely had time to celebrate that stunning victory when they received the astonishing news that Lisbon had fallen to the constitutionalists the day before. The combination of Terceira reaching the Tagus overland from the Algarve, Napier sailing in from the ocean, and a liberal uprising inside Lisbon on 24 July had thrown the absolutists there into a panic. The duke of Cadaval and his forces evacuated the capital city and retreated toward Santarém. In the North, Bourmont and Dom Miguel lifted the siege of Oporto on 2 August and marched their troops toward Coimbra. By that time Dom Pedro was already in Lisbon, having arrived on a steamboat from Oporto on 28 July.[65]

Dom Pedro and his cabinet of ministers arrived at Lisbon around noon on 28 July 1833 aboard the steamer *William the Fourth*. The salutes began at Fort São Julião as the regent's vessel crossed the bar. Alerted by the sound of the guns, city residents mobbed the quays and jammed the harbor in small boats to greet the hero, blue-and-white banners flying from every masthead. "It was, indeed, a brilliant sight," Admiral Napier recorded, "and what with rockets, fireworks and salutes from batteries and ships, there was more powder burnt than would have fought a general action." The admiral's launch was one of the first to reach the steamer, and as soon as they were tied, the regent rushed down the gangplank toward Napier and "fairly pulled me out of the boat and embraced me in the warmest Portuguese fashion." Dom Pedro landed at the Belém quay to the wild acclaim of the multitude, which doubtlessly included many who on earlier occasions had greeted his brother with comparable enthusiasm.[66]

While Dom Pedro asked for peace and reconciliation, liberals recently freed from Dom Miguel's prisons, whose possessions had been confiscated by the absolutists, demanded restitution and vengeance. The leading absolutists had fled inland, leaving property in Lisbon that, whatever the constitutional requirements, the new government was of no mind to safeguard—certainly not while the owners remained in arms against the liberal regime. Reluctantly, Dom Pedro agreed with his ministers that the time had not yet come for soft measures. The war continued, for aside from Lisbon, Oporto, and a few other coastal enclaves, the country was still solidly Miguelista. This was hard for Dom Pedro to accept; on 15 August he ordered elections held throughout Portugal for deputies to the Cortes, which was scheduled to meet in Lisbon on 1 October. It would be many months, however, before enough districts were liberated to elect a quorum and allow the parliament to convene. In the meantime, Dom Pedro and his cabinet ruled by decree. They expelled the Papal Nuncio—who had asserted that the conflict in Portugal was not a civil war, but rather the "struggle of a nation against a gang of bandits who want to loot the country and turn it over to foreigners"—and the Jesuits. The property of other regular orders was confiscated if abandoned, or if the monks refused to take oaths to Queen Maria II and to the constitution. The constitutional queen was summoned from Paris, but when she and her stepmother learned that absolutist forces were marching on Lisbon and threatening to reconquer the city, they stopped in London to await better news from the Portuguese capital.[67]

Dom Miguel and Bourmont arrived in Coimbra from Oporto on 10 August with 18,000 men. There they were joined by the duke of Cadaval and some 6,000 absolutists from the South. Bourmont organized them into three divisions and set out with them for Lisbon on 14

August. Unaccountably, they took three weeks to get there, marching 200 kilometers through friendly territory. This gave Dom Pedro, Terceira, Napier (acting as a major-general in the absence of an enemy navy to fight), and Saldanha (who had left Oporto for the capital without authorization and without troops) ample time to prepare the defenses of Lisbon. Dom Pedro had some 38,000 men under arms, half of whom were newly raised militia, and some of the rest converted Miguelista prisoners of war. The constitutionalist forces manned several forts on the south and north banks of the Tagus, and were strung out around Lisbon in a semicircular line that was anchored on the river at Alcântara in the west and Xabrega in the east. Along this line the liberals emplaced 184 field guns; Dom Pedro, as usual, worked on the fortifications from dawn until after dark. Admiral-General Napier admired the regent's energy—to which he attributed the salvation of Lisbon—but wrote in a letter to his wife that Dom Pedro "should confine himself to his own part, without putting his head where he had no business." When the attack came on 5 September, the regent, to Napier's dismay, insisted on stationing himself in a spot that was "just as hot as any amateur could wish."[68]

Bourmont sent 12,000 infantrymen, in six columns, supported by artillery and cavalry, against the liberal perimeter at Campolide early on the morning of 5 September. It was a bold operation, ably led by some of Dom Miguel's bravest Portuguese and French officers. The liberals' finest were there to meet them at Campolide, and the fighting was fierce. The duke of Terceira's horse was shot from under him; an officer standing close to Dom Pedro was killed by a cannonball. The constitutionalist line held, however, and the attackers withdrew with heavy losses. A second absolutist assault was mounted at two o'clock in the afternoon, but it was not as well organized as the first, and it floundered before the liberal ramparts. Absolutist cavalrymen tried to revive the attack with a gallant charge, but were slaughtered by Dom Pedro's gunners. Bourmont wanted to send in another wave, but Dom Miguel overruled him and the absolutists retired to the positions from which they had mounted the attack.[69]

Before Bourmont made his next attempt to crack the constitutionalist perimeter, Dom Pedro received a visitor from Brazil: Antônio Carlos de Andrada. He came at the behest of his brothers, José Bonifácio and Martim Francisco, and other members of Brazil's growing restorationist movement. They wanted Dom Pedro to return to Brazil to save the country from disintegration. In the midst of the exhausting struggle to liberate his native land, Dom Pedro was moved by the plight of his adopted country, of the independent state that he and the Andrada brothers, more than anyone else, were responsible for creating. But, he told Antônio Carlos, his abdication was irrevocable, as he had sworn it would be. He would sacrifice anything for Brazil "except my honor." If the Brazilian people wanted him to return and exercise the powers of regent during the minority of his son, Dom Pedro II, they would have to express their will through their representatives in the municipal councils and the national parliament. He would become regent of Brazil only in accordance with the constitution, by election of the General Assembly in a solemn vote, and upon the presentation of a petition to him in Portugal by an official delegation of the Brazilian parliament.[70]

Antônio Carlos knew that there was little likelihood that the Brazilian General Assembly would ever vote to recall Dom Pedro. Although the restorationists had won every parish but one in Rio de Janeiro in the 1833 elections, planter-slavocrats or regional interests hostile to centralized government held sway in the provinces. When the new parliament met in 1834, the resolution offered was not to recall Dom Pedro, but to banish him, to make it unlawful for him to set foot again on Brazilian soil. The bill offended not only restorationists elected from Rio, but also Dr. Antônio Ferreira França of Bahia, a philosophical republican and precursor of Brazilian abolitionism. "Dom Pedro was the author of the independence and the liberty of Brazil," he declared. "Suppose that this man had a need to come to Brazil, without antagonizing us. I, for certain, would have to open the door for him." But Vasconcelos and the slavocrats had the votes; the tally was sixty-one to nineteen in favor of barring Dom Pedro from Brazilian territory.[71] The worst fear of the restorationists, however, was not realized: Brazil did not come apart. Vasconcelos, Evaristo, Feijó, and their collaborators managed to hold the country together, although just barely. They "saved the society from ruin," Brazil's greatest abolitionist would write, "but it was from the ruin that [they themselves] arranged." The abdication of Dom Pedro I, Joaquin Nabuco believed, had been a setback for the "democratic cause" in Brazil.[72]

Although Dom Pedro had abdicated two thrones, he had given up only one citizenship, that of Portugal. He realized that his Brazilian nationality would cause trouble for him in the Portuguese Cortes, and decided that if that legislative body refused to confirm him as regent for his Brazilian-born daughter, he would leave Portugal and retire with his wife to Germany. But that problem would not have to be faced until the Portuguese parliament convened after the war. The military struggle was far from over when Dom Pedro wrote down for Antônio Carlos his conditions for accepting the Brazilian regency on 14 September 1833. Earlier that day, before dawn, the absolutists had made a determined, though ultimately unsuccessful, assault on the liberal perimeter around Lisbon. The failure of the 14 September attack led to the resignation of Marshal Bourmont and to his replacement as commanding general of the absolutist army by a Scottish veteran of Spanish service. Ranald MacDonell of Glengarry "was one of those hazardous Roman Catholic Highlanders who have always roamed the Continent as soldiers of fortune, lending a hand when and where they could against England the ancient foe."[73] A lull fell over the battleground as General MacDonell set about reorganizing Dom Miguel's battered forces. Meanwhile among the liberals the conviction grew that they were in Lisbon to stay; scarcely a week after the 14 September victory they welcomed their queen to the seat of the Portuguese monarchy.

The fourteen-year-old Queen Maria II arrived at Lisbon on the afternoon of 21 September aboard the steamer *Soho*, escorted by a steam frigate of the British navy. As the *Soho* approached the Belém quay, Dom Pedro came out to meet her in a magnificent galley painted blue and white, and manned by forty-eight oarsmen dressed in the same colors. The regent, who was accompanied by Napier and Mendizábal, was received on the gangplank by his wife, whom he joyfully embraced. The plump, blond queen stood by, dressed in pink instead of the expected blue and white, tears running down her cheeks. Waiting his turn to greet Dom Pedro was the ever-faithful Chalaça. Napier "thought that [he] had never seen a more happy party." The only discordant note was sounded by the nearly two-year-old Dona Maria Amélia, who was frightened by her father's bushy beard. They had dinner aboard the *Soho* that night, and the queen disembarked the next day, amid the usual pomp and ceremony.[74]

Little more than a month after Dona Maria II landed in Lisbon, another underage queen was acclaimed in Madrid, the three-year-old Doña Isabel II, daughter of King Fernando VII, who died on September 29. Doña Isabel was the child of Don Fernando by Queen Maria

Cristina, whom he had married after the deaths of Queen María Isabel (Dom Pedro's sister) and an intervening wife. Queen Mother María Cristina, who was from the Bourbons of Naples, had cultivated the goodwill of Spain's repressed liberals, to seek their support for her daughter's claim to the throne against that of her late husband's brother, Don Carlos, who cited not-so-ancient Spanish law to prove that females were barred from ruling Spain. Because it was the deceased king's will that his daughter (he had no sons) succeed him, Spanish absolutists were theoretically obliged to accept her, and most of them did—at least for a few days, until the ideologically suspect Doña María Cristina assumed the post of regent to rule Spain during the minority of Queen Isabel II. In October absolutists in various parts of Spain rallied to the standard of Don Carlos, who had been in Dom Miguel's Portugal since March, drumming up support for his cause, in anticipation of the final demise of the ailing Spanish king. Don Carlos was the uncle and brother-in-law of Dom Pedro and Dom Miguel, and a kindred spirit of the latter, who generously, though unwisely, backed his campaign for the Spanish crown. (Don Carlos's wife was Doña María Francisca, who joined her sisters—the widow Dona Maria Teresa, the unmarried Dona Isabel Maria, and Dona Maria d'Assunção—in choosing Dom Miguel over Dom Pedro; among the sisters, only Dona Ana de Jesus, wife of the marquis of Loulé, sided with their older brother.) With Dom Miguel allowing Carlist rebels to use his territory for operations against the Spanish regency, the new government in Madrid had reason to make common cause with Dom Pedro. And the British, who had practically written off the Portuguese constitutionalists before Napier's victory, were now proposing a joint military operation with Spain to finish off Dom Miguel, and, they hoped, to restore their influence over the independent-minded Dom Pedro.[75]

But the regent of Portugal well knew that he could not depend on the British government, which only months before had been urging him to scrap his constitution and promise to leave the country if Dom Miguel would do likewise. Dom Pedro would fight and win his own battles with Portuguese like Saldanha and Terceira and mercenaries like Napier. It was Saldanha who led a sudden attack on MacDonell's positions before Lisbon on 10 October. Saldanha, who knew MacDonell personally from exile days in Paris, appreciated his opponent's organizational genius and recognized the need to strike before the Scotsman could reconstruct Dom Miguel's army. Saldanha's attack came as a complete surprise to the absolutists, who nevertheless managed to hold their line during the day. That night, in a brilliant maneuver, they fell back to new positions at Loures; Saldanha did not learn that they were gone until after sunrise the next morning. In the final phase of the staged withdrawal, the success of which owed much to the cool courage of Dom Miguel, the absolutists redeployed at Santarém on 15 October, taking possession of the ancient but still formidable hilltop fortress that controlled access to the city from the lower Tagus River. Dom Pedro took part in the pursuit, exposing himself repeatedly to the fire of his brother's forces. New lines were formed between Santarém and Cartaxo, where Saldanha set up his headquarters. Actually, the liberals controlled only the Tagus and a thin strip on each bank up to Santarém; beyond this salient, the countryside remained solidly Miguelista. Dom Pedro divided his time between Lisbon, where he presided over an increasingly fractious liberal government, and Saldanha's camp upriver. He developed a fever and bronchitis, but kept to his busy pace; in Cartaxo, in November, his expectoration was flecked with blood.[76]

Across the line, in Santarém, Dom Miguel and his sister, Dona Maria d'Assunção, were stricken by cholera: he survived, but she died. Dom Miguel sent a sealed letter through the lines to his brother, to inform him of the death of their sister. But Dom Pedro refused to receive the letter and sent it back unopened. Although the regent would not correspond privately with the enemy chief, he was willing to communicate with him officially through intermediaries, like the British minister in Lisbon and the Spanish minister in Santarém. The British and Spanish, even as they were negotiating an alliance against Dom Miguel, offered themselves as mediators in the Portuguese civil war, and Dom Pedro's terms were relayed through them to the absolutist camp. In the winter of 1833–34 the regent demanded that Dom Miguel formally renounce his claim to the throne and leave Portugal; in return, his royal titles and pension would be guaranteed, and his officers would retain their posts in the Portuguese army. Dom Pedro would have an admiral of the British navy supervise the execution of the peace agreement. General MacDonell thought it wise for the absolutists to go along with the British-Spanish mediation effort, if only to buy time, but Dom Miguel disagreed, which prompted the Scot to resign his command on 20 December. He was replaced by a Portuguese general of no particular distinction and the war continued; Dom

Miguel reaffirmed his determination not to abandon his kingdom.[77]

The duke of Terceira assumed command of the liberal forces at Cartaxo in January 1834 as Saldanha undertook a campaign to the north, swinging to the west around Santarém. Saldanha won a great victory at Almoster on 18 February but was unable to exploit his success, he complained, because he got no cooperation from Terceira. Dom Pedro had to separate the two feuding generals; he sent Saldanha south of the Tagus, and Terceira north to Oporto to begin a drive eastward along the Douro. Without the regent's authorization, Napier went farther north, to the Spanish border, and liberated most of the province of Minho in March and early April. Terceira landed at Oporto on 3 April, occupied Amarante three days later, and threatened Vila Real, where Don Carlos and his Spanish absolutists had their headquarters. The pretender found himself between two fires, as Spanish loyalist forces massed along the border to the east. Don Carlos escaped south of the Douro with his court and Carlist guard before Terceira and the Spanish loyalists could join forces on Portuguese territory on 22 April, the day that the Treaty of the Quadruple Alliance was signed in London. The joint operations of Terceira and the Spaniards in northeast Portugal anticipated the provisions of the treaty, which was not ratified by Dom Pedro in Lisbon until 10 May.[78]

The Quadruple Alliance joined Britain, France, Spain, and Portugal in a mutual security pact. Under its terms Portugal formally requested military intervention by Britain and Spain to combat the forces of Dom Miguel, and pledged to aid its allies in the pursuit of Carlists in Portuguese territory. The treaty assured an early end to the Miguelista usurpation, but except for about 5,000 Spaniards cooperating with Terceira, allied troops were not directly involved in the final, victorious campaign of the Portuguese constitutionalists. The momentum built as liberal forces, now well provisioned with horses and matériel, drove through the country, collecting adherents from among freed political prisoners, exiles returning from Spain, closet liberals, and opportunists. Recoiling in disoriented horror was the larger population of Miguelistas, a people whose saints had failed them. Dom Miguel's faithful subjects could not cope with the audacity of men like Terceira, Saldanha, and Napier; the conservative society could not withstand the shocks of liberal enterprise. Terceira took Coimbra on 8 May, and Napier advanced inland from Figueira. On 16 May the Miguelistas made a gallant stand at Asseiceira, near Tomar, but the outcome of the day's fighting was a total victory for Terceira.[79]

With Terceira at Tomar, his Spanish partners at Abrantes, and Saldanha driving up from the south, the absolutist capital of Santarém was doomed. Dom Miguel and Don Carlos packed up their courts and left Santarém for Évora, and they received the enthusiastic cheers of the people of that conservative city on 22 May. It was the last hurrah for the Miguelistas, whose generals, the next day, voted in a council of war to suspend hostilities and sue for peace. Dom Miguel and Don Carlos accepted the decision, and messengers were sent from Évora under flags of truce to find Saldanha and Terceira. The two liberal generals arranged to meet their absolutist counterparts, in the presence of the first secretary from the British legation in Lisbon, at the town of Évora-Monte on 26 May. There the absolutists surrendered their forces and accepted the terms of Dom Pedro and his allies, which required the expulsion of Dom Miguel and Don Carlos from the Iberian peninsula. Don Carlos went to England, but later slipped back into Spain to continue the Carlist War. Dom Miguel embarked on a British warship at the little coastal town of Sines on 1 June; he went to Italy, eventually settled in Germany, and never returned to Portugal.[80]

9 Return to Queluz

Alas! good sir: Do not die, I pray you.
Sancho Panza to Don Quixote
Dom Pedro did not die. Only ordinary men die, not heroes.
José Bonifácio to Dom Pedro II and his sisters

"Don't believe that I feed on vengeance, blood, and death," Dom Pedro advised enemy troops in a proclamation issued during the last months of the civil war. "I pride myself on being true, human, and generous, and on being able to forget offenses committed against me."[1] During the fighting Dom Pedro personally went to great lengths to ensure that Miguelista prisoners were treated humanely, and that captured enemy wounded got the best medical care available. His flashes of anger were more likely to be directed against fellow liberals than against absolutist foes; such flare-ups could be kindled by old grudges, which typically would be dismissed after the flare-up. When Colonel Rodrigo Pinto Pizarro—who as an exile in France had tried to block Dom Pedro from assuming the leadership of the liberation expedition in 1831–32—landed in Portugal in June 1834, the regent ordered him expelled from the country. When Pizarro refused to leave, he was thrown in jail, but was soon released and went on to take a seat in the Cortes a few weeks later.

Against General Jorge de Ávilez, Dom Pedro had grievances dating from Brazil in 1821–22; the former commander of the Portuguese Division in Rio languished in absolutist jails in Portugal from 1828 until 1832, when he escaped and made his way to Spain. He recrossed the border early in 1834 and joined the duke of Terceira in his northern campaign, after which Dom Pedro appointed his old adversary military governor of the North. Though Dom Pedro did not forgive Dom Miguel, neither did he seek to wreak vengeance on his brother. He forgave his sister, Dona Isabel Maria, whom he had confirmed as regent in 1826, and who had sided with Dom Miguel after the usurpation; Dom Pedro personally welcomed her to Lisbon in June 1834.[2]

During the war Dom Miguel's followers suffered huge property losses. The confiscation of private property by the liberals was not a punitive measure—at least not as far as Dom Pedro was concerned—but a means of financing the war. The liberal fund-raising, however, was poorly regulated, especially where moveable goods were involved. In Lisbon there were sales on the Rossio, where furniture, pictures, and jewelry of proscribed nobles went for bargain prices; in combat areas, plunder was the order of the day as constitutional troops, especially unpaid mercenaries, scrambled for direct remuneration. Even so refined a gentleman as Colonel Bacon of the Lancers was known to rummage through private homes looking for gold and jewelry. Liberal Justice and Finance Minister Mousinho da Silveira, who opposed the confiscation of private property, was replaced in the cabinet during the siege of Oporto by José da Silva Carvalho, who favored it. Silva Carvalho and his colleague, War Minister Agostinho José Freire, were regarded as "corrupt and vindictive" by the British government, which took upon itself the task of curbing their abuses and, quite unnecessarily, of persuading Dom Pedro to institute constitutional rule in postwar Portugal.[3] Lord Palmerston might congratulate himself on winning generous terms for the Miguelistas in the April 1834 London negotiations that established the Quadruple Alliance, but the terms were not secured at the expense of Dom Pedro, whose views they mirrored.

Dom Pedro authorized his field commanders, Terceira and Saldanha, to accept the surrender of the Miguelistas on the terms laid down in London; there would be no negotiations. The document signed at Évora-Monte on 26 May was not a "convention," as it would be called, but a capitulation by the absolutists. It required Dom Miguel to leave the country within fifteen days, and guaranteed him an annual pension of 62,500 dollars. Although Miguelista military officers were to be retained in the Portuguese army, some priests and absolutist government officials stood to lose their employment; nobles who had violated their oath to the constitution by supporting the usurper forfeited their seats in the House of Lords. There was to be a general amnesty for political offenses committed since 1826, and confiscated private property was to be restored in accordance with formulae to be worked out by the Cortes.[4]

The final liberal triumph, the arrival of peace, and the amnesty, Dom Pedro felt, were well worth celebrating. He and his wife and the queen made plans to go to the São Carlos Theater, where a special program was arranged for the night of 27 May—Bellini's opera, *The Pirate*, and a ballet by Montani, *Clazimiro and Slawizza, or, The Usurper Punished*. The regent ordered his amnesty decree printed and had copies sent to the theater for distribution to the audience. But the peace of Évora-Monte did not please the multitudes of Lisbon, who wanted to see Dom Miguel hanged, along with the others who were responsible for executing more than one hundred liberals during the usurpation. Those who had acquired Miguelista property were horrified at the thought that they might have to return it; the masses wanted the confiscation continued, not reversed. They expressed their displeasure by pelting Dom Pedro's carriage with rocks and mud as it passed through the streets of Lisbon carrying the royal party to the theater. An exterior wall of the theater was plastered with a poster likening Dom Pedro to Dom Miguel, proclaiming that one was as bad as the other. Hoping to get a better reception inside, Dom Pedro stepped to the rail of the royal box and loosed some copies of the amnesty decree to the audience below; the gesture was greeted by the stamping of feet, by shouts and whistles of derision; some theatergoers threw coins at the regent. Dom Pedro's military aides tried to send troops into the theater to expel the leaders of the demonstration, but the soldiers refused to act. Already shaking and breathing hard, Dom Pedro broke into a coughing fit as he cursed the audience; he brought a handkerchief to his mouth, where it turned red with blood for all to see. A hush fell over the audience. The regent stopped coughing, put away his handkerchief, straightened up and then made a bow to the orchestra, and in the strongest voice he could muster, commanded, "Carry on." The performance began, but Dom Pedro left before it was over.[5] After the episode at the theater he spent more time at Queluz—the palace where he had been born, ten kilometers from Lisbon—and appeared in the city less frequently.

Eager to return the country to constitutional rule, Dom Pedro signed a decree on 28 May ordering elections for members of the Chamber of Deputies, now scheduled to convene on 15 August. In the meantime, Dom Pedro and his cabinet tried to impose as much of their program as possible, in order to present the Cortes with *faits accomplis* on the major social and economic questions. An order for the suppression of all monasteries and convents and the liquidation of their holdings was issued on 28 May; subsequent decrees provided pensions for the dispossessed monks and allowed most nuns to live out their lives on the convent premises. Dom Pedro favored the sale of monastic property to help pay off the huge public debt that Portugal had incurred during the war years, to make land available cheaply to private farmers —thereby promoting agricultural development and building a rural constituency for Portuguese liberalism—and to curtail the power of a privileged class that despised freedom and poorly served the liberating religion it professed. In a country where for more than 300 years everyone had been required to be Roman Catholic and to pay taxes to the Church, it was not unreasonable for liberals to view Church holdings as public property; the privatization of the holdings of the regular clergy was an essential step in the dismantling of the theocratic corporatist system. The liberal government also attacked other special interests: it abolished the state wine monopoly, and lowered the import duties on almost all goods, regardless of country of origin, to 13 1/2 percent, a point and a half below the formerly preferential rate enjoyed by the British. And the constitutionalist regime signaled its intention to end the extraterritorial privileges that British subjects enjoyed in Portugal. Lord Palmerston grumbled that Dom Pedro's government was ungrateful to Britain, but as a liberal himself, he had to acknowledge that "exclusive privileges . . . are far less beneficial to the nation that enjoys them than many persons may be inclined to suppose."[6]

As the liberal decrees flowed from Queluz palace, the regent's health deteriorated. Although Dom Pedro did not complain about his ailments in letters to family and friends, observers recorded that from the time of the siege of Oporto the regent sometimes had trouble breathing and suffered from fevers, trembling, chest pains, and edema in the feet. Symptoms of tuberculosis were evident by November 1833, after which Dom Pedro's physical decline accelerated, with periods of remission rarer and of shorter duration than before. By June 1834 horseback riding was almost impossible for him, and he had to give up hunting. He could no longer conceal his condition from absent friends and relatives, for the trembling precluded his writing personal letters in his own hand, as was his custom; by July he was dictating all his correspondence to the Chalaça. Ever optimistic, he took each remission as the beginning of complete recovery. He had great faith in the treatment of Dr. Tavares and his other physicians, who prescribed hot baths and caustics. But no improvement was noted by those who saw him on 8 July, when he drove into Lisbon with Dona Amélia and the queen to take part in festivities marking the second anniversary of the landing at Oporto. The famous dark beard of the hero was streaked with grey; his eyes were sunken, his nostrils flared, his coughing cavernous. Nevertheless, he survived the ceremonies and was well enough to return to Lisbon less than two weeks later to inspect work on the former Benedictine monastery that was being remodeled to house the Portuguese Cortes.[7]

The regent insisted on taking a steamboat trip to Oporto with Dona Amélia and the queen to introduce them to the heroic city and show them where he had spent the most difficult and glorious days of his life. The people of Oporto received the royal party with jubilation, and festivities lasted from 27 July to 6 August. Dom Pedro was greatly pleased with his reception in Oporto; he attended all the celebrations and met with everyone who requested to see him. The visit provided the triumphant note that enabled Dom Pedro to concede that the drama was coming to a close. "Goodbye, Oporto!" he exclaimed from the deck of the departing steamer, "I'll never see you again."[8] But there was still business in Lisbon to be concluded. Dom Pedro was determined to preside over the reestablishment of constitutional rule in Portugal, to open the first session of the Cortes on 15 August. He spent the night before at Necessidades palace in Lisbon, and on 15 August managed to climb the steps to the former monastery where the Cortes was assembled. He entered the parliament building red faced and gasping. Seated in the regent's chair, he looked, according to one witness, "more like a corpse than anything else."[9] In a faltering voice he delivered a long speech, reviewing the major developments since the 1828 usurpation and outlining the questions that remained to be resolved—principally that of the regency. Dom Pedro did not ask the Cortes to confirm him as regent for Dona Maria II, though that was what he desired. There were, however, constitutional problems with his holding the office of sole regent, since he was a Brazilian citizen and was not in the Portuguese royal line of succession. Palmela and the marquis of Loulé argued that Dona Isabel Maria was the one indicated by the constitution to rule during the queen's minority, and, should she decline, the Cortes was required to elect a regency of three persons, one of whom could be Dom Pedro. The liberator decided to leave the Lisbon area while the Cortes debated the question.[10]

Against the advice of his physicians, Dom Pedro rode eighty kilometers in a carriage to the hot springs of Caldas da Rainha. He was accompanied by the Chalaça and the equally dedicated Dr. Tavares, who hoped to salvage some benefit for his patient from the ill-advised trip. Under Dr. Tavares's supervision the regent undertook a regimen of hot baths and ingestion of the supposedly curative waters; it did him no good and his condition worsened. He returned to Queluz palace on 25 August, before the Cortes had completed its consideration of the regency question. The final ballot was in the House of Lords on 28 August, and Dom Pedro was elected sole regent with five dissenting votes—including that of his brother-in-law, the marquis of Loulé. Dom Pedro was sworn in as constitutional regent two days later, at Ajuda palace, because he was no longer able to climb the steps to the Cortes building. The deputies and lords were friendly and the crowds enthusiastic. Dom Pedro was fully vindicated: the constitution he had devised was in effect, the rights of his daughter to the throne were secure, and he had been elected by the representatives of the nation to rule in her name. He remained at Ajuda palace for a few more days, receiving an occasional visitor and taking short carriage rides through nearby city neighborhoods. After presenting this brave front to the people of Lisbon, the regent returned to Queluz on 10 September, certain that death was near, and went to bed in the illusorily circular room in which he had been born. Surrounded by painted images of the knight of La Mancha, Dom Pedro dictated his will to the marquis of Resende on 15 September, but his tremors prevented him from signing it. The liberator bequeathed his sword to Prince Auguste—the duke of Leuchtenberg, Dona Amélia's brother—whom he had chosen to marry the queen, to her great delight.[11]

Dom Pedro's hand was steady enough to sign his will on 17 September, the day that the regent received the last rites of the Church. The next day he informed the Cortes of the fact—in a note painfully transcribed in his own palsied hand—and advised the representatives that he was no longer physically able to perform the duties of regent; he invited them to take whatever measures they felt were necessary. Dom Pedro's desire, conveyed orally to members of the Cortes, was that no other regent be named and that Queen Maria II be declared reigning monarch immediately, though she was only fifteen years old. The Cortes acceded to the wishes of the dying hero and acclaimed Dona Maria that very day, 18 September. She presided over her first council of ministers meeting on 18 September at Queluz, and met with her council of state the next day in Lisbon, at Necessidades palace.[12]

As his daughter took over the reins of government, Dom Pedro was saying goodbye to friends and comrades, receiving a few select visitors at his bedside in the Don Quixote room. Among these was an enlisted soldier, veteran of the siege of Oporto, who left the meeting emotionally shaken, crying that he would have preferred death in battle to seeing his leader in such a condition. Death came peacefully to Dom Pedro at two-thirty in the afternoon of 24 September 1834. "He expired in my arms," Dona Amélia informed her stepchildren in Brazil. "He died like a holy martyr and Christian philosopher, and never was there a death more tranquil." Admiral Napier observed that the deceased had borne "his sufferings with Christian fortitude."[13] The hero was mourned by the multitudes who lined the route of his funeral cortege from Queluz to the Church of São Vicente de Fora in Lisbon. Although places were reserved for family members and three official mourners —Terceira, Saldanha, and Napier—people marched in the procession and attended the funeral without regard to rank or social status, in accordance with the will of Dom Pedro. It was also the deceased's wish that his heart be sent in an urn to Oporto, to be deposited in a church there. His body, without that organ, was interred in the São Vicente church in Lisbon on 27 September.[14] One hundred and thirty-eight years later the bones of the liberator were removed to Brazil, his chosen country, and buried at Ipiranga, on the site where he had declared Brazilian independence in 1822.

Notes

Abbreviations

ABN   *Anais da Biblioteca Nacional*, published by BNRJ
ADI   *Archivo Diplomatico da Independencia*, six volumes published by AHI in 1922–25
AHI   Arquivo Histórico do Itamarati (Foreign Ministry), Rio de Janeiro
ANTT   Arquivo Nacional Torre do Tombo, Lisbon
AIP   Arquivo Imperial, Petrópolis
BNL   Biblioteca Nacional, Lisbon
BNRJ   Biblioteca National, Rio de Janeiro
FO   Foreign Office Archive, Public Record Office, Kew Gardens, London
HAHR   *Hispanic American Historical Review*
JLAS   *Journal of Latin American Studies*
PAN   *Publicações do Arquivo Nacional*, Rio de Janeiro
PRO   Public Record Office, Kew Gardens, London
RIHGB   *Revista do Instituto Histórico e Geográfico Brasileiro*
USDS   United States Department of State, U.S. National Archives Microfilm
DD   Diplomatic Documents
CD   Consular Dispatches

1—The Exodus

1   Charles R. Boxer, "Brazilian Gold and British Traders in the First Half of the Eighteenth Century," *HAHR* 69 (1969): 454–72; George Kubler and Martin Soria, *Art and Architecture in Spain and Portugal and their American Dominions, 1500–1800* (Baltimore, 1959), pp. 110, 114.

2   Kubler and Soria, *Art and Architecture*, p. 114.

3   Ángelo Pereira, *D. João VI, Príncipe e Rei* (Lisbon, 1953), 1:18–22, 57–58; William Beckford, *The Travel Diaries of William Beckford of Fonthill* (Cambridge, 1928), 2:370–71.

4   Pereira, *D. João VI* 1:65–94; José Ferreira Borges de Castro, ed., *Collecção dos tratados, convenções, contratos e actos públicos celebrados entre a coroa de Portugal e as mais potências desde 1640 até ao presente* (Lisbon, 1857), 4:128–51. A secret provision of the 1801 treaty allowed British mail packets to call at Portuguese ports.

5   Laure Saint-Martin Junot, Duchesse d'Abrantès, *Mémoires de Madame la Duchesse d'Abrantès* (Paris, n.d.), 5:136–37, 372–75; António Caldeira Pires, *História do Palácio Nacional de Queluz* (Coimbra, 1926), 2:233–35.

6   Abrantès, *Mémoires* 5:373–77.

7   Ibid.

8   Ibid.

9 Raúl Brandão, *El-Rei Junot*, 3d ed. (Coimbra, 1974), p. 72; Pires, *História do Palácio* (1924), 1: 258, 275–76.
10 Pedro Calmon, *O rei do Brasil: Vida de D. João VI* (Rio, 1943), pp. 30–33; Caetano Beirão, *Dona Maria I* (Lisbon, 1944), pp. 320–22, 445–47, 451; Pereira, *D. João VI* 1:27–54.
11 Beckford, *Travel Diaries* 2:253, 374; Brandão, *El-Rei Junot*, p. 72. According to a rhyme that was popular at the time, Dom Miguel's father was "Neither Marialva nor João, But the caretaker at Ramalhão." Luiz Edmundo da Costa, *A côrte de D. João no Rio de Janeiro* (Rio, 1957), 1:217. Tobias Monteiro sees no physical resemblance in the portraits of Dom Miguel and Marialva, *História do Império: A elaboração da Independência* (Rio, 1927), p. 82. Beckford, who knew Marialva intimately, thought it noteworthy in discussing Dom Miguel's parentage that the marquis "was webfooted." Cyrus Redding, *Memoirs of William Beckford of Fonthill, Author of "Vathek"* (London, 1859), 1:283.
12 Calmon, *O rei*, pp. 77–79; Ángelo Pereira, *Os filhos de El-Rei D. João VI* (Lisbon, 1926), p. 28.
13 Pereira, *Os filhos*, pp. 71–72; Octávio Tarquínio de Sousa, *A vida de D. Pedro I* (Rio, 1972), 1:13–16.
14 Beckford, *Travel Diaries* 2:364–66.
15 Pereira, *Os filhos*, p. 14; Robert Southey, *Journals of a Residence in Portugal 1800–1801 and a Visit to France 1838* (Oxford, 1960), p. 120.
16 Redding, *Memoirs of Beckford* 2:55; Calmon, *O rei*, p. 21. Professor George D. Winius has located an early manuscript of "Adeste fidelis" in the handwriting of João IV.
17 Monteiro, *História do Império: Elaboração*, pp. 88–89; Southey, *Journals of a Residence*, p. 13; Beckford, *Travel Diaries* 2:365.
18 Abrantès, *Mémoires* 5:385; Pereira, *Os filhos*, pp. 90–91.
19 Beckford, *Travel Diaries* 2:253, 362–63, 374. Connoisseur and aesthete, enormously wealthy and extraordinarily talented as a writer and linguist, William Beckford nonetheless was often shunned by his countrymen at home and abroad because of his notorious habits. Even Lord Byron, who admired his novel *Vathek*, was moved to priggish indignation by Beckford's erotic eccentricities. An imaginative voluptuary, Beckford was bisexual and a pederast. Of greater concern to the historian is the fact that he was also a liar. Scholars have found significant discrepancies between published accounts of his travels and the unpublished diaries from which they were supposedly taken. Unfortunately, Beckford did not keep a diary at the time he visited Queluz, and whatever notes he made on that journey have been lost or destroyed; the published version, while probably "faked up here and there," according to Rose Macaulay, is generally believable. Beckford certainly knew whereof he wrote; he was especially well connected with the Marialva family. The marquis of Marialva had a homosexual relationship with Beckford dating from the latter's visit to Portugal in 1787, when the marquis was fifteen years old (the affair was interrupted when Beckford returned to England with a still younger boy). Marialva's relationship with Carlota Joaquina, Beckford suggests, began with their visit to Queluz. Thus, some of Beckford's animosity toward the princess could be due to the fact that she displaced him in the nobleman's affections. The young marquis's father—a pillar of Portuguese nobility —remained quite fond of the Englishman, whom he hoped to marry to his illegitimate daughter, Henriqueta. An excellent introduction to Beckford's Portuguese

escapades is in Rose Macaulay, *They Went to Portugal* (London, 1946), pp. 108–42, quotation at p. 136.

20 Abrantès, *Mémoires* 5:382–83.

21 Beckford, *Travel Diaries* 2:366.

22 Abrantès, *Mémoires* 5:450, 473–74; 6:76–87, 89–90, 408–21, 457–58, 530, 554.

23 Monteiro, *História do Império: Elaboração*, pp. 7–8, 15; Percy Clinton Sidney Smythe, Viscount Strangford, *Observations on some Passages of Lieut. Col. Napier's History of the Peninsular War* (London, 1828), p. 15.

24 M. de Rayneval to António de Araújo de Azevedo, and Conde de Campo de Alange to Araújo, 12 August 1807, in *Supplemento à collecção dos tratados, convenções, contratos e actos públicos celebrados entre a corôa de Portugal e as mais potências desde 1640*, ed. Júlio Fermino Judice Biker, (Lisbon, 1878), 6:228–32.

25 Araújo, *Relatório*, n.d. [November 1807], in *Supplemento*, ed Biker, 6:369–77.

26 Pereira, *Os filhos*, pp. 102–6; Lord Strangford to George Canning, 21 and 29 August 1809, FO 63, codex 55, folios 94–99, 108–15. Strangford learned of the deliberations of the council of state from an informant, probably Rodrigo de Sousa Coutinho.

27 George Gordon, Lord Byron, "English Bards and Scotch Reviewers," *The Complete Poetical Works of Lord Byron* (Boston, 1905), p. 246.

28 Abrantès, *Mémoires* 5:139, 389–90; Norwood Andrews, Jr., "Camões and Some of his Readers in American Imprints of Lord Strangford's Translations in the Nineteenth Century," in *Empire in Transition: The Portuguese World in the Time of Camões*, ed. Alfred Hower and Richard H. Preto-Rodas, (Gainesville, 1985), pp. 204–18. An early critic of Strangford as a diplomat was Henry Brougham, secretary to a British naval and military mission to Portugal in 1806, who reported back to London that the viscount was "too flighty and uncertain in his movements to gain my confidence. . . . My temper has been tried perpetually by his infinite childishness in doing business, and indeed in doing everything else; . . . there is a defect about him which I can still less pardon than his want of commonsense. I mean his *total want* of that first-rate quality which gives a man's words the right to be believed." Quoted in Macaulay, *They Went to Portugal*, pp. 367–68.

29 Strangford to Canning, 29 August and 8 September 1807, FO 63, codex 55, folios 116–24, 143–50.

30 Strangford to Canning, 26 September 1807, FO 63, codex 55, folios 205–16.

31 Ibid.

32 Borges de Castro, *Collecção* 4:237–62.

33 Dom João, Decreto ordenando que os portos de Portugal sejam fechados à entrada dos navios, assim de guerra como mercantes, do Grão Bretanha, 20 October 1807, in *Supplemento*, ed. Biker, 6:382.

34 Strangford to Canning, 17 and 20 November 1807, FO 63, codex 56, folios 208–15, 234–38; Araújo to Strangford, 6 November 1807, in *Supplemento*, ed. Biker, 6:355–56; Pereira, *Os filhos*, p. 108.

35 Araújo to Marialva, 10 and 13 November 1807, in *Supplemento*, ed. Biker, 6:358–61, 363–68; Monteiro, *História do Império: Elaboração*, p. 32; Brandão, *El-Rei Junot*, p. 77.

36 Canning to Strangford, 7 and 9 November 1807, FO 63, codex 56, folios 37–52, 68–72; Strangford to Canning, 20 and 24 November 1807, FO 63, codex 56, folios 234–38, 249–57; Strangford, *Observations*, pp. 31–34.

37 Pereira, *Os filhos*, pp. 111–12; Araújo to Strangford, 25 November 1807, in

Strangford, *Observations*, p. 34.

38 Pereira, *Os filhos*, pp. 129–32; Brandão, *El-Rei Junot*, pp. 104–5.

39 Pereira, *Os filhos*, pp. 129–32; Brandão, *El-Rei Junot*, pp. 104–7.

40 Maximilièn Sébastian Foy, *Histoire de la guerre de la péninsule sous Napoleón* (Paris, 1827), 2:387–88.

41 Brandão, *El-Rei Junot*, p. 107; Thomas, Count O'Neil, *A Concise and Accurate Account of the Proceedings of the Squadron under the Command of Rear Admiral Sir Sidney Smith in Effecting the Escape of the Royal Family of Portugal to the Brazils, on November 29, 1807* (London, 1810), pp. 15–16.

42 Francisco José da Rocha Martins, *A Corte de Junot em Portugal* (Lisbon, 1910), p. 21; Strangford to Canning, 30 November and 2 December 1807, FO 63, codex 56, folios 280–86; O'Neil, *Concise Account*, pp. 22–25.

43 Antônio Augusto de Aguiar, *Vida do Marquez de Barbacena* (Rio, 1896), p. 10.

44 Ellen Margaret Thompson, "Francisco Gomes da Silva: Advisor and Court Jester to Pedro I" (Master's thesis, University of Florida, 1975), pp. 1–2.

45 Pereira, *Os filhos*, p. 119; Brandão, *El-Rei Junot*, p. 109.

46 Abrantès, *Mémoires* 7:19–31; Adolphe Thiers, *Histoire du Consulat et de L'Empire* (Paris, 1849), 8:325–42.

47 Abrantès, *Mémoires* 7:31; Thiers, *Histoire* 8:342–44; Rocha Martins, *A corte de Junot*, p. 28. The picture of Junot arriving in Lisbon just in time to see the ships carrying the royal family slip down the Tagus beyond his reach—a standard feature of history textbooks—is charming, but totally false. Observers on the scene leave no doubt that the royal family was long gone before Junot appeared in Lisbon. Cf. Camilo Luís de Rossi, "Memória sobre a evasão do Núncio Apostólico Monsehor Caleppi, da corte de Lisboa para a do Rio de Janeiro (1808)," tr. Jerônimo de Avelar Figueira de Melo, *ABN* 61 (1939):21.

Lord Strangford's influence on the course of events was less than the British minister claimed. Strangford's "dispatch" of 29 November 1807, supposedly written aboard Smith's flagship *Hibernia* off the Portuguese coast, was actually composed in George Canning's apartment in London on 19 December 1807 as a press release. Although Strangford included in the document portions from an authentic report, he arranged and edited them so as to give the false impression that he, after conferring with Smith aboard the *Hibernia*, had returned to Lisbon and persuaded Dom João to embark. The "dispatch" appeared in the *London Gazette* on 22 December 1807. Discrepancies in Strangford's newspaper account were pointed out by Ralph Rylance in the pamphlet *A Sketch of the Causes and Consequences of the Late Emigration to the Brazils*, published in London early the next year, and by Hipólito da Costa in the August 1808 issue of the *Correio braziliense* (London). Hipólito suggested that Strangford could have made an honest error, getting his dates mixed up; the distinguished Brazilian journalist had difficulty believing that the viscount actually contrived so blatant a deception, risking certain exposure and possible grave consequences for his diplomatic career (*Correio braziliense* 1, 3 [August 1808]:207). But the matter was little noted in 1808 and was not fully aired in the English-language press until twenty years later. The controversy was sparked by the publication of W. F. P. Napier's *History of the War in the Peninsula* (London, 1828), which is uncomplimentary to Strangford. In the ensuing battle of pamphlets and lawsuits, Strangford admitted that when he returned to Lisbon on 28 November 1807, he found the

Portuguese court already embarked. However, Strangford maintained that it had been his encouragement, over a period of months, that prepared Dom João to take this bold step. Actually, Portuguese and British documents —including Strangford's dispatches—indicate that the Portuguese government had transformed the idea of moving to Brazil into a contingency plan as early as August 1807. The viscount certainly did not persuade the Portuguese to put the plan into operation; this they did, as they had long intended to do, after forces hostile to the Bragança monarchy actually invaded Portugal. Strangford was not in Lisbon on 23 November 1807, when word was received there that Junot had crossed the border, and when a copy of the 13 November issue of the French government gazette *Le Moniteur* reached the city, proclaiming that the Braganças had ceased to rule; nor was he there when the final decision to embark was made on 24 November.

British Foreign Minister Canning apparently felt that Strangford was somehow responsible for the escape of the Portuguese royal family, and with more pressing matters to attend to, did not object to the viscount's taking credit for it publicly. Privately, Strangford, in his report to Canning of 30 November/2 December 1807 (FO 63, codex 56, folios 280–85), acknowledged that the Portuguese court was embarked when he arrived in Lisbon on 28 November, but claimed that Dom João was having second thoughts about the project and was on the verge of disembarking and surrendering to the French. "I saw that not a moment was to be lost," declared Strangford, "that my duty was to destroy in [Dom João's] mind all hopes of accommodating matters with the Invaders of his Country, to terrify him with dark and gloomy descriptions . . . then to dazzle him suddenly with the brilliant prospects before him, to direct all his fears to a French Army and all his hopes to an English Fleet." Strangford succeeded, he said, because "I am acquainted with the turn and temper of the Prince Regent's mind." By his triumph in Lisbon, according to the viscount, "I have entitled England to establish with the Brazils the Relation of Sovereign and Subject, and to require Obedience to be paid as the price of Protection."

Reading Strangford's diplomatic correspondence disposes one to endorse Lord Byron's exhortation, evoked by the Hibernian's poetic efforts: "Mend! Strangford! Mend thy morals and thy taste." Byron, "English Bards," p. 246. See also Strangford, *Observations*, pp. 6–7, 28–31.

48 Angelo Pereira, *D. João VI* 1:172.

2—The New Kingdom

1 Strangford to Canning, 30 November/2 December 1807, FO 63, codex 56, folios 280, 284; O'Neil, *Concise Account*, pp. 22–24; Pereira, *Os filhos*, p. 113; Sir Sidney Smith to W. W. Pole, 1 December 1807, in *The Life and Correspondence of Admiral Sir William Sidney Smith, G.C.B.*, by John Barrow (London, 1848), 2:271–74; José Wanderley Pinho, *A abertura dos portos—Cairu—os ingleses—a Independência* (Salvador, 1961), pp. 15–16.

2 Eugène Garay de Monglave, *Correspondance du don Pédre Premier, Empereur Constitutionnel du Brésil, avec le roi de Portugal Don Jean VI, son pére, durant les troubles du Brésil* (Paris, 1827), p. 12.

3 O'Neil, *Concise Account*, pp. 25–26; Pereira, *Os filhos*, p. 113.

Notes

4 Smith to Secretary of the Admiralty, 1 December and 6 December 1807, in *Life and Correspondence*, Barrow, 2:274–76; Pereira, *Os filhos*, p. 113.

5 Pereira, *Os filhos*, p. 113.

6 Robert Walsh, *Notices of Brazil in 1828 and 1829* (Boston, 1831), 1:180–81; Monglave, *Correspondance*, p. 13; Pereira, *Os filhos*, p. 72; Lucas Alexandre Boiteux, *A marinha de guerra brasileira nos reinados de D. João VI e D. Pedro I (1807–1831)* (Rio, 1913), p. 9.

7 Pereira, *Os filhos*, p. 113; Wanderley Pinho, *Abertura*, p. 17.

8 O'Neil, *Concise Account*, pp. 68–71; Wanderley Pinho, *Abertura*, p. 21; Thomas Lindley, *Narrative of a Voyage to Brazil* (London, 1805), pp. 238–51.

9 Charles Darwin, *The Voyage of the Beagle* (Garden City, N.Y., 1962), pp. 31, 493–94; O'Neil, *Concise Account*, pp. 68–71.

10 Lindley, *Narrative*, pp. 252–53; Boiteux, *A marinha*, p. 9.

11 Alexandre José de Mello Moraes, *Historia da trasladação da corte portuguêza para o Brasil em 1807–1808* (Rio, 1872), pp. 67–68.

12 Strangford to Canning, 26 September and 30 November/2 December 1807, FO 63, codex 55, folios 205–16, and codex 56, folio 284.

13 Dom João, Carta Régia, 28 January 1808, in *Historia da trasladação*, Mello Moraes, pp. 71–72.

14 Mello Moraes, *Historia da trasladação*, pp. 69, 74; Lindley, *Narrative*, pp. 140, 273–74.

15 Guilherme de Melo, *A música no Brasil* (Rio, 1947), p. 106; Johann Maurice Rugendas, *Viagem pitoresca através do Brasil* (São Paulo, 1941), plates 1/27 and 2/8 (depicting Bahian capoeiras and bahianas); Manuel Antônio de Almeida, *Memórias de um Sargento de Milícias* (Rio, 1968), pp. 108–9; Lindley, *Narrative*, p. 55.

16 Pereira, *Os filhos*, pp. 113–14; O'Neil, *Concise Account*, p. 35; Walsh, *Notices* 1: 441–42; Mello Moraes, *Historia da trasladação*, pp. 75–81.

17 Luiz Gonçalves dos Santos, *Memórias para servir à história do Reino do Brasil* (Rio, 1943), 1:210–19; Tarquínio de Sousa, *Vida de D. Pedro I* 1:51–52; L. E. da Costa, *A corte* 1:83–101.

18 John Luccock, *Notes on Rio de Janeiro and the Southern Parts of Brazil taken during a Residence of Ten Years . . . 1808 to 1818* (London, 1820), p. 96.

19 John Mawe, *Travels in the Interior of Brazil, Particularly in the Gold and Diamond Districts of that Country* (London, 1812), pp. 105–6; Luccock, *Notes*, pp. 35–37, 41–42.

20 Tarquínio de Sousa, *Vida de D. Pedro I* 1:53–54, 64–66; Calmon, *Rei do Brasil*, pp. 34–35.

21 Loretta Sharon Wyatt, "D. Carlota and the Regency Affair" (Ph.D. dissertation, University of Florida, 1969), pp. 26–29. Don Pedro Carlos was the son of Don Gabriel Antonio, the fourth son of Spanish King Carlos III and Dom João's sister, Dona Maria Vitória.

22 Wyatt, "D. Carlota," pp. 55–95; Alan K. Manchester, *British Preëminence in Brazil: Its Rise and Decline* (New York, 1964), pp. 118–25; Barrow, *Life and Correspondence*, p. 301.

23 Luiz Norton, *A corte de Portugal no Brasil* (São Paulo, 1938), p. 66; Wyatt, "D. Carlota," pp. 55–95; Barrow, *Life and Correspondence*, pp. 301–4.

24 Strangford to Canning, 9 October 1809, quoted in Manchester, *British Preëminence*, p. 123.

25 Pereira, *Os filhos*, p. 78; José Presas, *Memorias secretas de la Princesa del Brasil* (Buenos Aires, n.d.), pp. 120–21; Monteiro, *Histório do Império: Elaboração*, p. 59.

26 Barrow, *Life and Correspondence*, pp. 328–36; Manchester, *British Preëminence*, pp. 122–25; Wyatt, "D. Carlota," pp. 96–131.

27 Pereira, *Os filhos*, p. 72.

28 João Rademaker held the military rank of lieutenant-colonel, and in English correspondence his first name was given as "John." His name and the fact that he was Strangford's agent apparently led Manchester to believe that he was an Englishman and an officer in the British army. Manchester, *British Preëminence*, p. 132; John Henry Hann, "Brazil and the Río de la Plata, 1808–1828" (Ph.D. dissertation, University of Texas, 1967), p. 214; Monglave, *Correspondance*, p. 16; João Rademaker to Rodrigo de Souza Coutinho, 15 October 1808, in *Os filhos*, Pereira, pp. 72–73; Alberto Pimentel, *A corte de D. Pedro IV*, 2d ed. (Lisbon, 1914), p. 12.

29 L. E. da Costa, *A corte* 1:199–202; Tarquínio de Sousa, *Vida de D. Pedro I* 1:59, 69–71; Alberto Rangel, *Dom Pedro I e a Marquêsa de Santos* (São Paulo, 1969), pp. 20–21; Monglave, *Correspondance*, pp. 16–17; Walsh, *Notices* 1:180–81.

30 Presas, *Memorias secretas*, pp. 120–21; Pimentel, *A corte*, p. 13.

31 L. E. da Costa, *A corte* 1:202–06, 220; Monteiro, *Histório do Império: Elaboração*, pp. 144–45.

32 F. W. O. Morton, "The Military and Society in Bahia, 1800–1821," *JLAS* 7 (1975):250.

33 A picture and description of such a rig is in Jean Baptiste Debret, *Viagem pitoresca e histórica ao Brasil* (Sao Paulo, 1949), 1:167–68.

34 Affonso de E. Taunay, *Do Reino ao Imperio* (São Paulo, 1927), pp. 100–101; James A. Henderson, *A History of the Brazil* (London, 1821), p. 63; Mawe, *Travels*, pp. 114–17; O'Neil, *Concise Account*, pp. 67–68; Monglave, *Correspondance*, pp. 18–20.

35 Calmon, *Vida de D. Pedro I*, p. 42; Luiz Lamego, *D. Pedro I, héroi e enfermo* (Rio, n.d.), p. 48; Taunay, *Do Reino*, pp. 107, 109–10.

36 D. Pedro to Conde dos Arcos, 13 September 1812, in *O último vice-rei do Brasil* by Francisco José da Rocha Martins (Lisbon, 1932), p. 97.

37 Monglave, *Correspondance*, p. 17; Walsh, *Notices* 1:183; Boiteux, *A marinha*, p. 55. In later years Dom Pedro would illustrate his bawdy verse with pornographic drawings, e.g., Sonetto sem pezo nem Medida, AIP, I-POB, s/d, PI.B. do (reservada).

38 David P. Appleby, *The Music of Brazil* (Austin, 1983), pp. 30–34, 60–61, 68–69; Luiz Heitor, *150 anos de música no Brasil, 1800–1950* (Rio, 1956), pp. 27–38; Gastão Penalva, "D. Pedro I, musico," *Revista Americana* (Rio) July 1919, pp. 155–58; Almeida, *Memórias*, pp. 57–60; Andrade Muricy, "Na Côrte de D. Pedro I," on jacket of Música na Côrte Brasileira, vol. 3, Angel records (Brazil, n.p., n.d.).

39 Walsh, *Notices* 1:182–83; Monglave, *Correspondance*, p. 16.

40 "Tratado de commércio e navegação . . ." and "Tratado de alliança e amistade entre o Principe Regente o Senhor D. João e Jorge III Rei da Gran-Bretanha," 19 February 1810, in *Colleção* Borges de Castro, 4:348–415. A third agreement bearing this date is a convention for the establishment of packet lines.

41 Caio Prado Júnior, *Formação do Brasil Contemporâneo: Colônia* (São Paulo, 1948), pp. 30, 100–101, 107; Leslie Bethell, *The Abolition of the Brazilian Slave Trade* (Cambridge, 1970), pp. 3–15.

42 Gonçalves dos Santos, *Memórias* 1:318–29, 368, 387–96; Luiz J. dos Santos Marrocos, *Cartas escritas do Rio de Janeiro a sua família em Lisboa, de 1811 a 1821* ABN 56 (Rio, 1934): p. 70; Calmon, *Rei do Brasil*, pp. 163–68.

43 Wyatt, "D. Carlota," pp. 194–208.
44 John Street, "Lord Strangford and Río de la Plata, 1808–1815," *HAHR* 33 (1953): 477–510; Hann, "Brazil and the Río de la Plata," pp. 129–60.
45 Hann, "Brazil and the Río de la Plata," pp. 160–85; Manchester, *British Preëminence*, pp. 129–33; John Street, *Artigas and the Emancipation of Uruguay* (Cambridge, 1959), pp. 136–74; Marrocos, *Cartas*, p. 102.
46 Henderson, *A History*, p. 50; Monteiro, *História do Império: Elaboração*, pp. 131–35.
47 Phil Brian Johnson, "Diplomatic Dullard: The Career of Thomas Sumter, Jr. and Diplomatic Relations of the United States with the Portuguese Court in Brazil, 1809–1821," *Studies in the Social Sciences* 17 (1978):21–35; Henderson, *A History*, pp. 50–51; Monteiro, *Histório do Império: Elaboração*, pp. 132–33.
48 D. João to Prince Regent of Great Britain, 20 February 1814, in *História do Brasil-Reino e do Brasil-Império*, by Alexandre José de Mello Moraes (São Paulo, 1982), 1: 437–38; Francisco de Almeida Portugal, Conde de Lavradio, *Memórias* (Coimbra, 1931), 1:46–47; Oliveira Lima, *D. João VI* 2:563–74.
49 Monglave, *Correspondance*, pp. 20–21; Gonçalves dos Santos, *Memórias* 1:450–51, 2:466–78, 488–99.

3—The Crown Prince

1 Monglave, *Correspondance*, p. 23; Walsh, *Notices* 1:267; Debret, *Viagem* 3:157; Rangel, *D. Pedro I e a Marquêsa*, pp. 4–5; Principal Sousa to Maria Genoveva do Rêgo e Matos, 15 November 1813, in *Os filhos*, Pereira, pp. 74–75; Maria Genoveva do Rêgo e Matos to Conde dos Arcos, 7 July 1814, in Rocha Martins, *Último vice-rei*, p. 98.
2 Eduardo Teodoro Bösche, "Quadros alternados de viagens terrestres e maritimas, aventuras, acontecimentos políticos, descrições de usos e costumes e povos durante uma viagem ao Brasil," *RIHGB* 83 (1919):204–5; L. E. da Costa, *A corte* 1:129–31.
3 D. Pedro to D. Carlota, n.d., AIP, I-POB, c. 1815/20, PI.B.c., nos. 14 & 15; Monglave, *Correspondance*, pp. 88–89; Monteiro, *Histório do Império: Elaboração*, pp. 135–37; Maria Graham, Lady Callcott, "Escorço biográfico de D. Pedro I, com uma notícia do Brasil e do Rio de Janeiro," *ABN* 60 (1938): 76, 129.
4 D. Pedro to D. Carlota, n.d., AIP, I-POB, c. 1815/20, PI.B.c., nos. 8, 9, 14, 16, 17 & 18.
5 L. E. da Costa, *A corte* 2:233; Marrocos, *Cartas*, pp. 143, 148, 162, 168–69, 235, 334; Pereira, *Os filhos*, p. 225. Don Pedro's skin infection was erysipelas, according to Marrocos.
6 L. E. da Costa, *A corte* 1:122–25, 142–48; Alexandre José de Mello Moraes, *Chronica geral do Brasil* (Rio, 1886), 2:154–55; Marrocos, *Cartas*, p. 37. Dom João's valet —*gentil homen da câmara*, or *camareiro*—was Miguel Rafael António de Noronha Abranches Castelo Branco, named count of Parati by Dom João. The three Lobato brothers, all of whom owed their noble status to Dom João, at various times served the royal family as chamberlain, or *guarda roupa da Casa Real*. They were Matias António de Sousa Lobato, first Viscount Magê; José Joaquim de Sousa Lobato, who became the second Viscount Magê on the death of Matias António in 1827; and José Rufino de Sousa Lobato, first Viscount Vila Nova da Rainha. There is much confusion about these personages in the secondary literature.
7 Mello Moraes, *Chronica geral* 2:155–57; Calmon, *O rei*, pp. 227–29; José Honório

Rodrigues, *O Conselho de Estado: O quinto poder?* (Brasília, 1978), pp. 35–36.

8   Debret, *Viagem* 2:12, plate 20; Luccock, *Notes*, p. 176.

9   Gonçalves dos Santos, *Memórias* 1:39, 88, 104–5, 168–69, 295–96; Luccock, *Notes*, pp. 76–79, 246; Mawe, *Travels*, p. 105; Luiz Edmundo da Costa, *Rio in the Time of the Viceroys* (Rio, 1936), p. 18. The word "carioca" comes from the Tupi Indian *kara'i*, "white man," and *oka*, "dwelling." Apparently, the fountain was built on the former homesite of some European. João Francisco de Sousa, *Origem e significação do apelativo "carioca"* (Rio, 1946). A waiting line and a fight at a smaller fountain is pictured in Rugendas, *Viagem*, plate 4/14.

10   José Honório Rodrigues, *Independência: Revolução e contrarrevolução*, vol. 2: *Economia e sociedade* (Rio, 1974), p. 92; Oliveira Lima, *D. João VI* 1:262–66; Heitor, *150 anos*, pp. 29, 35–39; Gonçalves dos Santos, *Memórias* 1:414.

11   Jacques Arago, *Narrative of a Voyage Round the World in . . . 1817, 1818, 1819* (London, 1823), pp. 79–80.

12   T. von Leithold and L. von Rango, *O Rio de Janeiro visto por dois Prussianos em 1819* (São Paulo, 1966), p. 21; L. E. da Costa, *Rio in the Time of the Viceroys*, pp. 57–61.

13   Agenor de Noronha Santos in his preface to Francisco Gomes da Silva, *Memórias* (Rio, 1939), pp. 18–20. He cites Francisco de Assis Cintra, *O Chalaça, Favorito do império* (Rio, 1934), pp. 26–27. See also, Thompson, "Francisco Gomes da Silva," p. 6.

14   Loosely translated. In the Portuguese the first and third lines also rhyme: Paulista e pássaro bisnau, / sem fé, nem coração: / é gente que se leva a pau, / a sopapo ou pescoção.

15   Rangel, *D. Pedro I e a Marquêsa*, p. 15; Sérgio Corrêa da Costa, *Every Inch a King: A Biography of Dom Pedro I, First Emperor of Brazil* (New York, 1953), p. 30; Noronha Santos in Gomes da Silva, *Memórias*, pp. 13–18, 20–21; Hélio Vianna, *Dom Pedro I, Jornalista* (São Paulo, 1967), p. 169.

16   Monteiro, *História do Império: Elaboração*, p. 142; Arago, *Narrative*, pp. 61–63; Leithold & Rango, *O Rio*, pp. 14–16; Maria Beatriz Nizza da Silva, *Cultura e sociedade no Rio de Janeiro (1808–1821)* (São Paulo, 1977), pp. 73–74.

17   Antônio Menezes Vasconcelos de Drummond, "Annotações . . . a sua biographia publicada em 1836," *ABN* 13 (1885–86):14; Monteiro, *História do Império: Elaboração*, pp. 142, 388; Rangel, *D. Pedro I e a Marquêsa*, p. 63; Mello Moraes, *Chronica geral* 2:173–74.

18   Monglave, *Correspondance*, pp. 23–24; Callcott, "Escorço," pp. 76–77; Mello Moraes, *Chronica geral* 2:173–74.

19   Damião Peres, *História de Portugal* (Barcelos, 1935), 6:329; Heitor, *150 anos*, p. 30.

20   Oliveira Lima, *D. João VI* 2:489–510; Charles-Maurice de Talleyrand, *Mémoires complets et authentiques* (Paris, 1967), 1:381–87.

21   Gonçalves dos Santos, *Memórias* 1:439–40; Bethell, *The Abolition*, pp. 12–14; Oliveira Lima, *D. João VI* 2:543–56. Dom João also had hopes of marrying the widow of Don Pedro Carlos, Dona Maria Teresa, to the Austrian crown prince. The Hapsburg emperor encouraged negotiations for a marriage alliance in a personal letter to Dom João at the time of the congress of Vienna. Franz I to D. João, 28 April 1815, ANTT, Cor. sob. Aust.-Port. (caixa forte), no. 162.

22   Marquis of Aguiar to Marquis of Marialva, 15 March 1816, AHI, lata 176, maço 5; Monteiro, *História do Império: Elaboração*, pp. 151–52; Oliveira Lima, *D. João VI* 2:485.

23 Hann, "Brazil and the Río de la Plata," pp. 221–24; Street, *Artigas*, pp. 284–89; Gonçalves dos Santos, *Memórias* 2:513–14; Charles K. Webster, *The Foreign Policy of Castlereagh, 1815–1822* (London, 1925), p. 18.

24 Gonçalves dos Santos, *Memórias* 2:514–22, 532–33; Hann, "Brazil and the Río de la Plata," pp. 241–48; Luccock, *Notes*, p. 550; Alberto Rangel, *Trasanteontem* (São Paulo, n.d.), pp. 56–57; Marrocos, *Cartas*, pp. 283–84.

25 Aguiar to Marialva, 15 March 1816, AHI, lata 176, maco 5.

26 Marialva to Aguiar, 14, 19 and 30 November 1816, AHI, lata 176, maço 5; Monteiro, *História do Império: Elaboração*, pp. 155–62.

27 Carlos H. Oberacker Jr., *A Imperatriz Leopoldina: Sua vida e sua época* (Rio, 1973), p. 62; Monteiro, *História do Império: Elaboração*, pp. 161–62.

28 Oliveira Lima, *D. João VI* 3:904–08; Monteiro, *História do Império: Elaboração*, pp. 171–79.

29 Emmi Baum, "Empress Leopoldina: Her Role in the Development of Brazil, 1817–1826" (Ph.D. dissertation, New York University, 1965), pp. 45–48.

30 Oberacker, *Imperatriz Leopoldina*, p. 71.

31 Oliveira Lima, *D. João VI* 3:908; Oberacker, *Imperatriz Leopoldina*, p. 92; Street, *Artigas*, pp. 295–306; Johnson, "Diplomatic Dullard," p. 28; Clemens von Metternich, *Memoirs of Prince Metternich, 1815–1829* (London, 1881), 3:29, 47–48; Robert C. Smith and Gilberto Ferrez, *Franz Frühbeck's Brazilian Journey* (Philadelphia, 1960), pp. 15–16; Johann B. E. Pohl, *Viagem no interior do Brasil . . . nos anos de 1817 a 1821* (Rio de Janeiro, 1951), 1:27–28.

32 Vamireh Chacon, *Abreu e Lima: General de Bolívar* (Rio, 1983), pp. 72–73; Oliveira Lima, *D. João VI* 3:815–33.

33 Arago, *Narrative*, pp. 89–91; Oliveira Lima, *D. João VI* 3:833–55; Rocha Martins, *Último vice-rei*, pp. 55–78; Cacon, *Abreu e Lima*, p. 73.

34 Metternich, *Memoirs* 3:43; Oberacker, *Imperatriz Leopoldina*, p. 93; Monteiro, *História do Império: Elaboração*, pp. 208–12; Oliveira Lima, *D. João VI* 3: 844–45, 909–10, 1055.

35 Pohl, *Viagem* 1:29–51; J. F. de Almeida Prado, *Dom João VI e o início da classe dirigente do Brasil (Depoimento de um pintor austriaco no Rio de Janeiro)* (São Paulo, 1968), pp. 8–16; Metternich, *Memoirs* 3:47–50.

36 Oberacker, *Imperatriz Leopoldina*, pp. 110–12, 124–25; Gonçalves dos Santos, *Memórias* 2:584–86.

37 Smith and Ferrez, *Franz Frühbeck*, pp. 19–20, 59–60, plate 7; Debret, *Viagem* 2: 230–32, plate 32; Gonçalves dos Santos, *Memórias* 2:586–96.

38 Mello Moraes, *Chronica geral* 2:176; Gonçalves dos Santos, *Memórias* 2:596–602.

39 Monteiro, *História do Império: Elaboração*, p. 164; Oberacker, *Imperatriz Leopoldina*, pp. 10–31.

40 Dona Leopoldina, Mes Resolutions, 1817, in *Imperatriz Leopoldina*, by Oberacker, pp. 467–70.

41 Baum, "Empress Leopoldina," pp. 63–66, 75–76; Oberacker, *Imperatriz Leopoldina*, pp. 147–56; Marrocos, *Cartas*, p. 305; Pereira, *Os filhos*, p. 139.

42 Walsh, *Notices* 2:459–62; Taunay, *Do Reino*, pp. 100–101, Baum, "Empress Leopoldina," pp. 76–77; Mello Moraes, *Chronica geral* 2:229.

43 Gonçalves dos Santos, *Memórias* 2:607–11; Arago, *Narrative*, pp. 84–86.

44 Calmon, *Rei do Brasil*, p. 149; Mello Moraes, *História da trasladação*, pp. 94–98;

Gonçalves dos Santos, *Memórias* 2:615–55; Debret, *Viagem* 2:12, 243–47, plates 37–38; Luccock, *Notes*, pp. 571–73.

45 Oliveira Lima, *D. João VI* 3:1033.

46 Oberacker, *Imperatriz Leopoldina*, p. 177; Talleyrand to Louis XVIII, 21 January 1815, in *Mémoires*, Talleyrand, 3:25; Denyse Dalbian, *Dom Pedro: Empereur du Brésil, Roi de Portugal (1798–1834)* (Paris, 1959), p. 21.

47 J. Prattle, Minute, 12 May 1834, *Parliamentary Papers*, cited in "Chinese and Tea in Brazil, 1808–1822" by Arlene M. Kelly (unpublished seminar paper, University of Florida, 1976), p. 4; Luccock, *Notes*, pp. 198, 574; L. E. da Costa, *A corte* 1:220–23; Presas, *Memorias*, p. 121; Arago, *Narrative*, p. 59; Baum, "Empress Leopoldina," pp. 75–79. Hunting people, as an amusement of young Portuguese nobles, is mentioned in A.P.D.C., *Sketches of Portuguese Life, Manners, Costume and Character* (London, 1826), pp. 162–63.

48 A.P.D.C., *Sketches*, p. 180; Arago, *Narrative*, pp. 53–71. L. E. da Costa, *Rio in the Time of the Viceroys*, p. 15, identifies A. P. D. C. as the duke of Chatelet.

49 Marrocos, *Cartas*, pp. 128, 138, 148, 176, 211, 216; Mello Moraes, *História da trasladação*, p. 96; Lavradio, *Memórias* 1:43; L. E. da Costa, *A corte* 2:395–405. Costa confuses Pastorino, the second count of Galvêas (Francisco de Almeida de Mello e Castro), with his brother, the first count (João de Almeida de Mello e Castro), who died in 1814.

50 Mello Moraes, *Chronica geral* 2: 176; Monteiro, *História do Império: Elaboração*, pp. 86–90; L. E. da Costa, *A corte* 1:186–89; Mello Moraes, *Chronica geral* 2:176–78.

51 Street, *Artigas*, pp. 296–311, 327–28; Monglave, *Correspondance*, p. 27; Baum, "Empress Leopoldina," pp. 76–79; D. Pedro to D. Carlota, 14 March 1818, and n.d., AIP, I-POB, 14.3.818 & c. 1815–20 no. 7, PI.B.c.; Henderson, *History*, p. 62.

52 L. E. da Costa, *A corte* 2:239–40; Anonymous, *Historia de la vida y reinado de Fernando VII de España* (Madrid, 1842), 2:132–33; Gonçalves dos Santos, *Memórias* 2:714–15.

53 Peres, *História de Portugal* 7:49–73; Oliveira Lima, *D. João VI* 3:1061, 1064–66; Gonçalves dos Santos, *Memórias* 2:757; Viscount Castlereagh to Edward Thornton, 5 May 1820, Thornton to Castlereagh, 31 May 1820 and 31 July 1820, in *Britain and the Independence of Latin America, 1812–1830*, by Charles K. Webster (London, 1938) 1:196–200.

54 D. João VI, Carta régia, 27 October 1820, in *História da Independência do Brasil* by Francisco Adolfo de Varnhagen (Brasília, 1972), pp. 40–42; Rocha Martins, *Último vice-rei*, pp. 108–14.

55 Count of Palmela to D. João, 2, 5 and 16 January 1821, in Duque de Palmella, *Despachos e correspondencia*, ed. J. J. dos Reis e Vasconcellos (Lisbon, 1851), 1:141–50; Manchester, *British Preëminence*, pp. 105–7; Tarquínio de Sousa, *Vida de D. Pedro I* 1:136–38; Christopher J. Herold, *Mistress to an Age: A Life of Madame de Staël* (Indianapolis, 1958), pp. 310–12.

56 D. Pedro to D. João, n.d., in *História da Independência*, Varnhagen, p. 64; Palmela to D. João, 16, 19, 26, and 27 January 1821, in *Despachos*, Palmella, 1:149–64; Thornton to Castlereagh, 31 January 1821, FO 63, 237:52–69, 74–76.

57 Mello Moraes, *História do Brasil-Reino* 1:51–56; *Idade d'Ouro do Brazil* (Bahia), 10 and 15 February 1821; W. Pennell to Edward Thornton, 10 February 1821, and Thornton to Palmela, 17 February 1821, in *Despachos*, Palmela 1:166–67; Thornton to Castlereagh, 3 March 1821, FO 63, 237:154–62; D. Leopoldina to G. A. von

Notes

Schäffer, n.d., in *A corte*, Norton, pp. 425–26; *Le Roi et la Famille Royale de Bragance doivent-ils, dans les circonstances présentes, retourner en Portugal, ou bien rester au Brésil?* (Rio, 1820), in FO 63, 237:104–13.

58 Palmela to D. João, 19, 21, 22, and 24 February 1821, in *Despachos*, Palmela, 1:167–77, 180–81; Silvestre Pinheiro Ferreira, "Cartas sobre a revolução do Brasil," *RIHGB* 51 (1888): 247–49.

59 D. João, Decreto, 18 February 1821, and Thornton to Castlereagh, 3 March 1821, FO 63, 237:144–45, 154–62; Mello Moraes, *História do Brasil-Reino* 1:136–42; Rocha Martins, *Último vice-rei*, pp. 115–28.

60 Varnhagen, *História da Independência*, pp. 74–75; Pinheiro Ferreira, "Cartas," p. 252.

61 Pinheiro Ferreira, "Cartas," p. 252.

62 Varnhagen, *História da Independência*, p. 75; Mello Moraes, *História do Brasil-Reino* 1:147–49.

63 Thornton to Castlereagh, 1 March 1821, FO 63, 237:133–35; Varnhagen, *História da Independência*, pp. 75–76; Monteiro, *História do Império: Elaboração*, pp. 316–17.

64 Varnhagen, *História da Independência*, p. 76; Pinheiro Ferreira, "Cartas," pp. 250–52; Mello Moraes, *História do Brasil-Reino* 1:61–62, 149.

65 Mello Moraes, *História do Brasil-Reino* 1:62, 107, 149–50; Thornton to Castlereagh, 1 March 1821, FO 63, 237:135–36; Pinheiro Ferreira, "Cartas," pp. 256–61.

66 Gonçalves dos Santos, *Memórias* 2:762–63; D. João, Decreto, 7 March 1821, FO 63, 237:186–87; Pinheiro Ferreira, "Cartas," pp. 256–61.

67 Monteiro, *História do Império: Elaboração*, pp. 306–7; Mello Moraes, *História do Brasil-Reino* 1:111–17; Varnhagen, *História da Independência*, pp. 79–81.

68 Pinheiro Ferreira, "Cartas," pp. 300–10; Monteiro, *História do Império: Elaboração*, pp. 331–32.

69 Johann B. von Spix and Karl F. P. von Martius, *Viagem pelo Brasil* (Rio, 1938), 1: 122–23; Mello Moraes, *História do Brasil-Reino* 1:107–9; Pinheiro Ferreira, "Cartas," pp. 280–84, 304–6.

70 Thornton to Castlereagh, 3 May 1821, FO 63, 237:251–55; Mello Moraes, *História do Brasil-Reino* 1:118–19; Varnhagen, *História da Independência*, pp. 87–88; Monteiro, *História do Império: Elaboração, pp.* 332–40; Manuel de Oliveira Lima, *O Movimento da independência, 1821–1822* (São Paulo, 1922), p. 56.

71 Monteiro, *História do Império: Elaboração*, pp. 340–46; Pinheiro Ferreira, "Cartas," pp. 312–18.

72 Monteiro, *História do Império: Elaboração*, p. 344; Varnhagen, *História da Independência*, pp. 89–91; Thornton to Castlereagh, 3 May 1821, FO 63, 237:253–54.

73 "Olho vivo e pé ligeiro/Vamos à nau buscar o dinheiro." Mello Moraes, *História do Brasil Reino* 1:119.

74 D. João VI, Decreto, 21 April 1821, in *História do Brasil-Reino*, Mello Moraes, 1:122; Pinheiro Ferreira, "Cartas," pp. 318–19.

75 Monteiro, *História do Império: Elaboração,* pp. 345–50; Pinheiro Ferreira, "Cartas," pp. 319–24.

76 Mello Moraes, *História do Brasil-Reino* 1:120–24; Monteiro, *História do Império: Elaboração*, pp. 350–51; Varnhagen, *História da Independência*, pp. 90–91; Thornton to Castlereagh, 3 May 1821, FO 63, 237:254–56.

77 D. João VI, Decreto, 22 April 1821, in *Colecção das leis do Imperio do Brasil desde a independência* (Rio, 1829), 1:70; Monteiro, *História do Império: Elaboração*, pp. 352–53;

Pinheiro Ferreira, "Cartas," pp. 325–27.

78 José da Silva Lisboa, Viscount Cairu, *Historia dos principaes successos politicos do imperio do Brasil* (Rio, 1830), 10:87; D. Pedro to D. João VI, 19 June 1822, in "Cartas autographas do Principe Real o Sr. D. Pedro de Alcantara," *RIHGB* 61 (1898):167; Mello Moraes, *História do Brasil-Reino* 1:125–29; Oliveira Lima, *Dom João VI* 3:1168; Boiteux, *A marinha*, p. 92. Cairu's version of Dom João's advice is: "Pedro, o Brasil brevemente se separará de Portugal: se assim fôr, põe a corôa sobre tua cabeça, ante que algum aventureiro lance mão della." Dom Pedro recalled his father's words as: "Pedro, se o Brasil se separa, antes seja para ti, que me has de respeitar do que para algum desses aventureiros."

4—Independence or Death

1 Boiteux, *A marinha*, pp. 88, 93.

2 Richard B. Morse, "Brazil's Urban Development: Colony to Empire," in *From Colony to Nation: Essays on the Independence of Brazil*, ed. A. J. R. Russell-Wood (Baltimore, 1975), p. 173; Luccock, *Notes*, p. 574; Roberto C. Simonsen, *História Econômica do Brasil (1500/1820)* (São Paulo, 1969), pp. 351–81, 434, 440; J. H. Rodrigues, *Independência* 2:92–98.

3 Walsh, *Notices* 1:168–69; Luccock, *Notes*, pp. 561–62; Simonsen, *História Econômica*, p. 459.

4 João Rodrigues de Brito, *A economia brasileira no alvorecer do século XIX* (Salvador da Bahia, n.d.), p. 132; Henderson, *History*, p. 76; E. Bradford Burns, "The Intellectuals as Agents of Change and the Independence of Brazil, 1724–1822," in *From Colony*, ed. Russell-Wood, pp. 216–29; Luccock, *Notes*, pp. 573–74.

5 Simonsen, *História econômica*, p. 375; Luccock, *Notes*, pp. 198, 567, 574; Spix and Martius, *Viagem* 1:97–103, 141–42.

6 J. H. Rodriguez, Independência 2:63, 65; Luccock, *Notes*, pp. 578–79; Manuel Aires de Casal, *Corografia brasílica* (Rio, 1945), p. 363; Spix and Martius, *Viagem* 1:128; Walsh, *Notices* 2:535.

7 J. H. Rodrigues, *Independência* 2:61, 64–67; Spix and Martius, *Viagem* 1:210–12, 222, 235—38; Casal, *Corografia*, p. 244.

8 Henderson, *History*, pp. 341–43; Catherine Lugar, "The Portuguese Tobacco Trade and Tobacco of Bahia in the Late Colonial Period," *Essays Concerning the Socioeconomic History of Brazil and Portuguese India*, ed. Dauril Alden and Warren Dean (Gainesville, 1977), pp. 26–55.

9 Simonsen, *História econômica*, charts following p. 382.

10 Arlene M. Kelly, "Family, Church, and Crown: A Social and Demographic History of the Lower Xingu Valley and Gurupá, 1623–1889" (Ph.D. dissertation, University of Florida, 1984), pp. 165–210, passim; Simonsen, *História econômica*, pp. 369, 377–81, 435; Casal, *Corografia*, pp. 266, 287, 293–94, 320–23.

11 Simonsen, *História econômica*, pp. 413–15, 420–26.

12 Henderson, *History*, pp. 583–84; Simonsen, *História econômica*, pp. 406–8, 426.

13 Simonsen, *História econômica*, pp. 409–14; John Armitage, *The History of Brazil from the Period of the Arrival of the Braganza Family in 1808 to the Abdication of Don Pedro the First in 1831* (London, 1836), 1.43–47; Luccock, *Notes*, pp. 580–82; Spix and Martius, *Viagem* 1:122–23.

Notes

14 D. Leopoldina to Franz I, 9 June 1821, in *A corte*, Norton, p. 441; Mello Moraes, *História do Brasil-Reino* 1:130–31, 154–55; Varnhagen, *História da Independência*, pp. 89–92, 131; Baron Wenzel von Marschall to Prince Metternich, 6 June 1821, in "A correspondencia do Barão Wenzel de Marschall," Part I, ed. Jeronymo de A. Figueira de Mello, *RIHGB* 77 (1914):176–77.

15 D. Pedro to D. João, 17 July 1821, in D. Pedro I, *Proclamações, cartas, artigos de imprensa* (Rio, 1973), pp. 223–27; Varnhagen, *História da Independência*, p. 122; D. Pedro, Decretos, 29 April, 11 and 13 May 1821, in *Collecção das Leis do Brasil de 1821* (Rio, 1889), 1:79–82.

16 D. Pedro, Decretos, 21 and 23 May, *Collecção das Leis 1821* 1:87–89.

17 Rocha Martins, *Último vice-rei*, passim; Arago, *Narrative*, pp. 64, 89–90, 94; Thornton to Castlereagh, 11 June 1821, in *Britain*, Webster, 1:211; Marschall to Metternich, 6 June 1821, in "Correspondencia," Part 1, p. 177.

18 Thornton to Castlereagh, 11 June 1821, in *Britain*, Webster, 1:211.

19 D. Pedro to D. João, 8 June 1821, AIP, II-POB 2.5.821, PI.B.c., anexo.

20 The dialogue is from D. Pedro's detailed account of the events of 5 June 1821, in his letter to D. João, 8 June 1821, AIP, II-POB, 2.5.821, PI.B.c., anexo. The Austrian diplomatic agent in Rio attests to D. Pedro's sangfroid. Marschall to Metternich, 6 and 17 June 1821, in "Correspondencia," Part 1, Figueira de Mello, pp. 177–87.

21 Monteiro, *História do Império: Elaboração*, pp. 381–83; D. Pedro to D. João, 8 June 1821, AIP, II-POB, 2.5.821, PI.B.c., anexo; Marschall to Metternich, 6 and 17 June 1821, in "Correspondencia," Part 1, Figueira de Mello, pp. 177–87.

22 D. Pedro to D. João, 8 June 1821, AIP, II-POB, 2.5.821, PI.B.c., anexo; Marschall to Metternich, 6 and 17 June 1821, in "Correspondencia," Part 1, Figueira de Mello, pp. 179, 183–88.

23 D. Pedro to D. João, 8 June 1821, AIP, II-POB, 2.5.821, PI.B.c., anexo; Marschall to Metternich, 6 June 1821, in "Correspondencia," Part 1, Figueira de Mello, p. 178; Count of Casaflores to Secretario del Despacho de Estado, 6 June 1821, in BNRJ, *Documentos para a historia da Independencia* (Rio, 1923), p. 354.

24 D. Pedro to D. João, 21 September 1821, in *Proclamações, cartas*, pp. 231–35; D. Pedro to D. João, 24 June 1821, AIP, II-POB, 2.5.821, PI.B.c., no. 4; Drummond, "Annotações," pp. 14–15; Marschall to Metternich, 27 August 1821, in "Correspondencia," Part 1, Figueira de Mello, pp. 212–13; Armitage, *A History* 1:47; P. Sartoris to John Quincy Adams, 30 July 1821, in *Diplomatic Correspondence of the United States Concerning the Independence of the Latin-American Nations*, ed. William R. Manning (New York, 1925), 2:722–23.

25 D. Pedro to D. João, 17 July and 9 November 1821, in *Proclamações, cartas*, 223–28, 249–50; Hann, "Brazil and the Río de la Plata," pp. 345–48.

26 Octávio Tarquínio de Sousa, *José Bonifácio, 1763–1838* (Rio, 1945), pp. 13–88; J. H. Rodrigues, *Independência* 4:23–40.

27 Tarquínio de Sousa, *José Bonifácio*, pp. 29–94; J. H. Rodrigues, *Independência* 5:271–73.

28 D. Pedro to D. João, 9 November 1821, in *Proclamações, cartas*, pp. 249–50; "Lembranças e apontamentos do Governo Provizorio para os Senhores Deputados da Provincia de São Paulo," in *Obras científicas, políticas, e sociaes de José Bonifácio de Andrada e Silva*, by José Bonifácio de Andrada e Silva (São Paulo, 1965), 2:95–102.

29 Monteiro, *História do Império: Elaboração*, pp. 381–82, 390–406; Armitage, *A History*

1:50–55.

30 D. Pedro to D. João, 4 October, 10 and 14 December 1821, in *Proclamações, cartas*, pp. 237–38, 251–54; D. Pedro to D. João, 30 December 1821, AIP, II-POB, 2.5.821, PI.B.c., no. 5; Marshall to Metternich, 27 August 1821, in "Correspondencia," Part 1, Figueira de Mello, p. 212.

31 São Paulo, Governo Provisório, to D. Pedro, 24 December 1821, in *Obras científicas*, J. B. de Andrada e Silva, 2:221–23.

32 Ibid., 223–25.

33 Mello Moraes, *História do Brasil-Reino* 1:241–45; Varnhagen, *História da Independência*, pp. 146–48; D. Pedro to D. João, 2 January 1822, in *Proclamações, cartas*, p. 259.

34 The People of Rio de Janeiro to D. Pedro, and Address by José Clemente Pereira, in *Correspondance*, Monglave, pp. 264–76; D. Pedro to D. João, 9 January 1822, *Proclamações, cartas*, pp. 261–62.

35 D. Pedro to D. João, 9 January 1822, in *Proclamações, cartas*, pp. 261–62. A longer version of Dom Pedro's reply to José Clemente, which was more conciliatory toward the Cortes, was published by the city council on January 9 and does not contain the word *fico*. The city council record was corrected the next day and made to conform to Dom Pedro's version of his words as reported in the prince's January 9 letter to his father. José Martins Rocha, Edital, 9 January 1822, and José Clemente Pereira, Edital, 10 January 1821, in *Proclamações, cartas*, D. Pedro I, pp. 61, 67.

36 "Great Reply!" Dom Pedro has a witness say in a four-page pamphlet he published anonymously on 21 January 1822, *Carta escripta pelo Sachristão da Freguezia de S. João de Itaboray ao Reverendo Vigario da mesma Freguezia, narrando os acontecimentos aos dias 9 e 12 de Janeiro deste anno* (Rio, 1822). The pamphlet is reproduced, and its authorship established, in *Dom Pedro I, Jornalista* by Hélio Vianna (São Paulo, 1967), pp. 13–29.

37 Maria Graham, Lady Callcott, *Journal of a Voyage to Brazil, and Residence There during Part of the Years 1821, 1822, 1823* (London, 1824), p. 180; Marshall to Metternich, 9 January 1822, in "Correspondencia," Part 2, by Figueira de Mello, *RIHGB* 53 (1916):15–16.

38 D. Pedro to D. João, 23 January 1822, in *Proclamações, cartas*, pp. 263–68; Callcott, *Journal*, pp. 178–81, 185. [D. Pedro], *Carta escripta pelo Sachristão*.

39 Callcott, *Journal*, pp. 182–83, 186; D. Pedro to D. João, 23 January 1822, in *Proclamações, cartas*, pp. 263–68; Marshall to Metternich, 14 January 1822, in "Correspondencia," Part 2, Figueira de Mello, pp. 17–18. [D. Pedro], *Carta escripta pelo Sachristão*.

40 D. Leopoldina to Grand Duchess of Tuscany, 12 February 1822, in *A corte*, Norton, p. 420; Marshall to Metternich, 14 January 1822, in "Correspondencia," Part 2, Figueira de Mello, pp. 17–21; Callcott, *Journey*, pp. 182–85.

41 Oberacker, *Imperatriz Leopoldina*, pp. 242–43; D. Pedro to Habitantes do Rio de Janeiro, in *Proclamações, cartas*, pp. 69–70; Callcott, *Journal*, pp. 183–84, 186; Varnhagen, *História da Independência*, pp. 157–58; Marshall to Metternich, 14 January 1822, in "Correspondencia," Part 2, Figueira de Mello, pp. 18–20; Mello Moraes, *História do Brasil-Reino* 1:266–70; D. Pedro to D. João, 23 January 1822, in *Proclamações, cartas*, pp. 264–66. [D. Pedro], *Carta escripta pelo Sachristão*.

42 Oberacker, *Imperatriz Leopoldina*, p. 243; Tarquínio de Sousa, *José Bonifácio*, pp. 56, 133–36.

43 José Bonifácio de Andrada e Silva, *O pensamento vivo de José Bonifácio* (São Paulo, 1961), p. 140; Tarquínio de Sousa, *José Bonifácio*, pp. 87, 95.

Notes

44 Marschall to Metternich, 27 August and 1 October 1821, in "Correspondencia," Part 1, Figueira de Mello, pp. 209, 220–21.

45 Oliveira Lima, *O movimento da Independência*, p. 179.

46 José Bonifácio, et al. to Martim Francisco Ribeiro de Andrada Machado, 21 January 1822, in BNRJ, *Documentos para a historia da independencia*, pp. 371–73.

47 Monteiro, *História do Império: Elaboração*, pp. 458–59.

48 D. Pedro to D. João, 2 February 1822, in *Proclamações, cartas*, p. 271; Mello Moraes, *História do Brasil-Reino* 1:92, 97; Varnhagen, *História da Independência*, pp. 161–62; Tarquínio de Sousa, *José Bonifácio*, p. 140; Marschall to Metternich, 22 January 1822, in "Correspondencia," Part 2, Figueira de Mello, p. 23.

49 D. Pedro to José Bonifácio, 3 February 1822, AIP, I-POB, 3.2.822, PI.B.ca.

50 D. Pedro to D. João, 14 February 1822, in *Proclamações, cartas*, pp. 275–76; D. Leopoldina to Franz I, 12 February 1822, in *A corte*, Norton, p. 450.

51 D. Pedro to D. João, 12 February 1822, in *Proclamações, cartas*, p. 273; Mello Moraes, *História do Brasil-Reino* 1:550–52; Pedro Calmon, *História do Brasil* (Rio, 1963), 5:1518.

52 Mello Moraes, *História do Brasil-Reino* 1:552–54; D. Pedro to D. João, 12 February 1822, in *Proclamações, cartas*, p. 273.

53 Varnhagen, *História da Independência*, pp. 170–73; D. Pedro to D. João, 14 and 19 March 1822, in *Proclamações, cartas*, pp. 284–85, 289.

54 D. Pedro to D. Miguel, 14 March 1822, AIP, I-POB, 14.3.822, PI.B.c., no. 1; D. Pedro to D. João, 11 March 1822, in *Proclamações, cartas*, p. 281.

55 D. João to D. Pedro, 7 August 1822, in Monteiro, *História do Império: Elaboração*, p. 427; D. João to D. Pedro, 3 August 1822, in "Cartas autographas do Principe Real o Sr. D. Pedro D'Alcantara," *RIHGB* 61 (1898):171.

56 D. Pedro to D. Miguel, 19 June 1822, AIP, I-POB, 14.3.82, PI.B.c., no. 2; D. Pedro to D. João, 19 June 1822, in *Proclamações, cartas*, p. 301.

57 Varnhagen, *História da Independência*, pp. 406–10; Mello Moraes, *História do Brasil-Reino* 1:320–44.

58 Tarquínio de Sousa, *Vida de D. Pedro I* 1:315–22; D. Pedro, "Briosos Mineiros," (speech) 9 April 1822, in *Proclamações, cartas*, pp. 81–84.

59 D. Pedro, Decree, 3 June 1822, in *História do Brasil-Reino*, Mello Moraes, 1:55–64; José Honório Rodrigues, ed., *Atas do Conselho do Estado* (Brasília, 1973), 1:3–10; José Bonifácio to D. Pedro, 6 April 1822, and D. Pedro to José Bonifácio, 6 April 1822, AIP, I-POB, 3.2.822, PI.B.ca., nos. 4 and 12.

60 Mario Behring, Introduction to Antonio Luiz de Brito Aragão e Vasconcellos, "Memorias sobre o estabelecimento do Imperio do Brazil," *ABN* 63 (1920):ix–xv; Drummond, "Annotações," pp. 43–44; Mello Moraes, *História do Brasil-Reino* 2:460–61; D. Pedro to José Bonifácio, 20 July 1822, AIP, II-POB, 20.7.822, PI.B.c., no. 1.

61 J. H. Rodrigues, *Independência* 3:136–45, 168–74, 204–9; Varnhagen, *História da Independência*, pp. 446–53; Armitage, *A History* 1:85–86.

62 Varnhagen, *História da Independência*, pp. 205–7; Francisco de Castro Canto e Mello, "Memoria sobre a declaração da independencia," *RIHGB* 41 (1878): part 2, 334; Gomes da Silva, *Memorias*, p. 54; D. Pedro, Manifesto . . . aos povos deste Reino, 1 August 1822, and Manifesto . . . aos Governos e Nações Amigas, 6 August 1822, in *Proclamações, cartas*, pp. 103–34.

63 Tarquínio de Sousa, *Vida de D. Pedro I* 2:15–23; Canto e Mello, "Memoria,"

pp. 334–37.

64 Rangel, *D. Pedro I e a Marquêsa*, pp. 31–32; Canto e Mello, "Memoria," p. 338.

65 Padre Belchior Pinheiro de Oliveira, Testimony, in *D. Pedro I e o grito da Independência*, by Assis Cintra (São Paulo, 1921), pp. 211–12; Canto e Mello, "Memoria," pp. 338–40; Manoel Marcondes de Oliveira Mello, Baron of Pindamonhangaba, in *História do Brasil-Reino*, Mello Moraes, 2:433–35; Gomes da Silva, *Memórias*, pp. 58–59; Rangel, *D. Pedro I e a Marquêsa*, p. 93; D. Pedro to José Bonifácio, 1 September 1822, AIP, II-POB, 20.7.822, PI.B.c., no. 2.

66 José Bonifácio to D. Pedro, 1 September 1822, in *José Bonifácio*, Tarquínio de Sousa, p. 178, and J. H. Rodrigues, *Independência* 1:248–49; D. Leopoldina to D. Pedro, 29 August 1822, in *História da Independência*, Varnhagen, p. 212; Mello Moraes, *História do Brasil-Reino* 2:435–40; Monteiro, *História do Império: Elaboração*, pp. 543–44. There is no authenticated letter from Dona Leopoldina in which she advises her husband that "the fruit is ripe; pick it before it rots." This celebrated counsel, like Dom João's to Dom Pedro about putting the crown on his own head—or even the "fico"—may be considered apocryphal. But the nonexistence of written words supposedly read is, for the historian, a matter rather different from disagreements over spoken words. See Oberacker, *Imperatriz Leopoldina*, p. 281; J. H. Rodrigues, *Independência* 1:248; Hélio Vianna, *D. Pedro I e D. Pedro II: Acréscimos às suas biografias* (São Paulo, 1966), pp. 11–12. Rodrigues's reading of José Bonifácio's handwriting in the 1 September letter is slightly different from Tarquínio's.

67 Pinheiro de Oliveira, in *D. Pedro I e o grito*, Assis Cintra, pp. 212–13; Marcondes de Oliveira Mello, in *História do Brasil-Reino*, Mello Moraes, 2:433–35; Gomes da Silva, *Memórias*, pp. 58–59; Canto e Mello, "Memoria," pp. 339–42.

68 Notes of Manoel Joaquim do Amaral Gurgel to Canto e Mello, "Memoria," pp. 342–44; Monteiro, *História do Império: Elaboração*, pp. 546–47. Canto e Mello and Gurgel, both present at the theater, differ on the music; Canto e Mello, who was with Dom Pedro earlier, testified that the prince wrote it that day; Gurgel thought it was a preexisting tune.

69 Canto e Mello (and Gurgel notes), "Memoria," pp. 344–47.

70 Gomes da Silva, *Memórias*, pp. 61–66; Octávio Tarquínio de Sousa, *Evaristo da Veiga* (Rio, 1939), pp. 33–39; Hélio Vianna, *Dom Pedro I e D. Pedro II*, pp. 12–13.

5—Constitutional Emperor

1 The Cortes originally, in 1820, put the total population of Brazil's eighteen provinces at 2,459,286, and that of Portugal's six provinces at 2,337,820 but provided for subsequent adjustments based on new provincial censuses. By mid-1821, Portugal was authorized one hundred deputies; Brazil, seventy-two; and other overseas provinces, nine. Monteiro, *História do Império: Elaboração*, pp. 400–401; J. H. Rodrigues, *Independência* 1:75–134; Varnhagen, *História da Independência*, pp. 97–101; Mello Moraes, *História do Brasil-Reino* 2:175–244 (includes the Portuguese constitution); Oliveira Lima, *O movimento da Independencia*, pp. 193–204.

2 D. Pedro to D. João, 22 September and 23 October 1822, AIP, II-POB, 22.9.822, PI.B.c., nos. 1–2.

3 José Honório Rodrigues, "O triunfo da lingua portuguêsa," (Paper presented at the

Notes

conference "The Portuguese World at the Time of Camões," University of Florida, 30 September 1980).

4 J. B. de Andrada e Silva, "Representação á Assembléa Geral Constituinte e Legislativa do Imperio do Brasil sobre a Escravatura," *Obras científicas* 2:115–58; Tarquínio de Sousa, *José Bonifácio*, pp. 190–215; Marschall to Metternich, 19 October 1822, in "Correspondencia," Part 2, Figueira de Mello, pp. 114–15; José Bonifácio to Felisberto Caldeira Brant Pontes, 4 October 1822, *ADI* (1922): 1:16–17.

5 J. H. Rodrigues, *Independência* 1:27–29, 262–63; Tarquínio de Sousa, *José Bonifácio*, pp. 183–86; Behring, Introduction to Aragão e Vasconcellos, "Memorias" *ABN* 63:xv–xvii; Drummond, "Annotações," pp. 44–47.

6 Mello Moraes, *História do Brasil-Reino* 2:460–63, 477–81; Marschall to Metternich, 19 October 1822, in "Correspondencia," Part 2, Figueira de Mello, p. 111; Behring, Introduction to Aragão e Vasconcellos, "Memorias," *ABN* 63:xv–xvii; Varnhagen, *História da Independência*, pp. 213–14, 219–27. Hélio Vianna's notes in Varnhagen give the correct dates for Masonic events like Dom Pedro's inauguration as grand master.

7 D. Pedro, Reposta de Sua Majestade Imperial e Real, 12 October 1822, *Proclamações, cartas*, p. 141; Mello Moraes, *História do Brasil-Reino* 2: 481–98; Debret, *Viagem* 2:270–71, plate 47.

8 J. H. Rodrigues, *Independência* 1:258–59; Debret, *Viagem* 2:270–71, plate 47; Marschall to Metternich, 19 October 1822, in "Correspondencia," Part 2, Figueira de Mello, pp. 111–12.

9 The pseudo-Masonic Apostolate, made up of close associates of Dom Pedro and José Bonifácio, continued to hold regular meetings until 15 May 1823, and was permanently disbanded two months later. Rangel, *Trasanteontem*, pp. 97–101; Drummond, "Annotações," pp. 51–53; Marschall to Metternich, 4 November 1822, in "Correspondencia," Part 2, Figueira de Mello, pp. 121–24; Tarquínio de Sousa, *José Bonifácio*, pp. 195–202; "Pedro Guatimozim" [D. Pedro] to Joaquim Gonçalves Ledo, 21 and 25 October 1822, AIP, I-POB, 21.10.822, PI.B.c., nos. 1–2.

10 Varnhagen, *História da Independência*, pp. 265–66; Marschall to Metternich, 3 December 1822, in "Correspondencia," Part 2, Figueira de Mello, p. 131.

11 J. H. Rodrigues, *Independência* 1:270; Debret, *Viagem* 2:272–73, plate 48. The crown, with the diamonds removed, is on display at the Imperial Museum in Petrópolis. The scepter is topped by the Bragança family dragon.

12 J. H. Rodrigues, *Independência* 1:270–71; Tarquínio de Sousa, *Vida de D. Pedro I* 2:76–78.

13 Hann, "Brazil and the Río de la Plata," pp. 342–51; Street, *Artigas*, pp. 334–37; Oliveira Lima, *O movimento da independencia*, pp. 206–10.

14 Condy Raguet to John Quincy Adams, 25 November 1822, and Woodbridge Odlin to Adams, 8 December 1822, in *Diplomatic Correspondence,* Manning, 2:751–53; Varnhagen, *História da Independência*, pp. 411–17.

15 J. H. Rodrigues, *Independência* 3:213–14; Monteiro, *História do Império: Elaboração*, pp. 581–82; Varnhagen, *História da Independência*, pp. 416–17.

16 J. H. Rodrigues, *Independência* 2:21–26; Raguet to Adams, 25 November 1822, in *Diplomatic Correspondence*, Manning, 2:751–52.

17 Raguet to Adams, 8 March 1823, in *Diplomatic Correspondence*, Manning, 2:754–55.

18 Thomas Cochrane, tenth earl of Dundonald, *Narrative of Services in the Liberation of Chili, Peru, and Brazil* (London, 1859), 2:6–9; Brant Pontes to José Bonifácio, May

1822, "Cartas sobre a Independencia do Brasil," *PAN* 7(1907):246–47; D. Pedro, Fala, 3 May 1823, in *Falas do Trono, Desde o ano de 1823 até o ano de 1889* (São Paulo, 1977), p. 34; Callcott, *Journal*, pp. 216–18.

19   Donald Thomas, *Cochrane: Britannia's Last Sea-King* (New York, 1978), pp. 27–28, 202–5, 242–43, 247–48, 320.

20   Ibid., pp. 348–49. Except where otherwise noted, the summary of Cochrane's career prior to 1823 is based on Thomas's biography.

21   Callcott, *Journal*, p. 220; Dundonald, *Narrative* 1:232–86.

22   Rodolfo Garcia, "O Rio de Janeiro em 1823, conforme a descripção de Otto von Kotzebue, official da Marinha russa," *RIHGB* 80 (1916):517.

23   Dundonald, *Narrative* 2:9–20; Callcott, *Journal*, p. 219.

24   Dundonald, *Narrative* 2:6, 13–21; Mello Moraes, *História do Brasil-Reino*, 2:49; Callcott, *Journal*, pp. 218–20.

25   Callcott, *Journal*, pp. 221–22; Callcott, "Escorço," p. 87; Manuel Moreira da Paixão e Dores, *Diário da armada da Independência* (Brasília, 1972), pp. 56–57.

26   Dundonald, *Narrative* 2:26–50; Paixão e Dores, *Diário*, pp. 70–98; J. H. Rodrigues, *Independência* 3:217–18.

27   Cochrane might well have used the British flag to gain entrance to Maranhão, as Padre Moreira Paixão e Dores, a chaplain aboard the *Pedro Primeiro*, recorded in his diary. (Paixão e Dores, *Diário*, pp. 98–121; cf. Dundonald, *Narrative* 2:50–74). But Brazilian historians consistently have supported Cochrane's claim that he entered the harbor at São Luís under Portuguese colors. Boiteux, *A marinha*, p. 178; Monteiro, *História do Império: Elaboração*, p. 631; J. H. Rodrigues, *Independência* 3:247.

28   J. H. Rodrigues, *Independência* 3:190–91; Varnhagen, *História da Independência*, pp. 540–44.

29   Varnhagen, *História da Independência*, pp. 277–82; José Honório Rodrigues, *A Assembléia Constituinte de 1823* (Petrópolis, 1974), pp. 28–29; "Dados biográficos de deputados que tomaram assento na Assembléia Constituinte (1823)" in *Diario da Assemblea Geral, Constituinte, e Legislativa do Imperio do Brasil, 1823*, fascimile edition (Brasilía, 1973), I: part A, unpaginated.

30   *Diario da . . . Constituinte* 1:5.

31   D. Pedro I, 3 May 1823, *Falas do Trono*, pp. 31–38; Callcott, *Journal*, pp. 230–32.

32   *O Espelho*, 30 May 1823, reprinted in *D. Pedro I, Jornalista*, Hélio Vianna, pp. 79–84; Chamberlain to Canning, 7 June 1823, in *Britain*, Webster, 1:225. The original draft of the article, in Dom Pedro's handwriting, is in the Imperial Archives in Petrópolis, where it is cataloged as a *fala* (speech). D. Pedro, Fala (rascunho) sobre a escravidão, AIP, I-POB, 1823, PI.B.fa.

33   Varnhagen, *História da Independência*, p. 287; Monteiro, *História do Império: Elaboração*, pp. 683–701; D. Pedro I, *Falas do Trono*, p. 36; José Bonifácio, *Obras científicas* 2:145–58.

34   Tarquínio de Sousa, *Vida de D. Pedro I* 2:103–09; Varnhagen, *História da Independência*, pp. 287–88, 291–92; Drummond, "Annotações," p. 62; Hélio Vianna, *Contribuição a história da imprensa brasileira* (Rio, 1945), pp. 512–15.

35   David St. Clair, *Drum and Candle* (Garden City, N.Y., 1971), p. 86; Michael D. Worth, "Epidemic Disease in Nineteenth-Century Bahia" (unfinished Ph.D. dissertation, University of Florida, ca. 1975); Callcott, "Escorço," p. 92; Tarquínio

de Sousa, *Vida de D. Pedro I*, 2:109–10; Rangel, *D. Pedro I e a Marquêsa*, p. 25; Varnhagen, *História da Independência*, pp. 293–94.

36 Varnhagen, *História da Independência*, pp. 294–96.

37 Drummond, "Annotações," pp. 60–61; Varnhagen, *História da Independência*, pp. 296–97; Rangel, *Trasanteontem*, pp. 99–101. Drummond is almost certainly mistaken in recalling, after forty years, that Domitila was at the palace, "in the next room," the night that José Bonifácio resigned. Her affair with the emperor later became notorious, but in 1823 it was well hidden and the mistress was kept a safe distance from the palace.

38 D. Pedro, "Habitantes do Brasil" (proclamation), 15 July 1823, *Proclamações, cartas*, pp. 177–79.

39 *Diario da . . . Constituinte* 1:689–99.

40 Monteiro, *História do Império: Elaboração*, pp. 764–65.

41 *O Tamoyo*, 12 August 1823; Drummond, "Annotações," pp. 63–66; Varnhagen, *História da Independência*, pp. 300–302.

42 Drummond, "Annotações," pp. 59, 67–68, 139, 145; Varnhagen, *História da Independência*, pp. 307–14; Gomes da Silva, *Memórias*, pp. 78–81.

43 *Diario da . . . Constituinte*, 2:369–70, 387; Drummond, "Annotações," pp. 72–74; Gomes da Silva, *Memórias*, p. 81; Varnhagen, *História da Independência*, pp. 322–25; Hélio Vianna, *D. Pedro I, Jornalista*, pp. 171–75; Raguet to Adams, 12 November 1823, in *Diplomatic Correspondence*, ed. Manning, 2:765.

44 *Diario da . . . Constituinte*, 2:389–93; *O Tamoyo*, 11 November 1823; Drummond, "Annotações," p. 74; Raguet to Adams, 12 November 1823, in *Diplomatic Correspondence*, ed. Manning, 2:766.

45 Varnhagen, *História da Independência*, p. 326; Drummond, "Annotações," pp. 74–75; Raguet to Adams, 12 November 1823, in *Diplomatic Correspondence*, ed. Manning, 2:766; Monteiro, *História do Império: Elaboração*, pp. 527–29.

46 Varnhagen, *História da Independência*, pp. 326–30; *O Tamoyo*, 11 November 1823; Gomes da Silva, *Memórias*, pp. 81–84; Raguet to Adams, 12 November 1823, in *Diplomatic Correspondence*, ed. Manning, 2:766–68.

47 *Diario da . . . Constituinte* 2:395–406; Drummond, "Annotações," pp. 75–76.

48 *Diario da . . . Constituinte* 2:406–8; D. Pedro, Proclamação, 12 November 1823, and Manifesto . . . aos Brasileiros, 16 November 1823, *Proclamações, cartas*, pp. 191–99; Monteiro, *História do Império: Elaboração*, p. 764; Drummond, "Annotações," p. 76; Gomes da Silva, *Memórias*, pp. 84–90.

49 Varnhagen, *História da Independência*, pp. 334–35, 350–53; Drummond, "Annotações," pp. 76–86; Raguet to Adams, 12 November 1823, in *Diplomatic Correspondence*, ed. Manning, 2:767–68. Padre Belchior, nephew of the Andrada brothers, received only half the pension of his fellow deportees, all of whom were married.

50 Dundonald, *Narrative* 2:94, 100–02.

51 Afonso Arinos de Melo Franco, "Introdução," to *O constitucionalismo de D. Pedro I no Brasil e em Portugal* (Rio, 1972), section 6 (unpaginated); Gomes da Silva, *Memórias*, p. 96; Varnhagen, *História da Independência*, pp. 350–51, 358; J. H. Rodrigues, *Conselho de Estado*, pp. 56–71.

52 Raguet to Adams, 19 November 1823, in *Diplomatic Correspondence*, ed. Manning, 2:768–70; Varnhagen, *História da Independência*, pp. 349–50; Monteiro, *História do Império: Elaboração*, pp. 832–33.

53 Dundonald, *Narrative* 2:100–07; Raguet to Adams, 20 January 1824, in *Diplomatic Correspondence*, ed. Manning, 2:775.

54 Tobias Monteiro, *História do Império: O Primeiro Reinado* (Rio 1939), 1:45–54; Gomes da Silva, *Memórias*, p. 96; Tarquínio de Sousa, *Vida de D. Pedro I* 2:156–59.

55 *Constituição Politica do Imperio do Brasil* (Rio, 1863); *Diario da . . . Constituinte* 1:689–99; J. H. Rodrigues, *A Assembléia Constituinte*, pp. 102–58.

56 *Constituição . . . do Imperio.*

57 Ibid.

58 Ibid.; Thomas Flory, *Judge and Jury in Imperial Brazil, 1808–1871: Social Control and Political Stability in the New State* (Austin, 1981), pp. 57, 116–17.

59 *Constituição . . . do Imperio*; Melo Franco, "Introdução," to *O constituicionalismo de D. Pedro I*, section 6; Paul Bastid, *Benjamin Constant e sa doctrine* (Paris, 1966), 2:917–27.

60 *Constituição . . . do Imperio*, artigos 98–101, 137–44; J. H. Rodrigues, *O Conselho de Estado*, pp. 72–74.

61 *Diario do Governo* (Rio de Janeiro), 26 March 1824; Monteiro, *História do Império: Primeiro* 1:45–54; Callcott, "Escorço," p. 82.

62 Monteiro, *História do Império: Primeiro* 1:73–109, 124–37.

63 Tarquínio de Sousa, *Vida de D. Pedro I* 2:172–74; Dundonald, *Narrative* 2:112–57.

64 J. H. Rodrigues, *Independência* 3:213; Monteiro, *História do Império: Primeiro* 1:151–256; Dundonald, *Narrative* 2:157–78. Economically, Pernambuco and the rest of the Northeast were severely disadvantaged within the Brazilian empire; the region probably would have done better as a separate nation. Nathaniel H. Leff, *Underdevelopment and Development in Brazil*, vol. 2, *Reassessing the Obstacles to Development* (London, 1982), pp. 23–32.

65 Thomas, *Cochrane*, pp. 290–316; Dundonald, *Narrative* 2:179–252; Monteiro, *História do Império: Primeiro* 1:259–317.

6—Misfortunes of Love and War

1 Baum, "Empress Leopoldina," p. 187.

2 Oberacker, *Imperatriz Leopoldina*, p. 219; D. Pedro to D. João, 23 June 1821, AIP, II-POB, 2.5.821, Pl.B.c., no. 3.

3 Rangel, *D. Pedro I e a Marquêsa*, pp. 76–113.

4 Ibid., pp. 7–8; Monteiro, *História do Império: Primeiro* 2:117–18.

5 Rangel, *D. Pedro I e a Marquêsa*, pp. 67, 90; Monteiro, *História do Império: Primeiro* 2:125; Walsh, *Notices* 1:266–67; Bösche, "Quadros alternados," p. 153.

6 Rangel, *D. Pedro I e a Marquêsa*, pp. 114–22; Certidões tirados dos autos findos do divórcio da marquêsa de Santos, BNRJ, Seção de Manuscritos, I-35, 31, 3. Domitila and Felício received one of the last divorces to be granted in Brazil until the late twentieth century. In 1827 the imperial government accepted the ruling of Dom Romualdo Antônio de Seixas, the archbishop-patriarch appointed by Dom Pedro, that such dissolutions of marriage were contrary to the doctrine of the established Roman Catholic Church, and were therefore unconstitutional. Not until 1977 did a republican government adopt a constitutional amendment permitting the legalization of divorce. Keith S. Rosenn, "Brazil's Legal Culture: The Jeito Revisited,"

Notes

Florida International Law Journal 1(1984):7.

7 Callcott, "Escorço," p. 125.

8 Dundonald, *Narrative* 2:139–41; Callcott, "Escorço," pp. 126–28. Adèle Bonpland told Maria Graham (later Lady Callcott) that the ministers had planned to kill Lord Cochrane and that she had saved his life. Mrs. Graham did not believe Madame Bonpland.

9 Tarquínio de Sousa, *Vida de D. Pedro I* 2:175.

10 Dundonald, *Narrative* 2:142.

11 Mello Moraes, *Chronica geral*, 2:229.

12 Monteiro, *História do Império: Primeiro* 2:11–23; Drummond, "Annotações," p. 59; Thompson, "Francisco Gomes da Silva," pp. 2, 15, 21–24; Callcott, "Escorço," pp. 99–118.

13 Callcott, "Escorço," pp. 105, 109; Oberacker, *A Imperatriz Leopoldina*, pp. 351–52; Drummond, "Annotações," p. 72; Christine Galbraith, "The Sorocaba Revolt of 1842" (unfinished Ph.D. dissertation, University of Florida, ca. 1979); Carlos Maul, *A Marquêsa de Santos (seu drama, sua epoca)* (Rio, 1938), pp. 107–11, 189–92.

14 Philipp von Neuman, *The Diary of Philipp von Neuman* (Boston, 1928), 1:153; Callcott, "Escorço," pp. 87, 98, 105–7.

15 Walsh, *Notices* 2:459; Bösche, "Quadros alternados," p. 153; Callcott, "Escorço," p. 98; Carl Seidler, *Dez anos no Brasil* (São Paulo, 1941), p. 75.

16 Callcott, "Escorço," pp. 107–20; Mello Moraes, *Chronica geral* 2:229, 250.

17 Callcott, "Escorço," pp. 110–11, 130; Callcott, *Journal*, p. 271; Tarquínio de Sousa, *Vida de D. Pedro I* 1:180; Tarquínio de Sousa, *José Bonifácio*, p. 246; Walsh, *Notices* 1:180–81, 2:450–51, 459–60.

18 Rangel, *D. Pedro I e a Marquêsa*, pp. 118–19; Heitor, *150 anos*, pp. 45–46.

19 Callcott, "Escorço," p. 87; Armitage, *A History*, 1:202; Bösche, "Quadros alternados," p. 204.

20 Raguet to Adams, 8 March 1824, in *Diplomatic Correspondence*, ed. Manning 2:778; Monteiro, *História do Império: Primeiro* 1:9–10, 2:9–13.

21 D. Pedro to Clemente Ferreira França, 14 October 1824, AIP, I-POB, 14.10.824, PI.B.c.

22 Raguet to Adams, 1 February 1824, in *Diplomatic Correspondence*, ed. Manning, 2:776.

23 D. Pedro to Georg Anton Ritter von Schäffer, 13 June 1824, and D. Pedro to Felisberto Caldeira Brant Pontes, 13 June 1824, in AIP, I-POB, 13.6.824, PI.B. do.; Baum, "Empress Leopoldina," pp. 172–74; Mário de Vasconcellos, "Schaeffer e Mello Mattos nos Estados da Allemanha," *ADI* 4(1922):xxxix–lv.

24 Henderson, *A History*, pp. 339–40; Antonio Augusto de Aguiar, *Vida do Marquez de Barbacena* (Rio, 1896), pp. 4–17; Braz do Amaral, note in *Memórias históricas e políticas da província da Bahia*, by Ignácio Accióli de Cerqueira e Silva, (Salvador da Bahia, 1931), 3:235.

25 Aguiar, *Vida do Marquez*, pp. 17–30.

26 Hilderbrando Accioly, "Brant e Gameiro em Londres," *ADI* 1(1922):xxxiii–lvii; Bethell, *The Abolition*, pp. 32–47.

27 Brant to Luiz Jozé Carvalho e Mello, 12 February 1824, *ADI* 2(1922):8.

28 Brant to D. Pedro, 7 September, 5 October, 9 November, 6 and 10 December 1824, AIP, II-POB, 7.9.824, Hor. c., nos. 1–5; D. Pedro to Brant, 11 August 1824, AIP,

I-POB, 11.8.824, Pl.B.c., no. 1.

29 Brant to George Canning, 3 August 1823, *ADI* 1(1922):289–89; Bethell, *The Abolition*, p. 42. Due to the war for independence, slave imports at both Rio and Bahia in 1823 were down from the previous year. In 1824 they totaled 26,712 in Rio and 3,137 in Bahia, according to the British Foreign Office sources cited by Bethell.

30 D. Pedro to Antonio Telles da Silva, February 1824, AIP, II-POB, .2.824, Pl.B.c.

31 Franz I to D. João VI, 12 July 1824, ANTT, Cor. sob. Aust.-Port., caixa forte, no. 196; Peres, *História de Portugal* 7:124–26.

32 Correspondence between Canning and Sir William à Court, 27 November 1824–24 January 1825, in *Britain*, Webster, 2:256–64; Brant and Manoel Rodrigues Gameiro Pessoa to Carvalho e Mello, 7 and 10 February 1825, *ADI* 2(1922):200–204; D. Pedro to D. João, 15 July 1824, AIP, II-POB, 15.7.824, Pl.B.c.

33 Ron Seckinger, *The Brazilian Monarchy and the South American Republics, 1822–1831* (Baton Rouge, 1984), pp. 17–20, 33–34; Raguet to Adams, 1 February 1824, in *Diplomatic Correspondence*, ed. Manning, 2:775–76; Manchester, *British Preëminence*, pp. 201–3.

34 Tratado do Reconhecimento da Independencia do Brazil, 29 August 1825, in *Historia da fundação do Imperio Brazileiro*, by J. M. Pereira da Silva (Rio, 1868), 7:410–12; also in *British and Foreign State Papers* (1824–25), 13:674–78.

35 Bethell, *The Abolition*, pp. 49–50; Convenção para ajuste de reclamações entre Portugal e Brasil, 30 August 1825, BNRJ *Documentos para a historia*, pp. 489–91.

36 Bethell, *The Abolition*, pp. 51–54; Manchester, *British Preëminence*, pp. 203–06.

37 Seckinger, *Brazilian Monarchy*, pp. 66–71; Street, *Artigas*, pp. 339–43; Monteiro, *História do Império: Primeiro* 2:233–36; Armitage, *A History*, pp. 236–37; D. Pedro to Antonio Telles da Silva, 27 January 1825, AIP, I-POB, 27.1.825, Pl.B.c.

38 Rangel, *D. Pedro I e a Marquêsa*, pp. 122–25; Ezekiel Stanley Ramírez, *As relações ente a Austria e o Brasil, 1815–1889* (São Paulo, 1968), p. 42; Armitage, *A History*, 1:222; Gomes da Silva, *Memórias*, p. 98; Thompson, "Francisco Gomes da Silva" pp. 22–23; Henrique Oscar Wiederspahn, *Campanha de Ituzaingó* (Rio, 1961), pp. 62–65.

39 Condy Raguet to Henry Clay, 17 January 1826, in *Diplomatic Correspondence*, ed. Manning, 2:840–42; Boiteux, *A marinha*, pp. 230–31; Street, *Artigas*, pp. 345–46.

40 Michael C. McBeth, "The Brazilian Recruit during the First Empire: Slave or Soldier," in *Essays Concerning the Socioeconomic History of Brazil and Portuguese India*, ed. Dauril Alden and Warren Dean (Gainesville, 1977), pp. 71–86.

41 Michael C. McBeth, "The Politicians vs. the Generals: The Decline of the Brazilian Army during the First Empire, 1822–1831" (Ph.D. dissertation, University of Washington, 1972), pp. 81–89; Manfred Kossok, *Im Schatten der Heiligen Allianz: Deutschland und Lateinamerika, 1815–1830* (Berlin, 1964), pp. 185–96.

42 Carl Schlichthorst, *O Rio de Janeiro como é, 1824–26: Huma vez e nunca mais* (Rio, 1943), p. 51; Bösche, "Quadros alternados," p. 163; McBeth, "Politicians vs. Generals," pp. 13, 84–92.

43 Calmon, *História do Brasil* 5:1590; Boiteux, *A marinha*, pp. 234–36.

44 Mello Moraes, *Chronica geral* 2:248–52; Rangel, *D. Pedro I e a Marquêsa*, pp. 128–30; Tarquínio de Sousa, *Vida de D. Pedro I* 2:205–8.

45 Monteiro, *História do Império: Primeiro* 2:29–33; Armitage, *A History*, 1:231–33; Rangel, *D. Pedro I e a Marquêsa*, pp. 131–33

46 Monteiro, *História do Império: Primeiro* 2:33–34; Viscount Rezende to Viscount

Paranaguá, 30 January 1826, *ADI* 4(1922):238–42; D. Miguel to D. Pedro, 6 April 1826, in *Supplemento*, ed. Biker, 16:159–61.

47 Monteiro, *História do Império: Primeiro* 2:35–38; Gomes da Silva, *Memórias*, pp. 126–30; Armitage, *A History*, 1:233–35; Melo Franco, introduction, sec. 7, and facsimiles of constitution with amendments and annotations by D. Pedro and Gomes da Silva, in *O constituicionalismo de D. Pedro I*, unpaginated.

48 Vianna, *Contribuição a história da imprensa*, pp. 39, 97–131, 431–32, 516–27; Walsh, *Notices* 1:426–33.

49 D. Pedro, Fala, 6 May 1826, *Falas do Trono*, pp. 97–98.

50 Armitage, *A History*, 1:246–51, 259–60; *Annaes da Camara dos Deputados do Brasil, 1826* (Rio, 1877), 4:99–112; Brant to D. Pedro, 12 January 1825, AIP, II-POB, 27.1.825, PI.B.c., no. 4.

51 Octavio Tarquínio de Sousa, *Bernardo Pereira de Vasconcelos e seu tempo* (Rio, 1937), pp. 45–49.

52 Bethell, *The Abolition*, pp. 56–57; Walsh, *Notices* 2:218–19.

53 Bethell, *The Abolition*, pp. 57–61; Manchester, *British Preëminence*, pp. 206–15.

54 *Annaes da Camara, 1827* 3:11.

55 Mello Moraes, *Chronica geral* 2:255; Rangel, *D. Pedro I e a Marquêsa*, pp. 138–42; Monteiro, *História do Império: Primeiro* 2:146.

56 Aguiar, *Vida do Marquez*, p. 136; Monteiro, *História do Império: Primeiro* 2:126–36; Rangel, *D. Pedro I e a Marquêsa*, pp. 140–41; Armitage, *A History* 1:286–87; Walsh, *Notices* 2:461–62; Callcott, *Journal*, p. 263.

57 Armitage, *A History* 1:254–60; McBeth, "Politicians vs. Generals," pp. 86, 118–19.

58 Tarquínio de Sousa, *Vida de D. Pedro I* 2:239; Mello Moraes, *Chronica geral* 2:255–56; Oberacker, *Imperatriz Leopoldina*, pp. 419–30; Aguiar, *Vida do Marquez*, p. 145.

59 Mello Moraes, *Chronica geral* 2:256–57; Monteiro, *História do Império: Primeiro* 2:155.

60 Tarquínio de Sousa, *Vida de D. Pedro I* 2:234, 236.

61 Aguiar, *Vida do Marquez*, pp. 146–51; Seidler, *Dez anos*, p. 79; Monteiro, *História do Império: Primeiro* 2:228–29; Gomes da Silva, *Memórias*, pp. 136–37.

62 Walsh, *Notices* 1:258. Arrábida quotation in *D. Pedro I e a Marquêsa*, by Rangel, p. 150.

63 Tarquínio de Sousa, *Vida de D. Pedro I* 2:243–47; Oberacker, *Imperatriz Leopoldina*, pp. 432–41; Rangel, *D. Pedro I e a Marquêsa*, pp. 148–50.

64 Rangel, *D. Pedro I e a Marquêsa*, pp. 159–62; Tarquínio de Sousa, *Vida de D. Pedro I* 2:246–47.

65 Street, *Artigas*, pp. 349–52; Boiteux, *A marinha*, pp. 309–11; Aguiar, *Vida do Marquez*, pp. 175–205; Seidler, *Dez anos*, pp. 95–98.

66 Robert Gordon to the Earl of Dudley, 17 January 1828, in *Britain*, Webster, 1:323–24; Street, *Artigas*, p. 352; Hann, "Brazil and the Río de la Plata," pp. 427–30.

67 Bethell, *The Abolition*, pp. 62–66; Walsh, *Notices* 2:322, 535.

68 Manchester, *British Preëminence*, pp. 209–10; Sérgio Buarque de Holanda, et al., *História geral da civilização brasileira* (São Paulo, 1962), 3:358–60.

69 Armitage, *A History* 1:288, 295–97; D. Pedro, Decreto, 3 July 1827, and D. Pedro to D. Miguel, 3 July 1827, in *Supplemento*, ed. Biker, 16: 298–99, 346–47; Earl of Dudley to Robert Gordon, 28 August 1828, in *Britain*, Webster, 1:320–21.

70 Walsh, *Notices* 1:278–79; McBeth, "Politicians vs. Generals," p. 92; Armitage, *A*

History 1:319–20.

71 Armitage, *A History* 1:320–21; Walsh, *Notices* 1:280–81; Bösche, "Quadros alternados," pp. 181–82.

72 Quoted in Bethell, *The Abolition*, p. 57.

73 Walsh, *Notices* 1:281–85; Bösche, "Quadros alternados," pp. 181–83; McBeth, "Politicians vs. Generals," pp. 93–95.

74 Bösche, "Quadros alternados," pp. 184–86; McBeth, "Politicians vs. Generals," pp. 95–96.

75 Bösche, "Quadros alternados," pp. 186–93; Walsh, *Notices* 1:288–89, 293.

76 Walsh, *Notices* 1:290; McBeth, "Politicians vs. Generals," p. 96.

77 Bösche, "Quadros alternados," pp. 192–97; Walsh, *Notices* 1:289–93; Armitage, *A History* 1:322–23.

78 Armitage, *A History* 1:323–28; Lord Ponsonby to the Earl of Aberdeen, 29 August 1828, in *Britain*, Webster, 1:325–26; Walsh, *Notices* 1:294–97.

79 Walsh, *Notices* 1:299–300; Bösche, "Quadros alternados," pp. 199–201; McBeth, "Politicians vs. Generals," pp. 1, 97–99.

80 Rangel, *D. Pedro I e a Marquêsa*, pp. 201–05; Mello Moraes, *Chronica geral* 2:286–87; Armitage, *A History* 1:318–19.

7—Abdication

1 Celso Furtado, *The Economic Growth of Brazil* (Berkeley, 1965), pp. 121–25.

2 Dundonald, *Narrative* 2:22; Callcott, *Journal*, p. 219; José Bonifácio D'Andrada e Silva, *Representação á Assembléa Constituinte e Legislativa do Imperio do Brasil sobre a escravatura* (Paris, 1825); João Severiano Maciel da Costa, *Memoria sobre a necessidade de abolir a introducção dos escravos africanos no Brasil* (Coimbra, 1821).

3 Debret, *Viagem* 2:233–34.

4 Tarquínio de Sousa, *Vida de D. Pedro I* 2:245–46; D. Pedro, Fala (rascunho) sobre a escravidão, AIP, I-POB, 1823, PI.B.fa.

5 [D. Pedro], *Carta escripta pelo sachristão*, in *D. Pedro I, jornalista*, Vianna, p. 19.

6 [D. Pedro], letter from "O Philantropo," in *O Espelho*, 30 May 1823, in *D. Pedro I, jornalista*, Vianna, pp. 79–84.

7 Drummond, 'Annotações," p. 140.

8 Walsh, *Notices* 2:215; Tarquínio de Sousa, *Bernardo Pereira de Vasconcelos*, pp. 7–34.

9 Armitage, *A History* 2:18–19; Flory, *Judge and Jury*, p. 15; Joaquim Nabuco, *Um estadista do Império* (São Paulo, 1949), 1:13.

10 Tarquínio de Sousa, *Bernardo Pereira de Vasconcelos*, p. 241.

11 João Pandiá Calogeras, *Formação histórica do Brasil* (São Paulo, 1938), p. 141; Armitage, *A History* 2:46–47.

12 *Annaes da Camara, 1827* 3:21–23; Romualdo Antonio de Seixas, *Memorias do Marquez de Santa Cruz* (Rio, 1861), pp. 3–50, 85–86; Bede A. Dauphinee, "Church and Parliament in Brazil during the First Empire, 1823–1831" (Ph.D. disseration, Georgetown University, 1965), pp. 1–2, 85–88, 183–92; Vitor de Azevedo, *Feijó: Vida, paixão e morte de um chimango* (São Paulo, 1942), pp. 11–136.

13 Nabuco, *Um estadista* 1.9–15.

14 Tarquínio de Sousa, *Evaristo*, pp. 13–83; Nabuco, *Um estadista* 1:13.

15 Armitage, *A History* 2:12; Flory, *Judge and Jury*, p. 52.

16 *Aurora Fluminense*, 10 March 1834, 1 February and 30 May 1828; McBeth, "Politicians vs. Generals," p. 94; Tarquínio de Sousa, *Evaristo*, p. 81.

17 Calmon, *História do Brasil* 5:715.

18 Tarquínio de Sousa, *Vida de D. Pedro I* 2:269, 271; Armitage, *A History* 1:322–24.

19 Walsh, *Notices* 2:218; Armitage, *A History* 1:324–25.

20 Armitage, *A History* 2:85–87, 99–101; Flory, *Judge and Jury*, pp. 109–10.

21 Tarquínio de Sousa, *Vida de D. Pedro I* 2:301–2; Session of 26 February 1829, *Atas do Conselho de Estado* (Brasília, 1973), 2:67–69.

22 Tarquínio de Sousa, *Vida de D. Pedro I* 2:302–3.

23 Ibid. 2:304–6.

24 Bethell, *The Abolition*, p. 68.

25 Armitage, *A History* 1:246, 273, 2:276–77; Tarquínio de Sousa, *Vida de D. Pedro I* 2:291; Aguiar, *Vida do Marquez*, pp. 317–21, 345–46.

26 Aguiar, *Vida do Marquez*, pp. 309–21; Tarquínio de Sousa, *Vida de D. Pedro I* 2:255.

27 Rangel, *D. Pedro I e a Marquêsa*, p. 194; Barbacena to D. Pedro, 1 January 1828, in *Vida do Marquez*, Aguiar, pp. 341–42.

28 Aguiar, *Vida do Marquez*, pp. 353–63; Rangel, *D. Pedro I e a Marquêsa*, pp. 194–99.

29 Aguiar, *Vida do Marquez*, pp. 379–434.

30 William Tudor, the very literary U.S. minister to Brazil, apparently translated the Portuguese *filhos de puta* as "whoresons," but the French minister only alluded to the emperor's use of an *injurieux et grossier* term. Tarquínio de Sousa, *Vida de D. Pedro I* 2:297; Metternich to Franz I, 22 September 1828, in *Memoirs*, Metternich, 4:524–33.

31 Rangel, *D. Pedro I e a Marquêsa*, pp. 211–19; Aguiar, *Vida do Marquez*, pp. 411, 513–24; Tarquínio de Sousa, *Vida de D. Pedro I* 2:322.

32 Armitage, *A History* 2:46–49; Dauphinee, "Church and Parliament," p. 123; D. Pedro, Falas, 2 April and 3 May 1829, *Falas do trono*, pp. 114, 119–20.

33 Tarquínio de Sousa, *Vida de D. Pedro I* 2:268, 308, 3:73; Armitage, *A History* 2:61, 77, 80, 103–4; Walsh, *Notices* 1:426–27.

34 Vianna, *D. Pedro I e D. Pedro II*, pp. 24–27; Tarquínio de Sousa, *Vida de D. Pedro I* 2:264–67; Ibid. 3:31; João Loureiro to Manuel José Maria da Costa e Sá, 17 June 1829, in "Cartas de João Loureiro escriptas de Rio de Janeiro ao Conselheiro Manuel José Maria da Costa e Sá, de 1828 a 1842," *RIHGB* 76, pt. 2 (1914):323–24.

35 Tarquínio de Sousa, *Vida de D. Pedro I* 2:293–95, 322, 3:3–8; Aguiar, *Vida do Marquez*, pp. 663–97; Resende to D. Pedro, 3 August 1829, in "Correspondencia de Antonio Telles da Silva, Marquez de Resende," *RIHGB* 80 (1916):353–55.

36 Tarquínio de Sousa, *Vida de D. Pedro I* 2:322–26; 3:4–6; Rangel, *D. Pedro I e a Marquêsa*, pp. 228–34.

37 Drummond, "Annotações," p. 140; Calógeras, *Formação histórica*, pp. 83, 141–42.

38 D. Pedro, Fala, 3 September 1829, *Falas do trono*, p. 123; Drummond, "Annotações," p. 146; Seixas, *Memorias*, pp. 64–65; Armitage, *A History* 2:51–53; *Annaes da Camara, 1829* 4:46–52, 56–75, 108–61.

39 Gomes da Silva, *Memórias*, pp. 139–60; Mello Moraes, *Chronica geral* 2:289–91, 295.

40 Aguiar, *Vida do Marquez*, pp. 704–06; *The London Times*, 5 July 1829; Resende to

D. Pedro, 3 August 1829, in "Correspondencia," Resende, p. 353; Seixas, *Memorias*, pp. 67–68; Mello Moraes, *Chronica geral* 2:288–91; Armitage, *A History* 2:64–65; Drummond, "Annotações," p. 142; Monteiro, *História do Império: Primeiro* 2:211–12; Maria Junqueira Schmidt, *A segunda imperatriz do Brasil* (São Paulo, 1927), pp. 40–41.

41 Drummond, "Annotações," p. 142; Tarquínio de Sousa, *Vida de D. Pedro I* 3:15–16.

42 Drummond, "Annotações," pp. 143–45; Armitage, *A History* 2:66–68, 144–47; Gomes da Silva, *Memórias*, pp. 163–67.

43 Drummond, "Annotações," pp. 143–44; Mello Moraes, *Chronica geral* 2:298.

44 Drummond, "Annotações," p. 144; Schmidt, *A segunda*, pp. 46–47.

45 Tarquínio de Sousa, *Vida de D. Pedro I* 3:27–28; Drummond, "Annotações," pp. 141–42.

46 D. Pedro to Barbacena, 7 April 1830, in *Vida do Marquez*, Aguiar, p. 741; Gomes da Silva, *Memórias*, pp. 167–78; Drummond, "Annotações," pp. 144–45; Vianna, *D. Pedro I e D. Pedro II*, pp. 59–63; João Loureiro to Costa e Sá, 27 February and 8 March 1830, in "Cartas," João Loureiro, pp. 342–43.

47 Gomes da Silva, *Memórias*, pp. 181–82; Enéas Martins Filho, "A missão Santo Amaro," *Anais do Segundo Congresso de História Nacional*, (1942), 2:523–50; João Loureiro to Costa e Sá, 8, 24 and 27 March 1830, in "Cartas," João Loureiro, pp. 343–46; Drummond, "Annotações," p. 145. Barbacena and Calmon also considered the possibility of dissolving parliament, changing the constitution, and calling on British and French troops to help impose the new order on Brazil—an idea similar to the one Dom Pedro had contemplated the year before. Apparently the emperor told them to discuss their idea with their ministerial colleagues, the marquises of Caravelas and Paranaguá, knowing that they would get a strong negative reaction from them. They did not, but gave Santo Amaro secret instructions to feel out the French and British on the matter anyway. D. Pedro to Miguel Calmon, 26 September 1830, in *D. Pedro I e D. Pedro II*, Vianna, pp. 74–75.

48 Aguiar, *Vida do Marquez*, pp. 727–39.

49 D. Pedro, Fala, 3 May 1830, and Projeto de voto de graças apresentado em sessão de 6 de Maio, and Emendas ofrecidas ao voto de graça, in *Falas do trono*, pp. 127–33.

50 McBeth, "Politicians vs. Generals," p. 173; D. Pedro, Falas, 3 September and 30 November 1830, *Falas do trono*, pp. 134, 137; Norman Holub, "The Liberal Movement in Brazil, 1808–1854" (Ph.d. dissertation, New York University, 1968), p. 78; Flory, *Judge and Jury*, pp. 109–10; Dauphinee, "Church and Parliament," p. 118; Bethell, *The Abolition*, p. 70.

51 Tarquínio de Sousa, *Vida de D. Pedro I* 3:16–17; Rangel, *Trasanteontem*, pp. 59–60.

52 Tarquínio de Sousa, *Vida de D. Pedro I* 3:64.

53 Vianna, *D. Pedro I e D. Pedro II*, pp. 66–77.

54 Ibid., pp. 78–81.

55 Chalaça had nothing to do with Barbacena's dismissal, as Hélio Vianna has shown. Vianna, *D. Pedro I e D. Pedro II*, pp. 66–108; Vianna, *Contribuição*, pp. 535–45; Barbacena, Exposição, 18 October 1830, in *Vida do Marquez*, Aguiar, pp. 787–98; Gomes da Silva, *Memórias*, pp. 181–93; W. D. Wright to Martin Van Buren, 12 February 1831, USDS/DD, M-121, roll 9.

It is not clear exactly when Dom Pedro concluded that Barbacena was a thief, but he was convinced of it by April 1831. Baron von Daiser, "Septe de Abril," *RIHGB*

84 (1920):302.

56 The draft of a long letter from Barbacena to Dom Pedro, dated 15 December 1830 and found among the marquis's papers some sixty years later, traces the writer's long struggle against the "secret cabinet" and Portuguese subversion; makes many self-serving comments; and concludes with a prediction that the emperor would fall from the throne within six months, unless he changed his Portuguese and "absolutist" ways. There is no evidence that this dramatic letter was received by its addressee, or sent to him, or composed prior to the event it predicts. The fact that it is in Barbacena's handwriting hardly dispels suspicions of fakery. It is printed in Aguiar, *Vida do Marquez*, pp. 803–10. See also Vianna, *D. Pedro I e D. Pedro II*, pp. 105–9; Monteiro, *História do Império: Primeiro* 2:273–86.

57 Tarquínio de Sousa, *Evaristo*, pp. 89–295; Armitage, *A History* 2:96–99.

58 José A. Muratti, "The Role of The Military in the Abdication of Dom Pedro I" (Master's thesis, University of Florida, 1972), pp. 36–42; Armitage, *A History* 2:93–96.

59 Muratti, "Role of the Military," pp. 53–54; Tarquínio de Sousa, *Evaristo*, p. 119; Hélio Vianna, *Vultos do Imperio* (São Paulo, 1968), pp. 155–56.

60 "Viagem do Imperador D. Pedro I a Minas-Geraes em 1830 e 1831," *RIHGB* 60 (1897):307–65; Lúcio José dos Santos, "Viagem do imperador a Minas," *Anais do Segundo Congresso de História Nacional* (1934), 1:569–90; Tarquínio de Sousa, *Vida de D. Pedro I* 3:77–84; Vianna, *Contribuição*, pp. 543–44; João Loureiro to Costa e Sá, 18 December 1830, 18 January and 5 March 1831, in "Cartas," João Loureiro, pp. 360–61, 365, 370.

61 Armitage, *A History* 2:62–63, 11–15; *Aurora fluminense*, 14 March 1831; Monteiro, *História do Império: Primeiro* 2:292–93; Tarquínio de Sousa, *Evaristo*, pp. 123–24; Luiz Gastão D'Escragnolle Doria, "Uma testemunha diplomatica do Sete de Abril," *RIHGB* 74, pt. 2 (1911): 186.

62 E. A. Brown to Van Buren, 19 March 1831, USDS/DD, M-121, roll 10; Brasil Gerson, *A revolução brasileira de Pedro I* (São Paulo, 1971), pp. 265–66; Monteiro, *História do Império: Primeiro* 2:293–94; Armitage, *A History* 2:117–18, 125–26; Arthur Aston to Lord Palmerston, 19 March 1831, FO 13, codex 81, folios 184–90.

63 Armitage, *A History* 2:120–23; Monteiro, *História do Império: Primeiro* 2:296–97; Bösche, "Quadros alternados," pp. 211–12; Aston to Palmerston, 19 March 1831, FO 13, codex 81, folios 184–90. The petition is in the *Aurora fluminense*, 18 March 1831.

64 Monteiro, *História do Império: Primeiro* 2:297–303; Vianna, *Contribuição*, p. 545.

65 Monteiro, *História do Império: Primeiro* 2:307, 312–13; Tarquínio de Sousa, *Vida de D. Pedro I* 3:98–102; Vianna, *Contribuição*, p. 545.

66 Doria, "Uma testemunha," p. 182.

67 Monteiro, *História do Império: Primeiro* 2:315–18.

68 Tarquínio de Sousa, *Vida de D. Pedro I* 3:106–9; Miguel Joaquim Ribeiro de Carvalho, "O 7 de Abril—O Feito," *Anais do Segundo Congresso de História Nacional* (1934), 1:602–03; Tarquínio de Sousa, *Evaristo*, pp. 136–43; José Egydio Garcez Palha, "Um episodio da revolução de abril de 1831," *RIHGB* 63 (1900):278–79.

69 Tarquínio de Sousa, *Vida de D. Pedro I* 3:109–12; Armitage, *A History* 2:128–30; Palha, "Um episodio," p. 279.

70 Doria, "Uma testemunha," p. 186; Aston to Palmerston, 10 April 1831, FO 13,

codex 81, folios 214–24.

71 Tarquínio de Sousa, *Vida de D. Pedro I* 3:114; Doria, "Uma testemunha," p. 187; "Abdicação do Imperador" and Aston to Palmerston, 10 April 1831, FO 13, codex 81, folios 206, 226–27.

72 Drummond, "Annotações," p. 48.

8—Dom Pedro vs. Dom Miguel

1 Armitage, *A History*, 2:133–34; Tarquínio de Sousa, *Evaristo*, pp. 143–49; W. H. Koebel, *British Exploits in South America: A History of British Activities in Exploration, Military Adventure, Diplomacy, Science, and Trade, in Latin America* (New York, 1917), pp. 342–47; Aston to Palmerston, 9 April 1831, FO 13, codex 81, folios 200–2.

2 Koebel, *British*, pp. 344–46; Tarquínio de Sousa, *Vida de D. Pedro I* 3:116–21.

3 Koebel, *British*, pp. 343, 351; Tarquínio de Sousa, *Vida de D. Pedro I* 3:138, 147, 312; Aston to Palmerston, 9 April 1831, FO 13, codex 81, folios 201–3.

4 Koebel, *British*, pp. 352, 355, 362–63; Tarquínio de Sousa, *Vida de D. Pedro I* 3:129–38; Vianna, *D. Pedro I e D. Pedro II*, pp. 41–42; Daiser, "Septe de Abril," p. 301.

5 D. Pedro, *Carta de despedida*, 12 April 1831 (facsimile print, Lisbon, 1972); Koebel, *British*, pp. 357–58.

6 The letters are in AIP and are extensively quoted in *Vida de D. Pedro I*, Tarquínio de Sousa, 3:145–299.

7 Tarquínio de Sousa, *Vida de D. Pedro I* 3:145–54; Neumann, *Diary*, p. 250.

8 Resende, "Correspondência," pp. 359–404; Oswaldo Corréia, "Telles da Silva em Vienna," *ADI* 4(1922):viii–xxxvi; Tarquínio de Sousa, *Vida de D. Pedro I* 3:64.

9 Dalbian, *Dom Pedro*, pp. 161–62; Charles K. Webster, *The Foreign Policy of Palmerston, 1830–41* (London, 1951), 1:237–42; Talleyrand, *Mémoires* 4:224; "Reclamaçôoes da França ao governo de D. Miguel," in *Supplemento*, ed. Biker, 18:17–19.

10 Dalbian, *Dom Pedro*, pp. 160–63; Talleyrand, *Mémoires* 4:248–49; Neumann, *Diary*, pp. 251–52.

11 Dalbian, *Dom Pedro*, pp. 162–64; Adelaide d'Orleans to Talleyrand, 30 July 1831, in *Mémoires*, Talleyrand, 4:252.

12 Dalbian, *Dom Pedro*, pp. 164–66, 198, 200; Webster, *Foreign Policy of Palmerston* 1:242.

13 Talleyrand, *Mémoires*, 4:273; Francisco da Rocha Martins, *Palmella na emigração* (Lisbon, n.d.), p. 136; Tarquínio de Sousa, *Vida de D. Pedro I* 3:168–70; Barão de Lagos, *O cavalheiro de Mendizabal e o thesouro de Portugal* (Lisbon, 1858), p. 7; Carlos de Passos, *D. Pedro IV e D. Miguel I, 1826–1834* (Oporto, 1936), pp. 268–69.

14 Rocha Martins, *Palmella*, pp. 23–88; Conde de Carnota, *Memoirs of the Field Marshal the Duke of Saldanha, with Selections from his Correspondence* (London, 1880), 1:1–44, 185–202, 217–18; Antonio da Costa, *Historia do marechal Saldanha* (Lisbon, 1879), 1:7–128, 199–209; Sergio Corrêa da Costa, *As 4 coroas de D. Pedro I* (Rio, 1972), pp. 196–201; Dalbian, *Dom Pedro*, p. 161.

15 Webster, *Foreign Policy of Palmerston* 1:240–45; Tarquínio de Sousa, *Vida de D. Pedro I* 3:170; Rocha Martins, *Palmella*, p. 156.

16 Webster, *Foreign Policy of Palmerston* 1:239–41.

17 Tarquínio de Sousa, *Vida de D. Pedro I* 3:154, 170; Peres, *História de Portugal* 7:186–87,

192; Corrêa da Costa, *4 coroas*, p. 157.

18   Passos, *D. Pedro IV*, p. 269; Rocha Martins, *Palmella*, pp. 138–40, 154–59.

19   Lagos, *O cavalheiro de Mendizabal*, p. 4; Vitorino Nemésio, *Exilados (1828–1832):
     História sentimental e política do liberalismo na emigração* (Lisbon, n.d.), p. 192; Charles
     Shaw, *Personal Memoirs and Correspondence* (London, 1837), 1:280–81; Dalbian, *Dom
     Pedro*, p. 177.

20   Dalbian, *Dom Pedro*, pp. 180–88.

21   Thompson, "Chalaça," pp. 47–49; Mello Moraes, *Chronica geral* 2:289–90, 295–97,
     299; Tarquínio de Sousa, *Vida de D. Pedro I* 3:184.

22   Tarquínio de Sousa, *Vida de D. Pedro I* 3:178–81; Dalbian, *Dom Pedro*, pp. 189–94;
     Gioacchino Rossini to D. Pedro II, 5 April 1866, in *Daumier e Pedro I*, Alvaro
     Cotrim (Rio, 1961), p. 131; José Trazimundo Mascarenhas Barreto, Marquês de
     Fronteira e D'Alorna, *Memórias* (Coimbra, 1926), 2:204.

23   Chacon, *Abreu e Lima*, pp. 47–112, 153–54, 187, 234.

24   G. Lloyd Hodges, *Narrative of an Expedition to Portugal in 1832 under the Orders of
     H.I.M. Dom Pedro, Duke of Braganza* (London, 1833), 1:2–3, 9–10; Thomas Knight,
     *The British Battalion in Oporto: With Adventures, Anecdotes, and Exploits in Holland; at
     Waterloo; and in the Expedition to Portugal* (London, 1834), pp. 42–43; Tarquínio de
     Sousa, *Vida de D. Pedro I* 3: 173–74, 185–88, 297–98.

25   Tarquínio de Sousa, *Vida de D. Pedro I* 3:188–98, 201; Passos, *D. Pedro IV*, pp.
     270–71; Shaw, *Personal Memoirs* 1:396.

26   D. Pedro, Decreto and Proclamação, 3 March 1832, in *Supplemento*, ed. Biker,
     18:311–14; Tarquínio de Sousa, *Vida de D. Pedro I* 3:200–202; Passos, *D. Pedro IV*,
     pp. 271–72; Nemésio, *Exilados*, pp. 200–212.

27   Tarquínio de Sousa, *Vida de D. Pedro I* 3:205–7; Corrêa da Costa, *4 coroas*, pp.
     209–13; D. Pedro, Decreto abolindo a escravidão nas ilhas dos Açores, 19 May
     1832, in *Supplemento*, ed. Biker, 18:317.

28   Hodges, *Narrative* 1:11; Knight, *British Battalion*, pp. 55–57; Passos, *D. Pedro IV*, p.
     278.

29   Charles Shaw to Patrick Shaw, 10 May 1832, in *Personal Memoirs*, Shaw, 2:148;
     Fronteira, *Memórias* 2:221–24.

30   Pimentel, *A corte*, p. 79.

31   Shaw, *Personal Memoirs* 1:340.

32   Raimundo José da Cunha Mattos, *Memorias da campanha do senhor D. Pedro
     D'Alcantara, Ex-Imperador do Brasil, no Reino de Portugal, com algumas noticias anterior
     ao dia do seu desembarque* (Rio, 1833), 1:137–57; Simão José da Luz Soriano, *Historia
     do cerco do Porto, precidida de uma extensa noticia sobre os differentes phazes politicas da
     monarchia desde os mais antigos tempos até ao anno de 1820, e desde mesmo anno até o
     começo do sobredito cerco* (Lisbon, 1846), 1:466–72; Pimentel, *A corte*, p. 97.

33   Passos, *D. Pedro IV*, pp. 290–93; Soriano, *Historia do cerco* 1:470–73; Mattos,
     Memorias da campanha 1:157–58. Mattos suggests that the Miguelistas withdrew
     according to plan, to trap D. Pedro and his expeditionaries in Oporto.

34   D. Pedro, Proclamação aos portuguezes, July 1832, in *Supplemento*, ed. Biker, 18:319;
     Knight, *British Battalion*, pp. 64–65.

35   Passos, *D. Pedro IV*, pp. 293–95; Mattos, *Memorias da campanha* 1:159–75; Lord
     William Russell to Lord Palmerston, 21 July 1832, FO 63, codex 368 (unpaginated).

36   Passos, *D. Pedro IV*, pp. 295–98; Mattos, *Memorias da Campanha* 1:176–96; Knight,

British Battalion, pp. 73–76.

37 Soriano, *Historia do cerco* 1:503–10; Mattos, *Memorias da campanha* 1:196–201; Fronteira, *Memórias* 2:247–54; Knight, *British Battalion*, pp. 73–76.

38 Passos, *D. Pedro IV*, pp. 299–302; Mattos, *Memorias da campanha* 1:201–9; Soriano, *Historia do cerco* 1:510–24.

39 Passos, *D. Pedro IV*, pp. 302–6; Soriano, *Historia do cerco* 1:535–51; Mattos, *Memorias da campanha* 1:216–18; Fronteira, *Memórias* 2:262–65.

40 Fronteira, *Memórias* 2:270–76; Lagos, *Cavalheiro de Mendizabal*, pp. 20–21; Tarquínio de Sousa, *Vida de D. Pedro I* 3:241–45; Webster, *Foreign Policy of Palmerston* 1:249; Palmerston to Russell, 29 August 1832, FO 63, codex 368.

41 Tarquínio de Sousa, *Vida de D. Pedro I* 3:241, 245.

42 Fronteira, *Memórias* 2:270; Passos, *D. Pedro IV*, p. 305.

43 Corrêa da Costa, *4 coroas*, pp. 164–65; Alexander Tolmer, *Reminiscences of an Adventurous and Chequered Career at Home and at the Antipodes* (London, 1882), 1:24; Fronteira, *Memórias* 2:277–83; Alnod J. Boger, *The Story of General Bacon: Being a Short Biography of a Peninsular and Waterloo Veteran* (London, 1903), pp. 191–92.

44 Russell to Palmerston, 12 October 1832, FO 63, codex 368; Soriano, *Historia do cerco* 2:35–47; Knight, *British Battalion*, pp. 94–98; Passos, *D. Pedro IV*, pp. 312–13; Fronteira, *Memórias* 2:277–83.

45 Tarquínio de Sousa, *Vida de D. Pedro I* 3:247.

46 Fronteira, *Memórias* 2:280.

47 Passos, *D. Pedro IV*, pp. 316–19; Tarquínio de Sousa, *Vida de D. Pedro I* 3:246–47, 251–52.

48 Passos, *D. Pedro IV*, pp. 312–14; Soriano, *Historia do cerco* 2:49–52.

49 Boger, *Story of General Bacon*, pp. 174–80, 190–91; Shaw, *Personal Memoirs* 2:2–12, 18–30, 220–44; James Edward Alexander, *Sketches of Portugal during the Civil War of 1834* (London, 1835), pp. 109–16; Knight, *British Battalion*, pp. 108–9; Lovell Badcock, *Rough Leaves from a Journal Kept in Spain and Portugal During the Years 1832, 1833, and 1834* (London, 1835), pp. 184–85, 232.

50 Passos, *D. Pedro IV*, pp. 314–16, 321–22; Soriano, *Historia do cerco* 2:60–63.

51 Tolmer, *Reminiscences* 1:17–18, 28; Badcock, *Rough Leaves*, pp. 184–85, 193; Shaw, *Personal Memoirs* 2:220–44; Knight, *British Battalion*, pp. 100–106.

52 Fronteira, *Memórias* 2:293; Shaw, *Personal Memoirs* 2:22–31; Boger, *Story of General Bacon*, pp. 182–90, 214, 234.

53 Boger, *Story of General Bacon*, pp. 213–14, 234; Badcock, *Rough Leaves*, pp. 140, 195–200; Soriano, *Historia do cerco* 2:100, 111.

54 Shaw, *Personal Memoirs* 2:119–20; Tolmer, *Reminiscences* 1:17, 31.

55 Boger, *Story of General Bacon*, p. 177.

56 Tolmer, *Reminiscences* 1:26–27.

57 Badcock, *Rough Leaves*, pp. 177–78, 200.

58 Charles Napier, *An Account of the War in Portugal between Don Pedro and Don Miguel* (London, 1836), 1:127–28; Passos, *D. Pedro IV*, pp. 326–28; Soriano, *Historia do cerco* 2:124–26; Badcock, *Rough Leaves*, pp. 189–92; Boger, *Story of General Bacon*, pp. 207–10.

59 Napier, *Account* 1:142–50; H. Noel Williams, *The Life and Letters of Admiral Sir Charles Napier, K.C.B.* (London, 1917), pp. 84–88; A. da Costa, *Historia do marechal Saldanha*, pp. 234–50; Boger, *Story of General Bacon*, pp. 212, 217–26; Shaw, *Personal*

Notes

Memoir 2:238−44; Soriano, *Historia do cerco* 2:127, 133−66

60 Napier, *Account* 1:151−59; Fronteira, *Memórias* 2:329; Soriano, *Historia do cerco* 2:189−91.

61 Napier, *Account* 1:160−76; A. da Costa, *Historia do marechal Saldanha*, pp. 269−74.

62 Napier, *Account* 1:176−96.

63 Carnota, *Memoirs* 1:324−25; A. da Costa, *Historia do marechal Saldanha*, pp. 275−94; Napier, *Account* 1:197−205.

64 Macaulay, *They Went to Portugal*, p. 300; Shaw, *Personal Memoirs* 2:260; Boger, *Story of General Bacon*, pp. 240−42; A. da Costa, *Historia do marechal Saldanha*, pp. 295−316.

65 Napier, *Account* 1:206−49; A. da Costa, *Historia do marechal Saldanha*, pp. 316−35; Tolmer, *Reminiscences* 1:31−49.

66 Napier, *Account* 1:248−51.

67 Tarquínio de Sousa, *Vida de D. Pedro I* 3:270−75.

68 Williams, *The Life*, pp. 88, 119; Napier, *Account* 1:269−88; A. da Costa, *Historia do marechal Saldanha*, pp. 337−41.

69 Peres, *História de Portugal* 7:212−13; Napier, *Account* 1:269−93; A. da Costa, *Historia do marechal Saldanha*, pp. 341−56.

70 D. Pedro to Antônio Carlos Ribeiro de Andrada Machado, 14 September 1833, in *D. Pedro I e D. Pedro II*, Vianna, pp. 47−49.

71 Gerson, *A revolução brasileira*, p. 251; Tarquínio de Sousa, *Vida de D. Pedro I* 3:282.

72 Nabuco, *Um estadista* 1:27, 32.

73 Macaulay, *They Went to Portugal*, p. 334; A. da Costa, *Historia do marechal Saldanha*, pp. 341−56; Tarquínio de Sousa, Vida de D. Pedro I, 3:280−84.

74 Napier, *Account* 1:299−301; A. da Costa, *Historia do marechal Saldanha*, pp. 357−63.

75 Webster, *Foreign Policy of Palmerston* 1:380−85.

76 Pimentel, *A corte*, pp. 214; Fronteira, *Memórias* 3:29−36; Tolmer, *Reminiscences* 1:55−57; A. da Costa, *Historia do marechal Saldanha*, pp. 366−81; Carnota, *Memoirs* 1:64, 339−43. MacDonell and Saldanha apparently first met in 1823 in jail in Lisbon, where the latter was a political prisoner of Dom João's restorationist regime, and the former was being held on suspicion of piracy. They renewed their acquaintance in Paris in 1832.

77 A. da Costa, *Historia do marechal Saldanha*, pp. 383−400; Tarquínio de Sousa, *Vida de D. Pedro I* 3:289−90.

78 Peres, *História de Portugal* 7:215−19; A. da Costa, *Historia do marechal Saldanha*, pp. 401−19, 435−65; Alexander, *Sketches*, pp. 132−43; Boger, *Story of General Bacon*, pp. 266−72; Napier, *Account* 2:126−59.

79 Napier, *Account* 2:193−204; Webster, *Foreign Policy of Palmerston* 1:386−98.

80 Peres, *História de Portugal* 7:220−27; Lord Howard de Walden to Palmerston, 27 May 1834 (2 dispatches), John McP. Grant to Walden, 26 May 1834, FO 63, codex 420.

9—Return to Queluz

1 Tarquínio de Sousa, *Vida de D. Pedro I* 3:293.

2 Peres, *História de Portugal* 7:189, 227, 235; Corrêa da Costa, *4 coroas*, pp. 220−23.

3 Webster, *Foreign Policy of Palmerston* 1:387−92; Thomas Knight, *Adventures in Holland and Waterloo; and Expedition to Portugal* (Sydney, 1867), p. 40; Boger, *Story of General*

Bacon, p. 251.

4 Grant to Walden, 26 May 1834, FO 63, codex 420; Peres, *História de Portugal* 7:222–25.

5 Pimental, *A corte*, pp. 214–15; Soriano, *Historia do cerco* 2:509–14; Walden to Palmerston, 30 May 1834, FO 63, codex 420.

6 Webster, *Foreign Policy of Palmerston* 2:406; D. Pedro, Decretos, 28 May (two) and 30 May 1834, in *Chronica Constitucional de Lisboa*, 31 May 1834; Walden to Palmerston, 17 May and 25 June 1834, FO 63, codex 420.

7 Tarquínio de Sousa, *Vida de D. Pedro I* 3:297–300, 302, 306; Badcock, *Rough Leaves*, p. 372; Walden to Palmerston, 24 May 1834, FO 63, codex 420.

8 Pimentel, *A corte*, pp. 227–28, 234–37.

9 Fronteira, *Memórias* 3:114.

10 Tarquínio de Sousa, *Vida de D. Pedro I* 3:300–301; Peres, *História de Portugal* 7:235–40.

11 Webster, *Foreign Policy of Palmerston* 1:379–405; Pimental, *A corte*, pp. 272–77; *Gazeta official do Governo*, 20 August 1834.

12 Walden to Palmerston, 18 and 20 September 1834, FO 63, codex 422.

13 D. Amélia to D. Januária, 29 September 1834, in Aleindo Sodré, "Imperatriz Amélia," *Anuário do Museu Imperial* 2(1941):129; Napier, *Account* 2:237; Pimental, *A corte*, pp. 253–57.

14 Napier, *Account* 2:240; Pimental, *A corte*, pp. 259–62.

Bibliographical Note

For study of the central figure of this book the indispensable source is in Petrópolis, Brazil, at the Imperial Archives (AIP). The AIP has the largest collection of original documents handwritten by Dom Pedro. Personal letters or drafts of letters that he wrote in Brazil to relatives, friends, and associates between 1815 and 1831 are filed under *D. Pedro I., correspondência remitida*. Letters written in Europe and sent to his children in Brazil from 1831 until shortly before his death in 1834 are included with the *correspondência recebida* of Dom Pedro II and his sisters. Other categories under Dom Pedro I's heading are *atos oficiais*, drafts of official pronouncements, like proclamations and speeches; *diversos*, drafts of orders and decrees; *escritos*, drafts of articles written for pseudonymous publication, and poetry; *correspondência recebida*, letters received from relatives, friends, anonymous informants, and petitioners; and *biografia*, reports by various individuals on such matters as Dom Pedro's education, health, and travel, dating from 1807 to 1831. For the biographer, the most fascinating of these papers are the ones in Dom Pedro's handwriting, especially the rough drafts, with their misspellings, strikeovers, and marginal doodles.

The major centers of documentation for the political and diplomatic history of the Luso-Brazilian world in the time of Dom Pedro are the Torre do Tombo National Archives (ANTT) in Lisbon; the National Archives in Rio de Janeiro (ANRJ); the separately housed Foreign Ministry Archives in Rio, the Arquivo Histórico do Itamarati (AHI); and the British Foreign Office Archives in the Public Record Office (PRO) in London. The archives in Lisbon and Rio are the official repositories for such documents as constitutions, registers of laws and decrees, and the paperwork generated by the various ministries and departments of government. The ANTT also holds the correspondence of Portuguese monarchs with other European sovereigns (in the *caixa forte*), and the ANRJ has the personal papers of certain public figures, like the marquis of Barbacena (códice 607, 7 volumes). Other important personal papers collections are in the national libraries in Rio (BNRJ) and Lisbon (BNL), in the *secção de manuscritos* (manuscript section) of each; useful items include the *memórias históricas* of J. F. T. Pereira d'Azambuja in the BNL, the four-volume (códices 597–600) diary and scrapbook of a prominent Miguelista in the 1820s and 1830s. The national libraries of Brazil and Portugal both have collections of early nineteenth-century newspapers that, though printed matter, are hard or impossible to find elsewhere. In London the Foreign Office section of the PRO houses the official correspondence of the British ministers and consuls in Lisbon, Rio, and other Portuguese and Brazilian cities. The dispatches of the British diplomats regularly include detailed observations of the local scene and supporting documentation, like broadsides and newspaper articles. Reports from United States representatives in Portugal and Brazil are not nearly so complete; they are available at the National Archives in Washington, and on U.S. Department of State microfilm (General Records, Series A). In Rio the archives of the Instituto Histórico e Geográfico Brasileiro contain originals of many of the documents published in its *Revista* (RIHGB).

There is a large body of printed primary source material on the Luso-Brazilian world of 1798–1834 that is available at major research institutions in the United States and in other countries. In the many cases where a document exists in both original manuscript and more accessible printed form, I have cited the latter, for it is the historian's duty to facilitate review of his scholarship and to show the way to others who would follow him on the same ground. The consulting rooms of most public archives are lined with volumes of documents published by those institutions. The *Publicações do Arquivo Nacional*, issued irregularly in Rio since 1886 by the ANRJ, contain useful material from the Brazilian independence period and the reign of Dom Pedro I, including some of the correspondence of the marquis of Barbacena (volume 7, 1907), the registry of foreign residents of Rio, 1823–30 (volume 49, 1961), and resolutions passed by Brazilian municipal councils, in the early 1820s (volume 71, 1973). The AHI has published the *Archivo diplomatico da Independencia*, 6 volumes (Rio, 1922–25), a compilation of Brazilian diplomatic correspondence relating to the achievement of Brazilian independence and its recognition by the major world powers. Portugal's Foreign Ministry has published the *Collecção dos tratados, convenções, contratos e actos publicos celebrados entre a coroa de Portugal e as mais potencias desde 1640 até ao presente*, edited by José Ferreira Borges de Castro, 14 volumes (Lisbon, 1881–87), and its companion, the *Supplemento à collecção dos tratatos, convenções, contratos, e actos publicos celebrados entre a coroa de Portugal e as mais potencias desde 1640*, edited by Julió Fermino Judice Biker, 22 volumes (Lisbon, 1872–79). The former contains Portugal's treaties and official foreign policy pronouncements; the latter reproduces internal government reports and correspondence related to foreign affairs, including almost all aspects of the internationalized Portuguese civil war of 1828–34. Less satisfactory are the limited selections of documents related to Brazilian independence chosen from British Foreign Office records by Charles K. Webster, *Britain and the Independence of Latin America, 1812–1830*, 2 volumes (London, 1933), and from the U.S. State Department files by William R. Manning, *Diplomatic Correspondence of the United States Concerning the Independence of the Latin American Nations*, 3 volumes (New York, 1925).

Portugal has published the record of the sessions of the Cortes of 1821–22, *Actas das sessões das Cortes Geraes Extraordinarias e Constituintes da nação portugueza, consagradas no anno de 1821*, 3 volumes (Lisbon, 1821–22), and the supplementary *Correspondencia oficial das provincias do Brasil durante a legislatura das cortes constitucionaes de Portugal nos annos de 1821–22*, 2d ed. (Lisbon, 1872) and *Documentos para a historia das cortes geraes da nação portugueza, 1820–1825* (Lisbon, 1883), the last two containing important letters and reports from the provinces of Brazil, including some by Dom Pedro. In Brazil the Federal Senate has published two volumes of the minutes of the council of state, 1822–34, edited by José Honório Rodrigues (*Atas do Conselho de Estado*, Brasília, 1973) and reissued the diary of the Constituent Assembly (*Diario da Assemblea Geral, Constituinte, e Legislativa do Imperio do Brasil, 1823*, 2 volumes, Brasília, 1973). The debates in the Senate during the empire are recorded in the *Annaes do Senado do Imperio do Brasil* (20 volumes, Rio, 1826–89), and the debates in the Chamber of Deputies during Dom Pedro I's reign are transcribed in the *Annaes da Camara dos Srs. Deputados, 1826–30* (20 volumes, Rio, 1874–78).

Primary sources published by the National Library in Rio include *Documentos para a historia da Independencia* (1923), one large volume of selected documents from the 1814–25 period, and *Revolução de 1817*, nine volumes on the 1817 revolt in Pernambuco, issued as volumes 101–9 (1953–55) of the BNRJ's serial *Documentos históricos*. Another BNRJ series, the *Anais da Biblioteca Nacional* (*ABN*), has published letters and manuscripts by important public figures and observers, like Antonio Menezes Vasconcelos de Drummond and the Andrada brothers (volumes 13–14, 1885–86), Francisco Sierra y Mariscal (volume 43, 1920), Luiz J. dos Santos Marrocos (volume 56, 1934), Maria Graham, Dona Leopoldina, and Friar Manoel Moreira da Paixão e Dores (volume 60, 1938). Other personal papers have been published by the Brazilian Historical and Geographical Institute in the *RIHGB*, including letters or testimony by Francisco de Castro Canto e Mello (volume 41, 1878), Silvestre Pinheiro Ferreira (volume 51, 1888), Dom Pedro (volume 61, 1898), José Egydio Garcez Palha (volume 63, 1900), Dona Leopoldina (volume 75, 1912), João Loureiro (volume 76, 1914), Baron Wenzel von Marschall (volumes 77 and 80, 1914 and 1916), the marquis of Resende (volume 80, 1916), Edward Theodor Bösche (volume 83, 1919), the baron von Daiser (volume 84, 1920), and José Antonio Lisboa (volume 213, 1951).

Some of Dom Pedro's most important writings of the independence period have been collected and published independently as D. Pedro I, *Proclamações, cartas, artigos de imprensa* (Rio, 1973). More titillating are the emperor's letters to his principal mistress, *Cartas do Imperador D. Pedro I a Domitilla de Castro (Marquesa de Santos)* (Rio, 1896). Dom Pedro instructed Domitila to destroy the letters, but she disobeyed, and after her death, her descendants allowed them to be published. Other associates of Dom Pedro who have left published papers or memoirs include Francisco Gomes da Silva (the Chalaça), *Memórias* (2d ed., Rio, 1939); José Bonifácio de Andrada e Silva, *Obras científicas, políticas e sociais*, 3 volumes (Rio, 1963); Thomas Cochrane, Earl of Dundonald, *Narrative of Services in the Liberation of Chili, Peru, and Brazil*, 2 volumes (London, 1859); Romualdo Antonio de Seixas, *Memorias do Marquez de Santa Cruz* (Rio, 1861); Pedro de Sousa Holstein, Duque de Palmella, *Despachos e correspondencia*, 4 volumes (Lisbon, 1851–69); José Trazimundo Mascarenhas Barreto, Marques de Fronteira e d'Alorna, *Memórias*, 5 volumes (Coimbra, 1926–32); and Charles Napier, *An Account of the War in Portugal between Don Pedro and Don Miguel*, 2 volumes (London, 1836). Not close to Dom Pedro, but with an inside view of some aspects of Luso-Brazilian politics, are Luiz Gonçalves dos Santos, *Memórias para servir à história do reino do Brasil*, 2 volumes (Rio, 1943); and Francisco de Almeida Portugal, Conde do Lavradio, *Memórias do Conde do Lavradio*, 2 volumes (Coimbra, 1932). General travel accounts and descriptions of Brazil and Portugal in the 1798–1834 period are numerous. The best for Brazil are Manuel Ayres de Casal, *Corografia brasílica: Facsimile da ed. de 1817*, 2 volumes (Rio, 1945–47); Maria Graham, *Journal of a Voyage to Brazil, and Residence There during Part of the Years 1821, 1822, 1823* (London, 1824); Henry Koster, *Travels in Brazil* (London, 1816); Theodor von Leithold, and Ludwig von Rango, *O Rio de Janeiro visto por dos prussianos em 1819* (São Paulo, 1966); John Luccock, *Notes on Rio de Janeiro and the Southern Parts of Brazil* (London, 1820); Johann B. E. Pohl, *Viagem no interior do Brasil, nos anos de 1817 a 1821*, 2 volumes (Rio, 1951); Augustin François César Provençal Saint-Hilaire, *Voyages dans l'interieur du Brésil*, 4 volumes (Paris, 1830–51); Carl Seidler, *Dez anos no Brasil* (São Paulo, 1941); Johann B. von Spix, and Karl F. P. von Martius, *Viagem pelo Brasil*, 4 volumes (Rio, 1938); and Robert Walsh, *Notices of Brazil in 1828 and 1829*, 2 volumes (Boston, 1831).

Some useful descriptions of Portugal during Dom Pedro's lifetime, including the 1828–34 civil war, are James Edward Alexander, *Sketches in Portugal during the Civil War of 1834* (London, 1835); the anonymous A. P. D. C., *Sketches of Portuguese Life, Manners, Costume and Character* (London, 1826), which also has some observations from Brazil;

Lovell Badcock, *Rough Leaves from a Journal Kept in Spain and Portugal during the Years 1832, 1833, & 1834* (London, 1835); G. Lloyd Hodges, *Narrative of an Expedition to Portugal in 1832 under the Orders of HIM Dom Pedro, Duke of Braganza* (London, 1833); Thomas Knight, *Adventures in Holland and at Waterloo; and Expedition to Portugal* (Sydney, 1867) and *The British Battalion at Oporto* (London, 1834); Raymundo José da Cunha Mattos, *Memorias da campanha do Senhor D. Pedro de Alcantara, ex-Imperador do Brasil, no Reino de Portugal*, 2 volumes (Rio, 1833); Hugh Owen, *The Civil War in Portugal* (London, 1836); Robert Southey, *Journals of a Residence in Portugal 1800–1801 and a Visit to France 1838* (Oxford, 1960); Charles Shaw, *Personal Memoirs and Correspondence*, 2 volumes (London, 1837); and Alexander Tolmer, *Reminiscences of an Adventurous and Chequered Career at Home and at the Antipodes*, 2 volumes (London, 1882).

One important primary source of information on life in Brazil during the second and third decades of the nineteenth century is visual: the pictures produced by the French and German artists brought to Rio by Dom João. The best paintings and drawings are reproduced in Jean Baptiste Debret, *Viagem pitoresca e histórica ao Brasil*, 2 volumes (São Paulo, 1949); Thomas Ender, *O velho Rio de Janeiro através das gravuras de Thomas Ender* (São Paulo, 1956); Johann M. Rugendas, *Viagem pitoresca através do Brasil* (São Paulo, 1940); and Robert C. Smith, and Gilberto Ferrez, *Franz Frühbeck's Brazilian Journey* (Philadelphia, 1960). Aside from the work of these professionals, some vivid scenes of everyday life in Rio are rendered by an amateur artist, Henry Chamberlain, in his *Views and Costumes of the City and Neighbourhood of Rio de Janeiro, Brazil, from Drawings Taken by Lieutenant Chamberlain, Royal Artillery, during the Years 1819 and 1820* (London, 1822).

The number of secondary works on the Luso-Brazilian world of 1798–1834 is enormous; only a representative few will be mentioned here. Among the most useful is John Armitage, *The History of Brazil from the Period of the Arrival of the Braganza Family in 1808 to the Abdication of Don Pedro the First in 1831*, 2 volumes (London, 1836); the author witnessed some of the events he describes, so part of his history may be considered a primary source. A work that is the source of much biographical data on Dom Pedro is Alexandre José de Mello Moraes, *Chronica geral do Brasil*, volume 2 (Rio, 1886), which is a collection of anecdotes and miscellaneous information supplied to the author by persons with some firsthand knowledge of the matters described. Mello Moraes's earlier works, like most Brazilian "histories" of the time, are composed of selected documents quoted at length, or in their entirety, and stitched together with a minimum of commentary. The first serious attempt to construct a comprehensive, integrated, and objective historical narrative of the Brazilian independence movement was undertaken by Francisco Adolfo de Varnhagen and resulted in his *Historia da Independencia do Brasil*, which was completed in the 1870s, but not published until 1916, in Rio. Varnhagen's view of Dom Pedro is favorable, but his book is marred by an antipathy for the Andrada brothers, political enemies of the author's father. A survey of the climactic phase of the independence process, with some attention to economic and social conditions, is Manoel de Oliveira Lima's *O movimento da Independencia, 1821–22* (São Paulo, 1922). Oliveira Lima's masterwork is his earlier (1909) *Dom João VI no Brasil, 1808–1821*, 3 volumes (2d ed., Rio, 1945), which presents an overall positive assessment of the activities of the Portuguese court in Brazil. Decidedly negative is the tone of Luiz Edmundo da Costa, *A corte de D. João no Rio de Janeiro, 1808–1821*, 3 volumes (2d ed., Rio, 1957), which, with a few exceptions, disparages the culture, intelligence, and character of the Portuguese in Brazil, pointedly including Dom Pedro. Somewhat more tolerant of the Braganças, and extensively researched in archives in Europe and Brazil, is Tobias Monteiro, *História do Império: A Elaboração da Independencia* (Rio, 1927), which deals with the 1808–23 period. Its sequel, *O Primeiro Reinado*, 2 volumes (Rio, 1934–46), is less satisfactory, covering unevenly Dom Pedro's reign as constitutional emperor of Brazil, 1824–31. The institutions established during this period are examined in various works by José Honório Rodrigues, whose magnum opus is *Independência: Revolução e contra-revolução*, 5 volumes (Rio, 1975–76), which treats broadly and deeply the major political, economic, social, and military developments in Brazil from 1808 to the Pernambuco revolt of 1824. Rodrigues is a conscientious scholar who does not hesitate to alert readers to facts that might contradict his own interpretations. His approach to his subject matter is basically patriotic Brazilian: he generally takes a dim view of the activities and motives of Britons and Portuguese, including Dom Pedro.

By far the best Brazilian biography of Dom Pedro is Octávio Tarquínio de Sousa, *A vida de Dom Pedro I*, 3 volumes (Rio, 1951), which is based on extensive research in the Bragança family papers, done soon after they were repatriated to Brazil from France and deposited in the AIP. But for all his diligence, Tarquínio overlooked some important aspects of Dom Pedro's life, notably his strong feelings against slavery. Having earlier written biographies of José Bonifácio and Evaristo da Veiga that praised their progressive ideas—and one of Vasconcelos that excused his retrograde ones—Tarquínio apparently could not believe what he was seeing in the documents: that Dom Pedro was out in front of them all. Tarquínio's overall view of Dom Pedro is favorable but hedged; the historian is the prisoner of his own past. The documents that Tarquínio missed in the AIP were found and published by Hélio Vianna in the 1960s in his *Dom Pedro I, Jornalista* (Rio, n.d.), *D. Pedro I e D. Pedro II: Acréssimos às suas biografias* (Rio, 1966), and *Vultos do Império* (São Paulo, 1968). In the following decade Brasil Gerson put the various pieces together and forcefully stated—in his *A revolução brasileira de Pedro I* (São Paulo, 1971)— what so many timid scholars had refused to acknowledge: that the emperor was not nude; he was decked out in the newest and finest clothes of nineteenth-century liberalism.

In 1953 readers of English were provided a lively introduction to the life of Dom Pedro with the publication in New York of Sérgio Corrêa da Costa's brief biography, *Every Inch a King*, the work of a distinguished Brazilian diplomat and scholar who has an understanding of the world in which his subject had to operate and no Lusophobia. A few years later French readers could refer to Denyse Dalbian, *Dom Pedro: Empereur du Brésil, Roi de Portugal (1798–1834)* (Paris, 1959), a biography based primarily on Tarquínio de Sousa's work, with added material on Dom Pedro's stay in France. A fairly well-balanced book about Dom Pedro from a Portuguese perspective first appeared in 1896, and was later reissued in slightly revised form: Alberto Pimentel, *A corte de D. Pedro IV* (2d ed., Lisbon, 1914). More important for the study of Portugal during Dom Pedro's lifetime is Simão José da Luz Soriano's monumental *Historia da guerra civil e do estabelecimento do governo parlamentar em Portugal . . . 1777 até 1834*, 19 volumes (Lisbon, 1866–93), the work of a liberal activist who had his differences with Dom Pedro. An academic work that reflects some of the illiberal, anti-Semitic, and fascistic notions of the early Portuguese Estado Novo—and has little sympathy for Dom Pedro—is Carlos de Passos, *D. Pedro IV e D. Miguel I, 1826–1834* (Oporto, 1936).

Diplomatic monographs based on research in the British Foreign Office Archives in the PRO, and dealing to some extent with the Luso-Brazilian world of 1798–1834, include Charles K. Webster, *The Foreign Policy of Castlereagh, 1815–1822* (London,

1925), and *The Foreign Policy of Palmerston, 1830–1841*, 2 volumes (London, 1951); Alan K. Manchester, *British Preëminence in Brazil: Its Rise and Decline* (Chapel Hill, 1933); and Leslie Bethell, *The Abolition of the Brazilian Slave Trade: Britain, Brazil and the Slave Trade Question, 1807–1869* (Cambridge, 1970). These monographs, with their concentration on a single source of primary documentation, often give a distorted picture of developments in Brazil or Portugal. When these scholars resort to sources outside the PRO, such sources are usually secondary and not the best; Bethell, for example, takes his account of the 1827 slave-trade debate in the Chamber of Deputies not from the Brazilian parliamentary record, but from the English translation of one of José Honório Rodrigues's more polemical books, *Brazil and Africa* (Berkeley, 1965). Far superior as diplomatic history is Ron Seckinger, *The Brazilian Monarchy and the South American Republics, 1822–1831* (Baton Rouge, 1984), which is based on extensive research in primary sources in all the countries involved.

In the field of intellectual history, E. Bradford Burns has revealed the extent of the penetration of enlightened and liberal ideas in Brazil before 1822 in "The Intellectuals as Agents of Change and the Independence of Brazil, 1724–1822," in A. J. R. Russell-Wood, ed., *From Colony to Nation: Essays on the Independence of Brazil* (Baltimore, 1975). The ideological conflict in Portugal after 1820 is analyzed in Victor de Sá, *A crise do liberalismo e as primeiras manifestações das idéias socialistas em Portugal (1820–1852)* (Lisbon, 1969). Thought patterns relating liberalism to revolution are examined in Carlos Guilherme Mota, *Idéia de revolução no Brasil (1789–1801): Estudo das formas de pensamento* (Petrópolis, 1979). Mota also is the editor and a contributor to *1822: Dimensões*, a volume of essays by Portuguese, French, and Brazilian scholars that was published in São Paulo in 1972. Most of the essays, shaped by class analysis and dependency theory, tend to view liberalism as a form of capitalist oppression. A decade and a half later, with Portugal in the European Common Market, the liberal restoration in Brazil surviving a traumatic first year, and Marxist–Leninists citing comparative advantage and extolling the benefits of the international division of labor, new interpretations may be expected.

Index

Index

Neill Macaulay is Professor of History at the University of Florida and is the author of *The Sandino Affair* (reprinted by Duke University Press, 1985) and *The Prestes Column: Revolution in Brazil*, among other works.